CONTESTING CANADIAN CITIZENSHIP

D1153558

CONTESTING CANADIAN CITIZENSHIP

HISTORICAL READINGS

Edited by Robert Adamoski,
Dorothy E. Chunn, and Robert Menzies

broadview press

Copyright © 2002 Robert Adamoski, Dorothy E. Chunn, and Robert Menzies

All rights reserved. The use of this publication reproduced, transmitted in any form or by any means, electronic, mechanical, photocopying, recording, or otherwise, or stored in a retrieval system, without prior written consent of the publisher — or in the case of photocopying, a licence from CANCOPY (Canadian Copyright Licensing Agency), One Yonge Street, Suite 1900, Toronto, Ontario M5E 1E5 — is an infringement of the copyright law.

NATIONAL LIBRARY OF CANADA CATALOGUING IN PUBLICATION

Contesting Canadian citizenship: historical readings / edited by Robert Menzies, Robert Adamoski, Dorothy E. Chunn.

ISBN 1-55111-386-4

1. Citizenship – Canada – History. 2. Canada – Social policy.
I. Menzies, Robert J., 1951- II. Adamoski, Robert L., 1963-
III. Chunn, Dorothy E. (Dorothy Ellen), 1943-

JL187.C67 2002   323.6'0971   C2002-902236-3

BROADVIEW PRESS, LTD.
is an independent, international publishing house, incorporated in 1985.
Broadview Press gratefully acknowledges the financial support
of the Book Publishing Industry Development Program,
Ministry of Canadian Heritage, Government of Canada.

North America	*United Kingdom and Europe*
Post Office Box 1243,	Plymbridge North (Thomas Lyster, Ltd.)
Peterborough, Ontario,	Units 3 & 4a, Ormskirk Industrial Park
Canada K9J 7H5	Old Boundary Way, Burscough Rd.
Tel: (705) 743-8990	Ormskirk, Lancashire L39 2YW
Fax: (705) 743-8353	Tel: (01695) 575112
	Fax: (01695) 570120
3576 California Road,	books@tlyster.co.uk
Orchard Park, New York	
USA 14127	*Australia*
customerservice@broadviewpress.com	UNIREPS
www.broadviewpress.com	University of New South Wales
	Sydney NSW 2052
	Tel: 61 2 9664099
	Fax: 61 2 9664520

Cover design by Zack Taylor. Typeset by Jeff Zuk.

Printed in Canada

CONTENTS

5

ACKNOWLEDGMENTS

As always, an edited collection of this sort is a true exercise in communitarianism.

Michael Harrison, Vice-President and Editor (Social Sciences) of Broadview Press, has been a bedrock of support from first contact to final binding. Suzanne Hancock, Broadview Editorial and Market Researcher and Assistant to the Vice-President, has facilitated our editing work in various ways. Barbara Conolly, Production Editor, and Judith Earnshaw, Assistant Production Editor, artfully shepherded the manuscript to completion; Martin Boyne copyedited the chapters with a rare combination of exactitude and restraint; Zack Taylor contributed an evocative and moving cover design; Tara Lowes coordinated marketing and publicity; and Joan Eadie composed the index.

Broadview's four anonymous reviewers of our book prospectus offered a wealth of insights and critiques that helped to sharpen our thinking about the citizenship concept and its place in Canadian social history.

Yvonne Klein produced an elegant translation of Denyse Baillargeon's essay, originally entitled "L'indispensable 'non-citoyenne': la ménagère des années 1930."

We are grateful to the University of Toronto Press Inc. for their permission to reprint a revised version of Chapter 5 in Mary Louise Adams' book *The Trouble With Normal: PostWar Youth and the Making of Heterosexuality* (© University of Toronto Press Incorporated 1997. Reprinted with permission of the publisher.) as Chapter 12 in this collection.

For their ever-present stimulation and support, we are beholden as always to our many colleagues, companions and co-travellers through the corridors of academe, including Susan B. Boyd, Susan C. Boyd, Joan Brockman, Mark Carter, Wendy Chan, Shelley Gavigan, Margaret Jackson, Hollis Johnson,

PART 1

CHAPTERS IN LEGAL AND SOCIAL HISTORY

Dany Lacombe, John Lowman, David MacAlister, John McLaren, Ted Palys, the late Barbara Roberts, Thomas Thorner, and Claire Young.

Our acknowledgments also go out to Kwantlen University College and Simon Fraser University for providing the resources and opportunity to complete this project. The SFU Publications Fund Committee generously supplied a grant to support production of the index.

Finally, we thank our thirteen contributors for having been such agreeable, efficient, well-regulated and productive citizens throughout the development of this book. Their inter-disciplinary historical scholarship is an inspiration to us all.

To my family for abiding my many absences during the various stages of this work, and particularly Evelina and Domenik, with whom I look forward to sharing more frequent walks in the park.

— ROBERT ADAMOSKI

For my parents, Margaret (Bain) Chunn (1915-2002) and Allen Chunn (1914-2001), for showing me through example what good citizenship is.   — DOROTHY E. CHUNN

For my mother, Audrey L. Menzies, and for my teachers and students, past and present.   — ROBERT MENZIES

PART I

CITIZENSHIP IN THEORY AND HISTORY

chapter one

RETHINKING THE CITIZEN
IN CANADIAN SOCIAL HISTORY

Robert Menzies
Robert Adamoski
Dorothy E. Chunn

There is one asset more important to the province than all the rest —
the human asset. No nation has attained permanence, whatever its
material wealth, unless inhabited by citizens of a superior type. To
my mind there are four traits necessary to the upbuilding of a
sound national character. They are: intelligence, industry, thrift,
and adaptability to conditions.

Premier John Oliver, British Columbia
(Trafalgar Day, circa 1925)[1]

The idea of discipline, of increasing social obligation, is a most fruitful clue to the study of citizenship. It sifts down to first principles,
defines the sphere of the State and the individual, and clarifies our
thinking on legal and moral issues.

Henry F. Munro, *Dalhousie Review* (1930)[2]

Our civilization has become one great comfy hostel where there are
no dangers, no temporations, a place where the sterner qualities are
no longer cultivated because they are no longer necessary in the
struggle to live. Mediocrity controls. ... Thanks to our mistaken,
unscientific and unoriented social welfare schemes, the drones and
wastrels of society are on the increase and in proportion as they
increase will the fit be hindered and impeded on the path to
knowledge, truth and betterment.

Professor William D. Tait, McGill University (1921)[3]

In Search of Canadian Citizenship

This book is about the diverse experiences of citizenship in Canadian social history. The project evolved out of our individual and collective encounters with the citizenship construct in theoretical and historical literatures, originating both in Canada and beyond, over the past fifteen years. As we and our contributors chronicle throughout this collection, the citizenship debates have soared to a place of prominence across a wide ambit of academic disciplines including political science, sociology, history, ethics, law, communications, women's studies, ethnic studies, and philosophy. In this country, renowned writers like Mark Kingwell,[4] Will Kymlicka,[5] John Ralston Saul,[6] and Charles Taylor[7] have played a leading role in our rediscovery of the Canadian citizen. More widely, a truly breathtaking volume of work has surged forth amid the global quest "for a more active conception of citizenship."[8] In its wake, this movement has spawned more than a hundred books, thousands of papers, and even a journal devoted exclusively to citizenship studies.[9] For many, citizenship has offered a rich medium for viewing contemporary political, philosophical and socio-cultural problems and concerns. Libraries overflow with a legion of works on citizenship and social theory,[10] along with myriad substantive topics and issues including globalization,[11] the economy,[12] the state,[13] sovereignty and nationalism,[14] democracy,[15] community,[16] identity,[17] population rights and obligations,[18] cultural, race and ethnicity,[19] multiculturalism and pluralism,[20] immigration and exclusion,[21] poverty and welfare,[22] communications and media,[23] education,[24] gender,[25] youth[26] and sexuality,[27] among assorted other preoccupations of modern life.

Needless to say, this vast body of work defies easy digestion or distillation. Any effort to bottle up the citizenship construct — or even to define or extract its main properties as it journeys through time and space — necessarily becomes a futile exercise in essentialism. In this collection of essays our aims will be far less lofty. For if one lesson has emerged from our latest romance with the modern citizen, it is that the concept itself is unremittingly fugitive, fragmented, culturally constituted, and politically contested. The more recklessly we pursue it, the more vexatiously it evaporates and retreats from view. Still, in this latter-day age of insecurity, we persist in this quixotic quest for the evasive grail of citizenship — for reasons that are much analyzed but never fully fathomed. "There appears to be a great yearning for it," as Philips observes, "even though no one actually knows what it is."[28]

But as fleeting as this thing called citizenship might be, it has long been embraced, and of late resanctified, as one of the great accomplishments of modernism, enlightenment and social progress. In its new incarnation since the 1980s, citizenship has come to offer beacons of hope — a reviving of past achievements and a mapping of future progress — in a world where democracy, community, human rights, and identity are under relentless siege. Amid the worldwide retraction of the Keynesian nation-state and its systems of social provision — in concert with recurrent transgressions against equality and social justice, the ascendancy of transnational corporatism, the hegemony of neo-liberalism and other ideologies of the right, the displacement and immiseration of countless millions, and the world's ongoing encounters with global terrorism and threats of war — there is a general belief that society must "renew and invigorate the powers of the citizen."[29] According to Kymlicka and Norman, these longings are accompanied by a conviction that "the health and stability of a modern democracy depends, not only on the justice of its 'basic structure' but also on the qualities and attitudes of its citizens."[30]

In our own corner of the world, citizenship crises and conflicts have been erupting in virtually every sphere of Canadian life. More than a decade of continental free trade has blurred the nation's economic frontiers, while neo-liberal politicians and lobbyists advance the idea of a currency union (if not a total amalgamation) with the United States — a process that may be accelerated by the events of September 11, 2001. Our public culture is littered with the icons of international corporate capitalism, from Nike to WalMart to the 500-channel universe. Canadian participation in the electoral process threatens to plummet to near-US levels. Meanwhile, our self-conception as a multicultural, progressive, "just" society is held up to question against images of Fujian migrants cast adrift, locked away in military barracks and summarily deported whence they came. Pepper spray in Vancouver and tear gas in Québec City have chemically and symbolically painted the boundaries of government's enthusiasm for collective political action and public dissent. Aboriginal Canadians persevere in their centuries-long struggle for autonomous nationhood, as treaty rights come under increasing onslaught and a Liberal administration in British Columbia contrives — in the name of "democracy" — to block the indigenous road to self-government. Domestic workers from Asia and the Philippines, and political refugees from around the globe, live and labour in a shadowy world of semi-citizenship. Women, working people, immigrants, racial, ethnic and linguistic minorities, youth, seniors, gays and lesbians, and disabled Canadians continue their struggle for unconditional access to the "national dream," and to the deserts of social justice that it promises to confer. And then, of course, there is Québec.

As the country agonizes over these unsettling questions, and untold others, history keeps invading the present. Twenty-first century projects of social reconstruction, democratization, peace, justice, and human rights are inevitably fuelled by the triumphs and tragedies of past generations. Legacies of prior citizenship struggles are everywhere apparent in contemporary discourses, structures, and events. Resounding throughout Canadian political life are the echoes of enduring debates — traceable back to Confederation and before — about the character and destiny of Canadian nationhood, the identity of its populace, the existing and aspired-to ambits of state power, the scope of civilian duties and entitlements, the experience of belonging, the relations between public and private, the hallmarks of social progress, and the constitution of civil and cultural communities. While the world has radically changed in every conceivable way since the country was founded, these myriad questions remain unresolved. Moreover, we ignore this heritage — and we adopt an ahistorical approach to political theory and practice — at our collective peril. As Barbalet writes, "the advent of the institutions of citizenship and their consolidation have a clear historical reality, a reality which must play a role in the continuing development of rights."[31]

It is this historical reality that we and the thirteen invited authors unveil in the chapters that follow. This anthology returns to a special time in Canadian history. In the late 1800s and through the first half of the twentieth century, the country was the testing ground for a plethora of new political ideologies and reform projects. These initiatives, and the values they represented, fundamentally recontoured the national landscape, just as they continue to capture the Canadian imagination after all these years. The historical inquiries comprising this book, therefore, seek to contextualize current citizenship debates by charting the genealogy of the citizen, and of relations of citizenship in which he/she has been immersed, back to these volatile times — back to the formative years of the Canadian state.

Reflecting the diversity and interdisciplinarity of our authors, we explore the origins and evolution of citizenship across a broad spectrum of social life. In doing so we describe the struggles that erupted in public and private realms over this most contested of political and legal concepts. We ponder both the ideals and the actualities of citizenship and nationhood; we chart transformations of the citizenry that occurred as the story of Canada unfolded; and we ground these studies in the institutions, practices, and discourses of welfare, warfare, justice, health, childhood, family, immigration, education, labour, media, popular culture, and recreation — in short, in the lived experience of everyday Canadians, and of those who aspired, too often in vain, to be Canadian.

Guiding our odyssey is the credo that geo-political and historical specificity is an integral precondition for the conduct of social theory, inquiry, and engagement. For a true understanding of modern citizenship, history is, quite simply, indispensable. With Charles Tilly, we maintain that "[s]ocial history gives us the means to think through how, why and with what effects citizenship forms, and more generally how struggles over identity have occurred in the past."[32] It is through the eyes of yesterday's citizens (and non-citizens), and of those who erected and patrolled the nation's gates, that the contemporary dilemmas of citizenship can be made visible and rendered subject to critical scrutiny.

figure 1.1

Immigrants waiting to go ashore, 1911.

WILLIAM JAMES TOPLEY /
NATIONAL ARCHIVES
OF CANADA / PA-010235.

Imagining the Historical Citizen

The modern citizen has a lengthy pedigree. As Shafir writes, "[c]itizenship, as the legal and social framework for individual autonomy and political democracy, has been a central axis of Western political philosophy."[33] From classical Greece to revolutionary France to welfare state Britain to the twenty-first century "global community," the citizen has consistently served as a "reference point"[34] for a remarkable historical ensemble of peoples, cultures, communities, and modes of government. And from Aristotle to Hobbes to Marx to Foucault, social theorists have wrestled with the citizenship concept and its many relevancies for the human species and the worlds it inhabits. "[F]rom very early in its history," Heater informs us, "the term already contained a cluster of meanings related to a defined legal or social status, a means of political identity, a focus of loyalty, a requirement of duties, an expectation of rights and a yardstick of good behaviour."[35]

There is no single historical conception of the citizen, or of her relationship to other people or the body politic. Arguably, citizenship can arise and thrive even in the total absence of a recognizable government or state. There is no doubt that, in modernity, "[d]ebates about citizenship ... are debates about nationhood"[36] and "[t]he majority of modern states establish a link between citizenship and nationality."[37] But it is equally apparent that "[t]he idea that citizenship in a nation-state should be a person's primary identity is a recent one on an historic scale."[38] Whether within or without a formal state apparatus, citizenship and the aspirations it invokes have exerted a powerful gravitational pull throughout history on peoples of immensely disparate backgrounds and cultures. Citizenship's greatest attraction, in fact, seems to inhere precisely in its capacity to function "as a unifying force in a divided world" — in its message that "[o]ur lives may be very different, but we are all equally citizens, and it is as citizens that we advance claims in the public realm and assess the claims made by others."[39] It is the benefits it imparts — ideological and material, imagined and real — that have allowed citizenship to survive the incessant upheavals of more than three millennia of history. At the same time, it is the chameleon-like qualities that it exudes — its endlessly shifting contents and meanings — that have rendered citizenship such a cryptic, opaque, internally contradictory, even paradoxical notion over the course of time. As Prokhovnik writes,

> Citizenship ... has involved an identification with the state, a sense of belonging to a whole, a definition of membership as equals, or entitlement to make a claim against the state. Citizenship has been seen as compulsory, or as voluntary, active or passive, moral or legal. It has been seen as a means of exercising freedom through participation with one's peers in a distinctively public, political realm of speech and action, in opposition to a 'dark' private realm of natural rhythms of material and biological necessity. It can mean having obligations as well as rights, or as going against one's self-interest.[40]

Up until the historical era straddled by this book, the two dominant — and violently oppositional — visions of the body politic and its constituents were civic republicanism and liberal individualism.

A creation of the Greek city state, and the ideal of political philosophers from Aristotle to Rousseau to Arendt, the republican citizen is an active participant in the public realm. Performativity, for republicans, is the key definer of citizenship. The individual's connection to civilization, and indeed to the community of humans more generally, equates with his (seldom her) participation in the structures and processes of governance.

In stark contrast, the republican's liberal counterpart is far less deeply immersed in, or even concerned with, political life. Within the archetypal models of liberalism, past and present, citizenship is a status, not an activity.

Rights, in turn, are negative not positive. Citizens are above all else autonomous, responsible, sovereign, economic men (seldom women) whose requirements from the state do not extend beyond "freedom and security."[41] As its critics have long observed, liberalism reduces citizens "to atomised, passive bearers of rights whose freedom consists in being able to pursue their individual interests."[42] The arbiter of citizen rights is, therefore, their capacity to gird the private domain — to shield people from the intrusions of state power. In turn, "[n]othing is enjoined upon the individual beyond a respect for the autonomy of others and the minimal civic duties of keeping the state in being — voting, paying taxes and, when the state itself is under threat, a readiness to come to its aid in some form of military service."[43] This liberal paradigm of citizenship reached its pinnacle in the nineteenth century, and in its neo-liberal form continues to perforate twenty-first-century life more than three centuries since Hobbes first conceived his Leviathan. It was hegemonic in Canada until — as many of the chapters in this book document — progressivism, welfarism, and scientific governance began to emerge as a competing, third, prototype of citizenship and state in the early and mid-1900s.

The most influential writing on this third citizenship paradigm surfaced precisely at the mid-point of the last century. Virtually every treatment of citizenship over the past 50 years has encompassed, at least in part, a conversation with the work of T.H. Marshall.[44] Through his meditations on the dilemmas and fortunes of post-World War II welfare-state Britain, Marshall became the architect of an ambitious blueprint aimed at recalibrating the one-sided, market-oriented, minimalist vision of liberalism that had left so many citizens — and especially the labouring classes — mired in destitution and despond. Marshall's main goal was to harmonize the needs of advanced capitalism with an expanded inventory of productive rights and entitlements for all citizens of the modern state.

As Marshall proclaimed in his celebrated 1949 Cambridge lectures, within the latter-day "hyphenated" social order spawned of liberal ideology, "citizenship and the capitalist class system [are] at war."[45] Neither the civil and political citizenships of eighteenth- and nineteenth-century origin, nor the rights of freedom and suffrage that they activated, were in themselves enough to ensure a lasting armistice between capital and labour. The only way to peace (and to a genuine working-class allegiance to the projects of nationhood) was through the promotion of a new social citizen within the framework of a fully democratic, progressive, welfarist,[46] rights-affirming political-economic order. According to C.B. Macpherson,[47] this social mode of citizenship was a radical departure from its antecedents, for the goods it bequeathed to the populace were not "rights *against* the state," but rather "claims for benefits guaranteed *by* the state."[48] For Marshall, social citizenship was a grand project aimed at reducing the inequalities borne of capitalism. It was a necessary precondition for the full realization of civil and political rights.[49] It was about securing equal membership in a class-inclusive political fellowship, about balancing entitlement with duty, and about offering assurances that all citizens would reap the rewards of their attachments and contributions to the democratic industrial complex. At its core, social citizenship was, for Marshall,

> ... a status bestowed on those who are full members of the community. All who possess the status are equal with respect to the rights and duties with which the status is endowed. There is no universal principle that determines what those rights and duties shall be, but societies in which citizenship is a developing institution create an image of an ideal citizenship against which achievement can be measured and towards which aspiration can be directed.[50]

Moreover, social citizenship required "a direct sense of community membership based on loyalty to a civilisation which is a common possession. It is a loyalty of free men endowed with rights and protected by a common law. Its growth is stimulated both by the struggle to win those rights and by their enjoyment when won."[51]

In the majority of so-called "western democracies," Marshall's social citizen has been the key agent and medium of political discourse throughout the latter half of the twentieth century and on into the present. But, as a rising chorus of dissent issuing from virtually every ideological corner has alleged, he (seldom she) is also, in part at least, a myth. According to the critics, even in its heyday social citizenship was a narrow and slippery notion. Having been concocted within the historically bounded confines of postwar social democratic Britain, it was directed at a finite population of male industrial labourers for the purpose of binding the wounds of mid-century capitalism. But in this millennial era of community-centred localism, expanding global corporatism, and a retreating welfare state, the social citizen is less and less a figure around whom projects of solidarity, peace, and justice can be advanced. It is scarcely surprising, then, that Marshall's vision is increasingly under assault. From neo-liberals and conservatives to post-Marxists, rights theorists, communitarians, and feminists, critics have come to view Marshall's social citizen as, variously, an anglocentric, statist, evolutionist, malestream, politically impotent anachronism.[52]

Particularly devastating for Marshall's vision of the citizen has been the historical observation — documented throughout this book — that, in their enactment, the rights cultures and doctrines of citizenship have promoted a frankly repressive and exclusionary praxis. For one thing, as Roche argues, after several generations the "western" welfare state has made little systemic progress toward the eradication of poverty, inequality, and injustice.[53] Moreover, Gorham observes that the very practice of social citizenship has a dark and dangerous side. "[T]he language of 'provision,'" he declares, "misleads. In 'providing' rights, society and the state do not simply give them to citizens *gratis*; citizens must subject themselves to the procedures and institutions necessary to ensure that the state can continue to provide rights."[54] Marshall's three mainstays of civil, political, and social rights, Gorham continues, all "ironically engendered their opposites — instead of creating greater freedom and power on the part of the individual 'citizen,' they helped subject that citizen to advanced techniques of discipline and control (modern forms of policing for civil, administrative machinery for political, managed production for socioeconomic rights)."[55]

figure 1.2

Inuit family looking at family allowance poster, 1948.

S.J. BAILEY / NATIONAL ARCHIVES OF CANADA /PA-167671.

Further, as we elaborate below — and as our contributors chronicle in their wide-ranging excursions through Canadian social history — however omnipresent it may appear, citizenship is finite, and is infinitely alienating of all those who circulate outside its boundaries. While "the logic of social citizenship" may be inclusionary, argues Gorham, in practice it "divides people as it unites them. ... States designate citizens by excluding outsiders. ... [S]tronger social rights for citizens disempower noncitizens, in order to protect jobs and ensure domestic tranquility in the welfare state."[56] Again and again, the authors in this collection show how the elevation of the citizen within progressive schemes of early Canadian welfare capitalism, relative to the liberal regimes they succeeded, functioned to disadvantage even further all those who, on account of alleged demographic, physical, mental or moral failings, found themselves on or beyond the shadowy outer edges of civil, political, and social citizenship.

In these ways, critics argue that the citizen in western nation-states is essentially a construction propagated by governments and economic elites to legitimize the unjust political orders that have flourished for decades under the banner of liberal democracy, the welfare state, and modernity. Far from being an autonomous repository of rights and obligations for individual citizens in their relations with the nation state, citizenship is indelibly infused with political practice and discourse. It is not oppositional to, but is rather interlaced with, the projects of a hierarchical social structure and exclusionary political order. To rehabilitate the citizen, it is necessary to rethink and rework governmentality itself.

With these goals in mind — and from a dizzying array of perspectives — philosophers, scientists, policy makers, and activists have collectively embarked on a heady pilgrimage in search of new, post-Marshallian modes of citizenship that would embrace a politic, ethic, and system of social justice for the twenty-first century. Here we mention just two.

The *first*, communitarianism, is associated with radical pluralist democratic initiatives of the new social movements, and seeks to forge populist models of citizen empowerment and responsibilization within an issues-driven, localistic politic. In the words of Mouffe, "[w]hat is at stake is the possibility and desirability of a return to the civic republican tradition in order to restore the idea of politics as the realm where we can recognize ourselves as participants in a community."[57] In contrast to (neo-)liberalism, in particular, communitarianism privileges "the notion of a public good, prior to and independent of individual desires and interests."[58]

Second, a formidable body of feminist writing on citizenship has emerged since the mid-1980s. This work has been concerned above all else with transcending the malestream public boundaries of conventional citizenship debates. From their encounters with the past, feminists have shown that the universal, faceless historical citizen of public discourse was almost universally male — not to mention white, heterosexual, and middle-class. The great citizenship movements recounted by Marshall had little meaning for the vast majority of women who were deeply entrenched within the private domain of family and domesticity. Far from being a liberating moment for women, "[p]olitical citizenship was the basis of the transformation from private to public patriarchy."[59] In more recent times, the ideals of social citizenship are perpetually undermined by the enduring hierarchies of a gender-divided social order. The challenge of feminist citizenship theory, therefore, is to activate a praxis that would have meaning and application across all lines of gender, social class, nationality, race, ethnicity, sexuality, generation, and (dis)ability. Two main preoccupations cut across the myriad streams of feminist citizenship literature: an effort to enlarge the realm of the political so that it might encompass all spaces where citizens participate and contribute to the common good;[60] and a search for "a public language capable of expressing ... ideas of solidarity, noncontractual reciprocity, and interdependence that are central to any humane social citizenship."[61]

Taken together, this brief and selective journey through the theoretical and historical fields of citizenship underlines one of the main themes of this collection — namely, that citizenship is an inescapably contested, unruly, fractionalized, and internally differentiated[62] construct that has carried a matrix of dissonant connotations throughout "western" history.[63] To be a citizen, or to be denied access to citizenship, is above all else a complex historical experience that is forged in human conflict. "[L]acking a fixed meaning," the citizenship concept always requires "specification in terms of its use by 'historical participants' in varying historical contexts."[64] Similarly, "this concept has no definition that is fixed for all time. It has always been at stake in struggles and the object of transformations."[65] As the subsequent chapters compellingly reveal, it is these contests over citizenship — along with the meanings that it harbours and the benefits it confers — that have shaped the relations between Canadians, and between Canadians and their government, throughout the course of this country's history.

Canadian Citizens Past and Present

The political and human content of Canadian citizenship is deeply rooted in our collective historical consciousness. Yet ironically, as Brodie observes in Chapter 2 of this book, there effectively *was* no Canadian citizen, in statute or substance, through the first eight decades of Confederation. Until the 1947 proclamation of the *National Citizenship Act*, native-born Canadians were first and foremost subjects of the British Empire, and their paramount allegiance was to the Queen or King. This colonial status, and the privileges and duties it bestowed, was indistinguishable from those enjoyed by individuals around the world who were lucky enough to broach this mortal coil under the welcoming folds of the Union Jack. For all others — the outsiders to British subjecthood — admission to the Canadian "nation" could be attained only by the establishment of domicile and the achievement of "naturalization" through the immigration machinery of the federal state.

Moreover, from the very first breath of Confederation there were manifold variations and hierarchies of civil, political, and social citizenship, and entire classes of subaltern peoples — among them Aboriginals, other racialized, cultural, and sexual minorities, francophones, immigrants, women, the labouring classes — whose belonging to the "nation" was either unconditionally denied or vigorously contested. During the period spanned by the essays in this book, for the majority of "Canadians" the rights to dignified work, a "citizen's wage," education, social provision, freedom of thought and movement, sanctity of private life, and participation in the public realm were at best the remote objects of unfulfilled longing. The historical threads of Canadian citizenship, as recounted throughout this collection, are inextricably woven into this country's dual legacies of colonialism and exclusion.

This book's historical expedition in search of the Canadian citizen is further confounded by the absence of a centralizing discourse around which an integrative sense of nationhood might have coalesced in this country. Unlike our neighbours to the south and other nations worldwide, argues Brodie, Canadians have had no recourse to a "foundational myth"[66] forged in revolution, conquest, a common theology or a charismatic leadership. A state whose identity has hinged, in rhetoric if not in fact, on "peace, order and good government" must find creative means for infusing its population with an ethic of fealty, patriotism, and public spirit. Throughout Canadian history, national problems of unity and identity have been all the more magnified by the centripetal forces of localism and regionalism; the triadic geometry of indigenous, francophone and anglophone heritage; the pluralistic forces of mass immigration; the geographic impediments to systems of transportation and communication; the myriad rifts borne of social class, gender, race, and culture; and the inhibiting effects of liberal ideology on interventionist projects of governance.

For these many reasons, Brodie asserts, Canadian citizenship has retained its shallow, soft, spectral character through the passage of time. A "moving target,"[67] continually reinventing itself, the concept has been at best a temperamental and capricious instrument in the hands of self-designated nation builders and social engineers. In compensation, successive governments, both federal and provincial, have sought to constitute and convey their own idealized visions of citizenship — to remake the populace, as it were, in their own image. In the late nineteenth and early twentieth centuries, as noted above, this constructed Canadian was an imperial male citizen — loyal, autonomous, rational, content, white, and British through and through. At the height of the welfare state these colonial beings transmogrified, as Brodie's analysis of Throne Speeches compellingly reveals, into Canadian variants of Marshall's social citizen — human embodiments of rights culture, and creations of scientific policy, whose mutual vulnerabilities and dependencies created a common, egalitarian, even universalistic relation to each other, nesting them ever further within the embrace of an expanding public realm. Since the 1980s, however, the entrepreneurial citizen of nineteenth-century liberalism, never fully cloaked from view, has multiplied and spread to encompass most of the population. This citizen-capitalist has gained centre stage as the chief protagonist of state myth-making — a creature of the marketplace, whose competitive initiative and capacity to engage in the global economy have become the signposts of his (and occasionally her) contributions to (inter)national corporatism.

In addition to this remarkable mutability of the Canadian citizen through time, our task is all the more complicated by our inevitable collision against citizenship's many hierarchical properties and stratified meanings, and by the political, cultural, and socio-legal contexts of struggle within which citizenships past and present have been won or lost, conferred or withheld. As Strong-Boag advises us in Chapter 3, miscellaneous groups of Canadians — and would-be Canadians — have stood in widely disparate relations to the nation-state based solely on their externally imputed and self-ascribed social class, gender, racial, and cultural identities.

Moreover, many of the commonly accepted stories of Canadian citizenship need to be challenged. From Mitchell's study of the 1919 National Conference on Canadian Citizenship,[68] for instance, we learn that populist scripts about a Canadian identity forged in the killing fields of Vimy Ridge and the Somme translate into at best an incomplete, and at worst a one-sidedly triumphalist, story of war and nationhood in the early twentieth century.[69] The inferno in Europe was indeed a crucible of Canadian citizenship, but for reasons that were as much attributable to social conflict at home as to carnage on the battlegrounds of Belgium and France. In effect, Canada's participation in the European holocaust unleashed a legitimacy crisis such as the young nation had never seen. The drums of war resounded back upon this country, argues Mitchell, ushering forth a wholesale "moral and political repudiation of the old order."[70] This "assault on the hegemony of the business class" was also "marshalled along the frontiers of class, ethnicity, region and gender."[71] It represented a critical turning point in relations of power between Canadians and their rulers.

Once the "wartime narrative of solidarity and sacrifice"[72] had dissipated — and with it any illusions about a post-bellum era of lasting peace and prosperity for all — the privileged and powerful needed new concepts and languages to cement their authority, to account for the burgeoning political and economic turmoil, and to fend off the mounting activism of socialism, labour, and other so-called "radical" elements. Citizenship served their purposes well. Mitchell recounts how state and industrial elites endeavoured, with varying degrees of success, to rearticulate their failures of leadership as a crisis of individual and collective citizenship. Drenched in the great ideas of the era — "social gospel, moral purity, progressivism, social engineering"[73] — the nation's ruling classes sought nothing less than to manufacture and maintain a new, improved citizenry. Through the application of scientific governance, reconstructed Canadian citizens would atone for the deficiencies and blunders of past generations. In exchange for the civil, political, and social entitlements conferred upon them by the state, they would be enjoined to identify with programs of government and industry, subscribe to the highest levels of ethics and virtue, and aspire to live and labour in the common interests of Canadian nationhood. In the process, social chaos could be averted and capitalism saved.

Not coincidentally, in various ways that arguably foreshadowed our courtship with the twenty-first-century citizen, projects and discourses aimed at elevating the citizenry in the 1920s and beyond also served to deflect attention from the structures of injustice that had exposed so many Canadians to the calamitous effects of war, oppression, and penury. According to prevailing citizenship languages and practices, the nation's health and progress depended far more on the uplifting of a deficient Canadian populace than on the reform of extant political and economic systems. In Mitchell's words, these citizenship discourses "were framed within a narrative of national development that did not challenge the boundaries of the liberal state or capitalist relations of production."[74] Canadianization was, and perhaps still remains in large part, a project of legitimation — a tinkering with the status quo, adapting people to structures more so than the converse. In the interwar years, the idea of citizenship therefore became synonymous with the manufacture of a faithful and compliant national population. In turn, the "happy, industrious, successful citizen"[75] came to be shaped and defined by the personal attributes of obligation, fealty, responsibility, self-governance, and above all else an abiding sense of duty to the "nation."

But for many, such adhering ideologies of patriotism, materialism, and domestic devotion harboured little meaning in political discourse, popular culture or everyday life. While nationalist debates and schemes were unfolding within an anglophone white male Canada, Québécois, Aboriginal, and other racialized peoples, and women, among many others, were confronting their own singular dilemmas of citizenship from coast to coast to coast.

Canadian citizenship narratives, for one thing, have never translated well into French. As Rudin writes in Chapter 4, "Québec sits somewhat oddly in a volume dealing with citizenship."[76] This very distinct society had very distinctive ways of engaging with ideas and identities of nationhood. Québécois strategies for conceiving self and society cannot be easily subsumed within the wider enterprises of Canadianism that were transpiring to the west, east, and north of *la belle province*. Generalization from the rest of Canada to Québec on the subject of citizenship (or anything else for that matter) inevitably occurs at the price of historical precision. The remarkable metamorphosis of its francophone inhabitants from Canadien(ne)s to French Canadians to Québécois(es); the enduring quest to be *maîtres chez nous* without a consensus about just who constitutes the *nous*; the experience of being eternally marooned in an ocean of Anglo-American culture; the mutual affinities and enmities of church and state; the undying tensions between ethnic and civic understandings of citizen and nation; and the resounding echoes of the quiet revolution — all of these factors require that questions of citizenship in Québec be studied on their own special terms.

Finally, what has citizenship meant over the years to Aboriginal Canadians? In Chapter 5, Denis observes how indigenous peoples have long faced a Hobson's choice when it comes to their prospects and conditions for winning sovereignty and status as full partners in the Canadian federation. As with francophone Québécois(es), the ethnic and civic identities of First Nations are in continuing conflict; the struggle for recognition within a Eurocentric politico-legal system is predicated on a partial eclipse, or even a total extinguishment, of Aboriginal cultural heritage. With assimilation and stereotype as the twin corollaries of legal citizenship, and with more than four centuries of subjugation as an historical subtext, it is small wonder that Native Canadians have been so ambivalent about sampling the promised fruits of Canadian nationhood.

Making Canadians and Excluding "Others"

A central theme of this collection is the wider context within which Canadian citizenship played out during the late nineteenth and early twentieth centuries. Viewed retrospectively, concerns about citizenship reflected anxieties about social and "race" purity that were expressed in the discourses of recurrent "crisis" — crises of "the family," public health crises, (un)employment crises, political crises, and so on. The (re)production of "good" citizens was inextricably linked to preventing such crises without effecting any fundamental structural change in Canadian society. Among reformers, authorities, and technocrats in developing welfare states such as Canada, an often explicitly articulated assumption was that good citizens would be found primarily among those who lived in or emulated "white," nuclear families based on a gendered/sexual division of labour and responsibilities. The corollary, and usually unarticulated, assumption was that good citizens would accept a society based on hierarchy and unequal life chances. For the most part, the middle classes had embraced these assumptions by the turn of the twentieth century. The challenge was to entrench the assumptions and "norms" of middle-class existence among the (white) working classes.

How was this objective to be achieved? Clearly, it was assumed that good citizens were (self-)made, not born — although some required more work than others. Thus, education, broadly defined, became key to the work of making good citizens in Canada during this period. According to one commentator of the day, for instance, the objective was to achieve "an aristocracy of mind as the highest ideal of democracy."[77] In more contemporary discourse, citizenship education has been defined as "a process of moral regulation and cultural production, in which specific subjectivities are constructed around what it means to be a member of a nation-state."[78] As several contributions to this book reveal, citizenship education in the developing Canadian welfare state was effected through myriad initiatives involving state and civil society in various capacities and in every sphere of social life — family, school, work, leisure, law, and politics. These multi-faceted efforts to nurture and sustain citizenship, as well as the struggles surrounding these emergent forms of (self-)regulation, had a powerful impact on the everyday lives of Canadians.

figure 1.3

Women's dormitory – Immigration Building, Saint John, N.B., ca. 1920-1930.

ISAAC ERB AND SON / NATIONAL ARCHIVES OF CANADA / C-045083.

Whether explicitly or implicitly, the analyses of citizenship in this collection speak to three broad issues. *First*, we consider the growing emphasis of citizenship initiatives on fostering self-control/self-regulation as much as possible in the formation of "subjectivities" conducive to the creation of a Canadian nation-state. Compulsion became the "last resort," reserved for separating the temporarily "deviant," and therefore salvageable, from the incompetent and incorrigible who were to be "expelled" from society through institutionalization or deportation. *Second*, we explore the criteria governing the citizenship selection process that informed decisions about inclusion/exclusion at different points in time. Who merited almost surefire inclusion and for what categories of citizenship? Who might possibly be included through assimilation? Who could be "refitted" for citizenship? Who could not be included? During a period when immigration law was *de facto* citizenship law in Canada, nationalism, patriotism, and the impact of gender/race/class/sexuality were critical to these decisions about who was "in" and who was "out." *Third*, we engage with the context and content of decisions about inclusion and exclusion. The developing welfare state in Canada as elsewhere marked a movement away from the explicit moralism of lay reformers and toward the scientific expertise of professionals and technocrats. Prevention of radicalism, delinquency, disorganization, and disorder, both individual and social, was increasingly viewed as a matter of technique rather than moral regeneration.

In keeping with the historical emphasis on the relationship between self-control/regulation and "good" citizenship, many of the studies in this collection examine inclusionary initiatives aimed at shaping and shepherding Canadian citizens during the early decades of the twentieth century. Not surprisingly, children were a major focus of such efforts. Although innocent at birth, they were also vulnerable, malleable and, if not properly socialized, potentially threatening to social order. Therefore, in keeping with developments elsewhere,[79] one of the most crucial targets for emerging forms of social regulation in Canada was the family. In gender-specific ways, parents were responsible for raising healthy children and future citizens. Because of the enormity of the task, however, they required education and training to fulfill their respective parenting and spousal roles. Thus, the impervious ideological boundaries between "private" and "public" which had both restrained and facilitated earlier liberal models of state activity started to give way, as both public officials and publicly-sanctioned professionals began to offer prescriptions that would ensure the creation of a vital, active young citizenry.

Women were inextricably bound to the (private) family, and motherhood was prescribed as the highest profession to which they could aspire. Indeed, the unpaid mother work, wife work, and housework that they performed within the family became the basis of their claim to citizenship status. As "mothers of the race," women were responsible not only for biological reproduction but also for the equally important social reproduction. By ensuring the physical, mental, and moral "fitness" of their off-spring, they were primary agents in moulding "good" citizens. Increasingly, however, women were deemed incapable of fulfilling this role using traditional child-rearing methods and practices. They needed education for "scientific" mothering by experts and professionals. Yet, if their children turned out badly, mothers were held solely accountable for this failure. Ultimately, then, women's citizenship status was partial, contingent, and deeply gendered — granted not in recognition of their participation as equal players in the public sphere, but rather, as Katherine Arnup illustrates in Chapter 11, "grounded in their role as mothers, a role they could fulfil with equal ease in the private and the public spheres."[80]

figure 1.4

Three proud
Aboriginal
mothers with
their prizewinning
babies, 1929.

NATIONAL ARCHIVES OF
CANADA / C-068995.

For men, engagement in paid labour outside the family was key to their claims for civil, political, and social rights and thus to their own status as citizens. Employment enabled a man to meet the "norms" of hegemonic masculinity — specifically, to marry, procreate, and assume the dual responsibility of being breadwinner and protector for his own (nuclear) family. "Good family men" thus contributed to the (re)production of future citizens and were likely to be immune to moral degeneracy, political radicalism, and other threats to the status quo. Just as women needed education to become "mothers of the race," men required assistance to become "good family men." Adoption of efficient, scientific approaches to employment aimed at the formation of a new, non-radical, primarily male industrial citizen,[81] the implementation of leisure rights by shortening the work day and introducing paid vacations that would increase worker productivity,[82] and the Canadianization and assimilation of non-Anglo male workers through a combined program of education and labour[83] would all, it was assumed, foster self-regulation/control among individual men and ultimately strengthen liberal democracy and nationhood.

In the final analysis, governance within and through "the family" was about the (re)production of "normality." Parents, teachers, scientific professionals, and experts (e.g., doctors, psychologists, psychiatrists), social reformers, politicians and others were involved in the same enterprise of creating "normal" citizens — that is to say, women and men who fulfilled their gender-specific roles and responsibilities within the context of heterosexual marriage and the nuclear family. In conjunction with the role-specific work of mothers and fathers, a diversity of other initiatives were developed to foster "normality." These included the dissemination of advice about sex to adolescents that was aimed at forming and reinforcing heterosexual subjectivity,[84] the construction of working class homes with basic amenities and adequate space to promote the development of healthy future citizens,[85] and the creation of healthy communities integrated through shared recreational facilities and programs that contributed to mental, physical, and moral "fitness."[86]

But not everyone can meet the "fitness" criteria required for citizenship status at particular historical moments. Those individuals and groups deemed "unfit" are invariably subject to exclusionary policies and practices. Despite the complex bases from which rights and entitlements claims have been advanced by various groups, and the assorted obligations that have flowed from their inclusion as citizens, exclusion from its civil, political, and social benefits has always been a key element in historical formulas of citizenship. From its very earliest conceptions within the Greek *polites* and Latin *civis*, citizenship has offered liberty and, in principle, a new ethic to only a very select, privileged segment of society. As Brodie asserts in Chapter 2, the original citizen was both ruler and ruled, while the majority who fell outside citizenship (whether women, children, slaves, or non-property-holders) were simply ruled. Observed in the context of nineteenth-century Canada, to quote Strong-Boag, "the line increasingly drawn among enfranchised and disfranchised subjects emerged as one critical measure of how those in authority imagined the humanity of those who came beneath their gaze. Those measured and found wanting were to remain subject to the government of those who were seen to wield authority naturally and properly."[87]

Perhaps even more fundamentally, citizenship operated — and continues to operate — as an "othering" practice. While there exist many attempts to define citizenship morally, ethically, and philosophically, in practice it is most often experienced simultaneously as a process of inclusion (or, to use Kaplan's term, "belonging"[88]) and exclusion. To be "abnormal" in any way was a primary marker of difference that was mobilized in powerful ways to separate those "unfit" for citizenship from those who met the fitness criteria. While the latter occupied a "position ... on the inside of the social body,"[89] those who failed to measure up faced ostracism, psychiatrization or incarceration.

Citizenship, Regulation, and Struggle

The essays that follow provide a survey of Canadian citizenship as it played out for various groups between the late nineteenth and early twenty-first centuries — a period which saw the rise, and later the retrenchment, of social citizenship in Canada. While the contributions are united by a desire to probe the social and political implications of a range of regulatory strategies that surrounded the rise of the Canadian welfare state, they offer a strikingly diverse range of approaches, and an equally varied collection of substantive and historical foci. What emerges is a complex collage. Hegemonic expressions of citizenship (the citizen-soldier, the citizen-mother, the active political and economic citizen), which were widely adopted, were also utilized in unanticipated ways by groups that found themselves on the margins of Canadian society. These oft-appropriated symbols appear here, surrounded by more contentious views of what constituted the privileges and burdens of citizenship.

As discussed above, Marshall's progressivist model — written at the high-water point in the development of western welfare states — seeded a torrent of more recent literature, some of it critical. The limitations of the model's generalizability, indeed, the resistance of the citizenship concept to any static typification, has been addressed above. We close this introductory discussion with two specific and interrelated challenges to traditional accounts of citizenship that are raised by the present collection: the role of social conflict and struggle in the development of citizenship regimes, and the contradictory nature of citizenship rights.

The histories gathered here demonstrate that the evolutionary conception of citizen did not square with Canada's past. As Giddens has observed, Marshall "fail[ed] to emphasize that citizenship rights have been achieved in substantial degree only through struggle."[90] The cry and clatter surrounding the construction and extension of Canadian citizenship are amply demonstrated in this collection. They emerge in the words and actions of those denied: the women who, perhaps sensing their objectification by legal and medical terminology, expressed their experience of rape in immediate, unmediated terms;[91] the vast constituencies of the disenfranchised who strained for a vote and, more so, for opportunity;[92] the housewives who laboured to keep their families intact and in the process ensured that the working class would survive the Great Depression;[93] the "women at the well" who gathered to organize and strategize against the systematic racism which denied Black Nova Scotians the most rudimentary education;[94] and the multi-faceted struggle to ensure adequate leisure time for Canada's workforce.[95] Roche evokes an entirely compatible vision of the challenges portrayed here when he contends that "[m]uch of the political history of the twentieth century has been a story of citizens' struggles, whether to defend their rights against tyrannical governments, ... to extend rights, ... or to give substance to civil and social rights."[96]

However, if these civil, political and social rights were often prizes that inspired the marginalized, they were not themselves incontestable. Canadian history is dense with examples of groups who regarded citizenship as perilous, and even potentially obliterative.[97] Similarly, many have found that the forms of citizenship open to them came at a significant price.

While a crucial political concept, citizenship was both polymorphous and the subject of great contention. Marshall's characterization of "citizenship and social class" as fundamentally oppositional is clearly called into question by the essays to follow. The structured inequalities existing in western societies (riven as they were — in the case of Canada — by colonialism, patriarchy, and capitalism) clearly had an impact on the form and substance of Canadian citizenship. There is a need to acknowledge the contradictory nature of the regime of social rights that gave content to modern citizenship. As Fraser and Gordon have noted, "[r]eceipt of 'welfare' is usually considered grounds for disrespect, a threat to, rather than a realization of, citizenship."[98] Drawing selectively from both republican and liberal traditions, the "social safety net" that was woven during the early twentieth century presented a multifaceted threat for those whose suitability for the rigours of full citizenship was questioned.

The fear of fostering dependency — widely regarded as toxic to the development of independent, free (male) citizens in the liberal mould — resulted in rights and benefit structures designed to mimic the contractual exchanges that supposedly characterized the market sphere. Not surprisingly, those benefits that extended to the "naturally dependent," while often presented (and sought) in the language of rights, were quickly colonized: first by the scientific charity movement, and thereafter by legions of professionals empowered to enforce standards of conduct ensuring the continued moral reproduction of the Canadian type.[99] In the United States, Fraser and Gordon argue, the regulatory regimes welded to social benefit schemes have paradoxically resulted in the direct compromise of the civil rights of claimants, particularly women and the chronically unemployed.[100]

Citizens, then, are often bearers of duties and obligations, and the subjects of regulation. The projects of the twentieth century imaged that, ideally, these proscriptions would be internalized as a component of the Canadian identity, but barring that, as noted by Foucault (in the European context), a series of "tiny, everyday, physical mechanisms ... of micro-power that [were] essentially non-egalitarian and asymmetrical"[101] crouched in the shadows of modern, juridical forms of citizenship.

Accounts of the historical development of Canadian citizenship which have limited their portrayal of citizenship to a status or benefit extended to selected groups of Canadians are challenged by the work that follows below. The authors who have contributed to this collection sharpen this traditional account by demonstrating that citizenship was not merely about rights and entitlements. The emergence of the Canadian state, and its nascent relationship with the citizenry, brought with it new understandings of the obligations of citizens, and a range of professional knowledges governing the surveillance and regulation of the social body.

Organization and Contents of the Book

The book is organized into five general parts: Citizenship in Theory and History; Constituting the Canadian Citizen; Domesticity, Industry, and Nationhood; Pedagogies of Belonging and Exclusion; and The Boundaries of Citizenship. As enumerated below, on the basis of our research and our knowledge of existing Canadian scholarship we have chosen specific topic areas that are subsumed within these five parts.

In addition to this introductory chapter, Part I includes Janine Brodie's insightful survey, discussed above, of the various ways in which the notion of Canadian citizenship has been mobilized in Speeches from the Throne, from Confederation onwards.

Part II, "Constituting the Canadian Citizen," brings together three diverse inquiries into some of the touchstones of the nation's citizenship experiences. Veronica Strong-Boag's analysis of the *Franchise Act* of 1885 is a nuanced account of a crucial moment in the ongoing struggle over political inclusion and expression in this country. While the *Act* marked a major extension of the franchise by eliminating the property requirement and ensuring universal suffrage for white working-class males, women and racialized Canadians suffered significant and enduring setbacks that would demarcate the terrain of struggle for future decades. Ronald Rudin's work contributes to this collection on a variety of levels. His analysis of the shifting identity politics evident among politicians and academics in Québec is an indispensable reminder of what has traditionally been regarded as the defining dichotomy of the Canadian experience. As a statement on the constitutive nature of historiography, his analysis casts an important hue of reflexivity on its neighbours in this collection. Of course, while it remains a central element in the hegemonic Canadian identity, the Eurocentric nature of "the two solitudes" has been widely challenged. Claude Denis' chapter concludes this section by contributing an account of the struggles of First Peoples to weather both the historical denial of the fruits of Canadian citizenship and its imposition at the expense of their Aboriginal identity. Analyzing key court rulings from the 1970s until the present, and incorporating the Nisga'a Accord, he argues that Canada may be headed toward a form of multiple citizenship which would effectively constitute Indigenous Canadians as "citizens plus" — although the basis, content, and progressive potential of such a construction are far from certain.

Part III of the book brings together a range of inquiries into the citizenship projects that were launched throughout the twentieth century. Organized primarily chronologically according to the period of study, this collection of chapters indicates how concerns about the integration, cultivation, and regulation of Canadian citizens shaped reforms in housing, unemployment, domestic labour, and leisure. The desire to rationalize and optimize the so-called domestic and productive spheres provides a common theme throughout these chapters. Sean Purdy's survey of housing reform in the first half of the century highlights how built space was manipulated to provide environments deemed optimal for the health and productivity of the working-class family. Similarly, Jennifer Stephen's study of the Ontario Commission on Unemployment, situated in the years following the First World War, documents the transformation of unemployment "from moral category ... to an area of scientific efficiency management." Characteristically, the commission saw expanded regulation by trained professionals as the solution to problems as diverse as immigration, population control, education/vocational training, labour organization, industrial relations, paid work for women, and scientific management of industry and human resources. Both of these authors also highlight the exclusionary nature of these various citizenship projects. Whether seeking affordable housing, or employment or training opportunities, those whose attributes, behaviour, or political leanings did not reach the standard for citizenship found few doors open to them.

The emerging Canadian welfare state had complex implications for the lives of most Canadians. As Denyse Baillargeon demonstrates, relief programs that operated in Québec during the Great Depression were both con-

tingent and reliant upon the unpaid domestic labour of women. These programs thus served as one important relay (along with the range of social, cultural, and legal restrictions on paid employment for women) reinforcing
women's dependency and confining them to the domestic sphere. Examining
the debates and implementation of hours of work legislation, annual paid
vacation, and publicly-funded recreational opportunities during the subsequent three decades, Shirley Tillotson argues that they collectively allowed
an increasing range of citizens the time and space required to participate
actively as citizens — although, even here, racialized difference persisted as a
category of exclusion.

Having sampled the wide range of interventions characteristic of the
Canadian state during the twentieth century, the book focuses, in Part IV, on
education. Spanning an impressive range of social settings, education represented perhaps the most crucial strategy in the development and cultivation
of Canadian citizens. The chapters gathered here describe educational programs targeting male immigrants working in isolated camps, new mothers
raising the next generation of Canadians, and young Canadians who were
beginning to explore their sexuality. In each instance, the pedagogical process
was facilitated by the appetites of its objects. Classes in the English language
and arithmetic offered advancement opportunities for many of the frontiersmen who people Lorna McLean's study of Frontier College. Nonetheless,
assimilation was the clear subtext to the College's efforts, and the fracturing
effects of the gender, racial, and ethnic divisions that underpinned the institution's mission reinforced the same divisions in early twentieth-century constructions of citizenship. In "Education for Motherhood: Creating Modern
Mothers and Model Citizens," Katherine Arnup describes a similar dynamic.
As Canadian women struggled with the material, economic, and social
changes that altered the experience of motherhood in the inter-war and postwar periods, advice literature and radio broadcasts provided "a friendly voice
in an otherwise lonely world." Too often, however, the advice that these
women received was contradictory and unrealistic. Failure to measure up to
the implicit standards engendered guilt and fear, as maternal success was
ultimately linked to women's access to political, civic, and social rights.

The final two contributions to Part IV focus on the education of young
people and share a thematic concern with the exclusionary dynamics that
infused education in general, and education for citizenship in particular.
Examining popular advice literature, and educational films dealing with sexuality and relationships which were directed at teens in the post-World War
II period, Mary Louise Adams' chapter links the wider trend toward normalization as a regulatory strategy with the powerful need to belong which

is often so definitive of the teen years. Adams' analysis highlights the boundaries of normality as constructed in these materials. The numbing homogeneity of the young people portrayed here is testimony to the exclusion experienced by teens who were other than white, middle-class, and "normal" in their expressions of gender and sexuality. Ostracism clearly functioned within the classroom, and in the schoolyard, as described by Bernice Moreau in her study of the educational experiences of Black Nova Scotian women. The women that she interviews describe how their great appetite for education, opportunity, and advancement was thwarted by their status as non-citizens. Doubly disqualified by racial and gender constructs, these women's voices provide a powerful reminder that education, despite its documented role in constructing and reinforcing structures of inequality, was still a beacon of opportunity for those most disadvantaged.

Part V of the book, "The Boundaries of Citizenship," continues our analysis of the exclusionary tendencies that characterized Canadian citizenship projects in the twentieth century, again highlighting the conflict between "insiders" and "outsiders" over the legitimate boundaries of the Canadian citizenry. The first two chapters of this section further the substantive focus on Canadian youth begun in Part IV. The chapters by Joan Sangster and Robert Adamoski peruse the historical experiences of delinquent and dependent youth in twentieth-century Canada, uncovering the hegemonic definitions of what constituted the "good" citizen and how this construct reflected and reinforced existing patterns of gender, race, and class inequality. "Delinquents," Sangster notes, "were caught up in contradictory definitions of citizenship: first, by virtue of their youth and their transgression of social norms, they were 'outsiders' to full, respectable citizenship, but *because of* their youth, they were seen simultaneously as potential, malleable 'insiders' to a future citizenship."[102] The threats apparently posed by children of differing gender, racial, and class attributes, and the varied responses to those threats provide both authors with the opportunity to examine the fractures internal to ideologies of Canadian citizenship during the past century.

The collection closes with two studies that examine efforts to patrol the extreme boundaries of the citizenship construct. Dorothy E. Chunn utilizes dossiers of over 450 sexual offence cases as a vehicle through which to examine the citizenship lessons dispensed by the British Columbia Supreme Court during the late nineteenth and early twentieth centuries. Noting the historical shift in regulatory strategies from criminalization to normalization which occurred during this period, her research emphasizes the role of professional discourse and expert testimony in differentiating between "potentially fit citizens and the unsalvageable/unredeemable."[103] Rounding out the collection, Robert Menzies' account of the British Columbia Royal Commission on Mental Hygiene offers an example of the impact that a new generation of public servants, social engineers, planners, professionals, and practitioners had on the far-reaching program of scientific governance that emerged in the first quarter of the twentieth century. His analysis details their "preoccupations with advancing modern civilization through the manufacture of good citizens and elimination of the unworthy."[104]

As this collection crosscuts several associated traditions, interests, and fields, it is designed to attract a wide interdisciplinary interest. In addition to Canadian history teachers, students, and researchers, those offering and undertaking courses on a range of topics — including the theory and practice of citizenship; welfare, health, and justice; the Canadian state; socio-legal and moral regulation; and gender, race, and ethnicity — should all find these essays to be applicable to their area of specialization. The impact of new socio-historical approaches evidenced in this book allows us to move beyond the often detached, esoteric manner in which debates surrounding conscription, multiculturalism, "the native question," and "the Québec question" have traditionally been addressed, to consider how citizenship practices had an impact on the daily lives of men, women, and children of differing ethnic and socioeconomic groups. From our perspective, the machinations of politicians, strategists, and advisors are crucial, but not sufficient for a full social understanding of the importance of citizenship for Canadians. Instead, like Friesen, many of the authors whose work is collected here revel in "the genius of common people working together in community."[105]

For the general population, the pronouncements of government represented only one element of the lived expression of their relationship to the state. Every day, Canadians also confronted institutionalized and cultural forces in the form of pronouncements on how they should work, parent, consume, occupy their leisure time, and express their sexuality and their rationality. At each of these interstices, the work collected here documents the manner in which various groups complied with or resisted these forces, and how they mobilized their own claims based on these experiences. Many of the analyses that follow profitably mine oral history, case files, correspondences, and other important sources common to social history to make even more palpable the impact of citizenship contests on daily life.

By adopting an historically informed focus on active, lived citizenship, this collection dovetails with some of the contemporary communitarian and feminist literature described earlier. Roche describes the "new sociology of citizenship" as being "concerned with issues of power, inequality and social change in social formations of rights and obligations, membership and identity in modernity."[106] For us, the authors gathered in this book provide an historical grounding crucial to this contemporary project. Citizenship has historically been an important expression of power, status, and identity for those who acquire or inherit entry. It has also functioned as a political weapon brandished against those deemed unfit. But there is danger in elevating the concept too far above the terrain of everyday life. Ultimately, much of the work presented here illustrates the relational nature of citizenship. As a status, or as a strategy, citizenship played out in relation to the many facets of people's lives. The casting of votes, the occupation of political office, and even access to social benefits, while clearly sought and even liberating, were more often relatively minor embellishments of life experiences fundamentally structured by gender, race, and social class.

Notes

1. James Morton, *Honest John Oliver* (London: J.M. Dent and Sons, 1933), 156.
2. Henry F. Munro, "Citizenship," *Dalhousie Review* 10 (April 1930-Jan 1931): 103-09, 106.
3. William D. Tait, "Democracy and Mental Hygiene," *Canadian Journal of Mental Hygiene* 3 (1921): 31-36, 33.
4. Mark Kingwell, *The World We Want: Virtue, Vice, and the Good Citizen* (Toronto: Viking, 2000).
5. Will Kymlicka, *Multicultural Citizenship: A Liberal Theory of Minority Rights* (Clarendon Press: Oxford, 1995); Will Kymlicka, *Politics in the Vernacular: Nationalism, Multiculturalism and Citizenship* (Oxford: Oxford University Press, 2001); *Citizenship in Diverse Societies*, ed. Will Kymlicka and Wayne Norman (New York: Oxford University Press, 2000).
6. John Ralston Saul, *Reflections of a Siamese Twin: Canada at the End of the Twentieth Century* (Toronto: Viking, 1997).
7. *Multiculturalism: Examining the Politics of Recognition*, ed. Amy Guttman (Princeton: Princeton University Press, 1994); Charles Taylor, *The Malaise of Modernity* (Concord, ON: Anansi, 1991); Charles Taylor, *Reconciling the Solitudes: Essays on Canadian Federalism and Nationalism* (Montréal and Kingston: McGill-Queen's University Press, 1993).
8. Chantal Mouffe, "Democratic Politics Today," in *Dimensions of Radical Democracy: Pluralism, Citizenship, Community*, ed. Chantal Mouffe (London: Verso, 1992), 5.
9. *The Journal of Citizenship Studies* (Abingdon, UK: Carfax).
10. Keith Faulks, *Citizenship* (London: Routledge, 2000); Herman R. van Gunsteren, *A Theory of Citizenship: Organizing Plurality in Contemporary Democracies* (Boulder, CO: Westview Press, 1998); Derek Heater, *What is Citizenship?* (Cambridge: Polity Press, 1999); *The Citizenship Debates: A Reader*, ed. Gershon Shafir (Minneapolis: University of Minnesota Press, 1998); *The Condition of Citizenship*, ed. Bart von Steenbergen (Thousand Oaks, CA: Sage, 1993); *Citizenship and Social Theory*, ed. Bryan S. Turner (London: Sage, 1993).
11. *Citizenship Today: Global Perspectives and Practices*, ed. T. Alexander Aleinikoff and Douglas Klusmeyer (Washington: Carnegie Endowment for International Peace, 2001).
12. *The Challenge of Restructuring: North American Labor Movements Respond*, ed. Jane Jenson and Rianne Mahon (Philadelphia: Temple University Press, 1993); *Production, Space, Identity: Political Economy Faces the 21st Century*, ed. Jane Jenson, Rianne Mahon and Manfred Beinfeld (Toronto: Canadian Scholars' Press, 1993).

13. *Extending Citizenship, Reconfiguring States*, ed. Michael Hanagan and Charles Tilly (Lanham, MD: Rowman and Littlefield, 1999); Bryan S. Turner, *Citizenship and Capitalism: The Debate Over Reformism* (London: Allen and Unwin, 1986).

14. David Miller, *Citizenship and National Identity* (Cambridge: Polity Press, 2000).

15. *Democracy, Citizenship and the Global City*, ed. Engin F. Isin (London: Routledge, 2000).

16. *Citizenship, Community and Democracy*, ed. Ellis Vasta (New York: St. Martin's Press, 2000); Henry Tam, *Communitarianism: A New Agenda for Politics and Citizenship* (Basingstoke: Macmillan, 1998).

17. Engin F. Isin, *Who Is the New Citizen? Class, Territory, Identity* (North York, ON: Urban Studies Program, York University, 1995); Engin F. Isin and Patricia K. Wood, *Citizenship and Identity* (London: Sage, 1999); May Joseph, *Nomadic Identities: The Performance of Citizenship* (Minneapolis: University of Minnesota Press, 1999).

18. J.M. Barbalet, *Citizenship: Rights, Struggle and Class Inequality* (Minneapolis: University of Minnesota Press, 1988); Thomas Janoski, *Citizenship and Civil Society: A Framework of Rights and Obligations in Liberal, Traditional, and Social Democratic Regimes* (Cambridge: Cambridge University Press, 1998).

19. *Cultural Identity and the Nation-State*, ed. Carol Gould and Pasquale Paquino (Lanham, MD: Rowman and Littlefield, 2001); Feliks Gross, *Citizenship and Ethnicity: The Growth and Development of a Democratic Multiethnic Institution* (Westport, CT: Greenwood Press, 1999); T.K. Oommen, *Citizenship, Nationality, and Ethnicity: Reconciling Competing Identities* (Cambridge: Blackwell, 1997); Jeff Spinner-Haley, *The Boundaries of Citizenship: Race, Ethnicity, and Nationality in the Liberal State* (Baltimore: Johns Hopkins Press, 1994).

20. *Citizenship, Diversity, and Pluralism: Canadian and Comparative Perspectives*, ed. Alan C. Cairns (Montréal and Kingston: McGill-Queen's University Press, 1999).

21. Veit Bader, *Citizenship and Exclusion* (Houndsmills: Macmillan Press, 1997).

22. Ian Culpitt, *Welfare and Citizenship: Beyond the Crisis of the Welfare State?* (London: Sage, 1992); Timothy J. Gaffany, *Freedom for the Poor: Welfare and the Foundations of Democratic Citizenship* (Boulder, CO: Westview Press, 2000); Maurice Roche, *Rethinking Citizenship: Welfare, Ideology and Change in Modern Society* (Cambridge: Polity, 1992).

23. *Communication, Citizenship, and Social Policy: Rethinking the Limits of the Welfare State*, ed. Andrew Calabrese and Jean-Claude Burgelman (Oxford: Rowman and Littlefield, 1999); Peter Dahlgren, *Television and the Public Sphere: Citizenship, Democracy and the Media* (London: Sage, 1995); Gerald Friesen, *Citizens and Nation: An Essay on History, Communication, and Canada* (Toronto: University of Toronto Press, 2000).

24. Stephen Heathorn, *For Home, Country and Race: Constructing Gender, Class and Englishness in the Elementary School, 1880-1914* (Toronto: University of Toronto Press, 2000).

25. *Gender and Citizenship in Transition*, ed. Barbara Hobson (London: Routledge, 2000); Ruth Lister, *Citizenship: Feminist Perspectives* (New York: New York University Press, 1997); Carole Pateman, *The Disorder of Women: Democracy, Feminism and Political Theory* (Palo Alto, CA: Stanford University Press, 1989).

26. *Youth, Citizenship and Empowerment*, ed. Helena Helve and Claire Wallace (Aldershot: Ashgate, 2001).

27. David T. Evans, *Sexual Citizenship: The Material Construction of Sexualities* (New York: Routledge, 1993).

28. Melanie Philips, "Citizenship Sham in Our Secret Society," *Guardian* 14 (September 1990), qtd. in Nira Yuval-Davis, "The Citizenship Debate: Women, Ethnic Processes and the State," *Feminist Review* 39 (Winter 1991): 58-68, 58.

29. Eric Gorham, "Social Citizenship and its Fetters," *Polity* 28, 1 (Fall 1995): 25-47, 26. See also Nancy Fraser, *Justice Interruptus: Critical Reflections on the "Postsocialist" Condition* (London: Routledge, 1997).

30. Will Kymlicka and Wayne Norman, "Return of the Citizen: A Survey of Recent Work on Citizenship Theory," *Ethics* 104 (January 1994): 352-81, 352.

31. Barbalet, *Citizenship*, 29.

32. Charles Tilly, "Citizenship, Identity and Social History," *International Review of Social History* 40, Supplement 3 (1995): 1-17, 3.

33. Gershon Shafir, "Introduction: The Evolving Tradition of Citizenship," in *The Citizenship Debates: A Reader*, ed. Gershon Shafir (Minneapolis: University of Minnesota Press, 1998), 2.
34. David Miller, "Citizenship and Pluralism," *Political Studies* 43 (1995): 432-50, 432.
35. Derek Heater, *Citizenship: The Civic Ideal in World History* (London: Longman, 1990), 163, cited in Angus Stewart, "Two Conceptions of Citizenship," *British Journal of Sociology* 46, 1 (March 1995): 63-78, 64.
36. Rogers Brubaker, "Immigration, Citizenship, and the Nation-State in France and Germany," in *The Citizenship Debates*, ed. Shafir, 132.
37. John Leca, "Questions on Citizenship," in *Dimensions of Radical Democracy: Pluralism, Citizenship, Community*, ed. Mouffe, 21.
38. William Alonso, "Citizenship, Nationality and Other Identities," *Journal of International Affairs* 48, 2 (1995): 585-99, 585.
39. Miller, "Citizenship and Pluralism," 432-33.
40. Raia Prokhovnik, "Public and Private Citizenship: From Gender Invisibility to Feminist Inclusiveness," *Feminist Review* 60 (Autumn 1998): 84-104, 90.
41. Adrian Oldfield, "Citizenship and Community: Civic Republicanism and the Modern World," in *The Citizenship Debates*, ed. Shafir, 76.
42. Lister, *Citizenship: Feminist Perspectives*, 23.
43. Oldfield, "Citizenship and Community," 77.
44. *Citizenship Today: The Contemporary Relevance of T.H. Marshall*, ed. Martin Bulmer and Anthony M. Rees (London: UCL Press, 1996); T.H. Marshall, *Citizenship and Social Class and Other Essays* (Cambridge: Cambridge University Press, 1950); T.H. Marshall and Tom Bottomore, *Citizenship and Social Class* (London: Pluto, 1992).
45. Marshall, *Citizenship and Social Class and Other Essays*, 94.
46. Maurice Roche observes that Marshall's concept of welfare was broadly inclusive, "taking 'welfare' in a broad sense to include such things as work, education, health and quality of life." Maurice Roche, *Rethinking Citizenship: Welfare, Ideology and Change in Modern Society* (Cambridge: Polity, 1992), 3.
47. C.B. Macpherson, "Problems of Human Rights in the Late Twentieth Century," in C.B. Macpherson, *The Rise and Fall of Economic Justice and Other Essays* (Oxford: Oxford University Press, 1985), 23, qtd. in Barbalet, *Citizenship*, 20.
48. Barbalet, *Citizenship*, 20.
49. Gorham, "Social Citizenship and its Fetters," 29.
50. T.H. Marshall, "Citizenship and Social Class," in T.H. Marshall, *Sociology at the Crossroads* (London: Heinemann, 1963), 87.
51. Marshall, "Citizenship and Social Class," 96, cited in Stewart, "Two Conceptions of Citizenship."
52. Mary G. Dietz, "Context Is All: Feminism and Theories of Citizenship," *Daedalus* 116 (Fall 1987): 1-24; Nancy Fraser and Linda Gordon, "Civil Citizenship Against Social Citizenship?" in *The Condition of Citizenship*, ed. van Steenbergen; Gorham, "Social Citizenship and its Fetters"; Michael Mann, "Ruling Class Strategies and Citizenship," *Sociology* 21, 3 (1987): 339-54; Pateman, *The Disorder of Women*; Roche, *Rethinking Citizenship*; Bryan S. Turner, "Outline of a Theory of Citizenship," *Sociology* 24, 2 (May, 1990): 189-217; *Citizenship and Social Theory*, ed. Bryan S. Turner (London: Sage, 1993); Sylvia Walby, "Is Citizenship Gendered?," *Sociology* 28, 2 (May, 1994): 379-95.
53. Roche, *Rethinking Citizenship*, 32.
54. Gorham, "Social Citizenship and its Fetters," 29.
55. Gorham, "Social Citizenship and its Fetters," 30. See also Anthony Giddens, "Class Division, Class Conflict and Citizenship Rights," in Anthony Giddens, *Profiles and Critiques in Social Theory* (London: Macmillan, 1982).
56. Gorham, "Social Citizenship and its Fetters," 39, 41.
57. Mouffe, *Dimensions of Radical Democracy*, 5.
58. Mouffe, *Dimensions of Radical Democracy*, 226.
59. Walby, "Is Citizenship Gendered?," 89.
60. Pateman, *The Disorder of Women*.

61. Nancy Fraser and Linda Gordon, "Contract versus Charity: Why Is There No Social Citizenship in the United States?," in *The Citizenship Debates*, ed. Shafir, 126. See also Lister, *Citizenship: Feminist Perspectives*, 23.

62. Will Kymlicka, "Multicultural Citizenship," in *The Citizenship Debates*, ed. Shafir; Joan Sangster, "Creating Social and Moral Citizens: Defining and Treating Delinquent Boys and Girls in English Canada, 1920-65," this volume, 337-58; Iris Marion Young, *Justice and the Politics of Difference* (Princeton: Princeton University Press, 1990).

63. Lister, *Citizenship: Feminist Perspectives*, 14; Anthony W. Marx, "Contested Citizenship: The Dynamics of Racial Identity and Social Movements," *International Review of Social History* 40, Supplement 3 (1995): 159-83; Stewart, "Two Conceptions of Citizenship," 64.

64. Stewart, "Two Conceptions of Citizenship," 64.

65. Etienne Balibar, "Propositions on Citizenship," *Ethics* 98 (July 1988): 723-30, 723.

66. Janine Brodie, "Three Stories of Canadian Citizenship," this volume, 55.

67. Alan Cairns, cited in Brodie, "Three Stories of Canadian Citizenship," 59.

68. Tom Mitchell. "'The Manufacture of Souls of Good Quality': Winnipeg's 1919 National Conference on Canadian Citizenship, English-Canadian Nationalism, and the New Order After the Great War," *Journal of Canadian Studies* 31, 4 (Winter 1996-97): 5-28.

69. On the impact of war on Canadian citizenship debates, see, *inter alia*, Marc Milner, *Canadian Military History: Selected Readings* (Toronto: Copp Clark Pitman, 1993).

70. Mitchell, "'The Manufacture of Souls of Good Quality,'" 9.

71. Mitchell, "'The Manufacture of Souls of Good Quality,'" 6.

72. Mitchell, "'The Manufacture of Souls of Good Quality,'" 9.

73. Mitchell, "'The Manufacture of Souls of Good Quality,'" 8.

74. Mitchell, "'The Manufacture of Souls of Good Quality,'" 19.

75. William E. Blatz and Helen Bott, *Parents and the Pre-School Child* (New York: William Morrow & Co., 1929), 275, qtd. in Harley D. Dickenson, "Scientific Parenthood: The Mental Hygiene Movement and the Reform of Canadian Families, 1925-1950," *Journal of Comparative Family Studies* 24, 3 (Autumn 1993): 387-402, 388.

76. Ronald Rudin, "From the Nation to the Citizen: Quebec Historical Writing and the Shaping of Identity," this volume, 95.

77. Tait, "Democracy and Mental Hygiene," 33.

78. Henry A. Giroux, *Schooling and the Struggle for Public Life: Critical Pedagogy in the Modern Age* (Minneapolis: University of Minnesota Press, 1988), 7, cited in Gorham, "Social Citizenship and its Fetters," 44-45.

79. Jacques Donzelot, *The Policing of Families* (New York: Random House, 1979).

80. Katherine Arnup, "Education for Motherhood: Creating Modern Mothers and Model Citizens," this volume, 251.

81. Jennifer Stephen, "Unemployment and the New Industrial Citizenship: A Review of the Ontario Unemployment Commission, 1916," this volume, 155-77.

82. Shirley Tillotson, "Time, Swimming Pools, and Citizenship: The Emergence of Leisure Rights in Mid-Twentieth-Century Canada," this volume, 199-221.

83. Lorna R. McLean, "'The Good Citizen': Masculinity and Citizenship at Frontier College, 1899-1933," this volume, 225-45.

84. Mary Louise Adams, "Constructing Normal Citizens: Sex Advice for Postwar Teens," this volume, 273-92.

85. Sean Purdy, "Scaffolding Citizenship: Housing Reform and Nation Formation in Canada, 1900-1950," this volume, 129-53.

86. Tillotson, "Time, Swimming Pools, and Citizenship," this volume.

87. Veronica Strong-Boag, "'The Citizenship Debates': The 1885 *Franchise Act*," this volume, 90.

88. William Kaplan, "Who Belongs? Changing Concepts of Citizenship and Nationality," in *Belonging: The Meaning and Future of Canadian Citizenship*, ed. William Kaplan (Montreal and Kingston: McGill-Queen's University Press, 1993), 245.

89. Adams, "Constructing Normal Citizens," this volume.

90. Giddens, "Class Division, Class Conflict and Citizenship Rights," 171.

91. Dorothy E. Chunn, " Sex And Citizenship: (Hetero)Sexual Offences, Law and 'White' Settler Society in British Columbia, 1885-1940," this volume, 359-84.
92. Strong-Boag, "'The Citizenship Debates,'" this volume.
93. Denyse Baillargeon, "Indispensable but not a Citizen: The Housewife in the Great Depression," this volume, 179-98.
94. Bernice Moreau, "Black Nova Scotian Women's Schooling and Citizenship: An Education of Violence," this volume, 293-311.
95. Tillotson, "Time, Swimming Pools, and Citizenship," this volume.
96. Roche, *Rethinking Citizenship*, 3.
97. In the present collection, the most evident examples include the construction of Québécois citizenship as detailed by Rudin, this volume, and the resistance demonstrated by First Nations peoples, some of whom long rejected British or Canadian citizenship under the terms in which it was offered. See Claude Denis, "Indigenous Citizenship and History in Canada," this volume, 113-26; and Veronica Strong-Boag, "'The Citizenship Debates,'" this volume.
98. Fraser and Gordon, "Contract versus Charity," 114.
99. Fraser and Gordon, "Contract versus Charity," 119.
100. Fraser and Gordon, "Contract versus Charity," 125. See also Roche, *Rethinking Citizenship*, 29 for a discussion of the problematic relationship between social citizenship and other dimensions of citizenship.
101. Michel Foucault, *Discipline and Punish: The Birth of the Prison*, trans. Alan Sheridan (New York: Vintage Books, 1979), 222.
102. Sangster, "Creating Social and Moral Citizens," this volume.
103. Chunn, "Sex And Citizenship," this volume.
104. Robert Menzies, "'Unfit' Citizens and the BC Royal Commission on Mental Hygiene, 1925-28," this volume, 387.
105. Gerald Friesen, *Citizens and Nation*, 228-29.
106. Maurice Roche, "Citizenship and Modernity," *British Journal of Sociology* 46, 4 (December 1995): 715-33, 730.

chapter two

THREE STORIES OF CANADIAN CITIZENSHIP[1]

Janine Brodie

Introduction

In November 1867, Governor-General Viscount Monck, reading from the Speech from the Throne, congratulated the newly elected members of Canada's first Parliament for completing the *Act of Union* which, he said, "laid the foundation of a new Nationality" and was "a fresh starting point for the moral, political and material advancement of the people of Canada." His Excellency the Governor-General referred to the people of Canada as "free and self-governing" and assured the House that "your new nationality enters on its course backed by the moral support, the material aid, and the most ardent wishes of the Mother Country."[2]

So marked the beginning of a new state, a new nationality, and a new community of citizens. The proclamation of statehood in the modern state system characteristically is a claim to national sovereignty, the supreme exercise of power over a bounded territory. State sovereignty also is meant to signal an alignment of territory, legitimate authority, citizenship, and identity. Yet the case of Canada is more complex. The territorial limits of the new state were still to be negotiated and sovereignty continued to be shared, both explicitly and implicitly, with Imperial Britain. Moreover, the very idea that the identity of Canada's inhabitants could be tied to a new and inclusive vision of "Canadianness" was confounded by the fact that the new political community contained, at least, three distinct cultural-ethnic groups, English, French, and Aboriginal, with different and, indeed, often antagonistic visions of self and nation. As a result, the embodiment in Canada of the fundamentals of modern statehood, concepts such as nation, state, sovereignty, and citizenship, was and continues to be elusive and contested.

This chapter traces the history of citizenship, which, as we shall see, involves much more than legal membership in a sovereign state. I will explore three different approaches to the history of Canadian citizenship. The legal, rights-based, and governance approaches all have a particular story to tell about being a member of the Canadian political community. I will attempt to unravel these stories through an exploration of state discourses about the Canadian character and the ideal Canadian citizen. To do so, I will draw on Speeches from the Throne from 1867 to the present. These historical transcripts, written by the government of the day and read by the Governor-General at the opening of a new session of Parliament, are unique records which document both the sitting government's perception of the "state of the nation" and its legislative agenda for the upcoming session. Published in Hansard, these speeches progressively unfold the drama of the Canadian experience from the threats of Fenian raids to those of the HIV/AIDS epidemic as well as the many historical foci of Canadian nation-building from the transcontinental railroad to the information highway. Before exploring these three stories, however, it is first necessary to discuss the conceptual underpinnings of the term "citizenship."

Citizenship: The Concept

The idea of citizenship has a long political history, initially describing a select few inhabitants of Ancient Greek city-states who claimed the privileges and responsibilities of self-government. The citizens of Ancient Greece were both rulers and ruled: collectively they established the law and procedures which governed the polis. The vast majority of others — slaves, children, and women, ineligible for citizenship privileges — were simply ruled.[3] Modern notions of citizenship, however, are tied directly to the emergence of the modern state system in the seventeenth century and to the ascendancy of the sovereign nation-state as the unchallenged unit of governance. Citizenship was the mark of formal legal inclusion within the nation-state as a specific and internationally recognized geopolitical entity. At a minimum, then, citizenship defined the population that could legitimately make claims on the state for protection as opposed to those, both inside and outside of a national territory, who could not. Membership in a nation-state became the defining mark of the modern political subject. As Gellner describes it, "The idea of a man without a nation seems to impose a great strain on the modern imagination. A man must have a nationality as he must have a nose and two ears."[4]

The modern ideal of citizenship was thus deeply implicated in the process of identity formation and the rise of nationalism which became the most potent political force of the twentieth century. Citizenship, i.e., identification with and loyalty to the nation state, required individuals to relinquish or subsume previous forms of allegiance, so-called "deep identities" such as religious, ethnic, and regional affiliations in favour of the universal status of citizen. These deep identities were seen as the totalizing products of traditional societies. The tribe, as Bauman explains, provided the fullest embodiment of the idea of belonging and total knowledge of the world and one's place in it. Any alternative identities were rendered invisible.[5] The birth of the modern nation state, however, saw the creation of national cultures as the principal source of cultural identification and as a good in its own right, indeed for some the supreme good. The ability to transcend particularisms in order to advance the collective good of the nation as a shared community of fate was the defining mark of the ideal citizen. Nationalism was a primary mechanism to adhere the citizen to the state and to give it popular legitimacy. Not surprisingly, all nationalist discourses are replete with various depictions of the ideal member of a political community. States also are deeply invested in these depictions insofar as they contribute to state authority and to social solidarity.

Although the history of citizenship and that of nationalism are closely interwoven, the two concepts are not interchangeable, as the Canadian case clearly attests. From its conception, this geopolitical unit has housed distinct nationalist visions grounded in different languages, cultures, and histories. These Native, francophone, and anglophone roots are what John Ralston Saul calls the "triangular foundations" of Canada. As Saul explains, "No matter how much each may deny the others at various times, each of their existences is dependent on the other two."[6] The Canadian story has been further complicated by successive waves of immigration which place many Canadians completely outside of Saul's triangle. However, the creation of an over-arching Canadian identity that would supercede this diversity has proved evasive, if not futile. Canadian citizenship does not coincide with a singular vision of nation, although, as discussed later in this chapter, our history abounds with attempts to evoke such a vision.

At the same time, citizenship represents much more than the right to hold a passport. The politics of citizenship, the shifting question of membership, of "who does and does not belong," involves more than accidents of birth, historical patterns of colonialization and settlement, or more systematic naturalization requirements. As Turner reminds us, citizenship is more properly understood as "that *set of practices* (juridical, political, economic and cultural) which define a person as a competent member of a society and which, as a consequence, shape the flow of resources to persons and social groups."[7] The range of public policies and state practices that contribute to defining competent membership in a political community are complex, often subtle, and shift across time. As such, the story of Canadian citizenship can be told in different ways. This chapter explores three possible perspectives. The legal, rights-based, and governance stories progressively expand our thinking about the multiple and dynamic underpinnings of the study of citizenship.

Three Stories of Canadian Citizenship

THE LEGAL STORY

Citizenship is first and foremost a legal status which identifies an individual as a full and equal rights-bearing member of the Canadian state and of Canadian society. For most countries, the formal story of citizenship is quite straightforward, involving a handful of laws specifying who has or may achieve citizenship status. In Canada, however, this formal story was complicated by its colonial origins. Although it was the first Commonwealth country to enact its own citizenship legislation independent of Britain, Canada did not have citizenship legislation in place until 1946, some 80 years after Confederation. Until then, the Canadian citizen as a legal entity did not exist in either national or international law. Instead, Canadians moved across borders as British subjects. However, the absence of explicit citizenship legislation did not mean that Canada's doors were open to the world as some nationalist myth-makers would have us believe. On the contrary, until the 1960s, immigration and naturalization legislation, especially the 1910 *Immigration Act*,[8] the 1914 *Naturalization Act*,[9] and the 1921 *Canadian Nationals Act*,[10] was explicitly designed to preserve and promote Canada's colonial identity as a white settler society.[11]

Canada's early legislators carefully monitored both the extent and origins of immigration to Canada, as the Speeches from the Throne from the 1880s until the 1920s readily demonstrate. Successive governments welcomed evidence of increasing flows of immigrants as a way to exploit the vast natural resources of Canada and as evidence of international recognition of Canada as a land of opportunity. At the same time, these speeches repeatedly note that it was "especially gratifying" that the stream of immigrants originated in the British Isles and, later, Continental Europe and the United States. By the early 1890s, these speeches also point to concerns about attracting immigrants of a "suitable type,"[12] "the unexpected influx of immigrants from oriental countries," and controlling immigration from India.[13]

These thinly-veiled racist sentiments were embodied in the *Immigration Act* of 1906[14] and strengthened in the *Immigration Act* of 1910. The latter legislation gave the federal cabinet the power to exclude, among others, "immigrants belonging to any race deemed unsuited to the climate or the requirements of Canada."[15] Following the passage of the act, the cabinet imposed a $500 head tax on immigrants of Asian origin, a sum exceeding the average annual wage of a Canadian manufacturing worker. Procedures also were devised, although not successfully executed, to exclude black immigrants. These racially-based practices were defended by William Scott, Superintendent of Immigration 1908-1924, who explained that "Canada ... is fully aware of sifting 'the wheat from the chaff' in the multitudes who seek her shores."[16] Canada's intent to exclude non-white immigrants was reconfirmed in the 1952 *Immigration Act*,[17] which enabled Cabinet to exclude immigrants using such subjective criteria as unsuitability to Canada's climate. Both formal and informal racially-based barriers to immigration and, consequently, to Canadian citizenship remained in place until the point-system was adopted in the 1970s. Thereafter, entry into Canada would be determined by, among other things, education, occupation and occupational demand, and language skills. Ostensibly these were non-racial criteria for immigration, but occupational preferences, levels of education, and language requirements still tended to favour immigration from Europe.

Although immigration policy served as proxy legislation, the apparent reluctance of Canada to enact its own citizenship legislation remains an historical curiosity. Part of the explanation for why Canadians maintained their status as Imperial subjects of the British Empire for so long was that Confederation was only a partial declaration of independent nationhood. And, indeed, Canada has been slow to strip away the vestiges of British colonialism. Canada's founding document, the *British North America Act (BNA)*, remained an Act of the British Parliament until the 1980s and the British monarch remains the Queen of Canada today. Nonetheless, most colonial ties were gradually frayed across the first half of the twentieth century, especially because of Canada's participation in the two world wars. Historians often have noted the strong linkages between the expansion of citizenship rights and participation in war. Groups previously excluded from such fundamental citizenship rights as voting and running for political office, especially working-class men, grounded their citizenship claims on their contributions to defending the country in times of war. Those willing to sacrifice their lives for their country, to embrace the ultimate obligation of citizenship, so the argument went, certainly deserved to enjoy the privileges of citizenship as well. An analogous process appeared to guide the achievement of the trappings of independent statehood among the British colonies during the twentieth century. After suffering staggering losses of their young men in the defence of the Empire in World War I, both Canada and Australia, for example, saw a rise of autonomous nationalism as well as a growth in sovereignty, increasingly with respect to foreign policy.

figure 2.1

Canadian Soldiers voting, France, 1916.

W.I. CASTLE / DEPT. OF NATIONAL DEFENCE / NATIONAL ARCHIVES OF CANADA / PA-000554.

Selected readings from Speeches from the Throne to Parliaments during World War I demonstrate this subtle transition in thinking from colony to statehood and from loyal imperialist subject to national citizen. In 1915, for example, the Speech paid tribute to "the people of Canada" who have "given most abundant and convincing evidence of their firm loyalty to our sovereign and of their profound devotion to the institutions of the British Empire." "Canadian soldiers," the Speech continued, "have shown conspicuous bravery and efficiency in the field of battle" and "have borne themselves worthily when fighting side by side with the best troops of the Empire."[18] In 1916, the Speech from the Throne again praised "the self-sacrificing and loyal spirit shown by all the Canadian people who have freely dedicated their manhood and substance to the common defense of the Empire."[19] By the end of the conflict, however, the federal government's assessment of the war effort had shifted to a more nationalist tone. The 1919 Speech from the Governor-General closing the Thirteenth Parliament noted the contributions of the Overseas Dominions and Dependencies to "those ties which bind the Empire in indissoluble union" but concluded with the following assessment of the war effort: "From the terrible struggle in which our country has borne so notable a part, Canada emerges with the proud consciousness that in fulfilling her duty to civilization and humanity she has taken a high place among the world's nations. ... Endowed with a vast heritage, we face the future with just confidence, firm in our determination to upbuild within our borders a great and prosperous nation."[20]

By the end of World War II, the obvious discrepancy between the legal designation of Canadians as British subjects and Canada's growing independent stature in the international community could not be sustained. The Speeches from the Throne during World War II did not frame Canada's contribution to the Allied effort as adolescent obligations to Mother Country and Empire. Instead, the Speeches applauded Canada's war effort with respect to "the maintenance of civilized society and the inheritance of human freedom,"[21] "the destruction of freedom throughout Europe," "civilization ... confronted with savagery,"[22] and the "titanic conflict between the forces of good and evil."[23] These wartime Speeches were full of references to Canadian nationalism, and the government's intention, once the conflict was over, to nation-build through national social security programs as well as by selecting a "distinctive Canadian flag" and by writing new citizenship legislation.

figure 2.2

First Canadian
Citizenship
Ceremony.

CHRIS LUND / NFB / NATIONAL ARCHIVES
OF CANADA / PA-129262.

In addition to a new-found sense of Canadian identity, there was another pressing reason why the federal government felt compelled "to revise and clarify the definition of Canadian citizenship, and to bring the legislation of respecting national status, naturalization and immigration into conformity with the definition of citizenship."[24] Although Canada was, throughout its first half-century, highly reliant on immigration, this inflow had dried up during the Great Depression of the 1930s and World War II. The war's end, however, saw an explosion of refugees whose homes and communities had been destroyed or who were fleeing from Soviet expansionism in Eastern Europe. Canada, as well as her allies, needed criteria to differentiate these desperate people — who were termed "displaced persons" (DPs in the pejorative) — from former Nazis and war criminals who also sought a safe haven and a new life.

In introducing the new *Citizenship Act* to the House of Commons in 1945, Paul Martin Sr., the architect of the legislation, explained the necessity of the legislation in terms of constructing a new national identity in the wake of the war. "For the national unity of Canada and for the future and greatness of this country," said Martin, "it is felt to be of utmost importance that all of us, new Canadians and old, have a consciousness of a common purpose and common interests as Canadians; that all of us are able to say with pride and say with meaning: I am a Canadian citizen."[25] The new law, however, was largely perfunctory, specifying the automatic right of entry of Canadians into Canada, a minimum residency requirement to qualify for Canadian citizenship, the conditions under which Canadian citizenship could be revoked, and a revised oath of allegiance. The 1946 *Citizenship Act*[26] was revisited in the mid-1970s to remove the preferential treatment of British subjects seeking Canadian citizenship and it has again been under reconsideration in the new millennium. Among the issues currently being re-examined is the question of whether citizens must be resident in Canada for a specified period in order to retain their citizenship.

THE RIGHTS-BASED STORY

The legal question of who is or can become a Canadian is one way of telling the citizenship story. Another approach is to inquire into the substance of citizenship: what rights come with being recognized as a full and competent member of a political community, and how have these rights changed with time? The structure of this "rights-based" story has been heavily influenced by T.H. Marshall's influential essay *Citizenship and Social Class*.[27] His evolutionary account of liberal-democratic citizenship was written during the formative years of the British welfare state and depicts the growing inclusiveness and substance of citizenship rights from this perspective. Nonetheless, many political scientists have embraced Marshall's work as a template to study the development of citizenship rights in all liberal democracies, including Canada.

The crux of Marshall's argument is that citizenship rights in liberal-democratic countries have evolved in three distinct stages, becoming an ever-more inclusive and substantial institution of governance in the process. He traces how citizenship rights have evolved from state recognition and protection of *civil rights* — relating to property, equal treatment under the law, and individual freedoms, to *political rights* — the right to vote, participate in politics, and hold governments accountable to *social rights* — the right to the collective provision of a minimum level of social security for all citizens as a right of citizenship. Marshall included among social rights "the right to a modicum of economic welfare and security to the right to share to the full in the social heritage and to live the life of a civilized being according to the standards prevailing in the society."[28] With few exceptions, fundamental civil rights were secured in the eighteenth century, political rights in the nineteenth century, and social rights in the twentieth century.

Marshall's work provides an historical account of the evolution of citizenship rights but it also has a strong normative component. Marshall was concerned about the uneasy relationship between the formal equality provided to all citizens through law and the many inequalities among these same citizens generated by capitalism. Characteristic of the intellectual climate of the period, Marshall celebrated the elaboration of social rights through universal social programs and the welfare state as a peaceful accommodation of class conflict as well as a prerequisite for the meaningful exercise of civil and political rights by all citizens. For him, individual freedoms and the formal right to participate in public life meant little if citizens were hobbled by the indignities and the powerlessness of poverty. Marshall saw social citizenship rights as a way of eroding the most glaring inequalities characteristic of industrial capitalism and of promoting social solidarity and social stability. The protection and promotion of the full range of citizenship rights, Marshall argued, nourished "a direct sense of community membership based on loyalty to a civilization which is a common possession. It is the loyalty of free men endowed with rights and protected by common law."[29]

A cursory review of the evolution of Canadian citizenship rights appears consistent with Marshall's historical analysis. Canada inherited the European civil rights legacy, largely achieved in the nineteenth century, when it adopted British Common Law tradition (as well as elements of France's Civil Law tradition in Quebec). In turn, political rights were conferred and expanded in the late nineteenth and early twentieth centuries. Indeed, between 1867 and 1919, issues of the franchise, electoral boundaries, and the conduct of elections were raised in 14 Speeches from the Throne. Admittedly, many of these early legislative initiatives had less to do with the recognition and expansion of political citizenship rights than with intricacies of establishing a workable electoral system in a new country with a federal system of government. There was much debate, for example, about whether there should be a separate standard for the federal franchise or whether provincial franchise legislation collectively would determine the composition of the national electorate.

Similarly, some of the debates about electoral boundaries were nothing more than veiled attempts by the governing party to seize partisan advantage.

From the perspective of the development of political citizenship rights, there were three important milestones. First, in 1876, the government announced the universal implementation of the secret ballot in order to obtain "an unbiased expression of the opinion of electors in selecting their representatives."[30] In 1885, the federal franchise was extended to non-propertied men — "numbers who have not hitherto enjoyed the right of voting for the election of members of the House of Commons."[31] And, in 1918, the federal franchise was extended to women. The Governor-General informed the House that "the extension of the franchise to women will notably broaden the basis and strengthen the stability of government and we may justly anticipate that it will exercise an important and wholesome influence upon many vital social problems confronting the nation."[32]

The idea of social problems and social programs began to appear in the Speeches from the Throne in the 1920s and increasingly during the Great Depression of the 1930s. The introduction of social legislation such as unemployment relief, assistance for the elderly, assistance for the provinces to meet their welfare obligations, work camps for homeless men, and security for sick workers were all framed as important to national development, the social and economic welfare of the dominion, and the national interest and the national good. No longer was falling on hard times interpreted as the lot of irresponsible individuals. Increasingly, the well-being of all citizens was seen to be the product of structural factors beyond the control of any one individual. In particular, condemnation of the capitalist system intensified during the most desperate years of the Great Depression. The 1935 Speech from the Throne explained the systemic liabilities of capitalism in terms that have been rarely heard in Canadian political debate. The Governor- General outlined the government's analysis of the Depression in the following way: "In the anxious years through which you have passed, you have been the witnesses of grave defects and abuses in the capitalist system. Unemployment and want are the proof of these. Great changes are taking place about us. New conditions prevail. These require modifications in the capitalist system to enable that system more effectively to serve the people."[33]

Government pronouncements of universal social programs as a right of citizenship followed later, especially in the mid-1940s when the foundations for the Canadian welfare state were first outlined. The idea of social citizenship rights was advanced in the 1943 Speech from the Throne. "It is in the general interest," it read, "*that freedom from fear and from want should be the assured possession of all*. A nation-wide plan which would provide insurance against the inevitable consequences of major economic and social hazards is essential if this objective is to be maintained." The government promised a "comprehensive national scheme of social insurance" which would "constitute *a charter of social security* for the whole of Canada."[34] The Canadian welfare state developed incrementally during the next two decades, for the most part without extravagant rights-based talk in the House of Commons. By Canada's centennial year, the cornerstones of social citizenship, especially universal medicare and the right to social assistance on the basis of need alone, had been set in place. The 1967 Speech from the Throne renewed the government's commitment to further pursuing the goal of citizen equality. The Speech declared that "the central concern of Canadian society must be the well-being of each individual, so that, regardless of his place or station at birth, he will have an equal chance to realize his full potential in the economic, social, political and cultural sense."[35] The linkage between citizenship and rights-based claims were further reinforced with the enactment of the *Canadian Bill of Rights* in 1960 and the entrenchment of the *Charter of Rights and Freedoms* in 1982.

Overall, the rights-based story of Canadian citizenship appears to correspond neatly with Marshall's evolutionary template, but his account has generated a number of criticisms that also find resonance in the Canadian experience. For example, Marshall's work leaves the false impression that citizenship rights were achieved in a systematic and peaceful manner. Such, however, was not the case in Canada or elsewhere. Comprehensive social programs, for example, were adopted only after a decade of social upheaval, the rise of new political parties that challenged the governing class, and the radicalization of the trade-union movement. Another well-founded criticism of Marshall's account is that his unfolding tale of the progressive elaboration of citizenship rights reflects only the experience of citizens from dominant social groups. The Canadian case shows that, for many groups, political rights were not achieved until well into the twentieth century, often after the advent of social rights. As already discussed, women did not gain the vote until 1918, while Chinese, East Indian, and Japanese Canadians could not vote in federal elections until after World War II. Status Indians were denied the federal franchise until 1960. Moreover, many racial and ethnic groups and, most especially, Canada's First Nations still have not realized the promise of social rights to social inclusion.

Others have argued that Marshall was short-sighted in suggesting that the achievement of social rights represents the full and final complement of membership in a political community. Turner, for example, suggests that cultural rights, i.e., the right both to distinctiveness and to participate in a complex culture, could be added to Marshall's list.[36] Indeed, a strong case can be made that Canada, in comparison with other liberal democracies, already has put flesh on the idea of cultural rights. Finally, after two decades of governmental restructuring, the erosion of social programs, and the hollowing out of the welfare state, it is fairly clear that Marshall's work reflects the optimism of another era and does not adequately appreciate the tenuous nature of citizenship rights. He applauded the achievement of social rights as an endpoint in governance which effected a necessary compromise between democracy and capitalism, the meaningful exercise of civil and political rights, and enduring foundations for social stability and social inclusion. The state of citizenship at the dawn of the twenty-first century, however, falls far short of Marshall's vision of the future and demonstrates that the scope and security of these rights are profoundly influenced by changes in the broader political and economic environment.

THE GOVERNANCE STORY

Our final story links citizenship, as a set of practices, to the broader study of governance. This latter term is meant to capture the historically shifting and politically negotiated (and enforced) relationships among the three principal domains of a liberal-democratic polity — the state, civil society, and the economy — as well as the ways in which citizens and groups articulate their interests, exercise their rights and obligations, and mediate their differences.[37] Students of governance, especially those drawing on Michel Foucault's essays on governmentality, begin with the premise that what governments do, the rationales behind their actions, and the objects of public policy are neither obvious nor static. Accordingly, neither citizens nor individuals exist as natural facts or prior to the act of governance. These and other social actors enter the political stage through dominant discourses and state practices that define certain characteristics and actions as governable entities or problems to be solved. To govern, in other words, "is to cut experience in certain ways, to distribute attractions and repulsions, passions and fears across it, to bring new facets and forces, new intensities and relations into being."[38] Different eras, moreover, are characterized by different philosophies of governance and thus cut experience in different ways.[39]

Governmentality theorists start with the premise that all government actions and, indeed, inactions are framed within particular political rationalities or discursive fields, each of which rests on its own particular vocabulary, ethical principles, and agreement on the nature and scope of political action and legitimate authority.[40] These rationalities prescribe what is a political problem and what and who is to be the object of governance. The governed do not exist outside of historically-specific political rationalities; instead, the governed are created by and speak through these rationalities. Citizenship is an instructive example. As already discussed, the modern citizen, as an object of governance, was created within the logics of the modern state system and gained identity as a member of a nation state. This and similar acts of identification, as Rose explains, are "simultaneously individualizing and collectivizing":[41] identifying with a collective tells us both who we are and who are not us.

Jane Jenson's development of the idea of citizenship regimes highlights the critical role played by states in creating identities of inclusion and exclusion. A citizenship regime, according to Jenson, consists of a broad range of institutional arrangements, rules, and understandings that 1) prescribe the boundaries of state responsibilities as well as those of markets, individuals, and communities; 2) set out formal citizenship rights and thereby identify those who are entitled to full citizenship and those who are not; 3) legitimize specific forms of political participation and modes of claims-making on the state; and 4) contribute to particular definitions of nation, nation-building, national identity, and the ideal citizen.[42] A citizenship regime is an integral element of the political rationality informing the governing practices of particular countries and specific eras.

The generation of a national identity has been instrumental in achieving and maintaining some level of social solidarity and state authority. Appeals to nation, rightly or wrongly, have provided the glue that holds diverse and unequal polities together as well as the force that mobilizes diverse populations into united actors, especially during periods of political crisis, social strain, and external threat. In this respect, the state has a large stake in promoting visions of national identity or what Castells calls a "legitimizing identity." Such identities help the state to maintain allegiance and social control as well as motivate concerted action.[43] The Canadian state, it is frequently argued, has played an inordinate role in trying to shape a national identity in order to transcend ethnic, religious, and regional conflicts and to build support for its many nation-building projects. Lacking a foundational myth, a story that locates the origin of a nation, a people, and a national character, successive Canadian governments have tried to create one.[44] Canadian journalist Richard Gwyn, in fact, has invented the term *state-nation* in order to convey the idea that the Canadian path to statehood was unique in that it was not the result of nationalist claims for self-government.[45] The state came first and it has actively and variously attempted to shape a singular vision of nation and national identity ever since.

Obviously, the story of Canadian citizenship told from the vantage point of political rationalities and citizenship regimes is a large, complex, and ongoing tale. In what follows, I will read the Speeches from the Throne with an eye to only one thread among many that weave through the history of Canadian citizenship regimes. My focus will be on how successive governments define Canada and what it is to be a Canadian. I am interested in the descriptors of both inclusion and exclusion, paying close attention to how the descriptor functions and how it connects with other things, especially the broader rationalities of governance. Elsewhere I have described in detail the three distinct political rationalities that have both informed governing practices since Confederation and provided the foundations for three distinct state forms and the configuration of nation and national identity.[46] My task in the remaining pages of this chapter will be less comprehensive. I will contrast the pre- and post-World War II eras to demonstrate the ever-shifting official constructions of citizens and of the Canadian experience.

The Imperial Subject

In Canada's first half-century, the over-riding focus of successive federal governments was nation-building: building transportation and other public infrastructures as well as recruiting a population to exploit the untouched resources of Canada's vast and expanding territory. The Speeches from the Throne during these years focus very much on these concerns: notions of national identity and of citizenship barely appear as objects of governance. In fact, between 1867 and 1930, the word "citizen" appears only three times: once with respect to the "citizen-soldiers'" contributions to quelling the 1885 Riel Rebellion;[47] again in 1900 with respect to the potential usefulness of immigrants "as citizens of the dominion";[48] and finally, in 1908, with reference to the citizens of France and the United States.[49] The absence of appeals to citizenship in these early years is perhaps not surprising considering that Canada had no citizenship act of its own and was still very much tied to the orbits of Imperial Britain. "The people of Canada" and "the Canadian people," as they are invariably referred to in the Speeches, are largely defined in reference to the Monarch and to Great Britain instead of to their own country. The object of governance was the *imperial subject* who was variously described as possessing "good intelligence,"[50] "enterprise, contentment and loyalty,"[51] "loyalty and good will,"[52] "loyalty and affection ... for her Majesty the Queen ... and the unity of the British Empire,"[53] and "happy and contented people, whose character and prosperity ... add strength to the great empire."[54]

The ideal Canadian, in other words, was a contented and, above all, loyal subject of the British Empire. This description might come as a surprise to many, given the francophone factor in Canada and the resistance that French Canadians mounted against Imperial Britain both when Canada created a navy in 1909 and again during World War I. Amazingly, there is not a single reference to French Canadians in these Speeches. References to the bilingual-cultural origins of the settler society do not appear until the 1960s. During these early years, provincial muscle-flexing over education had the effect of either assimilating francophones or pushing them back into the province of Quebec. There, *les Canadiens* were largely excluded from business, administered to by the Roman Catholic Church, regulated by a separate legal code, and governed by an inward-looking elite who dominated communication with the outside jealously guarding its jurisdiction and acting as an intermediary to the federal state. The early political bargain in Canada involved a coalition of anglophone and francophone elites, but ordinary French Canadians rarely fell directly into the governing spaces of the early federal government.

In addition to the Imperial subject, two other governable identities emerge as objects of public policy in these early transcripts — the immigrant and the Indian. As already noted, government policy aimed to exclude non-whites within the ideal categories of Imperial subject and the "Canadian people." During these years, immigrants also are objects of concerns with respect to their "thrift, energy and law abiding character,"[55] their contribution "to the wealth of the country,"[56] their "desirability" and "suitability,"[57] and their ability to be "absorbed into our population."[58] Then, as today, the immigrant was identified as an instrumental other — an outsider whose value depended both upon rapid assimilation and potential contribution to economic growth.

The case of the Indian provides an instructive example of how state discourses construct and manipulate the governable subject into second-class or non-citizens. During the 1870s and 1880s, when the federal government was rapidly negotiating treaties with Native populations and expanding the territorial sovereignty of the Canadian state, the "Indian" and "Indian Tribes" are recurring characters in the Speeches from the Throne. Moreover, these actors are represented as autonomous and competent. In 1875, for example, the Speech refers to "amicable relations with the Indian tribes [the Crees and Santeux of the North-West] and in the following year reference is made to "the interest taken by the people of Canada in the welfare of their Indian fellow-countrymen."[59] Again, in 1878, the Speech refers to the "peaceful negotiation with the native tribes, who place implicit faith in the honour and justice of the British crown."[60]

However, as the terrain of the Canadian state expanded and with the implementation of the *Indian Act* (1876), the identity of the First Nations was rapidly transformed from independent actors to faceless objects of administration. In the early 1880s, for example, the government lamented mounting evidence that tribes moved to reserves were starving. In a paternalistic tone, the Speech argued it was necessary to "induce [Indian bands recently settled on reserves] to betake themselves to the cultivation of the soil" and to "induce them to betake themselves to the raising of cattle."[61] "We can only expect," the government contended, "by a long continuance of patient firmness to induce these *children of the Prairie and the Forest* to abandon their nomadic habits, become self-supporting, and ultimately add to the industrial wealth of the country."[62] Later the government would congratulate Indian Industrial Schools, finding "the proofs of proficiency and intelligence on the part of children ... highly encouraging."[63] By the turn of the century, the Speeches no longer mention Indians or their social plight; instead, there are recurrent references to the government's intention to amend the *Indian Act*. Indeed, Indians re-emerge only in the 1960s, this time as indigenous people in need.

As already discussed, ties to Imperial Britain and, consequently, the validity of the Imperial subject began to unravel during the 1920s. A new rationale for governance, one based on state intervention and the provision of social welfare, would emerge after World War II. The rationale of governance in the 1930s and early 1940s can best be described as crisis management which, in turn, was accompanied by different depictions of the ideal citizen. Not surprisingly, the good Canadian in the 1930s was someone who could withstand the hardships of the Depression with "patience and fortitude" and with a "spirit of cooperation and mutual understanding." "These attributes of Canadianism," the 1931 Throne Speech read, "are national assets of real value" and "the surest bulwark of the nation's welfare and happiness."[64] The onset of World War II predictably called on the duty of the Canadian people to meet their responsibilities and to show determination in the defence of freedom and "civilization confronted with savagery."[65] The ideal citizens, of course, were "the fighting men of Canada" who, "at sea, on land] and in the air ... wherever they have served, have displayed the highest courage, endurance and skill."[66]

From Social Citizen to Entrepreneurial Citizen

I have already noted that, near the end of World War II, the government embraced both a new rationale for governance based on the provision of social programs and a new sense of Canadian nationalism. This second phase of nation-building during the 1940s and 1950s saw a flurry of initiatives aimed at creating the social and the symbolic infrastructures of the new Canadianism; however, any rhetoric that gave flesh to the substance of this identity was rare. During the 1950s, the Speeches announced, in rapid sequence, social legislation for families, the sick, the blind and disabled, the unemployed, veterans, women, students, the elderly, and the poor as well as initiatives to build up the cultural and symbolic infrastructures of citizenship. Successive governments announced their intention to select, among other initiatives, a Canadian flag and a national anthem; to pursue national development in the arts, letters, and sciences; to finance the Canadian Broadcasting Corporation (CBC); to protect historic sites and monuments; to launch the Canada Council for the arts, humanities, and social sciences; to enhance national museums; and, finally, to establish a Canadian Bill of Rights which would "manifest the intent that fundamental rights and freedoms shall prevail and remain inviolate in all matters within the competence of parliament."[67]

Since the early 1960s, the Speeches from the Throne have taken on a very different style and tone from their predecessors. They have become progressively longer, less focused on perfunctory legislative agendas, and more descriptive of core Canadian values, Canadian identity and national unity. This postwar preoccupation with establishing "who we are," of course, has coincided with the rise of Quebec nationalism and the separatist movement, the radical transformation of Canada from a predominantly and self-consciously white settler society to a multi-ethnic and multi-racial one, and the ever-intensifying pace of globalization. Distinguished Canadian political scientist Alan Cairns provides a succinct analysis of the volatility that has come to characterize Canadian identity and citizenship. "The definition of who we are as a people," he writes, "has been a moving target for the last half century. The federal state and Canadian society have been caught up in a vortex of pressures between new identities emerging from below and struggling for recognition and ... governmental attempts from above to refashion collectivities ... in light of state purposes. The transformation in political identity and conceptions of community since the Second World War have already been immense, but the end is not yet in sight."[68] I cannot detail all of the often nuanced attempts to fashion a coherent and encompassing vision of the Canadian citizen since the 1960s, but I will contrast two incarnations — the social citizen most visible during the golden years of the welfare state and the entrepreneurial citizen who has recently arrived on the political stage.

The social citizen was very much a product of the welfare state and the assumptions of liberal-progressivism which guided governing practices in

Canada until at least the mid-1970s. This governing philosophy mandated the state to intervene in the market, civil society, and the home in order to provide security for all citizens as a right of citizenship. The welfare state and the extensive bureaucracy built up around it were committed to the formal equality of citizens, impersonal procedures and, above all, the abiding belief that social progress could be realized through planning and the reasoned implementation of public policy. At its apex in the late 1960s, liberal-progressivism exuded a spirit of confident optimism and a sense of endless possibility. To today's reader, the announced intentions of the federal government, such as the "elimination of poverty among our people"[69] or the creation of a just society, appear overly optimistic, if not hopelessly naive. Liberal-progressivism promised that these outcomes were not only conceivable but, with planning and funding, within the government's grasp.

The social citizen was, above all, an individual bearer of rights and other state-based assurances of equality, as well as of equality of opportunity which, in turn, provided Canadians with their collective identity. The state would provide "a national minimum of social security and human welfare"[70] for *all Canadians*; "full equality of rights for *all Canadian citizens*"; "*all Canadians* [would] retire in security and with dignity";[71] "*all Canadians* [would] feel equally served by Confederation";[72] "*all Canadians* [would] obtain needed health services, irrespective of their ability to pay";[73] and "*each Canadian* [would have] the enjoyment of the maximum possible liberty, happiness and material well-being."[74] Jane Jenson has pointed out the underlying paradox in the construction of Canada's social citizen. This citizenship regime was grounded in individualization: the new collective identity rested on the rights guaranteed to abstract individual claims-makers.[75] However, the individual Canadian of the 1960s was differently conceived than the individual Canadian of the early twenty-first century. The former was assumed to be equal with respect to vulnerability to insecurity while the latter is assumed to be equal with respect to assuming personal security.

This idea of shared vulnerability also informed governmental attempts to ensure national unity during the early years of the Quebec Revolution. In 1963, the French fact was finally acknowledged in a Speech from the Throne. "The character and strength of our nation," it read, "are drawn from the diverse cultures of people who came from many lands ... The greater Canada that is in our power to make will be built not on uniformity but on continuing diversity, and particularly on the basic partnership of English speaking and French speaking people."[76] The programs informing the social citizen, however, provided uniformity at the level of the individual and were consistently linked to the national unity question. For successive governments, the challenge of national unity, whether related to Québécois nationalism, regionalism, or Aboriginal communities, could be quelled through the fulfillment of the promise of social citizenship. Indeed, in 1973, the government assured the Parliament that it remained "fully committed to two preeminent goals, national unity and equality of opportunity for all Canadians."[77]

The oil shocks, rising government debt, and stagflation of the 1970s, however, would soon strain this commitment and begin the gradual displacement of the social citizen. These years saw both the promise of social security shift away from all Canadians to Canadians in need and the promise of equality of opportunity redirected to the cultural and legal spheres. In 1974, for example, the government spoke of "extending equality before the law for all Canadians."[78] Two years later, the government noted that national unity was enhanced when "all Canadians believe we have an equal opportunity to be fully ourselves in a cultural sense."[79]

At the same time, the ideal Canadian was recast from a social citizen to a caring and sharing citizen who was willing to sacrifice when times were tough. Signals that the social-security regime would shift from a universal to a residual model were flagged in the mid-1970s when social security was designated first and foremost for those who could not work. By 1977, Canadians were told that it was "essential to the unity of the country" to show a "greater willingness to sacrifice ... to take less so that others may have enough."[80] In the 1980s, Canadians were informed that these actions were part and parcel of the national character. The 1980 Speech from the Throne, for example, noted that "Canada's tradition is one of sharing ... a country whose people share their wealth first with those who need it most." "Canadians will accept sacrifice," the Speech continued, and they understand that "the state cannot meet every demand or satisfy every group."[81] In 1986, the Speech represented Canada as "a modern, tolerant, and caring nation," adding that Canadians "want their governments to give the highest priority in social policy to those who are in greatest need."[82] The ideas of the universal vulnerability to insecurity and the socialization of risk were thus jettisoned.

During the 1980s, the assumptions motivating the welfare state were gradually replaced by those of neo-liberalism, specifically an uncompromising confidence in the superiority of the market and market mechanisms, privatization, decentralization, and the individualization of risk.[83] The transition from the welfare to the neo-liberal state also has been accompanied by the birth of the entrepreneurial citizen, whose realm of activity and responsibility increasingly stretches beyond Canada's borders. The persona of the entrepreneurial citizen can be traced back to the mid-1980s when the newly elected Mulroney government embraced neo-liberal assumptions and governing practices "and embarked on the long, complex and painstaking road of building a national economic consensus."[84] More recently, celebrations of the entrepreneurial citizen have been motivated both by the federal state's abandonment of universal social security and by the challenges of global competition in an ever-intensifying era of globalization.

Since the late 1980s, the Speeches have stressed that Canadians are living through fundamental changes that deem invalid the assumptions of the past. Moreover, "Canada is inescapably part of the global economy"[85] and Canadians are "citizens in a global economy."[86] Canada's ability to compete — indeed, national unity — requires a strong and innovative economy. In contrast to the postwar period when the state was central to realizing both citizen equality and national unity, these critical outcomes are now entrusted to the market. In 2001, the government represented an innovative economy as essential to creating opportunity for Canadians and for distributing it across sectors and regions. However, consistent with neo-liberalism's core premise, the state is not identified as taking a leadership role in the creation of the new economy. Instead, future success will depend on "people with advanced skills and entrepreneurial spirit."[87] And, similar to the loyal Imperial subject and the social citizen, the very future of the country has become dependent on the economic successes of the entrepreneurial citizen. As the government explained in the 1991 Speech, "there is much more to Canadian unity than amending the constitution. Our unity is strengthened by a strong economy."[88]

Fortunately, we also have been told that Canadians are well placed to succeed in the global market. In fact, the requisite qualities of the entrepreneurial citizen are embedded in our national tradition and value structure: "Canada's history is the history of builders and achievers."[89] Later in the decade, the national character was elaborated with respect to the perceived demands of global competition. The Speeches underlined that "our citizens have the qualities that are needed to succeed in the 21st century." Canadians "welcome innovation and new ideas"[90] and "have the self-confidence to act, and to act successfully."[91] "Change does not frighten us — we have always harnessed it to our advantage."[92] "Canada is proud, optimistic and strong ... and [can] face the challenges."[93] More than that, "Our country has a tradition of being a responsible, engaged, committed world citizen. ... This is a key characteristic of our national identity and a source of pride to Canadians."[94] Together, this inherited inventory of national values helps define what the government now terms "our Canadian Way."[95]

Such revelations about Canadian history and the Canadian character are the stuff of nationalist myth-making — the invention of a tradition and a foundational myth where none existed before.[96] And, like all national myths, it serves to contain dissent and to mobilize citizens around new philosophies of governance and new development strategies. In the present era, the ideal Canadian, indeed all Canadians, already brimming with entrepreneurial DNA, have been asked to play their part. "Canada's ability to prosper," according to the government's analysis, will be determined by our educational and management skills and "by our attitudes to work and to change."[97] To meet the challenges, the Speeches recommend that we work together, collaborate, partner, and volunteer — in effect, put our collective shoulder to the wheel: "Canadians must rise to these challenges."[98] "Every citizen can contribute to building our nation," we are told; indeed, "every Canadian is called upon to make a contribution to build our country."[99]

The pursuit of the "Canadian Way" rests on individual entrepreneurship with the state only acting in a steering role. The ideal citizen, however, understands that governments should recede in the current era: "Canadians understand that their governments simply cannot afford everything that is demanded of them"[100] and they "want their governments to work in partnership."[101] According to the logic of these neo-liberal public transcripts, government does have a role, and that is to draw lesser Canadians, so-called "at risk" groups, into the entrepreneurial fold. These include high-school dropouts, illiterate and under-skilled adults, single mothers, people with disabilities, and Aboriginal peoples. The government promises to work with the latter group, in particular, "to help strengthen their entrepreneurial and business expertise."[102] Otherwise, neo-liberal governance prescribes that the mantle of leadership fall outside of the public sphere, increasingly, in fact, to communities. Critics of neo-liberalism have argued that this divestiture of state power and responsibility effectively diminishes political citizenship rights and democratic governance because it shrinks the public sphere and the domain of collective decision-making. But the 2001 Speech from the Throne advanced an opposing view: "In a healthy democracy, leadership can come from everyone, because it is a sense of really knowing what you want and what you can contribute."[103]

Conclusion

The three stories of citizenship recounted here demonstrate the complex and dynamic nature of modern democratic citizenship and its close companion, national identity. However, while citizenship can claim a long genealogy and rich history, its future is increasingly clouded by neo-liberal governance and intensifying globalization of national economies and cultures. These inescapable political facts have upset most of the core concepts and practices that grew up within and beside the nation-state. Globalization, in particular, has been indicted for the pervasive erosion of state sovereignty which, in turn, has profound implications for the meaningful exercise of citizenship rights. In effect, globalization has disrupted the historically-grounded and over-lapping fit among national territory, sovereignty, democracy, citizenship, and identity.

The familiar liberal-democratic geography of power and representation has shifted away from the citizen in three distinct directions — upward to the international and transnational, downward to the local, and outward to the market and to civil society. Combined, these forces have weakened citizenship rights, nurtured a steady decline in democracy, and threatened social stability. As the importance of borders lessens and the capacity of the state to effect change within national boundaries weakens, the meaning of citizenship has rightly fallen into question. In all liberal democracies, citizenship practices have been powerful instruments of political mediation and social inclusion. In Canada, moreover, they also have been instrumental in constructing various visions of national identity and solidarity. As citizenship loses its coherence and force in this current climate of neo-liberal globalism, we might rightly ask if Canada can be far behind.[104]

Notes

1. I wish to thank Sam Tang for his valuable assistance in researching this chapter.
2. Canada, Speech from the Throne [hereafter SFT], 7 November 1867, 5-6.
3. Christina Gabriel, "Citizens and Citizenship," in *Critical Concepts: An Introduction to Politics*, 2nd ed., ed. Janine Brodie (Toronto: Pearson Education Canada, 2002), 261.
4. Earnest Gellner, *Nations and Nationalism* (Oxford: Basil Blackwell, 1983), 6.
5. Zygmunt Bauman, *In Search of Politics* (Stanford, CA: Stanford University Press, 1999), 161-62.
6. John Ralston Saul, *Reflections of a Siamese Twin: Canada at the End of the Twentieth Century* (Toronto: Viking, 1997), 81.
7. Bryan Turner, "Conceptual Problems in the Theory of Citizenship," in *Citizenship and Social Theory*, ed. Bryan Turner (London: Sage, 1993), 2, emphasis mine.
8. *Immigration Act*, S.C. 1910, c.27.
9. *Naturalization Act*, S.C. 1914, c.44.
10. *Canadian Nationals Act*, S.C. 1921, c.4.
11. Valerie Knowles, *Forging Our Legacy: Canadian Citizenship and Immigration, 1900-1977* (Ottawa: Public Works and Government Services, 2000), 31-40.
12. See, for example, SFT, 18 April 1995, 3.
13. SFT, 16 June 1899, 4.
14. *Immigration Act*, R.S.C. 1906, c.93.
15. Quoted in Knowles, *Forging Our Legacy*, 33.

16. Quoted in Knowles, *Forging Our Legacy*, 34.
17. *Immigration Act*, R.S.C. 1952, c.145.
18. SFT, 4 February 1915, 1-2.
19. SFT, 13 January 1916, 4.
20. Canada, House of Commons, Debates, 1919, 2.
21. SFT, 7 November 1940, 1.
22. SFT, 22 January 1942, 1.
23. SFT, 6 September 1945, 4.
24. SFT, 6 September 1945, 4.
25. Quoted in SFT, 6 September 1945, 65.
26. *Canadian Citizenship Act*, S.C. 1946, c.15.
27. T.H. Marshall, *Citizenship and Social Class* (Cambridge: Cambridge University Press, 1950).
28. Marshall, *Citizenship and Social Class*, 10.
29. Marshall, *Citizenship and Social Class*, 40-41; also quoted in Barry Hindess, "Citizenship in the Modern West," in *Citizenship and Social Theory*, ed. Bryan Turner (London: Sage, 1993), 22.
30. SFT, 10 February 1876, 2.
31. SFT, 20 July 1885, 3476.
32. SFT, 23 May 1918, 2559.
33. SFT, 17 January 1935, 3.
34. SFT, 28 January 1943, 1-2, emphasis mine.
35. SFT, 8 May 1967, 2.
36. Turner, "Conceptual Problems in the Theory of Citizenship," 7.
37. United Nations Development Program (UNDP), *Reconceptualizing Governance* (New York: UNDP Press, 1997), 9.
38. Nikolas Rose, *Powers of Freedom: Reframing Political Thought* (Cambridge: Cambridge University Press, 1999), 31.
39. Janine Brodie, "Meso-Discourses, State Forms and the Gendering of Liberal-Democratic Citizenship," *Citizenship Studies* 1 (1997): 223-42.
40. Rose, *Powers of Freedom*, 26, 28.
41. Rose, *Powers of Freedom*, 46.
42. Jane Jenson, "Social Citizenship in the 21st Century: Challenges and Options," The Timlin Lecture, University of Saskatchewan (February 2001), 4.
43. Manuel Castells, *The Power of Identity* (Oxford: Blackwell, 1997), 7.
44. Stuart Hall, "The Question of Cultural Identity," in *Modernity: An Introduction to Modern Societies*, ed. Stuart Hall et al., (London: Blackwell, 1995), 613.
45. Richard Gwyn, *Nationalism Without Walls: The Unbearable Lightness of Being Canadian* (Toronto: McClelland and Stewart, 1995).
46. Janine Brodie, *Politics on the Margins: Restructuring and the Canadian Women's Movement* (Halifax: Fernwood Publishing, 1995); Brodie, "Meso-Discourses"; Brodie, "The Rise and Demise of the Canadian Welfare State," in *West-East Comparisons of the Welfare State*, ed. Christina Aspalter (New York: Nova Science Publishing, 2002).
47. SFT, 20 July 1885, 347.
48. SFT, 1 February 1900, 3.
49. SFT, 20 July 1908, 13593-94.
50. SFT, 14 June 1872, 1144.
51. SFT, 4 February 1875, 2.
52. SFT, 2 January 1896, 3.
53. SFT, 25 March 1897, 4.
54. SFT, 12 January 1904, 6.
55. SFT, 1 February 1900, 3.
56. SFT, 20 July 1908, 13592.
57. SFT, 9 March 1922, 7.
58. SFT, 8 January 1926, 11.
59. SFT, 4 February 1875, 2.
60. SFT, 8 February 1878, 14.

61. SFT, 12 February 1880, 3.
62. SFT, 9 February 1882, 2, emphasis mine.
63. SFT, 20 August 1896, 6.
64. SFT, 12 March 1931, 1, 3.
65. SFT, 22 January 1942, 1.
66. SFT, 27 January 1944, 3.
67. SFT, 15 January 1959, 2.
68. Quoted in Policy Research Initiative (PRI), *Rekindling Hope and Investing in the Future: Report*, prepared for the Social Cohesion Network (Ottawa: Privy Council Office, 1998), 8.
69. SFT, 5 April 1965, 2.
70. SFT, 6 September 1945, 4.
71. SFT, 16 May 1963, 7, emphasis mine.
72. SFT, 16 May 1963, 7.
73. SFT, 5 April 1965, 2.
74. SFT, 18 January 1966, 9.
75. Jenson, "Social Citizenship in the 21st Century," 8.
76. SFT, 16 May 1963, 6.
77. SFT, 4 January 1963, 4.
78. SFT, 30 September 1974, 7.
79. SFT, 4 January 1973, 4.
80. SFT, 18 October 1977, 3.
81. SFT, 14 April 1980, 5.
82. SFT, 1 October 1986, 13.
83. Brodie, "Meso-Discourses."
84. SFT, 5 November 1984, 6.
85. SFT, 3 May 1991, 3.
86. SFT, 23 September 1997, 10.
87. SFT, 30 January 2001, 4.
88. SFT, 3 May 1991, 3.
89. SFT, 3 May 1991, 2.
90. SFT, 23 September 1997, 6.
91. SFT, 30 January 2001, 5.
92. SFT, 30 January 2001, 3.
93. SFT, 30 January 2001, 5.
94. SFT, 23 September 1997, 11.
95. This term is found in SFT from 1997 to 2001.
96. Hall, "The Question of Cultural Identity," 613.
97. SFT, 3 May 1991, 4.
98. SFT, 23 September 1997, 6.
99. SFT, 30 January 2001, 5.
100. SFT, 3 May 1991, 5.
101. SFT, 23 September 1997, 9.
102. SFT, 30 January 2001, 6.
103. SFT, 30 January 2001, 8.
104. Janine Brodie, "An Elusive Search for Community; Globalization and the Canadian National Identity," *Review of Constitutional Studies* (forthcoming).

PART II

CONSTITUTING THE CANADIAN CITIZEN

chapter three

"THE CITIZENSHIP DEBATES"
The 1885 *Franchise Act*

Veronica Strong-Boag

Introduction

In the years after Confederation, the character of the Canadian state and the relationships among its constituent parties, whether provinces, territories, genders, classes, or races, were far from settled. Canadians had to learn the specifics of citizenship under the new regime. From March to June of 1885 the House of Commons fought over the specifics of a federal franchise law to replace the provincial regulations that hitherto had determined voting eligibility. The exchanges among MPs, what I have termed the "citizenship debates," brought to the fore key issues of gender, race, and class, advantage and disadvantage.

In its original form, *Bill 103* proposed to enlarge the electorate with two new groups of voters: spinsters and widows, at least those of European origin, meeting male property qualifications; and Indians who occupied land in *fee simple* with improvements of $150 or more on their reserves anywhere in the Dominion. This latter group would no longer, as was required under the *Indian Act of 1868*, have to renounce tribal membership and annuities in return for the vote. As progressively amended, however, the *Franchise Act* ultimately excluded all women from the category of *persons* and all Natives "in Manitoba, British Columbia, Keewatin, and the North-West Territories, and any Indian on any reserve elsewhere in Canada, who is not in possession and occupation of a separate and distinct tract of land in such reserve, and whose improvements on such separate tracts are not of the value of at least one hundred and fifty dollars, and who is not otherwise possessed of the qualifications entitling him to be registered on the list of voters."[1] The final legislation, inspired by British Columbia's example and evidently at the request of that province's MPs, also explicitly excluded "Asiatics" or "Chinamen." While Wilfrid Laurier would return the determination of the federal electorate to the provinces in 1898, the exclusions of 1885 set the terms for decades-long conflict over the political rights of various groups living in Canada.

The Act passed on July 4, 1885 was a critical moment in the history of "rights talk" in Canada. The following pages examine its significance, beginning with a review of Canadian citizenship, nationality, and disfranchisement in the nineteenth century, next considering the resistance of marginalized communities to second-class status, and finally moving to a review of the House of Commons debates themselves. This last section assesses parliamentary treatment of the three groups — White women, Natives, and Chinese — whose right to enfranchisement was at issue. As we shall see, claims to Canada were far from settled in the decades after Confederation. One debater of the day spoke truer than he knew in declaring, "in reference to the Franchise Bill, there is certainly a great deal of excitement in regard to it, and the excitement is increasing."[2]

Citizenship, Nationality, and Disfranchisement

At the time of the *Franchise Act*, Native-born or naturalized Canadians were legal subjects, rather than citizens *per se*, of the British Crown in the Dominion. But, as Alfred Howell pointed out in his magisterial *Naturalization and Nationality in Canada* (1884), the rights of subjects "under a monarchy with free representative institutions and responsible government" were effectively no different from those of the citizens of a republic.[3] Canadian citizens nonetheless did not exist as such until the first *Citizenship Act* in 1947 and they remained British subjects in law and on passports until 1977.[4] In contrast to the American republic, Canadian nationality looked simultaneously in two directions, one imperial and the other national. Matters were still more complicated as many residents retained strong local loyalties to the provinces and to homelands elsewhere. In the case of the First Nations, their allegiance very frequently embraced bands, tribes, and, increasingly, pan-Indian communities. Such diverse loyalties distinguished Canadian identity from the very beginning.

In 1881 the Dominion passed the first legislation with regard to nationality. This *Act Respecting Naturalization and Aliens*, commonly referred to as *The Naturalization Act, Canada, 1881*, discriminated not only between aliens and subjects of the Crown but also among the latter. Regulating naturalization as well as denaturalization, it joined similar efforts by Britain and the United States to distinguish more effectively among those who might claim citizenship. It abrogated the old legal rule that one cannot expatriate oneself without the consent of the government.[5] The legislation also defined "disability" as "the status of being an infant, lunatic, idiot, or married woman."[6] Section 26 went on to specify that "[a]no married woman shall, within Canada, be deemed a subject of the State of which her husband is for the time being a subject." Section 27 identified a British-born widow, "who has become an alien by or in consequence of her marriage," as "a statutory alien."[7] Indians, the only *racial* group singled out *per se*, were "not entitled to all the privileges of British subjects unless they are enfranchised," a status that depended on holding property in *fee simple*, in other words the abandonment of the collective landholding of the tribal community.[8] Such distinctions were intrinsic to the efforts of the modern state to define and restrict its obligations and responsibilities. Those set beyond the pale could expect to be treated as lesser creatures within the law. Women and Indians might be British subjects (and the Six Nations of Ontario, for example, rejected even this status), but they were not the equals of White men.

Well before the 1880s the franchise was also used to distinguish groups of citizens as full or only partial participants in the community. Property was an influential determinant of the right to vote. Many poorer men, especially rural labourers and those in towns and cities, remained disfranchised at most levels until well after Confederation. While numerous, they were not the largest group shut out. As colonial jurisdictions reformed their electoral systems in the nineteenth century, women of every condition encountered formal exclusion on the basis of sex alone. Lower Canada explicitly barred them in 1834, PEI in 1836, New Brunswick in 1843, the Union of the Canadas in 1849, and Nova Scotia in 1851.[9]

Natives and Asians were also singled out. In enacting manhood suffrage in 1854, Nova Scotia rejected Indians, only to cancel this formal prohibition when it resorted to the assessment franchise in 1863. That same year the colony of British Columbia barred Indians and Chinese from voting; in 1875 the new Pacific province passed the *Qualification and Registration of Voters Act* that made it illegal to grant the franchise to any Chinese. While only Nova Scotia and B.C. in British North America specifically disfranchised Indians, rights under colonial regimes that honoured property as well as prejudice remained more theoretical than practised. When John Brant, a chief of the Six Nations Confederacy and son of the heroic Native Loyalist Joseph Brant, was elected to the Upper Canada Assembly in 1831, his election was subsequently nullified. Lease-holding, the proprietorship said to exist on Native reserves, was held not to count as property for the purpose of the suffrage. Thus many of Brant's supporters were disfranchised.[10] Although John A. Macdonald, as Attorney-General of Canada West, won near unanimous approval in 1857 for the enfranchisement of Indians possessing a freehold on reserves and income based on their share of tribal revenue, this option had little effect.[11] It was no coincidence that Confederation had only fathers, and White ones at that.

Resistance and Reform

In the decades after 1867, the monopoly of power by middle-class White men came under increasing attack. A movement politics emerged among workers, settler women, and Natives, and can be glimpsed as well among Asians. Across the Dominion, in settings as diverse as reserves, universities, and Chinatowns, prejudice's victims repudiated discrimination and disrespect. The franchise, whether municipal, provincial or federal, was but one, and rarely the most sought after, goal of protesters who often viewed freedom of employment or opportunity for education as better prizes. As the vote's significance in a modern, newly democratic state became clearer, however, its denial received increasing attention even from those preoccupied with other campaigns. Immediately after Confederation, as Gregory S. Kealey has noted, Canadian workers distinguished themselves from their enfranchised American counterparts by their demands to join the electorate.[12] By the 1880s the Knights of Labor and workers in general were struggling "to devise strategic directions to take towards politics."[13]

Many women were no more quiescent. By mid-century Canadians were debating the question of *proper spheres* with what one anti-suffragist characterized as "a freedom and a fierceness too which augur badly for its settlement in reasoned and scriptural grounds."[14] Settler women like Sara Anne Curzon, Agnes Maule Machar, and Emily Howard Stowe were activists in a broad-ranging movement for equality that targeted education, employment, marriage and sexual morality, and, ultimately, politics.[15] Women's political impotence was increasingly identified as the source of multiple ills. Emerging in the 1870s, the Canadian branches of the Woman's Christian Temperance Union readily became, as in the United States, associated with demands for suffrage. In confirmation of the connected nature of diverse issues, one angry Ottawa opponent of laws that forbade marriage to a dead wife's sister, a controversial cause throughout the English-speaking world in these years, drew a typical lesson in 1881:

> Our political disabilities ... are the greatest source of our greatest evil, and, having no voice in making the laws, we are bound to obey ... we contribute equally to the wealth of the nation — we are at all times exposed to the whims and decrees of the opposite sex.[16]

Women's suffrage was sufficiently in the air in these decades that a writer in a leading Canadian magazine could observe that "Today, how many of keenest politicians, quick to sense the coming breeze, are avowing themselves in its favour! Let us hope that it is not simply because they want votes."[17] Prime Minister Macdonald could hardly have been surprised, therefore, to receive a petition in 1883 from a group, founded in 1876 as the Toronto Women's Literary Society, which was clearly so concerned with the issue of disfranchisement that it now went by the title of the Dominion Women's Enfranchisement Association.

Propertied widows and spinsters began winning the municipal vote in 1873 in British Columbia. In 1884, Victoria extended the right to vote for school trustees to single women householders or freeholders, or wives of householders or freeholders, and Ontario extended the municipal franchise to spinsters with property. Indeed, the 1880s ushered in a string of such victories. It may well be that in Canada, as in Great Britain, such incorporation in local government spurred White women's growing interest in all aspects of political life.[18] The tide for reform was further fuelled in the same decade by the Dominion's pioneering generation of female university and medical students, expert in the art of breaching male monopolies.

While some women opposed their own enfranchisement, Natives appeared still more ambivalent. Until 1885 enfranchisement had meant effective assimilation. While women of European origin might hope to gain the vote without giving up claims to distinctiveness, the First Nations were not offered that option. Some individuals were, nevertheless, self-confident about negotiating the terms of their relationship with settler society. In the course of the debates Macdonald quoted an entire letter from Kahkwaquonaby, or Peter Jones, Chief of the Mississauga Band on the Credit River. On behalf of the Grand Council of Ontario of which he was secretary, he thanked the Prime Minister for making the Indian a "person." In September 1884 the Council, "composed of delegates from nearly every reserve in Ontario," had unanimously agreed "that the time had arrived when we should insist upon a representative or voice in the Dominion Parliament." It was hoped that the franchise, a "noble stand," would "elevate the aborigines to a position more approaching the independence of whites." The Mississauga chief also emphasized that the band earned whatever money it received from the government and that voters were thus independent.[19] The Mohawk Oronhyateka, or Peter Martin, as president of the Independent Order of Foresters and perhaps the most prominent Native of the day, was equally enthusiastic about the legislation.[20]

At the centre of the Iroquois Confederacy, the Six Nations in Ontario, the community was, however, divided.[21] While the *Brantford Expositor* believed that "quite a number" were "anxious to take advantage of this Act," the opinion of the majority ultimately was far from certain.[22] When Macdonald toured the territory in September 1886 on behalf of Tory candidates, he was disabused of his hopes by Chief William Smith, who spoke on behalf of the Council of the Six Nations that had "determined not to mix themselves up in the franchise." When he left the hereditary and elected chiefs to speak before the community as a whole, Macdonald found that the "open-air gathering was more receptive." In any event his candidate ultimately lost.[23]

On the Pacific Coast, Asian residents engaged in a wide range of protests against the efforts of provincial and local governments to restrict their rights. Victoria grew accustomed to receiving petitions and letters of condemnation; still other strategies included strikes and boycotts. In the nineteenth century support for political reform was often directed at China itself but the Canadian Asian community, as it grew more settled, had good reason to question its treatment. In time, disfranchisement would emerge as a powerful symbol of second-class status and trigger continuing dissent.

Such movements of protest were often isolated from one another, frequently practising their own versions of discrimination. Prejudices of class, of sex, and of race for the most part separated most reformers. And yet, increasingly, we catch glimpses of figures, like Pauline Johnson or T. Phillips Thompson,[24] who forged linkages. The language in which they claimed equality, the language often of "free-born British subjects" living in a parliamentary democracy, the language of justice and human equality more generally, was often remarkably similar. While they might never be in league with and were sometimes in opposition to one another, the late nineteenth century saw a blossoming of equality claims that together helped unsettle, even when they could not entirely dislodge, long-standing assumptions of privilege.

Disturbance was fuelled when Canadians looked elsewhere. As the 1885 debates themselves illustrate, residents of the new Dominion were frequently self-conscious observers of how other nations were constructing their electorates. To take only the case of English-speaking nations such as Britain, the United States, Australia, and New Zealand, voting rights preoccupied legislatures and significant numbers of their residents. There were the great refusals in Britain's Second and Third Reform Bills of 1867 and 1885, but English women received the municipal franchise in 1869 and Scottish women won the same right in 1882. The American territories of Wyoming and Utah enfranchised women in 1869 and 1870, rights retained in new state constitutions in 1890 and 1896. In 1871 the flamboyant feminist Victoria Woodhull made an eloquent plea to Congress. In the Pacific, New Zealand's Lower House debated the first suffrage bill in 1887.[25]

By the decade of the 1880s, "the growing prestige of suffrage and the outspoken support by such a figure as Frances Willard for the Knights of Labor encouraged expectations for an all-around reform alliance."[26] In short, the suffrage campaigns constituted a global phenomenon that linked crusaders around the world.[27] Workers and women were most visible but others also attracted occasional attention from legislatures in modernizing states that were attempting to define the rights and obligations of those who lived within their borders. New Zealand for example introduced a specific Maori property franchise in 1867. Such visible public developments, regularly remarked upon by MPs in the course of the 1885 debates, reminded Canadians that electorates were far from fixed.[28]

The 1885 Debates

The question of a federal franchise, to whom and under what conditions, had been haunting Canada since at least Confederation. Macdonald had talked of it in 1867. A bill appeared in parliament in 1869. In 1870 it gained second reading and went to committee. In 1873 the Speech from the Throne mentioned it. It was announced once more in 1883, again in 1884, and then in March 1885. While there was much grumbling on the Opposition benches and much sign of confusion on the part of the government, the franchise question was a familiar feature on the political landscape.

To many subsequent scholars, such as the political scientist Norman Ward, the 1885 legislation represented "an astonishing hodge-podge that discriminated between provinces, social classes and racial groups."[29] His classic 1950 text, *The Canadian House of Commons Representation*, summed up the frustration of early and subsequent commentators. The bill "was introduced in the legislature without a word of explanation as to its problems or possible effects on the constituencies, and indeed the whole debate ran its course with neither party in the House of Commons having any real knowledge of what the bill was going to do."[30] While some issues, such as Macdonald's support for women's suffrage, have provoked questions, the *Franchise Act* itself has been generally dismissed as one in the bag of tricks of a consummate politician. In the winter and spring of 1885 the Macdonald government was desperately trying to deal with multiple crises: the Northwest Rebellion, the near-bankruptcy of the CPR, and the growing demand for temperance legislation. The *Franchise Bill* proved a tremendous distraction, resulting in round-the-clock sittings of the House, considerable vituperation, and a great deal of confusion over both its exact character and its implications.

The bill that the Old Chieftain himself claimed to be "the greatest triumph of my life" has been neglected in favour of the turmoil that surrounded its introduction.[31] Yet the original bill, the debates it aroused, and the final act are all singularly instructive about the ways that citizenship was constructed in the young nation. At one obvious level, the arguments over the legislation, pitting, for the most part, Conservatives against Liberals, highlighted the ongoing struggle over federal-provincial rights. When he moved the second reading on April 16, John A. Macdonald claimed "simply to introduce as far as possible a system of representation which will be applicable to the different Provinces and will readily give an opportunity for the people of Canada as a whole to send representatives here for the purpose of representing Dominion interests as a whole."[32] As the champion of provincial rights, however, the Liberal Party saw the hand of the autocratic centralizer at work. Should Ottawa set the conditions for the federal franchise, the provinces would surrender significant power and patronage. Such threats ignited the outrage of the Opposition.[33]

Whatever the jurisdiction, wealth, the traditional mainstay of political rights, remained critical. Property or income was required for all classes of real and potential voters, yet its power was nevertheless fading. In the course of extensive debates, the Conservatives yielded to the existing male property franchises in Prince Edward Island and British Columbia and instituted a special fisherman's franchise.[34] Although property, also known as the *stake in the community* argument, never disappeared, provinces' steady enlargement of their own electorates and the examples of the British *Reform Acts* and the more democratic American model meant its heyday was drawing to a close. In the 1880s, increasing numbers of poorer White men could look forward to joining the better-off at the ballot box.[35] The decreasing significance of property qualifications, combined with the complications offered by new married women's property acts, meant that husbands' long-standing usufructuary claims to the vote, based on wives' property, became both restricted and increasingly irrelevant.[36] Yet, if property, and thereby class, at least with respect to the vote, lost currency after Confederation, democracy was far from triumphant. The 1885 law firmly marked women, First Nations, and Asians as outsiders in the masculinist settler state as it attempted to put its house in order.

WOMEN

Although speakers spent more time debating the merits of enlarging the male settler electorate — poor teachers, for example, received a good deal of sympathy — women of European origin were singled out early on. In his brief introduction to the bill, John A. Macdonald suggested their importance:

> There is one question, however, in this Bill in which, personally, I may be considered to be interested, and that is women's franchise. I have always and am now strongly in favor of that franchise. I believe that it is coming as certainly as came the gradual enfranchisement of women from being the slaves of men until she [sic] attained her present position, almost the equal of man. I believe the time is coming, though we are not any more than the United States or England quite educated up to it, [sic] I believe the time will come, and I shall be very proud and glad to see it, when the final step towards granting women the full enfranchisement is earned in Canada.[37]

A few days into the debate, the Prime Minister, a familiar of Kingston circles that included the noted feminist author Agnes Maule Machar ("Fidelis"),[38] went beyond the intent of his own bill to announce his personal support for enfranchising married women:

> Some people are apprehensive that if the wife holds one political view and the husband a different political view there might be family discord. ... I believe it is the chief argument that is used against giving married women votes. I do not believe in its force. ... if the law which allows women to have separate property has not produced such social discord ... I do not think that the fear of domestic discord on account of exercising the franchise ought to prevail ...

He also dismissed assertions that voting rights rested on the capacity to bear arms in defence of the nation. As he asked, "But why not, then, take away the vote of the clergymen who do not go to battle? Or the votes of the Quakers, Mennonites, and Tunkers who have conscientious scruples against going to war."[39]

Such declarations, while questioned, even ridiculed, by Edward Blake and the Opposition, placed Macdonald squarely within the pro-suffrage camp of the day. He was not, however, prepared to demand the acquiescence of his substantial majority. Conservative MPs were permitted a free vote and took the opportunity, for the most part, to narrow the range of the government-sponsored legislation. Only a few spoke in favour of female enfranchisement. Perhaps mindful of WCTU activities and the visits of American supporters like Susan B. Anthony in his own constituency, Noah Shakespeare, the junior Tory member from Victoria, B.C. stood up to insist upon women's support for the measure.[40] From King's, New Brunswick, a senior Conservative minister, the Hon. George Foster, an ardent temperance advocate, identified himself as sympathetic.[41] From Ottawa County, Ontario, another Conservative, Alonzo Wright, observed that "the question of woman suffrage is now exciting much attention in the world." He found it impossible to "understand how, in any country like this, rights, privileges, and the franchise should be conferred on one-half of the human race and denied to the other half." He went further still, locating, as had Macdonald, the proposed legislation in a broader emancipatory tradition: "We have lived to see slavery abolished, and Catholic emancipation granted in our own highly favored land; liberty of the press conceded, and liberty of conscience accorded. Let us trust that at no distant period we shall live to see this great injustice removed, this 'great wrong righted.'"[42] Despite such spirited interjections, as Catherine Cleverdon, the author of the first major treatment of the Canadian suffrage campaigns, pointed out, "a careful listener in the House galleries would have noticed that the chants of praise for the ladies were delivered almost exclusively by members of the Liberal Opposition, while Sir John's own followers maintained an ominous silence."[43]

The behaviour of the Opposition was no more consistent. As an outspoken reform-minded editor of *The Canada Citizen* observed of Blake, the Liberal Leader,

> He does not pose as an opponent of woman suffrage, but neither does he come frankly out in favour of it. ... On the contrary, he rather indicates his preference for Tennyson's somewhat vague philosophy, the fundamental idea of which is the fear that woman may have an independent development, a state of things, which, for better or worse, would certainly be promoted by her political enfranchisement.[44]

Like the British Liberal prime minister William Gladstone, who actively resisted women's inclusion in the Third Great Reform Bill, also in 1885, Blake proved no friend to the supporters of John Stuart Mill. His soon-to-be successor, Wilfrid Laurier, openly opposed the extension of the franchise, arguing that

> I do not believe that the emancipation of woman can be promoted so much by politics as by social reform. I believe that the action of women must be most influential in politics as in everything else, but I believe that action is more effective if exercised in the circle of the home, by persuasion and advice, than if woman is brought to the poll to vote.[45]

Among party leaders, Conservatives like Benjamin Disraeli in Britain and Macdonald in Canada, perhaps inspired by hopes for an increase in the influence of the propertied classes, had better claim to be women's champions.

The Prime Minister found the bulk of suffragists among the Liberal rank-and-file, whose contributions likewise invoked most of the pro-suffrage arguments employed over the next decades. They too appeared sensitive to signs of progress elsewhere. James Trow from South Perth, Ontario, attempted to edify the House by reading aloud an article by Millicent Garrett Fawcett, soon to be one of Britain's most prominent suffragists and wife of a British Liberal MP.[46] His colleague from North York, William Mulock, cited liberalism's commitment to "natural" rights and opposition to the hostile weight of "custom." Like Macdonald, he too dismissed the military argument: "it is just as reasonable to say that as to say that men should not have the franchise because they are not able to bear children."[47]

Canada's suffragist Grits joined opponents in paying homage to the *cult of true womanhood*. In contrast, however, they emphasized the purifying effect of potential new electors, pointing positively to female voters in Ontario and B.C. municipalities.[48] John Charlton, the Member for North Norfolk, looked forward to the creation "of a large vote which would be on the side of moral, social, and religious reform."[49] In response, Macdonald crossed the floor to shake his hand. Some commentators invoked the reality of women's labour as yet further justification. From West Elgin, George Casey asked, "If it is degrading to women to go quietly to the polling booths and deposit their ballots, say once in every five years, is it degrading to spend day after day at the washtub, until they are bent in body and weakened in mind, and have acquired the seeds of disease ... owing to exertions made to support, perhaps a lazy and drunken husband, or a family?"[50] From North Wellington, his colleague James McMullen chose to highlight the contributions of farm daughters: "when they undergo the amount of labor in this way, perhaps in the absence of sons, it is nothing but right they should be allowed the privilege of exercising their franchise and voting for those they want to elect." Still more in keeping with the general spirit of the House, he saluted "one of the noblest Queens who have ever occupied the throne of Great Britain."[51]

Liberal speakers also joined a handful of government members in voicing sympathy for the enfranchisement of married women. George Landerkin, the Member for South Grey, summed up the common sentiment:

> Now I cannot understand why it is that the mothers of this country are to be so treated by the gallant knight who leads this Government. I would like to know why it is that he will give the franchise to an unmarried female, who may be Chinese, or a squaw, or any other person naturalised, and deny it to the mothers of this country.

The bill, he went on to argue, constituted "a ban upon matrimony ... a blow at the most deserving class of people that are found in the Dominion of Canada to-day."[52] His brutal distinction between idealized White women, in effect "colonial ladies," and their supposedly wild and uncivilized counterparts among other races was also a commonplace of the imperial politics of the day.[53] Such appeals to racism, as well as to expediency, regularly joined the justice claims that marked the suffrage campaigns from their beginning to their conclusion.[54]

Anti-feminist sentiment ultimately, however, carried the day, in what the Tory Member for Algoma, Simon James Dawson, termed "a very dangerous step."[55] On the other side of the House, Québec Liberal Flavien Dupont dramatically invoked the French revolutionaries, Charlotte Corday and Louise Michel, in order to libel political women as sources of "indescribable trouble and disorder."[56] Despite Macdonald's dismissal of the argument, a Tory MP, Charles James Townshend from Cumberland, Nova Scotia, prophesied that a voting woman would no longer be "man's helpmate" but "his rival," and that "seeds of dissension" would enter "the family circle."[57] From the constituency of West Huron in Ontario, Liberal MP Malcolm Colin Cameron worried openly about a world turned upside-down. Raising the spectre of the clothing reformers of the day, he prognosticated that vote-minded women were motivated by the "desire to don the coat and pantaloons."[58] Such fears ensured that the provisions for the enfranchisement of settler women disappeared from the Bill on April 28.

FIRST NATIONS

The First Nations were the next potential voters to preoccupy the House in the spring of 1885. While off-hand references to feminist agitation had occasionally surfaced, MPs were riveted by the spectacle of the Indians and "halfbreeds" in what *Hansard* termed "the North-west disturbances." In 1868 federal legislation had provided for voluntary enfranchisement but required can-didates to surrender Indian status and to reside outside reserves. As some MPs noted in 1885, few Indians were prepared to make such sacrifices. Their resistance betokened the failure of political assimilation and suggested the need for other solutions. In 1884 the Macdonald Government passed the *Indian Advancement Act*, which envisioned the voluntary transformation of reserves into model municipalities, much like those of settlers. Ultimately only nine bands, some under pressure, succumbed to this approach.[59] The integration of potential Native voters also interested some provinces. Early in 1885, Queen's Park made Indians who lived off-reserve in Ontario but con-tinued to participate "in the annuities, interest moneys and rents of a tribe, band, or body of Indians" eligible for the vote on the same basis as Whites.[60]

Like the Ontario example, the federal *Franchise Bill of 1885* offered a solution to the dilemma created by Indian recalcitrance to surrender tribal rights in exchange for the promise of political assimilation. In effect, both legislative initiatives asserted an over-riding community of interest among Canadian property-holders. Prosperous Indian counterparts to settler neighbours were invited to cast ballots. Since they were not forced to surrender status or com-munity life, better-off Native voters might emerge as beacons of successful assimilation. Such at least seemed the hope. The implications of this possi-bility for an effective *dual citizenship* are provocative: such voters had the opportunity to be politically active in two nations simultaneously. This recognition of multiple identities mirrored that enshrined in the 1881 *Nationality Act*, which made Canadians both British and Canadian. Just as Edward Blake would sit in parliaments in both Ottawa and London, poten-tial voters from Six Nations, such as the hereditary and elected chiefs, might well exercise power in the Confederacy Council of the Iroquois at Ohsweken and then again in the House of Commons.

The possibility of Indian voters and perhaps also representatives stirred up a hornet's nest. Critics immediately questioned whether the potential legisla-tion involved Indians in all parts of the country, including the rebels Poundmaker and Big Bear. Macdonald's apparently casual affirmative response led to nightmares among his listeners of voters going "from a scalping party to the polls."[61] Subsequent debates rarely moved far from this apprehension. Since MPs, including the Prime Minister, never seemed entirely sure which Indians were to be enfranchised, early fear and confusion persisted. The Opposition continued to suggest that Indians on any and all reserves were eligible while Conservatives emphasized the privileged assimilated few. Numbers were important for a variety of reasons, but some MPs — those from western Ontario and the Grand River area in the same province were obvious examples — foresaw their futures as somewhat dependent on the Indian vote. Such practical concerns accompanied contradictory opinions about the civil and moral status of Canadian First Nations. Edward Blake himself introduced a recurring preoccupation with the dependency of Aboriginal peoples under the *Indian Act*.[62] A member of his party, Thomas Bain (North Wentforth), vividly summed up the widespread apprehension:

> It is not enfranchising the Indians. It is simply creating a number of voting machines. We do not enfranchise a Chinaman or a negro, or any other man, white or black, mixed or colored, unless he has qualified himself for the duties of citizenship, by taking all the responsibilities attached to it. Other men can be sued for their debts, but you cannot reach the Indian under the ordinary contracts. He is as much a minor as a child, and is absolutely under the control of the Government of the day.[63]

Opponents characterized Indians as slavishly dependent on the largesse on the Department of Indian Affairs. Enfranchisement was yet one more method of maintaining Conservative power, like an earlier act, commonly referred to by Liberals as the "gerrymander" act, which altered constituency boundaries.[64] From West Elgin, John Henry Wilson cited the partisanship of the Mohawk medical doctor and president of the Independent Order of Foresters, Oronyhtekha (also known as Peter Martin).[65] This "good Tory," like ninety per cent of enfranchised Indians, was identified as an Orangeman, and Grits knew "full well how they will vote."[66] For John Frederick Lister, the MP from West Lambton, Macdonald in his role as the Superintendent of Indian Affairs resembled "a southerner" controlling sixteen to eighteen thousand Indian "slaves" in Ontario.[67] From South Brant, the home of the Six Nations, another Liberal, William Patterson, drew yet another unfavourable comparison: "The position of an Indian is not like that of a woman under the control of her husband, if you use that expression, but it is like that of a child under twenty-one years of age, and under the control of his father. The Indians are minors in the eye of the law."[68] Such critics perceived Native enfranchisement on the basis of a proportional share in tribal lands as manifestly unfair. According to this perspective, Indians had no more than usufructuary rights to reserves. The federal government remained the real owner. This argument presents an interesting reversal of European usufructuary traditions that empowered husbands on the basis of the property of their wives.

Tempers raged all the more when speakers recalled young Canadian reservists fighting in the North-west.[69] Such heroes might very well lack property qualifications for the vote. In contrast the rebels, charged with making "widows and orphans in this country,"[70] both "murdering the settlers and subjecting their wives and daughters to a fate worse than death," in short "bloody vindictive barbarians," could be enfranchised.[71] The House of Commons might face the prospect of admitting "Pie-a-pot or Big Bear or Poundmaker." Worse still some "Blackhead [sic]" might emerge "to lead the Conservative Party." Angry parliamentary Jeremiahs foresaw even greater repercussions. Suppose Native MPs bring with them demands that "other languages [be] established in this House"?[72]

Opponents also castigated Macdonald's failure to give "suffrage to the workman, to the sailor, or mariner, to the lumberman, and to the sons of mariners and tenants," asking, "Have not these individuals as much right to vote as Indians?"[73] Women's disfranchisement was similarly remembered. The contrast angered many, like the MP for Prince Edward, Ontario, who pointed out that

> this House has declared that our mothers, wives, and sisters, no matter whether they pay taxes, or not, shall not have a vote, and yet the franchise is to be conferred on these Indians who are incapable of exercising that franchise, who have not asked for it, who are in receipt of annuities from the Government, and who would be influenced by the agents of the Government. ... The First Minister said that these Indians bought tea and tobacco and other taxable goods, but I venture to say that there are many females in this country, who are refused the franchise, and yet who buy as many taxable goods as a whole tribe of Indians. ... it is a monstrous proposition that we should, in the same parliament, refuse the same franchise to the women of this country and give it to the low and filthy Indians of the reserves.[74]

In another speech, gender surfaced rather differently. George Landerkin, the Liberal from South Grey, claimed to hold that "it would be a much better idea to give the squaws a vote than the Indians." In characterizing Native women as working hard while their mates, "neither more or less than brutes" in his mind, idled, this speaker joined the host of European commentators who, as scholars like Sylvia Van Kirk have observed, failed to understand Aboriginal economies.[75] The perceived exploitation of Indian women by their own communities was routinely accepted as proof of inherent savagery.

Many opponents of the bill appeared to lack any sense of a more inclusive future, wondering why "we are asked to legislate for a race that is gradually disappearing from the country."[76] The Liberal speaker, David Mills (Bothwell), berated Macdonald, a "gentleman" who knew full well that "the Indian is not a citizen; he does not mingle with the rest of the community; he forms a member of a tribe, and they stand apart."[77] Later he framed his objections still more brutally: "You know what would become of the Indian if the Government did not interfere on his behalf. You do not allow the natural law of the survival of the fittest to operate in regard to him. You prevent his extinction by want or disease."[78] When Opposition critics added that Indians were also essentially disinterested, they again confirmed a natural incapacity.[79]

Some Liberals attempted to disassociate themselves from the most extreme of their colleagues. From South Brant, the home of the Six Nations, Patterson demonstrated his knowledge of his constituents, reminding listeners that the Iroquois had continually insisted that they remained allies, "not subjects of the Crown," and that they wished "to preserve their identities as a separate people."[80] He doubted they wanted or would use the vote. Yet even when racial thinking was specifically repudiated, racism remained, as can be seen in the observations of the Liberal Peter Mitchell from Northumberland, New Brunswick:

> There is no exclusion of the Indian because of his race, or his blood, but it is because of his condition, his want of intelligence, his want of assimilation to the usages of civilised society ... I would give to everyone who has assumed the same position as the white man, who places himself in a position to contribute towards the revenues of the country, towards maintaining the institutions of the country ... the right to vote.[81]

Supporters mustered a variety of defences to such attacks. Property was a fundamental principle for many. As Macdonald suggested, "I fancy that an Indian who is qualified would have a vote if he is a British subject. If an Indian has an income of $300 a year, he will have a vote the same as any other person."[82] The Conservative minister George Foster also emphasized the effect of property-holding in creating rights:

> I hold ... in favor of the complete enfranchisement of women, married, single or widows, who have equal property qualifications with men, when once you fix the condition of a franchise by a property qualification. But, I say too, that I believe in enfranchising the Indian. I believe that the Indian who earns a living for himself, the Indian who has real property, who occupies a home, who has a salary or an income, who is looking forward to that greatest boon which men in

a civilised country can claim, and which men in a savage country
can aspire to — the boon of full and perfect citizenship — I say I
could not in justice to history and to my own convictions, deny the
right of the franchise to that man. ... it is not the intention nor is it
in the power of this Bill to enfranchise the wild hordes of savage
Indians all over the Dominion....

And, in a rather contradictory spirit, he rejected charges that Indians were
mere pauper wards of the government: "it is not upon the bounty doled out
by the white people that the Indians are living. It is but an infinitesimal part
of their own rights, which they have surrendered to us, that we return to
them."[83]

Despite his previous opposition to women suffrage, Dawson, the MP
from Algoma, a district with a large Native population that exercised household suffrage immediately after Confederation, was on this issue sensitive to
concerns of fairness. Citing the 1857 findings of the Imperial Commission to
inquire into State of Indians in Ontario, this Tory concluded,

So all the Indians have received from the white man they have repaid
ten fold. If the white man has kept the Indians in a degraded position, it is high time that he should adopt another system, and
endeavor to lead them forward and lift them up in the social scale,
and try to make good citizens of them.

He went so far as to attack the legislation of an earlier Conservative
administration: "The enfranchisement under the Indian Act ... is no enfranchisement at all. ... it is a merely a scheme to divide up the reserve and give
to each Indian his portion ... designed to break up the reserve and to do
away with the tribal system."[84] The 1885 Act in contrast promised opportunity without sacrifice.

Dawson claimed for Indians the rights of all free men. He went so far
against the temper of the House as to discover proof of Native "freedom,
independence and high spirit" in the North-west resistance of that year.
Contrary to critics, "They are certainly British subjects; they are certainly of
independent disposition, and through the whole history of all these Indian
tribes it was never possible to make slaves of them." Indians were

capable, with proper training, of higher and better things than rebellion. We have had examples which show that the Indians are quite
capable of exercising the franchise. Take the half-breeds, the same

class of people we have here [in the Northwest]; the franchise was allowed to them in Manitoba, and it did them a great deal of good. It kept them quiet, and they sent half-breed representatives to the Local Legislation of their Province, some of whom occupy the best offices ... These people who have been so sweepingly denounced we must admit are British subjects; they have the same rights.

Although he at first argued that "the whole Indian race, from the Atlantic to the Pacific, should have some sort of representation in the House,"[85] Dawson learned to curb his enthusiasm. In the course of Conservative search for broader support, he eventually denied that the legislation proposed to enfranchise "the wild Indians of the forests and the plains."[86]

Such champions emphasized the fundamental similarity, rather than the difference, of Indian voters. The Scottish immigrant prime minister put it this way: "They are educated men; many of them are doing business and have large property. They are traders or merchants, who have engaged in all sorts of business. But they prefer to stick to the clan system, just as, until lately, in my own country, the Highlanders stuck to their clan system in the highlands of Scotland." Both groups proudly title themselves "British allies."[87] Another Canadian Scot, Donald MacMaster, from Ontario's Glengarry County, extended the metaphor: "My own ancestors in the Highlands of Scotland had not escaped from the bonds of savagery 150 years ago." Only after British troops broke the northern clans "did my noble countrymen, having succumbed to the fortunes of war, acquire all the advantages of civilisation." Conquered Scots discovered "opportunities of empire" in enlisting in the British Army. Indians, as with the legendary hero Tecumseh, similarly fought for the Empire. Much like some advocates of woman suffrage, this Tory located Indian enfranchisement within a broader emancipatory tradition. Was it not, he asked, "one hundred years since women were burned as witches in Scotland and elsewhere[?] It is not one hundred years since a Roman Catholic, even in civilised England, was not entitled to the ordinary rights, the ordinary civil rights, that are so freely bestowed." His Conservative colleague, Pierre Armand Landry from Kent, New Brunswick, reflected on the "prejudices" of "ruling races." It was time "to place the Indians on an equal footing with other men."[88]

Even Noah Shakespeare from British Columbia, a province with a substantial Native population with a long history of resistance to settler demands, lined up with his leaders, assuring the House,

So far as the Indians in British Columbia are concerned ..., I, for one, would be glad to see them have the franchise ... to my mind the clause referring to the Indians was one of the most important clauses of the Bill. I believe it will be one of the greatest influences in the Dominion towards settling the disputes, the difficulties and the claims they may have, to allow these men to have votes, so that they would have some person or persons to look after their claims and insist upon their rights.[89]

Revealing of the final outcome, however, no other B.C. member echoed this enthusiasm.

Conservatives also rejected any claim that the legislation was merely self-serving. From Hastings, Ontario, John White defended the potential voters:

I say it is contemptible and mean for any hon. Gentleman to stand up here and throw slurs upon them. They are just as true, just as loyal, just as generous, just as sober and industrious, as many of the men who stand up here and utter such harsh, unkind words against them. They are just as loyal to the Government and true to one another.

The Mohawks of the Township of Tyendenaga could, he argued, be a credit to the House of Commons: "I wish to-day, from the inmost thoughts of my heart, that there was a member of an Indian band to stand up here and defend his race." Like any other voters, Indians might be Conservative or Liberal. The government was "not battling to get them enfranchised because we believe they are all Conservatives, but because we believe it is right and just."[90]

Despite such appeals, prejudice along with the bill's provisions for the preparation of voters' list, which seemed to offer every opportunity for partisanship, fuelled on-going opposition. Endeavouring to broaden his support, Macdonald conceded an amendment limiting franchise to the Indians of the old provinces on May 4. He had intended to retain also the B.C. franchise, since "One hon. Gentleman from British Columbia spoke in favour of their being allowed the franchise, and I had the impression that that was the general impression." After being reminded of other opponents, however, he excluded that province as well.[91] The Opposition was little happier. In 1898 Laurier would strike out the entire Native franchise.

CHINESE

While raised only late in the debates, the issue of Chinese electors also aroused racial prejudice in 1885. Noah Shakespeare, the erstwhile defender of women and Indians, was a long-time leader of opposition to Chinese settlement, labour, and enfranchisement in B.C.[92] That province's recurring racism found a comfortable home as the new state set out the terms of the new nationality. On April 10, just as the *Franchise Bill* was also preoccupying MPs, Dr. Joseph Adolphe Chapleau, one of two commissioners for the 1884 Royal Commission on Chinese Immigration, introduced *Bill #124* to restrict Chinese immigration. With its provision for a head tax, it quickly received royal assent on July 20. While scholars of Chinese Canadian history often focus on the immigration restrictions, the franchise provoked a great deal more debate that spring. On May 4, Macdonald proposed inserting, after the inclusion of Indians, the words "and excluding a Chinaman." Confident of support, he did not feel the need, as he explained,

> to discuss, at any length, the reasons for this amendment. The Chinese are not like the Indians, sons of the soil. They come from a foreign country; they have no intent, as a people of making a domicile of any portion of Canada; they come and work or trade, and when they are tired of it they go away, taking with them their profits. They are, besides, natives of a country where representative institutions are unknown, and I think we cannot safely give them the elective franchise.[93]

Such sentiments, while clearly in the majority, were nevertheless not unanimous. From Northumberland, N.B., the Honourable Peter Mitchell cited the example of Montreal's Chinese population, who were "spoken of as a responsible body of men — good, peace-loving citizens. ... If we can make Canada sufficiently attractive to them, I am not sure they will go back to China."[94] His Liberal colleague, Louis Henry Davies from Queen's, P.E.I., was also positive. From his point of view, it was unfair to exclude members of any race once naturalized.[95] Another speaker, Andrew H. Gillmore (Charlotte, N.B.), took much the same position: "For my part, I believe in the unity of the human race ... I should be sorry to see any man, of whatever race, receive anything but fair play in a British colony." Going further he turned the conventional comparison on its head. The Chinese in fact compared "favorably with those Christian people, the whites of British Columbia."[96]

Macdonald's original comparison with the Indians also sparked debate. Peter Mitchell spoke in favour of "Chinamen being placed on an equal footing with all other persons. Certainly a Chinaman is quite as good as an Indian."[97] From the constituency of Sunbury, New Brunswick, the Liberal Charles Burbee saw little to choose between two undesirable races:

> There is as good a reason to exclude the Indian as for excluding the Chinese. The Chinese who have acquired property, and have become British subjects, and are doing business in the country, are developing the country, and I think those portions of them have a better right to vote than the tribal Indian, who is not a free agent but a ward of the Government. I do not say that the Chinese are a desirable class of people to encourage, but I do say that if they are here and take an interest in the country and aid in its development, they are better fitted to be entrusted with the franchise than the tribal Indians.[98]

For Ontario Liberal David Mills, neither Chinese nor Indians had much to offer. He bluntly defined the Chinese as members of "the class we designate as non-progressive" and argued that the same could be said of "the Indian population, except in so far as they will show fitness to be enfranchised." The contrast with desirable settlers was sharp. When he applied the criteria of progress "to the young men of the country," a group he effectively designated as White, or "to the Europeans who come here to carve out homes for themselves," they passed unconditionally.[99]

Macdonald, however, stuck to invidious distinction between the two controversial populations:

> I cannot agree ... at all. Indians are sons of the soil; they are Canadians and British subjects; and, there, they have the proper qualification. ... they ought to be treated as other British subjects. The Chinese are foreigners. ... [with] no British instincts or British feelings or aspirations.[100]

Indians were not the only point of reference in the hierarchy of race that most members seemed to accept. From Islet, Québec, the Liberal Philippe Baby Casgrain suggested that "the Chinese are superior to the negroes; not that I would like to give a vote to the Chinese."[101] Fortunately the issue of disfranchising Canadian Blacks was not before the House.

Ultimately, MPs revealed significantly less sympathy for Chinese than for women or Natives. The vote to exclude them was passed without the extended defence the others had inspired. Indeed the exclusion was deliberately broadened. When queried about how to define the Chinese, given that they might well be British subjects, Macdonald responded, "I used the word Chinaman to designate a race." The Bill's wording was accordingly changed to read "Excluding a person of the Mongolian or Chinese race."[102] Whereas the *Naturalization Act* of four years earlier had not discriminated between those of European and Asian origin, the *Franchise Act* affirmed inferiority.

Conclusion

By 1885, the political elites of the newly confederated nation, if far from unanimous, were sufficiently in agreement to distinguish between men of European origin, the preferred British subjects, and those — women, Natives, and Asians — whom they designated as properly subordinated. The "ship of state," constituted as a result of the 1885 debates, was vividly summed up by one participant:

> As that beautiful craft came sailing in, we saw a fair spinster and a charming widow standing on the deck; the 'heathen Chinee' was in the cabin, and the banded Indian was concealed in the hold. Sir, we have quickly disposed of the ladies; we have kicked them on shore; the 'heathen Chinee' we have strangled; the banded Indian we have dragged from his concealment, and those of them that were of no immediate use, we have put on shore, but we will retain those in the old Provinces.[103]

The exclusion of all women, the vast majority of First Nations, and all Chinese marked the new nationality in crucial ways. In the nineteenth century the franchise as never before represented full membership in a national community. The line increasingly drawn among enfranchised and disfranchised subjects emerged as one critical measure of how those in authority imagined the humanity of those who came beneath their gaze. Those measured and found wanting were to remain subject to the government of those who were seen to wield authority naturally and properly.

That heritage of discrimination would be long-standing. Parliamentarians proved generally more prepared to extend their privileges to poorer men of their own race than to women of their own class and race or men of other races. On the other hand, White women invoked more sympathy than representatives of other races. Their enfranchisement some decades earlier than either Indians or Asians was predictable on the basis of the 1885 debates. And yet White women waited more than thirty years for a right that seemed in sight that spring. While White manhood suffrage was generally conceded in the nineteenth century, not until 1919 did women of European origins gain both the federal franchise and the right to election on an equal basis with men; not until 1940 was the last provincial bastion secured. Inclusion of non-White women and men was slower still: the last statutory disfranchisement of Asian Canadians ended only in 1948; the Inuit waited until 1950 for enfranchisement and status Indians until 1960.

And yet the power of elite settler males was never uncontested. Even within the House of Commons, as we have seen, the claims of settler women, First Nations, and Asian Canadians upon the emancipatory traditions of western civilization were sometimes admitted. While few MPs championed all three groups, the connections among the disadvantaged were there to be made. For all the persistence of racism and sexism, traditions of emancipation and human equality could be called upon on behalf of women, Natives, and Asians. The citizenship debates of 1885 invoked many versions of Canada. While prejudice was the immediate victor, the equality claims that would eventually transform the Canadian electorate also made their appearance, promising that the contest would continue.

Notes

My thanks to Christopher Ross for his efforts as a research assistant early in this project and to Women's Studies at York University which offered me the opportunity to present a preliminary version of this work.

1. Charles O. Ermatinger, *Canadian Franchise and Election Laws. A Manual for the Use of Revising Offices, Municipal Officers, Candidates, Agents, and Electors* (Toronto: Carswell & Co., 1886), 16.
2. John Charlton (North Norfolk), Canada, *House of Commons Debates* (henceforth *Debates*), 15 May 1885, 1856.
3. Alfred Howell, *Naturalization and Nationality in Canada* ... (Toronto and Edinburgh: Carswell & Co., Law Book Publishers, 1884), 12.
4. For a useful, albeit brief, review of changes see Joe Serge, *Canadian Citizenship Made Simple* (Toronto: Doubleday, 1993), ch.14.
5. Howell, *Naturalization and Nationality in Canada*, 4.
6. Howell, *Naturalization and Nationality in Canada*, 46.
7. Howell, *Naturalization and Nationality in Canada*, 72-74.
8. Howell, *Naturalization and Nationality in Canada*, 11.
9. John Garner, *The Franchise and Politics in British North America 1755-1867* (Toronto: University of Toronto Press, 1969), ch. 12.
10. Garner, *The Franchise and Politics in British North America*, 161.
11. Garner, *The Franchise and Politics in British North America*.

12. Gregory S. Kealey, *Toronto Workers Respond to Industrial Capitalism 1867-1892* (Toronto: University of Toronto Press, 1980), 368, fn 4.

13. Bryan Palmer, *Working-Class Experience: The Rise and Reconstitution of Canadian Labour 1800-1980* (Toronto: Butterworth & Co., 1983), 133.

14. Rev. Robt Sedgewick, "The Proper Sphere and Influence of Women in Christian Society" (1856), in *The Proper Sphere*, ed. Ramsay Cook and Wendy Mitchinson (Toronto: Oxford University Press, 1976), 8.

15. See Beverly Boutilier, "Women's Rights and Duties: Sarah Anne Curzon and the Politics of Canadian History," and Dianne M. Hallman, "Cultivating a Love of Canada through History: Agnes Maule Machar, 1837-1927," in *Creating Historical Memory. English-Canadian Women and the Work of History*, ed. Beverly Boutilier and Alison Prentice (Vancouver: UBC Press, 1997), 25-74.

16. 'Gunhilda,' *Marriage with a Deceased Wife's Sister: Letters of a Lady to the Right Rev., the Lord Bishop of Ontario* (Ottawa: Daily Citizen, 1881), Canadian Institute for Historical Microproductions (CIHM) 34239, 33.

17. "The Woman Question," *Canadian Monthly and National Review* (May 1879), in *The Proper Sphere*, ed. Cook and Mitchinson, 64.

18. See Claire Eustance, Laura Ugolini and Joan Ryan, "Introduction: Writing Suffrage Histories — The 'British' Experience," *A Suffrage Reader. Charting Directions in British Suffrage History*, ed. Claire Eustance, Joan Ryan and Laura Ugolini (London & New York: Leicester University Press, 2000), 1.

19. *Debates*, 8 June 1885, 2371.

20. On Oronhyatekha see G. Mercer Adam, *Prominent Men of Canada* (Toronto: Canadian Biographical Publishing Co., 1892), and Trudy Nicks, "Dr. Oronhyatekha's History Lessons: Reading Museum Collections as Texts," in *Reading Beyond Words: Contexts for Native History*, ed. Jennifer S.H. Brown and Elizabeth Vibert (Peterborough: Broadview Press, 1996).

21. For an excellent discussion of the Six Nations and the suffrage see Malcolm Montgomery, "The Six Nations Indians and the Macdonald Franchise," *Ontario History* 57 (1965): 13-25.

22. "The Indian Question," *Brantford Expositor*, 7 May 1885.

23. See Sheila Staats, "The Six Nations Council House: Historic Building at Ohsweken," *Ontario History* 85, 3 (September 1993): 219-20.

24. See Veronica Strong-Boag and Carole Gerson, *Paddling Her Own Canoe: The Times and Texts of E. Pauline Johnson* (Toronto: University of Toronto Press, 2000); Gregory S. Kealey and Bryan Palmer, *Dreaming of What Might Be: The Knights of Labor in Ontario, 1880-1980* (Cambridge: Cambridge University Press, 1982), 32; and T. Phillips Thompson, *The Politics of Labor* (1887, reprint with an Introduction by Jay Atherton, Toronto: University of Toronto Press, 1975).

25. On the international movement see the essays in the outstanding collection by Caroline Daley and Melanie Nolan, eds., *Suffrage and Beyond: International Perspectives on Women's Suffrage* (Auckland: University of Auckland Press, 1994).

26. *The Concise History of Woman Suffrage: Selections from the Classic Work of Stanton, Anthony, Gage and Harper*, ed. Mari Jo Buhle and Paul Buhle (Urbana: University of Illinois Press, 1978), 28.

27. On the links between the British and American campaigns, albeit one that fails even in the index to mention Canada, an extraordinary omission given the triangular trade in protest, see Patricia Greenwood Harrison, *Connecting Links: The British and American Woman Suffrage Movements, 1900-1914* (Westport, CT : Greenwood Press, 2000).

28. *Debates*, 16 April 1885, comments of Alonzo Wright, 1143-46.

29. Norman Ward, *The Canadian House of Commons Representation* (Toronto: University of Toronto, 1950), 218.

30. Ward, *The Canadian House of Commons Representation*, 217.

31. Donald Creighton, *John A. Macdonald: The Old Chieftain* (Toronto: MacMillan, 1966), 427.

32. *Debates*, 16 April 1885, 1133.

33. For a lengthy defense of provincial rights, much interrupted by cries from Government members, see the speech by John Charlton, *Debates*, 5 May 1885, 1608-18.

34. Ermatinger, *Canadian Franchise and Election Laws*, xvi.

35. On the decreasing importance of property see Ward, *The Canadian House of Commons Representation*, 225.

36. On the growing restrictions on traditional usufruct presented by *Married Women's Property Acts* and that available under Québec civil law see Ermatinger, *Canadian Franchise and Election Laws*, fn (b), 6-7 and fn (f), 8-9.

37. *Debates*, 16 April 1885, 1134. Every suffrage bill Macdonald introduced in the 1880s included provision for widow and spinster suffrage.

38. On this Kingston feminist and her circle see Dianne M. Hallman, "Cultivating a Love of Canada through History: Agnes Maule Machar, 1837-1927," in *Creating Historical Memory*, ed. Boutilier and Prentice, especially at 27.

39. *Debates*, 27 April 1885, 1389. He is presumably referring to the *Ontario Married Women's Property Act of 1884*, which provided that women marrying after July 1, 1884, or acquiring property after that date, held this as "femmes soles." Ermatinger, *Canadian Franchise and Election Laws*, 8-9.

40. *Debates*, 16 April 1885, 1142. For the opposing argument see the speech of Malcolm Colin Cameron (West Huron), 1142.

41. *Debates*, 2 May 1885, 1563.

42. *Debates*, 16 April 1885, 1144.

43. Catherine L. Cleverdon, *The Woman Suffrage Movement in Canada*, reprinted with an introduction by Ramsay Cook (Toronto: University of Toronto Press, 1970, [1950]), 174.

44. 'Onlooker,' "Men, Women and Things in General," *Canada Citizen*, 8 May 1885, 534.

45. *Debates*, 17 April 1885, 1171.

46. *Debates*, 29 April 1885, 1461. On Fawcett see David Rubinstein, *A Different World for Women: The Life of Millicent Garrett Fawcett* (New York: Harvester Wheatsheaf, 1991).

47. *Debates*, 28 April 1885, 1427-28.

48. J. Fleming. *Debates*, 16 April 1885, 1147. See also Shakespeare, 17 April 1885, 1391; McMullen, 17 April 1885, 1397; and Charlton, 17 April 1885, 1390. For the Conservative articulation of the "cult" in opposition to the vote see Joseph Royal (Provencher), 17 April 1885., 1390.

49. *Debates*, 27 April 1885, 1390.

50. *Debates*, 27 April 1885, 1405.

51. *Debates*, 27 April 1885, 1396-97. For a similarly positive reference to women's work see Casey, 27 April 1885, 1405.

52. *Debates*, 21 April 1885, 1356.

53. On the "colonial lady" and Native women see Jean Barman, "Taming Aboriginal Sexuality: Gender, Power, and Race in British Columbia, 1850-1900," *BC Studies* 115/116 (Autumn/Winter 1997/98): 237-66; and Adele Perry, "'Oh I'm just sick of the faces of men': Gender Imbalance, Race, Sexuality, and Sociability in Nineteenth-Century British Columbia," *BC Studies* 105/6 (Spring/Summer 1995): 27-43.

54. On the expediency and justice tensions within the suffrage movements see, for example, Veronica Strong-Boag, "'Ever a Crusader': Nellie L. McClung, First Wave Feminist," in *Rethinking Canada: Essays in Women's History*, 3rd ed., ed. Veronica Strong-Boag and Anita C. Fellman (Toronto: Oxford University Press, 1997); and Christine Bott, "The Ideas of British Suffragism," in *Votes for Women*, ed. Jane Purvis and Sandra Stanley Holton (London and New York: Routledge, 2000).

55. *Debates*, 16 April 1885, 1161.

56. *Debates*, 17 April 1885, 1235.

57. *Debates*, 21 April 1885, 1253.

58. *Debates*, 16 April 1885, 1142.

59. Olive P. Dickason, *Canada's First Nations. A History of Founding Peoples from the Earliest Times* (Toronto: McClelland & Stewart, 1992), 288.

60. Ermatinger, *Canadian Franchise and Election Laws*, 16.

61. David Mills (Bothwell), *Debates*, 30 April 1885, 1484. See also "Shocking," *Brantford Expositor* (5 May 1885), with its reference to the creation of "rotten boroughs."

62. *Debates*, 30 April 1885, 1486.

63. *Debates*, 11 May 1885, 1777.

64. "In addition, the glorious opportunities for patronage in a nation-wide electoral system, combined with the relative failure of the gerrymander act of 1882 to accomplish its purpose, no doubt quickened Sir John's interest in a project which he had openly favoured for two decades." Ward, *The Canadian House of Commons Representation*, 212.

65. See n.20 above.

66. *Debates*, 26 May 1885, 2121.

67. *Debates*, 27 May 1885, 2154.

68. *Debates*, 1 May 1885, 1492.

69. J.H. Wilson, *Debates*, 1 May 1885, 1515-16. See the argument that the Indian vote was intended "to stifle the voices of the white men of Ontario." *Brantford Expositor* (17 May 1885).

70. W. Mulock, *Debates*, 1 May 1885, 1521.

71. John Charlton, *Debates*, 1 May 1885, 1523.

72. John Milton Platt (Prince Edward), *Debates*, 1 May 1885, 1526.

73. Joseph E.A. De St. Georges (Pontneuf), *Debates*, 2 May 1885, 1533; see also Platt, *Debates*, 2 May 1885, 19 May 1885, 1977.

74. J. M. Platt, *Debates*, 1 May 1885, 1526.

75. *Debates*, 2 May 1885, 1540. See Sylvia Van Kirk, *Many Tender Ties: Women in Fur Trade Society, 1670-1870* (Winnipeg: Watson & Dwyer, 1980).

76. P.B. Casgrain (L'Islet), *Debates*, 1 May 1885, 1516.

77. *Debates*, 11 May 1885, 1747-48.

78. *Debates*, 27 May 1885, 2147.

79. J.H. Wilson, *Debates*, 1 May 1885, 1515.

80. *Debates*, 26 May 1885, 2125. See also Mills, 27 May 1885, 2144.

81. *Debates*, 19 May 1885, 1880. See also Wilson, 1 May 1885, 1515.

82. *Debates*, 30 April 1885, 1484.

83. *Debates*, 2 May 1885, 1562.

84. *Debates*, 26 May 1885, 2123.

85. *Debates*, 30 April 1885, 1491.

86. *Debates*, 20 May 1885, 2007.

87. *Debates*, 4 May 1885, 1574.

88. *Debates*, 2 May 1885, 1556.

89. *Debates*, 19 May 1885, 1976.

90. *Debates*, 20 May 1885, 2009.

91. *Debates*, 27 May 1885, 2160.

92. See *From China to Canada. A History of the Chinese Communities in Canada*, ed. Edgar Wickberg (Toronto: McClelland & Stewart, 1982), 46, 48, 49. This volume fails to note the provision of the 1885 *Franchise Act*.

93. *Debates*, 4 May 1885, 1582.

94. *Debates*, 4 May 1885, 1582.

95. *Debates*, 4 May 1885, 1583.

96. *Debates*, 4 May 1885, 1586.

97. *Debates*, 4 May 1885, 1582.

98. *Debates*, 26 May 1885, 2119.

99. *Debates*, 19 May 1885, 1967.

100. *Debates*, 4 May 1885, 1582.

101. *Debates*, 4 May 1885, 1588.

102. *Debates*, 4 May 1885, 1582.

103. J.H. Fairbank (East Lambton), *Debates*, 12 May 1885, 1783.

chapter four

FROM THE NATION TO THE CITIZEN
Québec Historical Writing and the Shaping of Identity[1]

Ronald Rudin

The Historian as Professional and as Advocate of Identity

Québec sits somewhat oddly in a volume dealing with citizenship, a subject that focuses upon the place of the individual within the nation-state. While there is a vast literature on the subject which grows daily in the face of challenges to the state in an age of globalization, the term is rarely employed in Québec by anyone other than those with an interest in Québec's accession to sovereignty. There is nothing that necessarily precludes the discussion of citizenship in the context of a province, and yet the term has been used almost exclusively by those associated with a particular political option, so strong is the association of sovereignty with the nation-state.[2]

Among historians, who provide the focus for the pages that follow, the discussion of citizenship in the Québec context has been raised most explicitly by Gérard Bouchard, arguably the most influential historian in Québec at the start of the new millennium. Bouchard has made little secret of his own preference for sovereignty, which he referred to as "the most desirable political option for the future of Quebec." In a fascinating exploration of the relationship between a population's view of its past and its securing of a common identity, Bouchard looked forward to the day when "all Quebecers feel like full-fledged citizens, regardless of their ethnic origins or constitutional preferences." While Bouchard was realistic enough to recognize that a sovereign Québec would have to accommodate those who were not sympathetic to that option, his use of the term "citoyen" was grounded in the anticipation that such a political goal was attainable if only a common identity might be fostered. Bouchard observed that "some people claim that it is impossible to construct a memory for the Québec nation that would be embraced by all because the various constituent groups do not have a common sense of history." Nevertheless, he was confident that historians were capable of projecting his vision for the future back upon the past.[3]

There is nothing particularly extraordinary about Bouchard's call for historians to put their tools at the disposal of a particular direction for Québec. Societies do not develop a sense of their identity by chance; rather, identities are constructed, usually by leaders capable of crafting images that have some meaning to the larger population. As Bouchard understood, historians can play an important role in the construction of an identity by giving people a sense of where they have been so that they might be able to imagine where they are headed.[4]

Over the course of the twentieth century, the involvement of historians in this process has been complicated by their self-identification as professionals engaged in a scientific act. Accordingly, there has been considerable tension between their commitment to the presentation of a reasonably objective view of the past and their own preferences regarding the future of the society in which they lived. Speaking directly to the dilemma facing historians throughout the twentieth century, Peter Novick has observed:

> I don't think that the idea of historical objectivity is true or false, right or wrong: I find it not just essentially contested, but essentially confused. Many philosophical assumptions of the concept seem to me dubious; some of the key elements in the objectivist synthesis I consider psychologically and sociologically naive. As a practical matter, I think it promotes an unreal and misleading distinction between, on the one hand, historical accounts 'distorted' by ideological assumptions and purposes; on the other, history free of these taints. It seems to me that to say of a work of history that it is or isn't objective is to make an *empty* observation.[5]

In order to respond to observations such as Novick's, Gérard Bouchard has argued that his own view of the past was grounded in something that approached "objectivity." He claimed to be engaged in a process of "objectification," which entailed the historian developing "interpretations which were theoretically coherent, methodologically verifiable and significant in terms of the contemporary concerns of the society in question."[6] He contrasted this perspective with that of earlier Québec historians, who were also involved in presenting views of Québec society that might provide direction for the future, but who were guilty of offering nothing more than "false representations."[7]

In particular, Bouchard condemned Québec leaders, including historians such as Abbé Lionel Groulx, the first professor of Canadian history in a French-language university in Québec, who emphasized such aspects of the French-Canadian experience as its rural nature. Bouchard criticized Groulx for projecting the image of a rural society, in the process ignoring the fact that Québec had long been in the process of urbanizing in step with the rest of North America.[8] In phrasing the issue in this manner, however, Bouchard pushed aside the fact that French-speaking Québec was more rural than the Canadian norm early in the century, when Groulx began his career.[9] So was it fair to refer to Groulx's characterization as "false"? On another level, however, one wonders if Bouchard was fair in referring to historians such as Groulx as members of an "elite looking for a nation," dismissing them as leaders who needed to impose a false view of the past upon a people who would not have otherwise followed their lead. Given Bouchard's own admission that he hoped to shape Quebecers' view of their past in order to forward his own political option, could one not say the same about his writings?

In the end, Groulx and Bouchard, at opposite ends of the twentieth century, represented the dilemma faced by all historians: the desire to remain fair to the facts while at the same time being influenced, in one way or another, by the world in which they lived. More specifically, each had a perspective upon Québec society in the past that might serve to direct that society into the future. In Groulx's day, the society in question was referred to as French Canada, defined by its language and religion, but not by provincial boundaries, while Bouchard's "nation québécoise" included all who lived within the territory of Québec; or, to put it in other terms, Groulx projected an ethnic form of nationalism, while Bouchard projected the image of the citizen in a sovereign state. In between the two, still other historians looked at the past in a manner that was consistent with the projection of a civic understanding of nationalism. As we will see in the sections that follow, various perspectives on the nation have been developed by historians committed to both the "truth" and an understanding of the world in which they lived.

The Paradigm of Difference

While Gérard Bouchard may have exaggerated the distinctiveness of the historians who preceded him, there is no escaping the fact that those who wrote up to the middle of the twentieth century were marked, as he put it, by their "preoccupation with difference. For the writers, journalists and essayists of this era, it was crucial to present French Canada as if it were radically different from their English-Canadian and American neighbours."[10] Long before historians who thought of themselves as professionals took centre stage, the Québec past was being presented by a series of "amateurs" who wrote in order to stiffen the resolve of their people to survive by explaining to them what made French Canada unique. This tradition began with François-Xavier Garneau, often referred to as French Canada's *historien national*, who wrote his *Histoire du Canada depuis sa découverte jusqu'à nos jours* in the immediate aftermath of the Rebellions of 1837. Fearing the assimilation of his people following the forced union of Upper and Lower Canada, Garneau depicted a people who were defined by their language, their religion, and their common ancestry that stretched back to France and who had shown resilience in the past when abandoned by their mother country or assailed by new masters after their Conquest.

In urging his compatriots to remain true to their roots, Garneau provided the model for the professional historians of the first half of the twentieth century who would bring new tools to their efforts, but who were still largely concerned with understanding the plight of a people who could be defined in ethnic terms. In particular, Groulx recognized his debt to Garneau, with whom he differed regarding the place of Catholicism in French-Canadian society, but with whom he could identify in terms of providing the picture of a people who had not betrayed their roots in the past and who needed to avoid doing so in the future.

Groulx, who dominated the Québec historical profession from his appointment at the Université de Montréal in 1915 until his retirement at the end of the 1940s, faced different challenges than Garneau had encountered. By the first half of the twentieth century, French Canadians constituted a minority population scattered among various provinces and American states. Moreover, they constituted a people who had not shared in the profits of the economic changes that had moved most people to the cities by the early 1900s. From Groulx's perspective, French Canadians had little hope of achieving either political or economic power, and so needed to focus upon their cultural survival, their *survivance*. Accordingly, Groulx tended to focus upon the rural roots of the population, in the process downplaying the distinctions of class that divided them internally and reminding French Canadians of what had distinguished them from the English-speakers who surrounded them. This distinctiveness had served them well in the past and, if they only remained true to their traditions, they would continue to survive well into the future.

While Groulx had not been trained as an historian, he tried during his long career to acquire the skills required by a professional. In his early writing, he presented a people who had sprung from "a superior race" of farmers devoted to Catholicism.[11] Over time, however, while Groulx never abandoned either his emphasis upon difference or his hopes for the future of his people, he did alter his vision of the past as he became familiar with the techniques of the professional historian. In his last work, prepared following his retirement from the Université de Montréal, he no longer focused exclusively upon the almost mystical farmer, as he adopted the emphasis upon material concerns that were becoming dominant in the profession. He now insisted that it was important to abandon "this false impression of a society consisting entirely of the peasantry .... We can never forget that the peasants of the St-Lawrence valley were never very distant from the far-flung lands of the [French] empire, which provided numerous opportunities for merchants, manufacturers, explorers and soldiers."[12]

Although Groulx's depiction of the past evolved over time, he never abandoned his vision of a French-Canadian nation consisting largely of relatively poor French-speaking Quebecers; nor did he necessarily object to this poverty which had kept French-speakers distinct from the more successful English-speakers who surrounded them. However, by the end of the 1940s, as French-speakers were finding themselves with considerably more money at their disposal as a result of the war and the boom that followed, their view of who they were and where they were heading began to change. This increased prosperity did not close the rather considerable wage gap that existed between Canada's two major linguistic groups; nevertheless, the increase in disposable income made it possible for some French-speakers to further their education, sometimes outside Canada, and for the population more generally to become receptive to a more materialistic view of the world. Among historians, this shift was most noticeable at the Université de Montréal, Groulx's own university, where a new generation of historians emerged on the scene in the late 1940s and early 1950s.

These historians, most notably Guy Frégault (Groulx's handpicked successor), Michel Brunet, and Maurice Séguin, followed in their *maître's* footsteps in continuing to focus upon a people defined in ethnic terms. Moreover, their interest in the past, as in the case of Groulx, had been inspired by a desire to explain why French Canadians had been different and to understand how they might survive into the future. However, they parted company with Groulx when it came to their understanding of this distinctiveness and what it implied for their *survivance*. While Groulx had been content simply to accept the economic domination of others, the new historians reflected their own connection to the consumer society in which they came of age by trying to understand the roots of French-Canadian economic "inferiority," an exercise that quickly led them to focus upon the implications of the Conquest that had destroyed a French-Canadian bourgeoisie. As Frégault put it, "The Conquest disrupted Canadien society, destroyed its political structure, and thoroughly drained its resourcefulness." Other historians such as Groulx might have had illusions regarding the prospects for *Canadiens* following the Conquest, believing that simple devotion to their traditions would allow their survival. Frégault thought that this was naive; he simply noted that, following the Conquest, *les Canadiens* constituted a "broken" people.[13]

Distance from power was no longer a badge of honour, but rather a problem to be overcome. The new historians at the Université de Montréal began to imagine the route to empowerment through the strengthening of the one government over which French Canadians might be able to exercise power. The Québec government had traditionally been a rather ineffectual tool for advancing French-Canadian interests, frequently looking after the interests of English-run business. In the 1960s, however, the view of Montreal historians would play a role in shifting the perspective of French-speakers who supported the redefinition of the role of the state in Québec via the Quiet Revolution so that they might rise up from the "broken" condition described by the Montreal historians. Even so, in the context of the 1950s, Groulx's successors had only one of two perspectives on the causes of French-Canadian economic inferiority.

As part of the process that had created a much better educated population, history emerged as a "scientific" discipline taught by members of an autonomous department not only at the Université de Montréal but also at the other French-language university, Université Laval in Quebec City. The historians associated with Laval, individuals such as Marcel Trudel, Jean Hamelin, and Fernand Ouellet, agreed with their Montreal counterparts that French Canadians had traditionally wielded relatively little power. However, they placed the blame for this situation squarely upon French-speakers, who had proven to be ill-suited for economic success in the world, to a considerable degree because of their own failings. These historians looked back to New France, but failed to find a successful bourgeoisie. Accordingly, the Conquest had not resulted in the destruction of this class; rather, it provided opportunities for profit that French Canadians managed to squander due to poor business practices that some attributed to the influence of Catholicism. According to Ouellet, the most outspoken of the Laval historians, if the French Canadian farmer had had difficulties it was due to his "lavish spending and unproductive investments [which] constituted a characteristic of his mentality and a lasting element in his culture."[14]

The Laval view of the past did not see the advancement of French-Canadian interests through the creation of a strong provincial government which, following in the footsteps of the Catholic church, would serve only to cut French-speakers off from the larger world. Over the course of the 1960s, several of the most important Laval historians, feeling that they were out of step with the more assertive nationalism that was leading to the construction of a powerful Québec state, left the province altogether. Their message ultimately found a receptive ear, but not among the leaders in Quebec City. Rather, it was well received by French-Canadian leaders who viewed participation at the federal level as the key to the advancement of their people's best interests.

In the end, however, while the Montréal and Laval historians may have differed from each other, they formed part of a tradition that had begun with Garneau and had continued with Groulx, in which the study of the past was focused upon what had made French Canadians different from the other inhabitants of North America. Having phrased the issue in this manner, these historians were interested in an ethnic group that lived primarily, but not exclusively, within the confines of Québec. Ultimately, by the 1960s the impact of the Quiet Revolution, for which historians bore some responsibility, would transform the self-image of French-speaking Quebecers as well as the focus of historical analysis.

The Paradigm of Normalcy

In the 1960s, Québec society was significantly transformed with the arrival of what is commonly called the Quiet Revolution. Within a relatively short period of time, the Québec state came to play a powerful role in the lives of the population, most notably through assuming control over education, previously run largely by the Catholic church, and hydro-electricity, heretofore controlled largely by English-dominated corporations. The 1962 Québec provincial election was designed as a referendum regarding the government's handling of the hydro-electricity dossier, but the Liberal party's use of the slogan "Maîtres chez nous" (Masters in our own house) indicated that there was more at play here than control over electrical power.

French-speaking Quebecers, who voted overwhelmingly in favour of the Liberals, were in the midst of a re-evaluation of their own identity, which had long been based upon membership in a group that had no clear territorial identity, but which instead was grounded in language, religion, common ancestry, and a legacy of powerlessness. By the 1960s, following more than a decade of increased prosperity and improved educational standards, French-speaking Quebecers were no longer interested in viewing themselves primarily as members of a weak Canadian minority, but rather as the self-confident and successful members of the majority group within Québec. As French-speakers abandoned Catholicism, which they viewed as an obstacle to their material success, they embraced the construction of the Québec state, which came to be viewed as the primary tool for their advancement as a modern people.

What remained unresolved, however, was the precise meaning of the "nous" in that 1962 election slogan; or to put if more pointedly, what did it take to be considered a "Québécois," an ambiguous term that was a further product of the Quiet Revolution? Some who occupy a rather marginal place in Québec society forty years after the start of these profound changes would insist that only French-speaking Quebecers can really be considered Québécois, in a sense perpetuating French-Canadian nationalism, but with a limited territorial reach.

The most obvious advocate of such a perspective is Jacques Parizeau, the former premier of Québec, who on the night of the 1995 referendum made his now infamous speech about the causes for the narrow loss of the sovereigntist option: "Friends, we have lost, but not by a lot. It was successful in one sense. Let's stop talking about the francophones of Québec. Let's talk about us. Sixty per cent of us have voted in favour. It's true we have been defeated, but basically by what? By money and the ethnic vote." In his insistence that the term francophone was irrelevant, Parizeau made it clear that when he referred to Quebecers, or "us," he meant French-speakers; no qualifier was needed, because all other Quebecers were non-citizens. He further marginalized "them" by the reference to "money," a not very subtle way of linking the non-francophone population with the wealthy English-speakers who had dominated Québec before the Quiet Revolution. In 1995 the average incomes of French-speakers were indistinguishable from those of non-francophones, but this made little difference to Parizeau, who made his ethnic understanding of nationalism perfectly clear for all to hear.

In contrast to Parizeau's view, the dominant view over the past forty years has seen the emergence of a more territorial understanding of "nous," with French-speakers playing a dominant role, but with the presence of other groups also taken into account, although perhaps not as much as the latter would like. Accordingly, over the course of the 1960s and 1970s successive Québec governments, under the control of both the Liberals and the Parti québécois, tried to accommodate both Native people and English-speaking Quebecers. In the first instance, the Québec government, following some ill-advised efforts to develop hydro-electric facilities upon Native lands in Québec's north, signed the James Bay and Northern Québec Agreement in

1975 by which Natives were to be partners in future developments. In a similar manner, when language legislation was implemented in the 1970s, attention was given to the acquired rights of English-speakers who had long lived
in the province. However, perhaps the clearest sign of the existence of a territorial understanding of what it meant to be Québécois came from René
Lévesque on the night of the first sovereignty referendum in 1980. Unlike
Parizeau fifteen years later, Lévesque did not question the legitimacy of the
outcome because of the overwhelming opposition from non-francophones.
Instead, he recognized his defeat at the hands of citizens whose votes needed
to be valued equally.

Lévesque projected the image of a modern and self-confident French-
speaking population whose identity was linked to a territory within which
the interests of non-francophones also had to be taken into account. This
image came to occupy centre stage in the new narrative of Québec's past that
emerged in the wake of the Quiet Revolution. With the greater prosperity of
Quebecers and the establishment of an interventionist state that encouraged
the expansion of the province's educational system, the ranks of professional
historians expanded dramatically. Many of the new professors came of age
during the Quiet Revolution and subsequently approached the past from the
perspective of a French-speaking population that was self-conscious about
the strides that it had made, both individually and collectively. Gone was the
sense of defeat that had led earlier historians, from Groulx to Frégault and
Ouellet, to try to make sense of French-Canadian weakness. Accordingly,
debates about the meaning of the Conquest that had long dominated historical writing disappeared from view, replaced by discussions of the roots of a
modern Québec that had long been in the mainstream of developments
across the western world. If previous historians had been obsessed by difference, the new historians were interested in projecting an image of normalcy.
As Gérard Bouchard has remarked, these historians, whom he has referred
to as modernists, were intent upon showing that Québec was "in the mainstream of developments both in North America and across the western world.
From this perspective, Québec was as industrial, as capitalistic, as liberal, as
developed, in short as modern as other societies."[5]

As one of the leading post-Quiet Revolution historians, Paul-André
Linteau, has observed, "Coming of age in a Québec where everyone was talking about modernization, living in an urban-industrial society, it was natural
that we would want to understand the roots of contemporary Québec. The
historical writing of the time, focusing upon New France and the early years
of British rule, was not responding to our concerns. Accordingly, we set off
to explore the various factors that led to the emergence of an industrial, cap-

italist society in Québec by the middle of the nineteenth century."[16]
Ultimately, Linteau, along with Jean-Claude Robert and René Durocher, produced the single work that best reflected the historians' post-1960 understanding of Québec's past. *Histoire du Québec contemporain* was a synthesis of
the various studies that their generation had been carrying out since the late
1960s.[17] The authors dealt exclusively with the period since Confederation,
thus setting themselves apart from Québec historians, going back to Groulx,
who had been preoccupied with an earlier period where the roots of
Quebecers' inferiority might be found. These earlier historians had focused
upon a rural society in which French-speakers had been strongly influenced
by Catholicism and little interested in issues pertinent to the world of business. Linteau, Robert, and Durocher disputed this characterization, giving
primary attention to urban issues and within this context making reference
to "the dynamism of the French-speaking bourgeoisie," in the process questioning the power of Catholicism to block the entrepreneurial instincts of
Quebecers. As Jocelyn Létourneau has put it, the French Canadian, "conquered, humiliated and demoralized," was replaced in the historical record
by the Québécois, "successful, entrepreneurial and ambitious."[18]

The significance of *Histoire du Québec contemporain* extended, however,
beyond its characterization of the French-speaking majority. Linteau, Robert,
and Durocher also reflected the territorial focus of nationalist discourse since
the Quiet Revolution in proclaiming in the preface to their work, "The
Québec that we are studying here is defined in territorial, rather than ethnic,
terms. We are interested in phenomena which were experienced by the men
and women who inhabited this territory. We have consistently used the
word 'Québécois' in a very precise sense. It pertains to all residents of
Québec including those whose ancestors came from the northwest thousands of years ago, those who came from France in the time of Jean Talon,
those who came from Scotland in the late eighteenth century or from Ireland
during the Great Famine, those Jews seeking refuge from the pogroms of
Eastern Europe, and those emigrating from a southern Italy which had little
to offer them."[19] Here was a clear expression of a civic understanding of
nationalism that departed dramatically from the "nous" that had previously
marked Québec historical writing.

Quite aside from the substantive significance of the modernist approach,
it also signalled a shift from previous Québec historical writing, which was
marked by a certain polemical tone. While historians from Groulx to
Frégault and Ouellet believed that they were, on some level, engaged in seeking the "truth," they did not hesitate to be explicit about their social and
political preoccupations. The modernists, by contrast, at least at the rhetori-

cal level, were circumspect about campaigning for any particular political option. In a sense, they projected the image of a modern people by presenting a seemingly value-free approach to the past. They took on the image of the modern professional, as opposed to that of the embattled partisan which had previously been the norm. In this regard, Serge Courville, Jean-Claude Robert, and Normand Séguin, three leading modernists, distinguished themselves from previous Québec historians whose work had been deformed by "preconceived notions and value judgements." For his part, Yves Gingras argued that Québec historians since the 1960s had turned from polemical writing to scientific research which kept a certain distance "from current social or economic concerns."[20]

The Paradigm of the Citizen

At the start of the new millennium, the modernist perspective upon the past remains the dominant approach to Québec historical writing, roughly thirty years after its leading practitioners began their careers. Nevertheless, much like the Quiet Revolution that spawned it, the modernist paradigm has received criticism from various quarters.[21] In particular, some critics have focused upon the modernists' efforts to help redefine the identity of Quebecers as inhabitants of a territory, in the process drawing attention away from the particular problems of the French-speaking majority.

In this regard, Jocelyn Létourneau has pointed to the general failure of the modernist approach to dislodge earlier narratives of Québec's past from the minds of ordinary Quebecers. Over the past few years, Létourneau has been asking his students at Université Laval to describe their conception of Québec history prior to taking his course on the subject. Almost invariably, the students have focused upon the difficulties of French-speakers in the face of conflict with their English-speaking counterparts. As one student put it, "As far as I go, the history of Québec ... is the struggle of French Canadians to avoid assimilation by the more numerous and powerful English-speakers. It is the history of a proud and united people who have been dominated." Another student remarked, "I see the history of Québec as the story of constant English-French tension ... Quebecers have always been dominated by another people; they have been too reluctant to take control of their own land." On the basis of a steady stream of such observations, Létourneau concluded that there was "no real connection between the [modernist] interpretation and the persistent representations of the past in the collective memory."[22]

While Létourneau indicated no interest in a return to the earlier depiction of Québec history as the saga of French Canadians, such a longing was present in the last writings, prior to his death in 1997, of the sociologist Fernand Dumont. On several occasions, Dumont complained about the impact of the Quiet Revolution, which had so systematically rejected everything from the past that French-speakers were left with little sense of their own history. As he put it, "It appeared to our elites that in order to take charge of the future, it wasn't enough to set off in new directions; they also insisted upon denying our past." Dumont was disturbed that the "collective memory [had] been devastated," as French-speakers were taught a history that did not speak directly to their needs and which had been purged of meaningful references from their past:

> It should still be possible to admire the soldiers and missionaries from New France, as well as the men who cleared the land and laboured in the distant past ... It should still be possible to recognize that our older form of nationalism had its merits ..., because it proclaimed the existence of a people during their darkest hours and, for better or worse, provided us with a tool, however inadequate, to defend ourselves ... Quebecers today are not facing the same challenges that were present a century ago. Nevertheless, I believe that an understanding of our beginnings can help us in our own times.[23]

Among historians, Dumont's interest in integrating some aspects of the earlier French-Canadian perspective on the past has been most forcefully presented by Gérard Bouchard, whose willingness to use history as a tool to mould a citizenry that might be more sympathetic to sovereignty, an option also dear to Dumont's heart, was briefly discussed at the start of this chapter. On a rhetorical level, Bouchard's explicit linking of historical analysis with political argument was a return to the language of historians prior to the Quiet Revolution. While he distinguished himself from the modernists in this regard, much of his conceptualization of the Québec population was inspired by the modernist emphasis upon normalcy. However, where the modernists viewed Quebecers as a "normal" people in the mainstream of social and economic developments across the western world since the rise of industrialization, Bouchard chose another basis for asserting normalcy. He insisted that Québec society needed to be considered as "une collectivité neuve" (a new people), much like Latin America, English Canada, the United States or Australia, all lands where an Aboriginal population had been pushed aside by Europeans who created new societies and ultimately achieved independence. Bouchard has made this last point, about the normal route toward sovereignty for any "société neuve," in various contexts, thus delivering a political message clear for all to hear. As he put it in one such reference, "If we compare Québec and Latin America, one very large question emerges: How can we explain that of all the peoples [of the Americas] ... Québec alone has failed to achieve its political independence?"[24] The question was rhetorical, designed to suggest what Québec should become on the basis of past experience.

Having departed from the modernists' political neutrality, Bouchard was drawn into redefining the relationship between the various groups within the territory of Québec. In order to see the direction of history as leading Quebecers toward sovereignty, he also needed to redefine the territorial "nous" that the modernists had proposed in order to give precedence to the place of French-speaking Quebecers. As he put it, "In terms of our identity, we have moved from being 'Canadiens,' to being French Canadians, and now 'Québécois,' a term which has come to include a large percentage of non-francophone citizens ... In spite of all these changes, one constant has remained: that of a French-speaking people which, in spite of some very difficult circumstances, has managed to survive in America and which has made this sense of survival a part of its identity."[25] This conceptualization of Québec society stood in stark contrast to Linteau's interest in shifting the focus of historical analysis from "an ethnic group" to "the inhabitants of a territory."[26]

If Bouchard wanted to redefine Quebecers so as to put French-speakers once again at the centre of the picture, where did this leave the other 20 per cent of the population? In a sense, he answered that question when he remarked, "It is necessary to open up the history of French Canada so as to insert the experiences of groups which have traditionally been excluded from the historical record."[27] He provided some clue about how he might insert the history of groups such as Native people into the history of French Canadians in his discussion of the experience of other, now-independent "sociétés neuves" that had managed to develop a common view of the past. He expressed particular admiration for the efforts in Mexico and Australia, where Native people were not conceived as the first occupants of a territory, but rather as the first members of the dominant group that now inhabits that territory. He admitted that, in the latter case, "this initiative has to date received little more than the support of certain intellectuals." Nevertheless, he thought that the model might be adopted in Québec: "If native people are going to form an integral part of the [Québec] nation, it is only logical to depict them as the first Quebecers, and not as a 'foreign' population or as the first occupants of the territory of Québec."[28]

One might well ask what Native people would have to say about the proposition that *their* history was really the start of the history of Bouchard's "nation québécoise," but such concerns about cultural appropriation did not seem to bother the historian. Moreover, Bouchard was not particularly troubled about assimilating the experience of the various non-native minorities into the history of the nation that he wanted to project into the future, in the process marginalizing the considerable conflict from the past and ignoring the desire of groups such as English-speakers to see themselves as members of a Canadian nation. As Jocelyn Létourneau has put it, "Bouchard has gone overboard in minimizing the significance of one of the major constants in Québec's past, namely the sometimes difficult relationship between French-speakers and the other linguistic groups in the province ...." Létourneau went on to criticize Bouchard for viewing non-francophones only in terms of their ties to "a welcoming French-speaking population," ignoring in the process "the real-life experiences of the various groups."[29]

Bouchard clearly parted company from the modernists who were prepared to convey a certain legitimacy to the various non-francophone groups in Québec, quite aside from their relationship with the linguistic majority. In the process, the modernists projected a civic understanding of nationalism into the past. For his part, Bouchard saw the road to sovereignty via the assertion that Québec formed "a diverse French-speaking population" which had been created as a result of the successful integration of immigrants into the French-speaking majority. He imagined a cohesive society in which citizens might share the fruits of the nation-state, and he explicitly rejected an historical vision nourished by "a guilty ethnic conscience inspired by the current popularity across the world for the concept of the civic nation."[30]

Plus ça change, plus c'est la même chose

It is rather easy to be critical of Gérard Bouchard's desire to construct the past for political ends. Létourneau, for instance, has condemned the manner in which "a partisan outlook has provided the starting point for the historian's interpretative approach."[31] Such a criticism, however, removes historical writing from the context in which it has been produced over the past century, ever since it emerged as a scientific endeavour. Throughout this period, historians have produced works based upon a certain search for the "truth," but moulded at the same time by the society in which they lived. Historians sometimes take on the posture of the "impartial" observer, as was the case with the modernists, while at other times they will be open about their hopes for the future of their society, as was the case for the historians of "difference" as well as for Gérard Bouchard. In either case, however, historical writing provides an occasion for leaders of a society to project an image from the past onto the future.

In the case of Québec, this exercise has had considerable significance for a French-speaking population trying to make sense of the various challenges it has faced. Prior to the Quiet Revolution, when most leaders conceived of francophone Québec as part of a larger French-Canadian nation, there was little reason to think about the "others" who inhabited the territory of Québec. Rather, historians as diverse as Lionel Groulx, Guy Frégault, and Fernand Ouellet wanted to understand why a particular ethnic group had not developed in the same way as the English-speakers who surrounded them in North America. With the coming of the Quiet Revolution and the development of a nationalism that was closely linked to a political territory, a civic understanding of nationalism blossomed through the writings of the modernists who wanted to integrate the experiences of all Quebecers into the historical narrative. Most recently, in light of a certain disenchantment with the Quiet Revolution, Gérard Bouchard has abandoned the modernists' approach so as to put an ethnic group back at the centre of the picture, albeit with a territorial slant and with a vision of various groups living in harmony as citizens of a sovereign state. While the various options grounded in the past changed over the course of the twentieth century, they were all articulated by historians with one eye on the past and the other eye upon the future of their society.

Notes

1. Many of the ideas in this chapter appeared in my *Making History in Twentieth Century Quebec* (Toronto: University of Toronto Press, 1997). The discussion of the recent writings of Gérard Bouchard has not appeared in my previous publications on historiographical issues and constitutes an updating of some of the arguments that I presented in *Making History*.

2. See, for instance, the essays pertinent to Québec in the following anthologies: William Kaplan, *Belonging: The Meaning and Future of Canadian Citizenship* (Montreal: McGill-Queen's University Press, 1993); *Le pays de tous les Québécois*, ed. Michel Sarra-Bournet (Montreal: vlb, 1998); *Penser la nation québécoise*, ed. Michel Venne (Montreal: Québec-Amérique, 2000).

3. Gérard Bouchard, "Construire la nation québécoise: Manifeste pour une coalition nationale," in *Penser la nation québécoise*, ed. Venne, 52, 56; Bouchard, *La nation québécoise au futur et au passé* (Montreal: vlb éditeur, 1999), 126. Over the past few years, Bouchard has received the highest prizes of both the Canadian Historical Association and its Québec counterpart, the Institut d'histoire de l'Amérique française, in addition to winning the Governor-General's award. This and all subsequent passages that were originally in French have been translated by the author.

4. The role of elites in constructing identity has been dealt with in a vast literature. See, for instance, *The Invention of Tradition*, ed. Eric Hobsbawm and Terence Ranger (Cambridge: Cambridge University Press, 1983).

5. Peter Novick, *That Noble Dream: The Objectivity Question and the American Historical Profession* (Cambridge: Cambridge University Press, 1988), 2, 6. The emphasis is his.

6. Gérard Bouchard, *Genèse des nations et cultures au nouveau monde* (Montréal: Boréal, 2000), 75.

7. Bouchard, *Genèse des nations*, 178. He has also expressed the same sentiment in *La nation québécoise au futur et au passé*, 130, and in *Entre l'ancien et le nouveau monde* (Ottawa: University of Ottawa Press, 1996), 3.

8. Bouchard, *Entre l'ancien et le nouveau monde*, 3-23.

9. In 1921, for instance, 54% of French-speaking Quebecers were rural dwellers, a figure that had fallen to 53% for Canada as a whole and 42% for Ontario. Only 20% of English-speaking Quebecers lived in rural areas, but they are not the individuals under discussion here.

10. Bouchard, *Entre l'ancien et le nouveau monde*, 13.

11. Lionel Groulx, *La naissance d'une race*, 1st ed. (Montréal: Bibliothèque de l'Action française, 1919), 181.

12. *Histoire du Canada français depuis la découverte*, 4th ed, 2 vols. (Montréal: Fides, 1960), I, 306.

13. Guy Frégault, *La guerre de la conquête* (Montréal: Fides, 1955), 457-58.

14. Fernand Ouellet, *Economic and Social History of Quebec*, trans. (Toronto: Gage, 1980), 463.

15. Gérard Bouchard, "Sur les mutations de l'historiographie québécoise: les chemins de la maturité," in *La société québécoise après 30 ans de changements*, ed. Fernand Dumont (Québec: Institut québécois de recherche sur la culture, 1990), 262. In various other publications, including *Making History*, I referred to these historians as "revisionists" for the way in which they revised the earlier paradigm of difference. My use of this term has raised hackles among critics who, wrongly, thought I was trying to equate these contemporary Québec historians with those, particularly in France, who have denied the Holocaust. Bouchard's use of the term "modernist" conveys the same sense, without the political baggage (Bouchard, *Genèse*, 70).

16. Paul-André Linteau, "La nouvelle histoire," *Liberté* 147 (1983): 44-45.

17. Paul-André Linteau, René Durocher and Jean-Claude Robert, *Histoire du Québec contemporain: de la Confédération à la crise* (Montréal: Boréal, 1979); Linteau, Durocher, Robert and Ricard, *Histoire du Québec contemporain: le Québec depuis 1930* (Montréal: Boréal, 1986); a new and revised edition of the two volumes was published by Boréal in 1989. All references (hereafter *HQC*) are to the second edition of the work.

18. *HQC*, I, 192; Jocelyn Létourneau, "La production historienne courante portant sur le Québec et ses rapports avec la construction des figures identitaires d'une communauté communicationnelle," *Recherches sociographiques* 36 (1995): 12.

19. *HQC*, I, 7.

20. Serge Courville, Jean-Claude Robert and Normand Séguin, *Atlas historique du Québec: le pays laurentien au 19e siècle, les morphologies de base* (Québec: Presses de l'Université Laval, 1995), 2; Yves Gingras, "Une sociologie spontanée de la connaissance historique," *Bulletin d'histoire politique* 4 (1996): 41.

21. I have been critical of certain aspects of the modernist approach. See *Making History*, ch 5.

22. Jocelyn Létourneau, "La production historienne," 30-32.

23. Fernand Dumont, *Raisons communes* (Montréal: Boréal, 1995), 104; *Genèse de la société québécoise* (Montréal: Boréal, 1993), 335, 331. Dumont also dealt with similar questions in *L'avenir de la mémoire* (Montreal: Nuit Blanche, 1993).

24. Dumont, *Genèse de la société québécoise*, 219. See, in the same volume, pp. 173, 176, 308, 396.

25. Dumont, *Genèse de la société québécoise*, 81.

26. Linteau, "La nouvelle histoire," 44-45.

27. Bouchard, "Construire la nation québécoise," 62.

28. Dumont, *Genèse de la société québécoise*, 298; *La nation québécoise au futur et au passé*, 117.

29. Jocelyn Létourneau, *Passé à l'avenir* (Montréal: Boréal, 2000), 73. Létourneau was also critical of Bouchard's handling of native issues: "To view native people as the first Québécois or to view the beginning of the history of the Québec people with the Amerindian and Inuit immigration to North America, is to violate one of the cardinal rules of rigorous scientific research" (69).

30. Bouchard, "Construire la nation québécoise," 60, 63.

31. Létourneau, *Passé à l'avenir*, 76.

chapter five

INDIGENOUS CITIZENSHIP AND HISTORY IN CANADA
Between Denial and Imposition[1]

Claude Denis

Toward "Citizens Plus"?

From the arrival of Europeans in the Americas until the War of 1812 between the British Empire and the recently independent United States, Indigenous peoples were partners to the newcomers in what became Canada. They began as senior partners, becoming gradually equal and then increasingly subordinated. From at least the adoption of the *Indian Act* by the Canadian parliament in the late nineteenth century, and up until 1960, they were left with a difficult choice: on the one hand, they could maintain a devalued but meaningful Indian status and, on the other hand, they could abandon their Indigenous identities as the price for acquiring Canadian citizenship.

A person could not, in other words, at once be "Indian" and a Canadian citizen. And there was no talk of an Indian/Indigenous citizenship: Indians were wards of the Canadian state, as they could not be expected to take care of themselves. To the extent that an otherwise Indian person learned/decided to run her own life in a more or less whitestream[2] manner, the law considered that she stopped being an Indian. The *Indian Act*'s goal was cultural *and political* assimilation, the political means of which was marginalization — a system that served as the model for South Africa's Apartheid system after World War II.

In the last thirty years, the will to assimilate has been partly displaced by a degree of recognition of Indigenous peoples, but this displacement has remained ambivalent and very much incomplete. Canada may be heading toward a recognition of Indigenous peoples as "citizens plus,"[3] which is to say that, in addition to enjoying full Canadian citizenship, persons of Indigenous descent would also carry a form of Indigenous citizenship.[4] It is far from certain, however, what form such Indigenous citizenship would take — if it comes to life at all.

The Courts began the process of recognition with the 1973 *Calder* decision, and have continued to define it with decisions in the last twelve years such as *Sioui* (1990), *Sparrow* (1990), *Badger* (1996), *Van der Peet* (1996), *Delgamuukw* (1997), *Marshall* (1999)[5] and *Mitchell* (2001).[6] These decisions have been accompanied by (failed) constitutional discussions and by self-government/treaty[7] negotiations between federal and provincial governments and some First Nations. The Nisga'a Accord, finalized in 1999, is generally recognized as the model (to be either followed or avoided) for such contemporary agreements. Dozens of self-government agreements — mostly in British Columbia — are currently being negotiated, but this is a very young and fragile process. It has become even more fragile since the election in the summer of 2001 of a Liberal government in British Columbia that opposes the so-called "treaty process" and has promised a referendum aiming to bring it to an end.[8] Even the Nisga'a Accord, ratified by all parties and in the process of being implemented, may be put into question.

With the constitutional process permanently stalled and the "treaty process" in danger of being shelved, law courts seem, once again, to be the only way to go for Indigenous peoples seeking the recognition of their rights. But where do courts lead? And where, for that matter, would the Nisga'a model be taking Canada's Indigenous peoples? Are their members on their way to becoming Canadian *citizens, plus* citizens of sovereign, self-governing Indigenous communities? As we will see below, in a strictly legal sense the courts' work of recognizing (or denying) Aboriginal rights is not going in the direction of making Indigenous citizenship possible. But we may think that the courts' legitimizing Indigenous distinctiveness *in law* produces an ideological effect of making Indigenous self-government more plausible politically.

For the most part, this chapter focuses on what the courts are doing to keep the issue of Indigenous citizenship out of the picture, while recognizing Aboriginal rights. The Nisga'a model will be discussed briefly at the end of the chapter to provide a counterpoint — in both its positive and negative aspects — to the kind of rights that the courts are affirming.

In addition to these questions and uncertainties, there is the philosophical issue of the terrain, as it were, on which Indigenous peoples stand as they negotiate: it is an historical rootedness that grounds the Indigenous claim, much more than a claim to cultural difference.[9] Basically, the rights of Indigenous peoples in Canada are problematized *in law* on the basis of a people having occupied, in an unchanging manner, a particular geographical space *since time immemorial*. This historical anchoring must be proved before either a court or government negotiators if a particular Indigenous people is to have the least hope of seeing some rights recognized. After seeing their history/histories long denied by Eurocentric conceptions of civilization and historical progress, Indigenous peoples in Canada are now being subjected to a heavy historical burden of proof.

Citizenship — Of the Individual and the Community

No matter what else it may involve, citizenship has to do with the general political rights of a self-governing or sovereign political community — that is, the political rights of the community members and the political rights of the community itself, including the authority to grant and deny citizenship to individuals.

In political theory, citizenship is typically thought of in individual terms — but this takes for granted the community within which these individuals may be included (as citizens) or from which they may be excluded. Debate thus arises around the criteria for admissibility and other such issues: What individual characteristics does one need in order to be granted citizenship rights? To what practices does citizenship entitle? To what practices does it obligate? What competences does one acquire as a result of being a citizen?[10] Questions asked less often deal with the community's capacity (social, political, and legal) to grant or deny citizenship. Generally overlooked is the issue of what right a community has to constitute itself as a *city*, so as to be recognized as such by other *cities* and exercise the authority to designate *citizens*. The stock answer to this type of question is that peoples have the right to self-determination. But what founds a people?

The troubled Québec-Canada relationship has raised these questions explicitly, especially since the 1995 sovereignty referendum and the federal government's resultant strategy toward Québec nationalism. A significant literature in political theory has developed around these issues. Today a debate is raging in Québec regarding the definition of the Québec people. This debate is couched with explicit reference to the development of a Québec citizenship, regardless of whether Québec becomes a sovereign state, and one key question is whether identity is to be thought of as primarily ethnic or primarily civic.[11] But, despite what some consider the romance of New France and of "la Laurencie," no one would think of founding the Québec people on any kind of historical fixity, some set of unchanging cultural practices or occupation of the land. Everyone involved in these debates takes for granted that Québec's political space changes, and that Québécois identity does the same.

A demand for permanence, fixity, is nonetheless the criterion that applies to Canada's Indigenous peoples as they attempt to obtain recognition for their rights. Indeed, what people of Indigenous descent might think about this — whether or not they want to affirm a substantive sameness with their ancestors — does not really matter: the Canadian state, through its governments and courts, is imposing its own terms of reference on that quest for recognition.

This is important because the autonomous government — or, more boldly, the sovereignty — of Indigenous peoples in Canada today raises the issue of political capacity for their communities. Included here are questions such as how might the citizenship-granting capacity develop? And how does the conceptual and jurisprudential frame defining such eventual capacity, as imposed by Canadian law, promote a culturalist, even ethnicist and essentialist, identification to the community? Again, no matter how Indigenous peoples might view the question for themselves, they are practically forced to present their case in those terms if they are to have any hope of being acknowledged by their whitestream counterparts.

History, in this sense, can be a rhetorical tool not only for nationalist representatives of the oppressed groups. It can be imposed equally well as a discursive modality by a dominant group: as the dominant defines itself by its own history of change and development, it defines the oppressed (as "primitive") by its immutability.

History, Social Change, and the Courts

Up until the 1960s, more or less, in what now looks like a prehistory of social sciences, a division of labour existed between the various disciplines, based on (among other things) the geopolitics of their application and their understanding of social change. While history's domain was Europe, neo-European societies, and a few other "great civilizations," anthropology's was made up of "primitive societies." And whereas history dealt with the past of fast-changing societies, anthropology studied "cold" societies thought to be basically unchanging. (Sociology, meanwhile, was interested in the present — and future — of "warm," fast-changing, societies.)

Over the years, we have learned to read change in supposedly cold societies, making it possible to (re)construct histories of peoples that can no longer be called primitive. Conversely, not only have we noticed the remarkable stability of certain underlying structures in "warm" societies, but anthropology has also developed a habit of doing ethnographies of Euro-American social spaces. Of course, sociology has also become interested in historical development. But while many substantive distinctions between disciplines have vanished, this has not brought about an actual merging of disciplines.

The Canadian state, through its courts, is now more or less ready to recognize the rights of Indigenous peoples, but only out of a sense of the immutability of their culture. Considered against the background of the history of the social sciences, and in light of current understandings that all societies develop and change, this legal doctrine is worth pondering. But one should not be surprised by the lack of connection between legal doctrine and the state of research/knowledge in the social sciences: British (and, by extension, Canadian) law remains reticent toward social-scientific knowledge.[12] More generally, the ideology of the "primitive/civilized" duality is far from having been abandoned, despite shallow acknowledgements of pluralism in liberal circles.[13] That said, in the coming pages I will focus on the legal doctrine.

What is it, then, that underpins this doctrine? When we put aside the many subtleties of the dozen relevant decisions made in the past thirty years, the simplicity of the courts' reasoning is striking: the rights of Indigenous peoples exist insofar as they are *Aboriginal* or *Indigenous*, which is to say that these rights are contingent on a provable claim that the people in question have always lived in the place and in the way that they live now. If a given Indigenous people has always lived in a particular place and way, it follows that Euro-Canadian/British law has superimposed itself upon pre-existing practices. It is such practices that are subject to recognition as rights. If, on the other hand, an Indigenous people has moved, if it has changed in the time between "contact" and now, then nothing fundamental distinguishes it from other groups of colonists or immigrants who have settled various parts of Canada over the centuries: this is, anyway, what is claimed by current legal doctrine in Canada. From this perspective, an Indigenous people that has migrated either in its way of life or in its geographical space is no longer to be considered an *Indigenous* people; and it is *Indigenous-ness* that founds a right in Canadian law.

If the general reasoning is straightforward, things become complicated when we ask what type of right is involved in the recognition of Indigenous practices. Indeed, it is a specific practice in a specific place by a specific group that *may* obtain recognition as a right: fishing in Lac Saint-François by a Mohawk band, for instance. If these Mohawk prove to a court's satisfaction that they have always fished in this lake, they may get their right; but the decision has not the slightest bearing on whether a Cree band in Alberta gets a similar right to fish in an Alberta lake.

Cultural Practices and Indigenous Rights Since *Baker Lake*

In the *Baker Lake* (1980) decision, Justice Mahoney developed a four-part test that provides the criteria allowing a court to decide whether an Aboriginal right exists in a particular case.[14] Only the first two tests will concern us here. The first one aims to ascertain the state of culture attained by the Indigenous people making the claim; the second deals with the permanence of occupation of the territory on which a right would be exercised.

The explicitly evolutionist aspect of the first part of the test (i.e., that certain peoples might not be sufficiently advanced culturally in order for them to be rights-bearing subjects) has been repudiated by the Supreme Court of Canada as recently as 1997, in the *Delgamuukw* decision — but only after the court of first instance had specifically affirmed it. In its insistence on cultural traits and their stability, however, the *Baker Lake* test remains at the heart of decisions such as *Van der Peet* (1996), *Delgamuukw* (1997), *Marshall* (1999) and *Mitchell* (2001).[15] In order to found an Indigenous right in Canadian jurisprudence, a cultural practice must not have varied over time — but that is not enough. It must also be considered an integral part of the culture of the Indigenous people in question. A stable but marginally important cultural practice cannot be established as a right.

In the *Van der Peet* decision, Justice Lamer explained that Aboriginal rights apply to specific cultural practices insofar as those practices have contributed to the distinctive cultural character of a particular people and continue to do so. As the same practice (e.g., fishing or trading) will play a different role from one people to another, it may be protected in some cases and not in others. For example, in the *Pamajewon* (1996) case, a group of First Nations claimed an Aboriginal right to organize casinos on their reserves.[16] The Supreme Court rejected this claim, arguing that the First Nations involved had not succeeded in proving that games of chance had played a significant part in their pre-contact cultural practices. In other celebrated cases such as *Delgamuukw* and *Marshall*, the Supreme Court has concluded that the Indigenous claimants had proven their case, and, as a result, it recognized an Aboriginal right. But in each case the right recognized or denied is specific to a particular activity by a particular group in a particular place. No consideration is given to the possibility of a general right, an *abstract political right*. Indeed, such rights are specifically excluded by Justice Lamer in *Van der Peet* and by Chief Justice McLachlin in *Mitchell*.

Since at least the *Baker Lake* decision in 1980, jurisprudence has established Aboriginal rights as, more or less, ethnic rights to certain locally distinctive practices. Faced with the practically unwavering resistance of governments to recognize abstract political rights, Indigenous peoples, their leaders, and their lawyers have tended to consider gains in the judicial arena as better than nothing — or perhaps as the lesser of two evils. The fact is that there is no conceptual continuity between rights as formulated in jurisprudence and Indigenous claims to sovereignty — or at least to an inherent global right to self-government. For Indigenous strategists, the key question is the same as that faced by all liberation movements: are punctual, reformist gains a step in the right direction, in the direction of freedom, or do they help in maintaining the dominant's hegemony by adapting it to circumstances? Surely there is no general answer to this question.

Indigenous Peoples *in* Canadian History — The *Marshall* Decision

Michael Asch has shown eloquently that Canadian law's way of distinguishing between important and marginal cultural practices belongs to the past of anthropology.[17] More generally, the Canadian state reproduces in law, in a contradictory way, an outmoded conception of anthropology. This is because the necessary stability of Indigenous-ness is inscribed in the dynamism of Canadian history: as Canadian society develops and changes, Indigenous peoples must stay the same. As with yesterday's anthropology, Canadian law needs "cold," "primitive" societies in order to recognize Indigenous peoples. But anthropology saw "hot" and "cold" societies existing independently of each other, each in its own time and space. Now it is in its relation with a dynamic Canadian history that Indigenous stability must be read: jurisprudence is established through a reading of Indigenous peoples' situation relative to the French Crown, then the British Crown, and finally the sovereign Canadian state.

At this point, two considerations come into play in our reading of the situation, depending on whether a treaty exists between the Canadian state (and its royal predecessors) and a given Indigenous people. The 1999 *Marshall* decision, for instance, confirms the current validity of an eighteenth-century treaty between the British Crown and the Miqmaw people, to the extent that it is applied in a way that respects its original spirit (as understood by the Court).[18] Thus, as the treaty established a Miqmaw right to sell the catch from their fishing activities *for subsistence purposes*, the *Marshall* decision recognizes a limited right of twenty-first-century Miqmaw to fish commercially, so as to allow the fishers a "moderate" income.

There is nothing simple in this understanding of a treaty. Indeed, whereas the Court narrowly translates the concept of *subsistence in the eighteenth century* into *a moderate lifestyle in the twenty-first century*, it is much bolder with regard to the location of this commercial activity. The treaty gave the Miqmaw permission to bring their catch to a Crown "truckhouse," a commercial counter operated by agents of the government; such truckhouses, of course, vanished a long time ago. Some analysts and intervenors before the Supreme Court took this to mean that the treaty had died with the truckhouses. The Court chose instead to broaden the application of the right to trade, by permitting the emerging Miqmaw commercial fishery to integrate with contemporary commercial fishing on the Canadian east coast.

The Supreme Court does not consider, however, that the Miqmaw treaty might permit or accommodate the accumulation of capital: Indians must not change. As the Court sees it, in order to have any meaning, the treaty must be given effect (by broadening the means of trade), but, two hundred and forty years after its signing, the mode of life that it envisaged is not permitted to change to a significant degree. How is this insistence on stability consistent with the Court's flexibility regarding the truckhouse? It could be that the Court is simply being inconsistent, arbitrary in its apportioning of what can change and what must stay the same. Or the Court might be saying that while it is expected that *Canadian* means of commerce should change (from the truckhouse to our abstract marketplace), the same logic does not apply to *Miqmaw* practices. The treaty, then, would be adaptable so as to remain consistent with evolving Canadian practice, but without allowing for Miqmaw change.

As R.L. Barsh and J. Youngblood Henderson argue in a sharply worded critique of *Marshall*,[19] the eighteenth-century Miqmaw Chiefs who signed this treaty surely did not want their people (and their members, individually) to become increasingly poorer relative to their colonist neighbours.[20] While the lifestyle of the colonists' descendants has changed profoundly since 1760 (including for some of them a considerable accumulation of capital), their Indigenous neighbours would be bound to a "moderate" lifestyle that rules out accumulation. If the treaty is to "live," Barsh and Youngblood Henderson ask, shouldn't its terms be adjusted in accordance with the transformations that have taken place since its signing, and with a concern for the equality between Indigenous peoples and the whole of Canadian society?

The Desperate Quest for a "Treaty": The Nisga'a Claim

How, in such conditions, might an Indigenous citizenship be founded which would make possible a genuine Indigenous *government*? There is no simple answer to this question. As argued above, it is clear that an Indigenous citizenship is unlikely to arise through the courts; this leaves only the stalled constitutional process and the "treaty" process in British Columbia that may or may not also be stalled. This is why the recourse to courts is such an ambivalent strategy for Indigenous peoples seeking recognition of their rights. While in many ways it is "the only game in town," it is clearly the wrong game.[21]

The second consideration in our reading of the relationship between the state and an Indigenous people arises when no treaty exists between the two. This was the case of the Nisga'a people, whose Chief, Frank Calder, took the Canadian government to court in the 1960s. It is the *Calder* decision that first established (albeit in an ambiguous way) that Indigenous peoples could have certain rights in Canada, and that governments had a duty to negotiate with them.[22] Once the legitimacy of the Nisga'a claim was established (through the proof that they have been occupying the Naas valley since time immemorial), the door was open for the negotiation of an agreement[23] between the Nisga'a, the Canadian government, and the government of British Columbia. It took more than 25 years for this negotiation to lead to an agreement. As I indicated at the beginning, what happens to the Nisga'a Agreement — and to the several dozens that should follow it — is very much unclear, given the statements of the new provincial government elected in British Columbia in 2001.

The first thing to note here is that negotiating the agreement was dependent on the same kind of stability that the courts look for: the Nisga'a had to prove that they had lived in the Naas valley forever. The second important fact is that it took nearly forever for the Nisga'a to reach their goal, in a fashion. In the early 1990s, for the first time in a century, the British Columbia government became interested in negotiating. But it approached that negotiation in a very tough-minded way and found that the federal government was willing to accommodate it at least as much as it wanted a deal with the Nisga'a.

The fundamentally good things about the Nisga'a Agreement are that it exists, that it is about Indigenous self-government, and that it explicitly establishes a "Nisga'a citizenship."[24] While negotiation of the Nisga'a claim was, eventually, a direct outcome of the *Calder* decision, nothing in that decision or in the many decisions since mandated that such self-government and citizenship develop. It is not a legal dynamic that has produced the Nisga'a Agreement, but rather a political one: it is a dynamic that breaks with legal precedent by providing for the abstract political rights of Nisga'a citizens, the members of the Nisga'a political community.

The troubling parts of the Nisga'a Agreement stem from the fact that the Nisga'a representatives were negotiating from a position of weakness, which the federal and B.C. government exploited to full advantage. In order to obtain an agreement, the Nisga'a negotiators (and, later, the Nisga'a voters who ratified the deal) had to swallow a variety of non-negotiable demands from both governments that sharply limit the nature and extent of self-government and citizenship. By contrast, court decisions that affirm Aboriginal rights impose settlements on governments, countering, to a significant degree, the power imbalance favouring government. The panicked reaction of the federal government to the *Marshall* decision is a good example of this.

In effect, Nisga'a self-government and citizenship now exist, but in a position that remains subordinate to the authority of both whitestream governments. Why did the Nisga'a assent to this? They agreed because there was a widely shared sense that it was now or never: the political climate seemed likely to worsen, it was not at all obvious it would improve again in the foreseeable future, and the Nisga'a could not wait another fifty years. It can hardly be said, in this sense, that the Naas valley has now been decolonized: it is the site of a kind of "home rule" that satisfies some members of the Nisga'a people, and not others. Similarly, some other Indigenous peoples throughout Canada would be satisfied with this kind of limited self-government, but many others would not. However, the federal and provincial governments are not becoming more accommodating. Therefore, between an imperfect and embattled Nisga'a model and the courts' insistence on recognizing ethnic rights, there is little room for Indigenous citizenship to develop in Canada.

Conclusion: *Mitchell*, the Mohawk and the St. Lawrence River

In the spring of 2001, the Supreme Court of Canada confirmed the legal doctrine that had been developing since the 1970s — both its culturalism, and its political aporia. In the *Mitchell* decision, the Court denied a claim by the Grand Chief of the Akwesasne Mohawk community to a right to trade freely between Canada and the United States through the territory of the reserve, which straddles the border between the two countries.[25] The Court ruled that the Mohawk must pay custom duties, just as other Canadians do. The Court recognized that commerce was an integral part of Mohawk culture at the time of contact with the Europeans, and that Mohawk sometimes travelled north of the St. Lawrence River, which generally marked the limit of their own territory. But the Court was not satisfied that commerce north of the St. Lawrence constituted a significant part of Mohawk culture. The consequence of this last part of the Court's findings is that the Mohawk have no Indigenous right to trade freely between Canada and the United States (i.e., across the St. Lawrence).

In *Mitchell*, as in other recent decisions, the Supreme Court insisted on the idea that, in order to found a right, a practice does not have to be absolutely unchanging over time: it is allowed to have changed so as to remain relevant to its time, but it must demonstrate a definite continuity. This is consistent with the Court's interpretation of trade in the Miqmaw treaty as considered in *Marshall*, in which it accepted the disappearance of the truckhouse and its replacement by a whole range of commercial relations. In *Mitchell*, however, the border marked by the Saint-Lawrence River is absolute: while changes to the way trade is carried out are permitted, the Court explicitly refuses to apply the same dynamic reasoning with regard to the territory on which such trade takes place.

It is not the first time that the relationship to the St. Lawrence River turns out to be crucial — and problematic — for the Mohawk people. The very well-known "Oka crisis" of 1990, of which the Mohawk community of Kanesatake was the central player, owes its origin to the fact that this community established itself just north of the St. Lawrence in the days of New France, i.e., outside traditional (pre-contact) Mohawk territory. Because of their post-contact migration north of the Saint-Lawrence, the Kanesatake Mohawk have never been able to secure their land base through the institution of a reserve, which is the settlement that other Indigenous communities have been obtaining since the mid-nineteenth century. As a result, the Kanesatake Mohawk occupy land that is in no way protected or "reserved" for their use. In 1990, when the Oka municipal government tried to expand a golf course onto land that the Mohawk claim as a sacred burial ground, the Mohawk had no intention of letting the expansion go ahead. However, they had no legal means of stopping it — hence the crisis.

How does the Supreme Court articulate the relationship to the St. Lawrence in *Mitchell*? Chief Justice McLachlin, who wrote the unanimous opinion, argues that Grand Chief Mitchell quite simply did not establish the existence of a Mohawk tradition or cultural practice of transporting goods, for the purpose of trading, from one side to the other of the Canada-U.S. border. If there was no such tradition, no right founded on it could be affirmed. Given this reasoning, the Chief Justice chose not to comment on the possibility of a conflict of sovereignties between the Canadian state and a Mohawk political community bent on affirming its autonomy to conduct international trade.

This brings us back to the truckhouse question. If it is possible for a practice to evolve somewhat within the terms of an Indigenous right, why does that flexibility not include accumulation of capital in one case and a degree of geographical mobility in the other? Why is the St. Lawrence uncrossable, as it were? For Kanesatake/Oka, the federal government has simply relied on the argument that no Mohawk reserve was to be established outside of traditional Mohawk territory. In *Mitchell*, the Chief Justice's reasoning is more involved. It hinges, in fact, on the political importance that she grants to the border between two states that have been successful in claiming sovereignty — a border that the Mohawk claim they can cross at will. If it were only a matter of crossing a river, Mitchell would never have found himself in court because he refused to pay customs duties. As he affirmed the right to cross not a river but a *political border*, he needed to show that there was a Mohawk tradition of carrying out this kind of *international* trade — as opposed to mere cross-river trade.

It is the very assertion of Canadian sovereignty that lends importance to the geographical mobility claimed by the Akwesasne Mohawk. In a complementary opinion to that of Chief Justice McLachlin, Justice Binnie comes clean: it is, he says, the Canadian assertion of sovereignty, and therefore the establishing of the Canada-US border, that negates the possibility of the right claimed by Grand Chief Mitchell. Beyond the existence, the importance, and the stability of a particular cultural practice, it is, then, the issue of political autonomy/sovereignty that is in question.

In the end, attempts to limit the implications of Indigenous claims by imposing an historical and/or cultural frame of reference can do no more than sidestep what remains the decisive issue: the sovereignty of political communities and citizenship. Need it be said that any advance on this issue will have to come from a political dynamic rather than from a legal one? After all, in his claims before the courts, including the Supreme Court of Canada, Grand Chief Mitchell presented himself as a citizen of the Iroquois confederacy, not as a Canadian citizen. For the Supreme Court, this was simply irrelevant.

Notes

1. A paper forming a large part of this chapter was presented, in French and in a different form, at the colloquium "Désirs d'histoire," organized by the Centre national de recherche scientifique (France), the Max Planck Institute (Germany), and the University of Erfurt, in Erfurt, Germany, 7-9 June 2001.

2. This term refers to Euro-dominance in Canadian society (among others), which has presented itself as "white," even when a significant part of the population has not been anything like white. On this issue, see Frances Abele and Daiva Stasiulis, "Canada as a 'White Settler Colony': What about Natives and Immigrants?," in *The New Canadian Political Economy*, ed. Wallace Clement and Glen Williams (Kingston, Montréal, London: McGill-Queen's University Press, 1989). I introduced the concept of "whitestream" in my *We Are Not You. First Nations and Canadian Modernity*, Coll. Terra Incognita (Peterborough: Broadview Press, 1997).

3. *Citizens Plus* is the title of a report by the Alberta Indian Federation, written in reaction to the federal government's 1969 White Paper aiming to end the special status of Indians and assimilate them into whitestream society. On the White Paper and the reactions that it provoked, see Olive Patricia Dickason, *Canada's First Nations: A History of Founding Peoples from Earliest Times* (Toronto: McClelland & Stewart, 1992).

4. For an interesting discussion of the complexities of multiple citizenship, see Joseph H. Carens, *Culture, Citizenship, and Community. A Contextual Exploration of Justice as Evenhandedness* (Oxford: Oxford University Press, 2000).

5. The same Donald Marshall was involved in a prior, unrelated, Supreme Court decision, so that there are two *Marshall* decisions. The other Marshall case is not considered in this chapter, and as such all references to *Marshall* are to the 1999 decision.

6. *Calder v. Attorney General of British Columbia* [1973] S.C.R. 313; *Baker Lake v. Minister of Indian Affairs and Northern Development* [1980] 1 F.C. 518; *R. v. Sioui* [1990] 1 S.C.R. 1025; *R. v. Sparrow* [1990] 1 S.C.R. 1075; *R. v. Badger* [1996] 1 S.C.R. 771; *R. v. Van der Peet* [1996] 2 S.C.R. 507; *R. v. Pamajewon* [1996] 2 S.C.R. 821; *Delgamuukw v. British Columbia* [1997] 3 S.C.R. 1010; *R. v. Marshall* [1999] 3 S.C.R. 533; *Mitchell v. M.N.R.* [2001] SCC 33.

7. Whether or not the self-government agreements sought by First Nations and governments are properly called "treaties" is an open, and very political, question. A number of (Indigenous and other) scholars argue that a treaty can only be conceived as an *international* agreement and that, since governments insist on the domestic nature of their agreements with Indigenous peoples, such agreements are not treaties. This is politically important because, among other reasons, many treaties signed in the past 400 years between Indigenous peoples and the French/British Crowns are claimed by the Indigenous side as international agreements between sovereign peoples. Not surprisingly, the Canadian government wants to avoid recognizing the sovereignty of Indigenous peoples. In recognition of the contested status of the agreements being negotiated, the term "treaty" will generally be avoided in this chapter, except in the cases of historical agreements that are uncontested treaties. Otherwise, contemporary agreements may or may not count as treaties, but they are unambiguously self-government agreements. For contrasting takes by two Indigenous authors on the concept of treaty, see Andrew Bear Robe, "Treaty Federalism," *Constitutional Forum Constitutionnel* 4, 1 (Fall 1992): 6-11; and Sharon Venne, "Treaty Indigenous Peoples and the Charlottetown Accord: the Message in the Breeze," *Constitutional Forum Constitutionnel* 4, 2 (Winter 1993): 43-46.

8. As this volume goes to press, the B.C. government is conducting its referendum, through a mail-in ballot. The eight yes/no questions on the ballot are all heavily loaded toward restricting indigenous rights. The results of the vote are expected to be announced in July 2002.

9. On the relationship (and difference) between historical rootedness and cultural difference as Indigenous grounds for making claims, see my *We Are Not You*.

10. On the range of issues dealt with in contemporary literature on citizenship see, for instance, *Citizenship in Diverse Societies*, ed. Will Kymlicka and Wayne Norman (Oxford: Oxford University Press, 2000). See also n.11 below.

11. For a wide-ranging survey of the issues in this debate, in a comparative and theoretical perspective, see *Droits fondamentaux et citoyenneté. Une citoyenneté fragmentée, limitée, illusoire?*, ed. Michel Coutu et al. (Montréal: Éditions Thémis, 1999). In the summer of 2001, the newspaper *Le Devoir* published a series of articles by leading intellectuals and a Quebec cabinet minister on whether the National Assembly should establish a "National Commission on Quebec Citizenship." See, all in *Le Devoir*, Alain G. Gagnon, "Plaidoyer pour une Commission nationale sur la citoyenneté québécoise, " 15 June 2001; François Rocher and Micheline Labelle, "De la légitimité d'une loi fondamentale québécoise: La citoyenneté et l'unité canadienne," 20 June 2001; Jocelyn Létourneau, "Collectivité québécoise: Le temps des espérances lucides," 22 June 2001; Joseph Facal, "Trop tôt pour une Commission sur la citoyenneté," 26 June 2001; Jocelyn Maclure, "Commission nationale sur la citoyenneté: Pour une politique des relations civiques," 8 August 2001.

12. Michael Asch, "The Judicial Conceptualization of Culture after *Delgamuukw* and *Van der Peet*," *Review of Constitutional Studies / Revue d'études constitutionnelles* 5, 2 (2000): 119-37.

13. This critique of liberalism is developed in *We Are Not You*.

14. *Baker Lake v. Minister of Indian Affairs and Northern Development* [1980] 1 F.C. 518

15. *R. v. Van der Peet* [1996] 2 S.C.R. 507; *Delgamuukw v. British Columbia* [1997] 3 S.C.R. 1010; *R. v. Marshall* [1999] 3 S.C.R. 533; *Mitchell v. M.N.R.* [2001] SCC 33.

16. *R. v. Pamajewon* [1996] 2 S.C.R. 821.

17. Asch, "The Judicial Conceptualization of Culture."

18. *R. v. Marshall* [1999] 3 S.C.R. 533.

19. Russel Lawrence Barsh and James (Sa'ke'j) Youngblood Henderson, "Marshalling the Rule of Law in Canada: Of Eels and Honour," *Constitutional Forum Constitutionnel* 11, 1 (Fall 1999): 1-18.

20. This is a rather risky argument, on several grounds. First, as with any "original intent" claim, in this case we just don't know what the Chiefs would have made of later socio-economic developments, including in particular capitalist accumulation. Second, the argument is made from within an accumulationist point of view: given current ecological/native politics, a counterargument can easily be imagined whereby the Chiefs would have wanted to keep their people from engaging in the ecologically destructive practices of capital accumulation. They might have wanted to affirm, instead, the maintenance of a lifestyle consistent with an ecologically "light footprint" upon the earth. Third, the original intent of the Chiefs (which in any case shall remain unknown) is not a necessary part of the argument for allowing the treaty to evolve so as to allow for capital accumulation. Indeed, if a Court were to consider seriously what that intent was, and if it came to the conclusion that the Chiefs would spurn accumulation, then the Chiefs' (purported) original intent would serve to constrain severely — for good or ill — the evolving life of the treaty. For epistemological (we just cannot know) as well as practical and strategic reasons (of avoiding unnecessary interpretive constraints), it is just better not to engage into "original intent" debates.

21. On this issue, see Patrick Macklem and Roger Townshend, "Resorting to Court: Can the Judiciary Deliver Justice for First Nations?," in *Nation to Nation. Aboriginal Sovereignty and the Future of Canada*, ed. Diane Engelstad and John Bird (Concord: Anansi, 1992), 78-87.

22. *Calder v. Attorney General of British Columbia* [1973] S.C.R. 313.

23. A treaty? On this issue, see n.7 above.

24. Government of Canada, Government of British Columbia, and Nisga'a Nation, *Nisga'a Final Agreement*, initialled 4 August 1998.

25. *Mitchell v. M.N.R.* [2001] SCC 33.

PART III

DOMESTICITY, INDUSTRY AND NATIONHOOD

chapter six

SCAFFOLDING CITIZENSHIP
Housing Reform and Nation Formation in Canada, 1900-1950

Sean Purdy

There is no more sacred word in the English language than 'home,' and on the retaining of the sacredness and significance of our homes depends the future of our municipality and our Nation.[1]

Dr. Charles Hastings,
Medical Officer of Health, Toronto, 1918

Hastings's evocative statement came at a time of severe housing crisis, marked by widespread concern over shoddy dwelling construction, poor sanitary conditions, and critical housing shortages for Toronto's burgeoning population. His emphatic language also highlights the crucial link in the propaganda of housing reformers between dwelling conditions and citizenship. For state officials such as Hastings believed that nothing was more suitable for the building of sound citizens than proper housing conditions. Constructing healthy homes for the country's working class was explicitly linked with a developing concept of what constituted a "proper" Canadian citizen. To build good homes was to build good citizens.

Historians have frequently emphasized the importance of national economic and administrative policy as the principal apparatus of nation-building. But recently an impressive body of literature has demonstrated that nation formation involved far more than governmental policies regulating the economy.[2] These studies have convincingly shown that as state formation proceeded in the first decades of the twentieth century, governments resorted to more subtle efforts to create a common national character with requisite forms of behaviour and attitudes. Researchers have chronicled how the state attempted to mould virtuous Canadian citizens through intervening in various facets of social life such as immigration, Aboriginal affairs, unemploy-ment policies and leisure.

This chapter centres on the role played by housing reform in the first half of the twentieth century in the construction of an ideology of Canadian cit-izenship.[3] The distressed state of working-class housing in Canada consti-tuted a pivotal concern of a diverse body of social reformers and state agen-cies in this period. From the first stirrings of reform consciousness at the turn of the century to the development of sizeable housing projects in major urban centres in the 1940s-1950s, housing betterment ideas and practices were imbued with distinct notions of what constituted a proper nation and a suit-able citizenry. Central to this ideological thrust was the belief that housing reform could assist in "Canadianizing" the working class to prop up class cooperation and maintain social hierarchy in the tumultuous first decades of the century. This would be accomplished through constructing ideological notions of what constituted legitimate "families" and "races." Through reform propaganda and practical implementation of various housing reforms, it proved useful for reformers and governments to blame social and economic problems on the so-called inferiority and "un-Canadianness" of both immi-grant and native-born working families.

Intensifying pre-existing English-Canadian nationalism and racism was a useful means to assuage the bruising social conflicts of the era. As a ruling-class ideology, nationalism served to eclipse other social divisions, especially class, by positing an overarching national identity that facilitated relations of domination and discouraged united challenges to the system by scapegoating "others." In the nationalist discourse of the housing-reform movement, con-cepts of race and nation were fused and simultaneously based on the princi-ples of inclusion and exclusion. As Robert Miles argues for the similar British case, racism formed "the lining of the cloak of nationalism."[4] Gender ideals — women's "respectable" role as domestic manager, reproducer, and nurturer — also interacted with concepts of nation, race, and class in the reform proj-ect as women's proper location in the domestic sphere was considered cru-cial to "Canadianizing" the working class.

Reform in this period can be defined as an approach advocating state intervention in the economy and society to alleviate the social problems of capitalism and thereby preserve the system itself.[5] Nevertheless, it is impor-tant also to trace how housing "experts" and policy officials groped through the contradictions of urban society in a creative manner that they themselves saw as more or less disinterested. Based on growing beliefs in the necessity of state intervention and the capacity of the trained expert to alleviate social conflict, the reform movement in the housing sphere centred on a notion of community that ostensibly stood above labour and capital, aiming to smooth out social relations for the greater national good. Reformers criticized unbridled capitalism in the urban setting — rampant land speculation, unscrupulous practices by developers and landlords, and self-destructive laissez-faire government policies. Yet we must not disentangle reformers from the structural imperatives and concrete social relationships of capitalist society. As the Italian Marxist Antonio Gramsci aptly noted of European middle-class reform, "The intellectuals are breaking loose from the dominant class in order to unite themselves to it more intimately."[6]

Housing and the State before World War I

Modern social policy, the concentrated and systematic regulation of labour-force reproduction, initially emerged as a response to the adverse effects of international migration and perceived political threats to the social order, and as a pre-emptive measure against military and economic deterioration. In this turn-of-the-century context, commentators on urban housing problems tended to emphasize individual responsibility and moral virtue. As the crisis deepened, however, questions of economic performance and social harmony came to the fore, prompting reformers to begin looking to wider structural problems of the economy. This set the stage for calls for active state intervention.

As the twentieth century opened, reformers first drew attention to the increasing dangers of infectious diseases and "immorality" which, in their estimation, spread from the slums to wealthier neighbourhoods. Paul Rutherford aptly sums up the reformers' fears: "Disease did not respect social standing."[7] Squalid housing conditions served as an important impetus to the emergence of the public-health project around the turn of the century. While most public-health officials at the time incorporated elements of both schools of current medical thought — environmentalism and eugenics[8] — they tended to emphasize that once these slovenly blots were removed the housing problem would vanish. In tandem with this ecological emphasis, house inspections, construction standards, and sanitary regulations formed the early groundwork for public-health activity.

There was a pronounced interest in eradicating the moral failings of slum dwellers as well. The metaphor of disease itself was applied to the moral degeneration of the urban environment. Discussing Vancouver, R.M. Fripp told the readers of a building trades magazine that slums brought "overcrowding, discomfort, inconvenience, decreased health, physical and moral degeneration, increased criminal population, more police, more jails, more jailbirds. All these evils multiply like bacilli in a cess-pot and constantly spill over and spread contagion."[9] Social purity campaigns of the era and sensationalist critiques in newspapers were wedded to a traditional focus on moral depravity. A 1906 editorial in the *Toronto Daily News* stated that one particularly "degenerate" slum in Canada's leading industrial city "constitutes a constant menace to the physical and moral health of the city. It is an open sore from which flow fetid currents which cannot but be corrupting the whole community."[10] The physical degeneration of slum areas was directly related to moral contamination, adding ideological remedies to the reform crusaders' attempt to cure the modern city.

Soon business people added their voice to the chorus of concern for working-class housing conditions. Manufacturers were first troubled by the threat to workplace efficiency that substandard dwellings posed. They discerned that there was a direct link between the home and the factory: "It is the best class of philanthropy that which results in raising the condition of our citizens and thereby increasing their efficiency," the editor of *Industrial Canada*, the journal of the Canadian Manufacturers Association, argued in 1911.[11] Manufacturers were also worried about class conflict — a growing problem brought about by an intensification of large-scale capitalist development and the emergence of working-class political alternatives such as trade unions and socialist organizations.[12] So threatening was this social disorder that *Industrial Canada* warned that "Out of the slums stalk the Socialist with his red flag, the Union agitator with the auctioneer's voice and the Anarchist with his torch."[13] Recognizing that the improvement of the home environment of their workers would help create a healthy, moral and contented workforce, sections of the business community joined reformers in calling for action on the housing question.

Reformers were also concerned that the family — the prime site of social reproduction and community life — was threatened by urban dislocation. As a result, the first furtive attempts to "improve" home life were made. Household inspectors, whose job was to inspect and condemn "unfit" houses, were hired in Ottawa in the 1870s, Hamilton in 1884, and Toronto in 1885.[14] Calls for sanitary standards, laws regulating construction, and improvement of the domestic regime within the home were frequently framed in terms of the central role of women within the family. The early domestic science movement aspired to apply rational techniques to living in order to reinforce the "proper" nuclear family form and enhance workplace efficiency.[15]

The stability of the family was intricately related to concerns for the working-class home. The home in the intellectual discourse of the time was far more than a physical structure; it also expressed and maintained "the ideology of prevailing social orders."[16] The relation between the condition of women in the working-class home and larger questions of society and state was repeatedly underscored in the literature of the period. J.J. Kelso, founder of the Children's Aid Society and a key figure in urban questions early in the century, echoed the sentiments of many in the reform community when he described the family home as the "foundation stone of the state."[17] Helen Cameron Parker, an early advocate of domestic science, stated that "upon the health and morals of its citizens depends the prosperity of a nation, and the health and morals of the people depend mainly upon the food they eat and the homes they live in."[18] The key traits of the ideology of home — stability, efficiency, and morality — were extended to the ideal organization of the state. Indeed, *Canadian Homes and Gardens* "celebrated housing renovation and innovation as signs of an evolving *national* culture."[19]

For the majority of middle- and upper-class commentators, it was still convenient to attribute poverty and miserable living conditions to individual weaknesses rather than structural flaws in the economy. Nevertheless, the Victorian creed of the "inexorability of material and moral progress"[20] and faith in individualistic solutions were gradually succumbing to the palpable threats of class conflict and recognition of the increasingly interdependent nature of the economy. The crucible of World War I would accelerate the appeal of social-scientific analysis,[21] meshing neatly with a growing state prepared to take action on the housing front.

The Early Interventionist State: Housing Reform 1914-1930

The first state interventions in the housing sphere occurred before World War I, but the incentive for more direct action received a great boost during wartime as governments faced the exigencies of voracious international economic and military competition. There was a heightened sense of the urgency of state intervention, based on the belief that only a state-assisted approach to urban-industrial problems would offset the hazards of social and economic crisis. The period from 1914 to 1930 saw the establishment of a town planning profession with housing as a chief component and expanding government initiatives to improve national housing conditions.

The Commission of Conservation, 1909-1921, was the first federal organization established to study Canadian urban conditions and make policy recommendations to governments.[22] It founded an impressive array of publicity organs, published books and studies, organized lecture courses at universities, and devoted much time to studying urban problems, punctuating its recommendations with the urgency of active state intervention. Under the guidance of the noted British planner Thomas Adams, the Commission wrote most of the provincial planning legislation of the war years. Moreover, Adams was instrumental in designing the Federal Housing Program of 1918 and the Halifax Reconstruction Commission,[23] the first major government initiatives in the housing sphere. The Commission played a central role in providing ideological legitimacy for the emerging theory and practice of town planning and helped promulgate its merits to a wide network of reformers, academics, and politicians. Indeed, an appreciative editorial in *Saturday Night* proclaimed that in the area of town planning the Commission had "shouldered the burden of creating, so to speak, a *national* conscience."[24]

The *efficiency movement*, exemplified in the sphere of production relations by scientific management guru Frederick Taylor, was applied with equal diligence by Adams and the Commission to urban reform. "This is an age in which efficiency is a great catchword," A.G. Dalzell, a former assistant to Adams, told real estate agents in 1920. "Industrial efficiency, commercial efficiency, national efficiency and personal efficiency are terms constantly before us."[25] The war provided a solid impetus for improving the efficiency of home life. "As a result of the past three years experience," Adams noted in 1918, "we have been made to see very clearly the extent to which the output of war industries and the production of food depends not only on the organization of labour but also on the conditions under which the labourer lives."[26] The Hydrostone housing scheme in Halifax, built as part of the reconstruction effort after the Halifax Explosion of 1917, was designed with these considerations in mind: "To properly house the worker, to give him air, space and light, pure water, and efficient means of transportation to this work, is merely exercising enlightened self-interest in the interests of our industries — for labour is the most costly and important factor in production, although it is frequently least considered."[27]

Concern for social stability went hand-in-hand with worries about efficiency. The National Industrial Conference (1919) and the Royal Commission on Industrial Relations (1919) both underscored the poor dwelling situation in the country as one of the chief causes of working-class upheaval and recommended immediate measures to deal with the problem. Thomas Rodens, President of the Canadian Manufacturers Association, warned his fellow industrialists about the urgency of housing reform in 1918, stressing "it was that condition that brought about the downfall of Russia, the indifference of the *guiding* classes to these conditions."[28] G. Frank Beer, the moving force behind the pioneering Toronto Housing Company scheme (1913-1921), stressed that urban reform was essential for social solidarity. Linking the efforts on the battlefield with social relations at home, he stressed: "Social work is not, cannot be philanthropy, but should be accepted as part of the natural duties of citizenship, arising from the solidarity of society. Let us translate the noble passion of Flanders into a passion for our own people. That must be our war heritage — a truer insight into the comradeship of our people."[29]

Beer's comments summed up reformers' concept of citizenship in this period. Deteriorating urban environments and the increasing militancy of the working class posed a challenge to reform endeavours to prop up Canadian capitalism, leading them to formulate and apply a specific conception of national citizenship premised on the social values of the middle and upper class. In a vein characteristic of British liberal reform thought, Beer insisted that where private enterprise fails, the government should help, but only in conjunction with the "voluntary cooperation of citizens," by which he meant reform-minded individuals and the worthy working class, both willing to endure sacrifice and work together for the betterment of society as a whole.[30] In *Garden Cities and Town Planning Magazine*, the renowned British housing-reform organ, he argued for the right balance necessary to uplift the working class: "To weaken self-reliance is to weaken self-respect, and too extended an activity upon the part of the State may end in a loss of virility, initiative, and perseverance in the class which needs these qualities most."[31] The house-building initiatives of the period were restricted to subsidized home owner-ship or co-ownership schemes. These ventures epitomized the sense of moderation deemed essential to harmonious social relations.

Consequently, citizenship rights in the emerging capitalist social order were expected to be exercised through private individual consumption. This expectation explains the near-universal support for individual home owner-ship among reformers. All municipalities, Dr. Charles Hastings advised, "must have a keen sense of the *social* and *national* significance of the term 'home' as being of one-family dwellings."[32] Reformers strongly held to the belief that single-family homes would uphold stable family life in a manner consistent with private-market principles. Tommy Church, mayor of Toronto, praised the federal housing program of 1919 because "there is no condition which will promote good citizenship than home ownership, and every aid should be given to encourage this."[33] Despite differences of opinion on the precise level and nature of state involvement, reformers viewed owner occupation as the most appropriate tenure because it fuelled capital accumulation and ostensibly encouraged the dominant material and ideological tenets of bourgeois society.

The growing importance of consumer goods for the household functioned in a similar capacity to individual home ownership. Veronica Strong-Boag has detailed the massive advertising campaign in the 1920s directed increasingly at working-class women that promoted the latest in "labour-saving" household technology, furniture, and plumbing and heating supplies. Although the benefits of such innovations were ambiguous, middle-class *élites* "celebrated housing renovations and innovations as signs of an evolving *national* culture."[34]

figure 6.1

An advertisement which ran in the magazine *Industrial Canada*, in 1922.

REPRODUCED FROM *INDUSTRIAL CANADA* (OCTOBER 1922): 1. REPRODUCED BY PERMISSION.

Victorian views of the "deserving" and "undeserving" working class were also evident in middle-class social critics' interpretation of what constituted a true "Canadian." The Toronto Housing Company consciously strove to classify applicants according to *degrees* of citizenship. Company directors emphasized that only "financially self-dependent" workers were eligible to rent their model flats. As a result, a restrictive tenancy policy was followed. Two references were required, rent was payable in advance, and a damage deposit was requested — requirements that were unusual and restrictive in the context of the rental housing sector in the war years.[35] The projects' backers believed that shining examples of upright working-class tenants living in an efficient and morally virtuous manner would trickle down to the lower strata of workers. "With an efficient citizenship," Beer concluded, "... there will be a levelling up and a levelling down."[36] It was in the interest of the reform movement to structure social policy so that "respectable" workers would be rewarded while the rest would be ignored or disciplined. In this way, a divided working class would be fostered.

Appealing to nationalism was another preferred strategy to ensure a harmonious and pliable citizenry. Social policies were a particularly convenient means of shaping the contours of nationhood. Social policies worked to define the boundaries of the "national" working class by sanctioning a specific model of class structure — what constitutes a proper "citizen" — and by attempting to shape social relations within the nation — what constitutes the proper behaviour of these officially defined citizens. The discourse of hous-ing betterment, along with its counterparts in other areas of government pol-icy such as immigration control, helped to cultivate the popular fiction of Anglo-supremacy and spread the racist message that "outsiders" were to blame for the nation's difficulties.

"Race" was a loosely defined term used extensively by commentators to designate the peculiar social attributes that allegedly derived from the biology or culture of a particular people. In the English-Canadian case, the ideology of race was rooted in a sense of the inherent superiority of British "stock."[37] Whether one was an environmentalist who believed that active intervention could uplift the social and moral conditions of the socially "misfit" or a hereditarian who envisioned social problems as originating in immutable biological traits, there was a common opinion that the Canadian "race" could be markedly improved.[38]

The menace of "race suicide" loomed large in the outlook of housing reformers as it did in all the social improvement campaigns of the period.[39] It was widely believed that the miserable health of the working class would imperil the future of the British "race." Authorities agreed that the physical, mental, and moral state of the "race" faced grave danger unless quick action was undertaken. William P. Struthers, a noted public health official, punctu-ated reformers' concerns succinctly: "Poor housing conditions, lack of light and ventilation, uncleanliness, ignorance of proper care of the body and the laws of health ... are rapidly producing a degenerate race."[40] Another reformer, Charles Hodgetts, argued that temporary shacktowns, built on the margins of cities, were becoming the "overcrowded permanent homes of a foreign population — hot beds of parasitic and communicable diseases and breeders of vice and inequity."[41] The distinguished psychiatrist C.K. Clarke even described many native-born workers as "failures at home" who "are often so because of congenital defects. Their progeny may rise above their own level, but they never cease to suffer from their misfortunes of birth."[42] It was not the wretched housing conditions under which immigrant workers suffered that were isolated as the chief problems, but rather the immigrants themselves.

If many Canadian-born workers did not qualify as deserving citizens, then immigrants could hardly expect better treatment from social policy thinkers and makers. Immigration controls aspired to stop the flow of physically, mentally, and morally "unfit" immigrants at the border, while restraints in social policy provisions effectively limited or barred social services to those second-class citizens — immigrants and aliens — already residing in the coun-try. The director of the Ontario Housing Committee (OHC), established to implement the 1919 Federal Housing Program in the province, wrote to

Premier Hearst arguing that the scheme should be confined to British subjects only. "Persons who are not British subjects," he brusquely noted, "are often undesirable occupants of any home."[43] As a result of this thinking, the federal government's 1919 housing program was almost exclusively limited to veterans who were British subjects.[44]

Small wonder that "restrictive covenants" — informal rules prohibiting certain minorities from renting or buying property — were integrated into federal housing programs and in suburban housing developments. Although their origins were corporate, these covenants were a particular reflection of a generalized opinion in the reform movement that non-British or non-white immigrants posed a threat to the racial norms of Canadian society. There is clear evidence that municipal officials wilfully ignored such practices until the 1950s.[45]

It was at the municipal level that the most concrete practices of racial exclusion were developed. "Ticketing and raiding" a house — identifying and labelling a residence for condemnation — was one common method of supervising the behaviour of Canada's immigrant and working-class population. From 1911 to 1918, Dr. Charles Hastings reported that 1,682 homes had been destroyed by such means in Toronto.[46] Hamilton's public-health officer proposed that the city hire a battalion of inspectors to "systematically go looking for trouble."[47] Winnipeg authorities boasted that they dealt with the "overcrowding evil by dint of stern repression and frequent prosecutions." Asian shanty towns in Vancouver and New Westminster were frequently inspected and destroyed with no concern for the inhabitants.[48] Drastic action such as slum clearances temporarily eliminated bad environments and ensured "racial purity" by preventing foreign slum conditions from spreading to other areas. But house inspection and condemnation also served as a form of pre-emptive state repression and a way of enforcing suitable standards of conduct.

In the classification of the growing problem of working-class housing, identity and place were firmly intertwined. Local boards of health targeted the most disreputable slum areas, creating a sensational and negative image of these areas which served to generalize racist exclusion. As David Ward argues, slums expressed "the presumed causal links between social isolation, and adverse environment and deviant behaviour."[49] Located next to City Hall and the wealthy neighbourhood around Queen's Park, Toronto's "Ward" was always a convenient target of the city's reform elite. In a 1911 study, Hastings squarely placed the blame for the Ward's shabby tenements on the "foreign element": Jews, Poles, and Italians, with their "dirty habits."[50] The persistence of the Ward in reform thought was such that it was located in different areas in various studies over the years. For Hastings and his colleagues, the Ward was more than a geographic area; it was a "condition, an attitude of mind toward life, a standard of living...."[51] Similar conflations of place and race occurred in other cities. Kay Anderson persuasively argues that the geographical and ideological construction of Vancouver's Chinatown was efficiently used by the local state to frame a "divisive system of racial classification."[52]

The construction of the preferred Canadian "race" was developed in relation to external economic and political pressures as well as internal conflicts. In an era of competing imperialisms, the perils posed by harmful living conditions on economic and military strength caused great apprehension among social commentators and policy-makers. The *Contract Record and Engineering Review*, a building-industry magazine, argued in June 1918 that "proper housing not only means better health and more comfort, but also a greater fitness for the day's work, which in its turn, means a more vigorous and optimistic prosecution of the war."[53] In an article entitled "Defective Children," Dr. Helen MacMurchy, a respected Ontario paediatrician and leading eugenicist,[54] favourably paraphrased British Prime Minister Lloyd George's quip, "You cannot have an A1 army on a C3 population."[55] The experience of wartime mobilization was clearly a crucible in the struggle for national action on the housing front. As the OHC recommended: "The provision of good houses for the people is not a fad for philanthropists. It is a command duty which cannot be shirked without national dishonesty and peril."[56] By war's end, housing reform was no longer considered a local issue of concern only to the poor but rather was seen as a major obstacle to the advancement of an industrial nation.[57]

Since the home was regarded as the principal unit of social organization, it was chosen as the chief site in the battle for thoroughly "Canadianizing" women and workers. Racial and ethnic assumptions intersected with the widely-held view that women were the "nurturers" of the race.[58] Henry Vivian, a visiting British MP and authority on town planning, spoke to a receptive Calgary audience, arguing that "the future of our Empire, the future of our race depends upon the preservation of those conditions that make for the retention and the strength of that individuality, and upon that our future really exists. The individual home, the individual family, the individual brought up in the home, and the association of home life — upon that all our success depends."[59]

Domestic life was to be improved by programs directed at regulating the labour of working-class and immigrant women, focusing on child-raising and household work. To social imperialists, as Anna Davin argues, "population was power."[60] As a result, motherhood needed to be reconstructed on a scientific basis to ensure the continuation of the Anglo-Saxon race and to bring unhealthy immigrants up to scratch. If Taylorism promised to increase efficiency in the labour force, domestic science aimed to "modernize" daily life in the home. A properly kept, compact family home fitted with the recent inventions of electric lighting, water, cooking appliances, and indoor toilets offered a certain future, free from the vagaries of cramped, unsanitary lodgings. It is clear that many reformers were motivated by genuine feelings for the casualties of industrial capitalism. But altruistic concerns were overshadowed by the vital national effort to create a stable family comprised of fit and complacent workers.

In combination with the crude procedures of house inspections and condemnations, the emerging public health campaign was utilized to instil the values of thrift, efficiency, and "Canadianness" into workers. In 1911, housekeepers were hired by the Industrial Hygiene and Housing Division of the Toronto public health department to advise on "cleanliness, sanitation and Canadian methods of housekeeping."[61] Speaking of the Ward, Joseph Howes of the Bureau of Municipal Research recommended that since the "majority of the residents are usually foreigners, often not speaking our language, not fully understanding our laws, and frequently without the Anglo-Saxon ideas of sanitation," the reform effort should be concentrated on the process of "education and Canadianization."[62] With this in mind, Dr. Charles Hastings instructed female sanitary inspectors to go into immigrants' houses to "teach them how to clean up and keep clean their homes and environments. ... Many of these people, by reason of birth and environments, have neither the moral stamina or the intellect to rid themselves of their vices and shortcomings."[63] Marilyn Barber has discovered that immigration literature intended for British domestic servants, while promoting Canada as a British country, also stressed that British women must "learn Canadian ways."[64] Only the "Canadianization" of housewives could combat the process of racial "degeneration" and equip families with the tools of citizenship needed to build a strong nation.

The promotion of housing designs drafted to rationalize and improve women's domestic labour served a similar purpose and was distinctly noticeable in the co-partnership and government-sponsored ventures of the period. The architects for the OHC, for instance, drafted house plans with space allocated in a compact fashion to make domestic management more efficient. The kitchen, the OHC Report recommended, is "a workroom and should be planned for comfort and convenience in handling work."[65] An essentially middle-class design — what Gwendolyn Wright calls the "minimal house"[66] — promised efficiency and social stability.

The ideal single-family dwelling included not only well-designed facilities for efficient labour but also morally sound organization of internal space.

Believing that licentious sex among the working class was contributing to "race suicide," architects and planners aimed to reinforce prevailing definitions of Victorian morality and sexuality. Hence, they provided for clearly defined thresholds between bedrooms and between houses to ensure privacy. Furthermore, health officials and reformers were adamant in condemning boys and girls sleeping with each other in the same room or with their parents.[67] "One of the most important on the list of essential items is the provision of a bedroom for parents, and a separate bedroom for children of each sex," the architects of the OHC recommended.[68] By the same token, they planned for spaces of at least twelve feet between houses, and fences were advocated to "seal" the private dwelling.[69] Sealing off houses aimed to shift the borders between the encapsulated working-class family — with its historical traditions of communality — and the surrounding community, revealing the social import attributed to atomized family and domestic life by bourgeois reformers.[70]

Despite the decline of the reform impulse in the 1920s, housing reformers could boast that their efforts sparked the first comprehensive country-wide planning legislation, several co-partnership housing schemes, and a national housing program. Most important, however, was that the ideological and political precedents had been set for the recognition of the necessity of state intervention in the housing realm. While some state involvement was advocated, few of the intellectuals and philanthropists supporting housing progress saw the need to directly contradict the private market. Fewer still believed that capitalist society itself was responsible for the lack of decent shelter. It would take the most devastating economic crisis in the history of world capitalism and changing political alternatives to advance beyond this limited outlook.

The Coming of the Welfare State: Housing Reform in the 1930s-1940s

Just as the economic and political uncertainty of World War I motivated a push for state intervention in the housing sphere, so too did the stormy ordeal of the Depression and World War II advance the cause of the housing-reform movement. Reflecting both political exigencies and broader developments in the social sciences, housing reformers found a more attentive audience in government circles and universities during this era. Throughout the 1930s and 1940s, there was a plethora of reports at all levels of government and academia dealing with the housing question. Wartime mobilization and the critical fear of economic depression and social unrest after the war precipitated significant legislative and regulatory interventions in housing and sustained ventures in government housing provision.[71] Much of the reform discourse of the period was interwoven with social-democratic viewpoints, embracing a conviction that governments should permanently intervene through technocratic planning *within* the capitalist system to ensure that decent housing was available to all people. But there were decidedly conventional solutions proposed to the question of women's role in the home, and assumptions of moral and nationalistic respectability stood alongside deeper critiques of the system.

The 1930s marked a coming-of-age of the new social sciences as academics and policy-makers were given renewed incentive to apply practical "scientific" knowledge to social problems because of the abject failure of governments to solve the world economic crisis. Social scientists forcefully asserted that laissez-faire policies were anachronistic in the context of a complex, interdependent industrial economy.[72] A cooperative relationship between government, business, and academia hinging on sensible intervention in the workings of the market was therefore deemed essential to remedy the crisis. These developments resulted in a slight reworking of the concept of citizenship proposed by the reformers of the World War I period.

Social democracy found intellectual expression in the League for Social Reconstruction (LSR), an eclectic group of intellectuals associated with the Cooperative Commonwealth Federation (CCF). The LSR's platform combined redistributive economic policies under the rubric of technocratic central planning with social policies intended to deliver essential services for victims of the market economy. The League worried that the unchecked profit motive of monopoly capitalism rode roughshod over stable family life and overall social and economic progress.[73] The most prominent housing activists of the era — Harry Cassidy, Leonard Marsh, and Humphrey Carver — were all members of the LSR, and theories of state-directed economic regeneration found a larger audience in liberal political circles.

The inclusion of a separate housing program in the LSR's manifesto, *Social Planning for Canada*, attests to the importance accorded to housing in the grander scheme of social-democratic modernization. Written by Humphrey Carver, a Toronto architect and later a key official in the Central Mortgage and Housing Corporation (CMHC), it confined itself to the LSR's general critique of the "unrestrained system of profit-making enterprise" in capitalism, encouraging the mass production of low-cost rental units for the working class to improve work habits and uplift family life. The capitalist, Carver chastised, "is ready enough to scrap obsolete machinery in his plant [but] is not interested in the domestic equipment of his employees."[74] The only solution was to reject the principles of "private profit" and "remunerative invest-ment" by providing direct grants for public housing projects.[75] The existing building industry was to remain the chief instrument of this program, but if private contractors were found to be unwilling, nationalization of the build-ing industry was *threatened* (if not planned). Unlike earlier reformers, Carver was also amenable to using the full powers of an interventionist state to expropriate slum lands for public housing ventures.[76]

The concept of technical expertise was also fully extended to include the standardization of building production methods and materials. Carver recog-nized the obstacles that inefficient construction processes posed for proper dwelling conditions: "it is necessary to apply to the design and construction of homes the same scientific rationalisation that has been applied, for instance to automobile plants; to reduce the costs of fabrication and assembly so that modern living conditions may become the normal possession of every house-holder."[77] In a 1948 CMHC study, Carver suggested that governments should take an active role in the formation of a large-scale building industry to expe-dite standardization, reduce labour costs, and generally smooth out the build-ing labour process to allow cheap, competent residential construction.[78] Carver and his contemporaries spurned the views on home ownership pro-motion espoused by liberal policy-makers, but shared their opinion that dwelling forms should be refined through rationalized designs in order to facilitate mass production and consumption standards.[79] This "Fordist" route was seen as the best road to national prosperity in a time of economic crisis.

figure 6.2

Slum Housing,
Toronto, 1947.

ALEXANDRA STUDIO / NATIONAL
ARCHIVES OF CANADA / RD-001058.

Extensive studies of Halifax, Hamilton, Ottawa, Winnipeg, Montreal, and Toronto in the early 1930s showed a proliferation of critical slum conditions and rampant social distress. The ground-breaking Toronto study, known as the Bruce Report, was considered a milestone in the movement for housing betterment. Written by University of Toronto professors Harry Cassidy and Eric Arthur, it identified the heavily skewed distribution of income, high unemployment, and anarchic land development as the main culprits of slum housing. Leonard Marsh, a McGill University economist who later gained fame as a key player in the federal government's postwar reconstruction plans, endorsed the Report's call for a National Housing Commission to oversee and implement reform measures.[80] In the depths of economic crisis, expert opinion reiterated once again that housing was a national concern.

The establishment of an informal housing advocacy group to follow up the recommendations of the Bruce Report speaks to public housers' (the term adopted from reformers in the United States) recognition of the importance of merging grass-roots activism with conventional lobbying to spur action on the public housing front. A drop-in housing centre was set up on the University of Toronto campus "to gain community interest and support" for public action in slum clearance, public housing, and centralized planning. A number of Toronto academics, architects, and reform-minded politicians used this forum to discuss and debate housing betterment, and eventually the group organized two national conferences in 1939 that criticized the federal government's *Dominion Housing Act* (1938). As Humphrey Carver argued, "a stimulating force" was needed "to galvanise and mobilise the nation into a united, peaceful and creative program of housing."[81]

A sense of balanced community life, deep-seated trust in the efficacy of centralized intervention, and citizen participation formed key planks in the public housers' platform. Carver believed that efficient community planning would "promote loyalty to local government, churches, recreation centres, institutions."[82] The Citizens' Housing and Planning Association (CPHA), formed during the war to promote subsidized rental housing in Toronto, endeavoured to elevate citizen participation in the reform process through continuous propaganda and lobbying of government officials. Regent Park North, the first fully-fledged public housing project in Canada, was the successful conclusion of what Carver called the CPHA's "sustained evangelistic effort...."[83] Despite their reservations about the eventual outcome of the project, the new breed of idealistic public housers, termed "Citizens in Action" by Albert Rose, a main proponent of Regent Park and noted social work professor at the University of Toronto, considered their efforts an eminently patriotic contribution to national democratic life.[84] Indeed, Harry Cassidy, who later became director of social welfare for the Province of British Columbia and professor of social welfare at the University of California, Berkeley, and Humphrey Carver saw social-welfare measures such as public housing as a bulwark against fascism and class conflict.[85] University of

Toronto architect E.G. Faludi argued during the war that "Today we are undergoing a social transformation and the securing of a tolerable standard of housing for all citizens has become a definite national obligation."[86]

The necessity of dealing with widespread slum conditions found in civic investigations brought out the crudely environmentalist streak in 1930s-1940s planning ideology. Direct slum clearance had been bandied about by public-health officials decades earlier, but the political will for comprehensive action was not yet paramount. The genuine social concerns of most planners differed from the routine insensitivity of government officials. Yet callous urban renewal strategies were the preferred initial course of action in public housers' strategy, since they thought that the removal of slums would stimulate the development of public housing projects by freeing up cheap land for municipal housing authorities.[87] Furthermore, it was held that the elimination of slum dwellings would mitigate the "pathology" of slum areas. It would not do, Carver contended, to simply renovate the affected areas. Only slum elimination integrated with a comprehensive approach to city planning would be adequate: "It is as unwise as it ever was to put new wine into old bottles; a repaired slum still remains a slum."[88] Albert Rose worried that Regent Park might become "a half-way station for many families with more or less chronic personal, social and economic problems."[89] As a result, the tenant selection processes for Regent Park were partially based on the desire to have "high-grade" tenants.[90] The repressive aspects of the technocratic initiative thus went hand-in-glove with the creed that every citizen had a right to decent housing.

If professional housers more or less discerned class divisions in the housing questions, they certainly retained restrictive views of women's proper social role, especially in the domestic sphere. In the name of the preservation and bolstering of the family, reformers paid particular attention to domestic architecture. Simplicity, efficiency, and economy were the key words in the arrangement of domestic environment as well as external housing design. As Carver put it, "the mechanisation of household equipment and the economy of bedroom space to be cleaned would help to liberate the housewife from the monotonous servitude of domestic chores and allow her to develop family life in more fruitful directions."[91] Albert Rose seconded Carver's optimism, lauding the Regent Park scheme for raising "maternal efficiency."[92] The proposed model of social relations within the home still hinged on a strict notion of nuclear family life, delimiting individual aspirations, especially those of women. If women were mentioned at all outside the strict realm of family life it was to champion their skills as housing estate managers which called for a combination of "social worker and business manager,"[93] pointing to the common judgement that women's "natural" home management skills could be transferred to the community as a whole to ensure the smooth functioning of the national polity.

Federal government housing policy during this era, especially the Home Improvement Plan (HIP) launched in the 1930s, clearly encapsulated many of the principal ideas of reform discourse concerning women, workers, and citizenship. The HIP was solely a home-improvement loan program, yet it embodied generalized ideas about women and workers in Canadian society. As Ruth Roach Pierson and Margaret Hobbs have shown, the HIP distinguished between the *rough* and *respectable* segments of the working class, favouring only stable workers who owned property.[94] As John Belec persuasively argues, federal government policy in the 1930s and 1940s aimed to embed citizenship rights within individualized consumption practices.[95] The HIP totally excluded non-citizens. Moreover, it made loans to home-owners in areas that had "racial convenants"[96] — continuing this long-standing racially-exclusive policy. Moreover, the whole HIP apparatus was premised on an ideal version of the nuclear family that obscured unequal relations within the family. The HIP's propaganda, loan procedures, and recommended house designs were thoroughly imbued with a traditional "gender-specific pitch that contributed to the perpetuation of an inequitable distribution of domestic labour...."[97]

A lecture series on town planning and housing instituted by the University of Toronto's School of Architecture in 1944 furnishes an illuminating glimpse of the accumulated experience of the 1930s-1940s housing-reform movement. In a survey of Canada's housing-policy history, Leonard Marsh — now executive secretary of the federal government's Committee of Reconstruction and author of the influential 1943 study, *Report on Social Security*,[98] which provided the intellectual framework for the postwar Canadian welfare state — presented the most articulate expression of the attitude that sustained government commitment was necessary for superior shelter provision. Favourably citing American houser Catherine Bauer on the progressive social vision of Marx, William Morris, and Roosevelt's New Deal, Marsh, while no Marxist, insisted that "[h]ousing cannot be regarded as an isolated or departmentalized field, but only as a basic part of the modern social environment, and also as a product of all the social forces at work."[99] While he separated economic needs and social criteria in the housing policy realm, he underscored the connection between employment, income distribution and decent shelter opportunities — all necessary for the collective vitality of the nation.

Eric Arthur similarly emphasized the need for a comprehensive and integrated public housing plan. Reflecting his personal admiration for the New

Deal housing projects in the US, he suggested that public housing schemes should include community centres, health clinics, and laundries under the close supervision of well-trained housing managers.[100] In contrast to early twentieth-century reform currents, the strict regulatory thrust was tempered by social democratic reformers' support for citizen participation and inclusive community development schemes.[101] Nevertheless, Canadian housers endorsed the view emanating from the social-work literature of the United States that tenants needed strict supervision. Arthur, for example, argued that tenants could not be entrusted to look after their own lawns. He seemed to sympathize with an American public housing manager's statement that "poison ivy, surrounded by barbed wire would be a godsend" in maintaining lawns in public housing projects.[102] Combining confidence in the benefits of well-planned public dwelling provision with a clear accent on the regulation of inhabitants, wartime housing reform thought would presage the dominant thrust of postwar social housing practices in the major projects of Toronto, Montreal, Halifax, Vancouver, and Ottawa.

Conclusion

The role that housing reform could play as part of the larger project of securing social consent by stabilizing family structures and contributing to the construction of a distinct national identity constituted pivotal concerns in the discourse of the housing-reform effort. To an anxious middle class and government in a time of political uncertainty, the push for industrial efficiency, moral righteousness, and social stability in workers' homes and neighbourhoods pledged to ameliorate the urban crisis by providing suitable shelter for workers, striving to shape a stable and productive workforce. A wide range of intellectuals and government officials, while differing on the extent of intervention, believed housing policy could allay the impact of industrialization and preserve class cooperation and social hierarchy. The scientific uplifting of home life on "Canadian" lines through various state-directed reform measures promised to check urban deterioration and reinforce the nation. In this way, housing reformers, in concert with the reform effort in other areas of government social policy, helped to construct the scaffolding of the nation by shaping healthy, productive, but divided citizens.

Notes

I would like to acknowledge the help of Tom Lambert, Doralice Assirati, and the editors of this collection for many useful suggestions and recommendations.

1. City of Toronto Archives (hereafter cited as CTA), City of Toronto, Minutes of the City Council, *Report of the Board of Health 1918,* Appendix A, 711.
2. For a small sample of work that engages with these arguments see Alan Sears, "Immigration Controls as Social Policy: The Case of Canadian Medical Inspection, 1900-1920," *Studies in Political Economy* 33 (Autumn 1990): 90-110; George Steinmetz, "Workers and the Welfare State in Imperial Germany," *International Labour and Working Class History* 40 (Fall 1991): 18-23; Cynthia Comacchio, *The Infinite Bonds of Family: Domesticity in Canada, 1850-1940* (Toronto: University of Toronto Press, 1999); Tom Mitchell, "The Manufacture of Souls of Good Quality: Winnipeg's 1919 National Conference on Canadian Citizenship, English-Canadian Nationalism, and the New Order after the Great War," *Journal of Canadian Studies* 31, 4 (1997): 5-28.
3. This chapter focuses on housing-reform initiatives "from above." For the important responses of workers to social policy initiatives, which fall outside the scope of this chapter, see Sean Purdy, "Building Homes, Building Citizens: Housing Reform and Nation Formation in Canada, 1900-1920," *Canadian Historical Review* 79, 3 (September 1998): 499-504.
4. Robert Miles, "Recent Theories of Nationalism and the Issue of Racism," *British Journal of Sociology* 38 (1987): 38. See also Alex Callinicos, *Race and Class* (London: Bookmarks, 1993).
5. For a similar usage note the fine article by Ian McKay, "The 1910s — The Stillborn Triumph of Progressive Reform," in *The Atlantic Provinces in Confederation,* ed. Ernest R. Forbes and Delbert A. Muise (Toronto and Fredericton: The University of Toronto and Acadiensis Press, 1993): 192-232.
6. Antonio Gramsci, "Some Aspects of the Sexual Question," in *The Gramsci Reader,* ed. David Forgacs (London: Lawrence and Wishart, 1988), 281, 296. See also David Harvey, "Labor, Capital, and Class Struggle around the Built Environment in Advanced Capitalist Societies," in *Urbanization and Social Conflict in Market Societies,* ed. Kevin Cox (Chicago: Maaroufa Press, 1978), 23.
7. Paul Rutherford, "Tomorrow's Metropolis: The Urban Reform Movement in Canada, 1880-1920," in *The Canadian City: Essays in Urban History,* ed. Gilbert Stelter and Alan Artibise (Toronto: McLelland and Stewart, 1977), 370-71.
8. Sears, "Immigration Controls," 105-06, n.5.
9. "Speculations on the Problem of Housing and the Working Classes in Vancouver," *Contract Record* 28, 41 (1914): 1276.
10. *Daily News,* 8 November 1906. See also in another Toronto newspaper "Forced to Live with Crime and City Lands are Vacant," *Toronto Globe,* 2 December 1906. For a study that also analyzes moral reform and disease see Marianna Valverde, *The Age of Light, Soap and Water: Moral Reform in English Canada, 1885-1925* (Toronto: McClelland and Stewart, 1991).
11. *Industrial Canada* (August 1911): 52. While questions of the development of social scientific analysis are largely beyond the scope of this paper it is worthwhile noting two early studies that applied more rigorous investigative methods. See Herbert Ames, *The City Below the Hill* (1897; repr. Toronto: University of Toronto Press, 1972) and the late-nineteenth and early twentieth-century studies of household budgets by University of Toronto professor James Mavor. James Mavor Papers, MS 119, Thomas Fisher Rare Book Library, Box 70.
12. For an outline of the well-documented working-class militancy see Bryan Palmer, *Working-Class Experience,* 2nd ed. (Toronto: McClelland and Stewart, 1992), 196-98, 211-13.
13. *Industrial Canada* (May 1912): 3.

14. Heather MacDougall, *Activists and Advocates: Toronto's Health Department, 1883-1983* (Toronto: Dundurn Press, 1986), 73-79. On the brutal anti-Asian dimension of these house-to-house inspections see Kay Anderson, *Vancouver's Chinatown: Racial Discourse in Canada, 1875-1980* (Kingston-Montreal: McGill-Queen's University Press, 1991), 83-84.

15. For a thorough analysis consult Veronica Strong-Boag, *The New Day Recalled: Lives of Girls and Women in English Canada, 1919-1939* (Toronto: Copp Clark Pitman, 1988), chap. 4 passim.

16. James S. Duncan, "Introduction," in *Housing and Identity: Cross-cultural Perspectives*, ed. James S. Duncan (London: Croom Helm, 1981), 1. See also Richard Harris, *The Family in Working-Class Life*, Research Paper No. 171, Centre for Urban and Community Studies (Toronto: University of Toronto, 1989), 3-8; Susanni Magri, *Politique du logement et besoins en main d'oeu-vre* (Paris: Centre de Sociologie Urbaine, 1972); Caroline Andrew, "Women and the Welfare State," *Canadian Journal of Political Science* 27 (1984): 667-84.

17. J.J. Kelso, "Can Slums be Abolished or Must We Continue to Pay the Penalty?," in *Saving the Canadian City: The First Phase, 1880-1920, An Anthology of Early Articles on Urban Reform*, ed. Paul Rutherford (Toronto: University of Toronto Press, 1974), 167.

18. Helen Cameron Parker, "Training for Housework," cited in "Technical Schools for Women," *Canadian Magazine* 1 (1893): 152-53.

19. Cited in Strong-Boag, *The New Day Recalled*, 121 (my emphasis).

20. David Ward, "The Progressives and the Urban Question: British and American Responses to Inner-city Slums, 1880-1920," *Transactions, Institute of British Geographers* 9 (1984): 303.

21. On this point note Doug Owram, *The Government Generation, Canadian Intellectuals and the State, 1900-1945* (Toronto: University of Toronto Press, 1986), 57.

22. For general histories of the Commission see Walter Van Nus, "The Fate of City Beautiful Thought in Canada, 1893-1930," in *The Canadian City*, ed. Gilbert Stelter and Alan Artibise; and Michael Simpson, *Thomas Adams and the Modern Planning Movement* (London: Mansell, 1985).

23. For information on Adams' activities see Oiva Saarinen, "The Influence of Thomas Adams and the British New Town Movement in the Planning of Canadian Resource Communities," in *The Usable Urban Past*, ed. Gilbert Stelter and Alan Artibise, Carleton Library No.119 (Toronto: Macmillan of Canada with the Institute of Canadian Studies, Carleton University, 1979), 273. Also consult the various issues of *Commission of Conservation, Annual Meetings* (hereafter *COC Annual Meetings*) and the Commission's journals *Conservation of Life* (hereafter cited as *COL*), later renamed *Town Planning and Conservation of Life* (hereafter cited as *TPCL*).

24. "The Commission of Conservation," *Saturday Night Magazine* (January 1921): 9 (my emphasis).

25. A.G. Dalzell, *TPCL* (July-September 1920): 66.

26. Thomas Adams, "The Housing Problem and Production," *COL* (July 1918): 49.

27. Thomas Adams, "Civic and Social Questions in Canada," *COL* (April-June 1916): 54-55.

28. Cited in John Bacher, *Keeping to the Marketplace: The Evolution of Canadian Housing Policy* (Kingston-Montreal: McGill-Queen's University Press, 1993), 79-80 (my emphasis).

29. Thomas Adams, *Social Welfare* (hereafter cited as *SW*) (March 1, 1919): 128.

30. Toronto Housing Company, "Better Housing in Canada: The Ontario Plan," in *First Annual Report* (Toronto 1913), 11.

31. G. Frank Beer, "Housing in Canada," *Garden Cities and Town Planning Magazine* (November 1914): 262.

32. Charles Hastings, "Suggestions for the Housing Problems," *Industrial Canada* (August 1912): 66 (my emphasis).

33. Mayor's Inaugural Address, CTA, Toronto City Council, City Council Minutes, 1920, Appendix C, 53.

34. Strong-Boag, *The New Day Recalled*, 117-21 (my emphasis).

35. Beer, "Housing in Canada," 262.

36. G. Frank Beer, "Working Men's Houses and Model Dwellings in Canada," *Garden Cities and Town Planning* 4 (May 1914): 109.

37. Frances Abele and Daiva Stasiulis, "Canada as a 'White Settler Colony': What about Natives and Immigrants?" in *The New Canadian Political Economy*, ed. William Clement and Glen Williams (Kingston and Montreal: McGill-Queen's University Press, 1989), 241.

38. See Angus McLaren, *Our Own Master Race: Eugenics in Canada, 1885-1945* (Toronto: McClelland and Stewart, 1990).

39. See Carol Lee Bacchi, "Race Regeneration and Social Purity: A Study of the Social Attitudes of Canada's English-Speaking Suffragists," in *Interpreting Canada's Past*, Vol.2, After Confederation, ed. J.M. Bumsted (Toronto: Oxford University Press, 1986), 192-207.

40. W. Struthers, "The Point of View in Medical Inspection of Schools," *Public Health Journal* 4, 2 (1913): 67.

41. Charles Hodgetts, "Unsanitary Housing," *COC Annual Meeting* (1911): 56.

42. C.K. Clarke, "The Defective Immigrant," *COL* (April 1919): 37. Alan Sears explains why British immigrants were not spared the rancour of social imperialists. See Sears, "Immigration Controls," 92-93, 99, 107 n.5.

43. Ontario Archives (OA), Sir William Hearst Papers (HP), MU 1307, Ellis to Hearst, 12 February 1919.

44. Bacher, "Keeping to the Marketplace," 79-82.

45. See John Bacher and David Hulchanski, "Keeping Warm and Dry: The Policy Response to the Struggle for Shelter among Canada's Homeless, 1900-1960," *Urban History Review* 16 (October 1987): 151; Michael Doucet and John Weaver, *Housing the North American City* (Montreal and Kingston: McGill-Queen's University Press, 1991): 99, 123; Anderson, *Vancouver's Chinatown*, 127, 269, n.63.

46. CTA, City of Toronto, Minutes of the City Council 1918, Appendix A, 726.

47. Bacher, "Keeping to the Marketplace," 48.

48. Information on Winnipeg and British Columbia cited in John Weaver, "'Tomorrow's Metropolis' Revisited: A Critical Assessment of Urban Reform in Canada," in *The Canadian City*, ed. Stelter and Artibise, 407.

49. David Ward, "The Progressives and the Urban Question," 304.

50. CTA, Toronto Board of Health, *Slum Conditions in Toronto* (Toronto: Toronto Board of Health, 1911), 8, 10, 14, 20-24.

51. Hastings cited in John Weaver, "The Modern City Realized: Toronto Civic Affairs, 1880-1915," in *The Usable Urban Past*, ed. Stelter and Artibise, 43.

52. Anderson, *Vancouver's Chinatown*, 84, 91.

53. *Contract Record and Engineering Review* 5 (June 1918): 443.

54. On MacMurchy's life and work see Kathleen McConnachie, "Methodology in the Study of Women in History: A Case Study of Helen MacMurchy, M.D.," *Ontario History* 75 (1983): 61-70; McLaren, *Our Own Master Race*, 28-45; Veronica Strong-Boag, "Canada's Women Doctors: Feminism Constrained," in *A Not Unreasonable Claim*, ed. Linda Kealey (Toronto: Women's Press, 1979).

55. Helen MacMurchy, "Housing and Health," *SW* (March 1919): 67. Admiration for Germany's efforts in welfare capitalism was also widespread before and during the war. For one of the various examples of Canadian reform support for German urban planning see Public Archives of Canada (hereafter PAC), Cauchon Papers, MG30 C105, Vol.1, Address to the Rotary Club of Hamilton, August 2, 1917.

56. Ontario, *Report of the Ontario Housing Committee* (hereafter OHC Report), Legislature of Ontario, Sessional Papers, Part 10, Report 65, 61.

57. On this important point see the ground-breaking article by Susanni Magri and Christian Topalov, "'Reconstruire': l'habitat populaire au lendemain de la première guerre mondiale, étude comparative France, Grande-Bretagne, Italie, Etats-Unis," *Archives Européennes de sociologie* 29 (1988): 319-70.

58. For insightful treatments of the literature on the history of women and the family in Canada see Joan Sangster, "Feminism and the Making of Canadian Working-Class History: Exploring the Past, Present and Future" (127-65), and Cynthia Comacchio, "'The History of Us': Social Science, History and the Relations of Family in Canada," (167-220), *Labour/Le Travail*, 46 (Fall 2000).

59. NA, MG28 I275, Vol.16, Papers of the Canadian Institute of Planners, Report of an Address to the Calgary City Planning Commission, "Town Planning and Housing," 9 April 1912, 15.

60. Anna Davin, "Imperialism and Motherhood," *History Workshop* 5 (1978): 10.

61. MacDougall, *Activists and Advocates*, 79.

62. Joseph Howes, "Housing Needs in the Ward; and their Relation to the General Housing Situation in Ontario," *SW* (October 1920): 15.

63. Charles Hastings, "The Modern Conception of Public Health Administration," *COL* (October 1917): 89, 90.

64. Marilyn Barber, "Sunny Ontario for British Girls, 1900-1930," in *Looking into My Sister's Eyes: An Exploration in Women's History*, ed. Jean Burnet (Toronto: Multicultural History Society of Ontario, 1986), 63.

65. OHC Report, 8-9.

66. Gwendolyn Wright, *Building the Dream: A Social History of American Housing* (Cambridge: MIT Press, 1981), 161-76.

67. Valverde, *The Age of Light, Soap and Water*, 136-37.

68. OHC Report, 59.

69. OHC Report, 89.

70. Martin Daunton, *House and Home in the Victorian City* (London: Edward Arnold, 1983), 37. Nuclear-family privacy is something Lizabeth Cohen has found American reformers sought to inculcate in working-class homes. See "Embellishing a Life of Labor: An Interpretation of the Material Culture of American Working-Class Homes, 1885-1915," *Journal of American Culture* (1980): 759.

71. For a comprehensive bibliography of reform literature and government housing studies as well as an outline of government legislation in the 1930s-1940s see David Hulchanski, *Canadian Town Planning and Housing, 1930-1940: A Historical Bibliography* (Toronto: Centre for Urban and Community Studies, University of Toronto, 1978) and *Canadian Town Planning and Housing, 1940-1950: A Historical Bibliography* (Toronto: Centre for Urban and Community Studies, University of Toronto, 1979).

72. Barry Ferguson and Doug Owram, "Social Scientists and Public Policy from the 1920s through World War II," *Journal of Canadian Studies* 15 (Winter 1980-81): 3-17.

73. Michiel Horn, "Leonard Marsh and the Coming of the Welfare State in Canada," *Histoire sociale/Social History* 9 (May 1976): 197-204.

74. Humphrey Carver, "A Housing Programme," in The League for Social Reconstruction, *Social Planning for Canada* (1935; repr. Toronto: University of Toronto Press, 1975), 451-52.

75. Carver, "A Housing Programme," 458. It is worth noting, however, that Carver did not oppose private enterprise in the housing market as a whole. For this point and a general critique of the reform movement and government policy at the time see Bacher and Hulchanski, "Keeping Warm and Dry," 151.

76. Carver, "A Housing Programme," 461.

77. Carver, "A Housing Programme," 459.

78. Humphrey Carver, *Houses for Canada, A Study of Housing Problems in the Toronto Area* (Toronto: University of Toronto Press, 1948), 61-63.

79. On this point, note the fine article by John Belec, John Holmes and Tod Rutherford, "The Rise of Fordism and the Transformation of Consumer Norms: Mass Consumption and Housing in Canada, 1930-1945," in *Housing Tenure and Social Class*, ed. Richard Harris and Geraldine Pratt (Gavle: Institute for Building Research, 1988), 227-28.

80. Leonard Marsh, Review of the "Report of the Lieutenant-Governor's Committee on Housing Conditions in Toronto," *Canadian Journal of Economics and Political Science* 1 (February 1935): 119-22. Like most municipalities, Toronto City Council considered housing a "government problem," meaning the *federal* government, and consequently did nothing. See CTA, "Special Committee on Housing, 1936," RG32, B1, Box 1.

81. Humphrey Carver, "The Architecture of Democracy," *Journal, Royal Architectural Institute of Canada* (October 1938): 227. Interestingly, Carver also highlighted the role of architects here, arguing that "[n]o international profession can contribute more to intellectual cooperation and social reconstruction than the profession of Architecture" (221).

82. Humphrey Carver, "Analysis of Planning and Housing," *Journal, Royal Architectural Institute of Canada* (September 1937): 195.

83. Humphrey Carver, *Compassionate Landscape* (Toronto: University of Toronto Press, 1978), 82.

84. See Albert Rose, *Regent Park, A Study in Slum Clearance* (Toronto: University of Toronto Press, 1958).

85. Harry Cassidy, *Social Security and Reconstruction in Canada* (Toronto: The Ryerson Press, 1943), 3-6; Carver, "The Architecture of Democracy," 221.

86. E.G. Faludi, "Housing the Nation," *The Canadian Forum* (November 1941): 243.

87. See Carver, "A Housing Programme," 460-61. This analysis is expounded upon by Marc Weiss, "The Origins and Legacy of Urban Renewal," in *Urban and Regional Planning in an Age of Austerity*, ed. Pierre Clavel et al. (New York: Pergamon Press, 1980), 54.

88. Carver, "A Housing Programme," 460. See also Cassidy, *Social Security*, 59. On the notion of slum "pathology" note Gerald Daly, "The British Roots of American Public Housing," *Journal of Urban History* 15 (August 1989): 417. The notion of "slum pathology" was used to argue for the slum clearance of a large area of downtown Toronto in order to build Regent Park. It also underlay the unscrupulous relocation of African Canadian residents in Africville near Halifax in the 1950s and 1960s. See Donald H. Clairmont and Dennis W. Magill, *Africville: The Life and Death of a Canadian Black Community*, 3rd ed. (Toronto: Canadian Scholars' Press, 1999). On urban renewal in Toronto after World War II see the comprehensive analysis of Kevin Brushett, "Blots in the Face of the City: The Politics of Slum Housing and Urban Renewal in Toronto, 1940-70," Ph.D. Thesis, Department of History, Queen's University, 2001.

89. Rose, *Regent Park*, 80. Yet Rose's views were changing: in an article a decade earlier, he criticized the top-down approach of social workers, arguing that the feelings of tenants should be taken into consideration. See Albert Rose and Alison Hopwood, "Regent Park: Milestone or Millstone?," *The Canadian Forum* 24, 340 (May 1949): 34-6.

90. The social history of Regent Park housing project in Toronto is fully explored in my forthcoming Queen's University Ph.D. thesis, "Life in the Projects: The Welfare State, Poverty and Resistance, 1945-1985." See also the outstanding exhibition catalogue by David Zapparoli, *Regent Park: The Public Experiment in Housing, A Photographic Exhibition at The Market Gallery, March 13-July 11, 1999* (Toronto: The Author, 2000).

91. Carver, "A Housing Programme," 463. He also shared the same concerns of World War I era reformers over separating boys and girls in housing projects. See his "Analysis of Planning," 195.

92. Rose, *Regent Park*, 108.

93. Carver, "A Housing Programme," 458.

94. Margaret Hobbs and Ruth Roach Pierson, "'A Kitchen that wastes no steps...': Gender, Class and the Home Improvement Plan, 1936-1940," *Histoire sociale/Social History* 21 (May 1988): 18.

95. John Belec, "The Dominion Housing Act, A Study of the Origins of Canadian Federal Housing Policy," Ph.D. Thesis, Department of Geography, Queen's University, 1988, 57.

96. See Bacher and Hulchanski , "Keeping Warm and Dry," 149. Also see Anderson, *Vancouver's Chinatown*, 127.

97. Hobbs and Roach Pierson, "Gender, Class and the Improvement Plan," 29-33.

98. Leonard Marsh, *Report on Social Security for Canada* (1943; repr. Toronto: University of Toronto Press, 1975).

99. Leonard Marsh, "Industrialization and Urbanization in Canada With Their Implications for Housing," Lecture 3 in *Planning of Canadian Towns with Special Reference to Post-War Opportunities in Town Planning and Housing*, Volume 1, A Course of Lectures Arranged by the School of Architecture in the University of Toronto (Toronto: School of Architecture, University of Toronto, 1944), 11-12.

100. Eric Arthur, "Housing for Canada," Lecture 16, School of Architecture lectures (see n.98 above), 1-16. It is interesting to note that many of these basic facilities were not provided in Canada's public housing projects until tenants organized and fought for such rights in the 1960s and 1970s.

101. For a minority view that stressed individual responsibility and the private market, see Charlotte Whitten, the conservative social worker, writer, and long-time mayor of Ottawa, in *The Dawn of Ampler Life* (Toronto: The Macmillan Company, 1943). This book was a conservative response to Marsh's *Report on Social Security*. Historian Frank Underhill criticized the reform movement for its policy of "nice genteel agitation," placing his hopes for housing reform in a powerful labour party. See "The Housing Fiasco in Canada," *The Canadian Forum* (October 1937): 228.

102. Eric Arthur, "Housing for Canada," 10. For a penetrating look at the top-down approach of Viennese social democrats in the housing sphere see Helmut Gruber, *Red Vienna, Experiment in Working-Class Culture, 1919-1934* (Oxford: Oxford University Press, 1991), 46-65, 146-79.

chapter seven

UNEMPLOYMENT AND THE NEW INDUSTRIAL CITIZENSHIP

A Review of the Ontario Unemployment Commission, 1916

Jennifer Stephen

Miss Edith Leach, of the Canadian Commission of Conservation, was determined to do her part to help solve one of the most serious problems facing the young Dominion of Canada in the days following the end of the Great War. The problem was the high number of British industrial women workers facing a lonely life of widowhood and spinsterdom. These women were threatening the employment prospects of returning British men demobilized and ready to reintegrate into the towns and cities of postwar Great Britain. Why not bring the women to Canada, and to rural Canada at that? Such a modest suggestion seemed to serve all interests equally well. The "racial stock," with which Leach and many of her contemporaries were so concerned, would not be diluted — after all, these were British women. This would help solve both the labour problem in Great Britain and the domestic question in rural Canada. Who could oppose such a sensible strategy?

The Social Service Council of Canada (SSCC) could, for one. Reporting on Leach's plan, the editors of the SSCC's monthly publication, *Social Welfare*, soundly denounced the idea:

> The importation of such large numbers of non-Canadian wives, and the loss of so many potential Canadian fathers cannot but endanger the maintenance of the national and distinctive Canadian type, especially in consideration of the post-war foreign immigration ....
>
> Further, the necessary maintenance of lifelong work for the thousands of women workers is not the greatest factor of the situation, but for the sake of the national ideal, some safeguarding against the

natural cynicism and bitterness of a life of labour, without satisfaction of the eternal 'homing instinct' of the woman, must be provided. Canada's problem in this connection would seem to be complicated tremendously, rather than aided, by Miss Leach's suggestion.[1]

Reconstruction was to be a very complex business indeed.

In the years immediately following World War I, self-styled social reform advocates set themselves the task of leading the young Dominion through a period of social reconstruction. This was to be the dawn of a new era, a New Day[2] for family, industry, community, and — above all — the nation. Efficiency was the watchword: national efficiency, industrial efficiency, individual and social efficiency. The lines connecting the individual to community, to work and industry, to family and to nation were closely drawn and even more closely guarded. Too much had been left to chance, to the market, and to the selfish actions of individuals. And where had it led? The war, according to commentators in the pages of *Social Welfare*, signalled the timely breakdown of the old social order. If Canadian "boys" had died for anything, their lives had to be understood as a sacrifice to and for democracy. And democracy surely could not be left to find its own way:

> *Social efficiency* has a place of honour it never before enjoyed. Social efficiency, to reach its maximum, requires individual efficiency. Yet individual efficiency is not enough. Individuals must be organised, led, trained in co-operation, given a mighty motive and therefore ready to lay aside all handicap that might hinder .... Commerce and industry must be considered in relation to the national life as a whole and be received as essential national service. The creation and maintenance of physically sound and mentally developed men and women must be regarded as a definite object for which the community as a whole is responsible and commerce and industry must be reorganised to serve this end.[3]

One of the clearest indices of inefficiency was unemployment. From the economic downturn during 1915-16, to the recession following the war in 1920-21, social-reform advocates took on the task of identifying the causes of, and the ultimate solution to, the evils of unemployment. Unemployment accompanied the young nation into the war and beyond it. At a time when uncontrolled speculation found some enjoying huge profits, thousands more were seen to be lining up for outdoor relief. So-called vagrant men wandered from town to city, while single young women drifted from factory to factory.

In the meantime, the Dominion government, the provinces, and municipalities were moving deeper into debt to finance imperial war on the one hand and local relief efforts on the other.[4]

In this chapter, I approach the phenomenon of massive unemployment in the decades surrounding the Great War as a crucible, in which social practitioners worked up their plans for the New Day. Unemployment devastated the lives of thousands of working women and men. It was also, however, to become a focus — a problem — of "the social" through which relations around work, nation, the state, and the individual were disrupted and transformed.

This was more than a process of negotiations, to the extent that the lived experiences of working-class, immigrant, and single women and men were differentially affected by the actions and programs of the social practitioners considered here. Working-class women and single immigrant men were targeted through an emerging discourse about unemployment which shaped and was shaped by notions about culture and ethnicity, race and gender, production and reproduction, paid work, social worth, and leisure. "Unemployment" came to represent the worst excesses of industrial capitalism, of so-called "uncontrolled" immigration, and Canada's alleged vulnerability as a "dumping ground" for the Empire, the mark of inefficiency: in sum, all that threatened the very purpose and rationale for the war.

I will explore how the phenomenon of unemployment was taken up by key proponents of social "reform" during the brief but tumultuous period from 1916 to 1921. I examine the testimony and final report of the Ontario Commission on Unemployment, appointed during the economic depression of 1914-15. By the time the final report of the Commission was released in 1916, what had previously been characterized as a pressing social problem had been transformed into a matter of how best to administer the market for predominantly "unskilled" male labour. However, the regulatory framework proposed by the Commission itself implicated and reconfigured the range of social relations involved in the dynamics of waged labour: in particular, women's relationship to paid employment and the "market" for labour; immigration, population control policy and the relations of empire; education and vocational training; labour organisation and industrial relations; scientific management of industry and of human "resources." From the Commission's report, I turn to a review of the principal journal of the Social Service Council of Canada, *Social Welfare*. I examine how unemployment was taken up in articles and reports written by leading social practitioners of the period, concentrating on the years 1918-21, supplemented by key reports from the *Canadian Journal of Mental Hygiene*, the publication of the Canadian National Committee for Mental Hygiene (CNCMH).

I have selected these key periods for two reasons. First, the 1916 Commission initiated a series of debates and discussions about matters of policy and administration which, I believe, would subsequently have profound implications for how unemployment was approached as a social "problem" and a "problem of the social" during the inter-war period. Second, the period of "social reconstruction" following the war was similarly influential as a time of great excitement and even greater prospects. The net was widely cast, as social practitioners debated new roles for industry, for community, for the state and the new nation they sought to forge on the ruins of the old social order.

Canada's place in the Empire was a subject of considerable discussion, in view of the newly formed League of Nations. Industrial relations and trade union/labour organizations began to assume a mantle of respectability and legitimacy, at least in the light of the new International Labour Office negotiated into the terms of the Peace Treaty of Versailles. Discussion turned to the need for national policy standards from Quebec to British Columbia: a single standard for working conditions, wages, and hours of work for women; mothers' pensions; and vocational guidance for girls and boys.

The old solutions to unemployment were cast very much on the basis of a conventional understanding of the causes of unemployment. For a young, newly industrializing "nation," industrial capitalism brought with it social problems which were less than welcome. The assumption that rural farm and domestic labour could absorb the many young men and women who needed paid work was as much a social as it was an economic solution. The "hinterland" was written into the mythology, absorbing and cleansing the pressures of the urban social order. But here was the contradiction. It was out on the hinterland that the problems were manifested: homesteaders ill-suited for the rigours of life and climate in the young, northern nation; and young men and women, drawn by the magnetism of the city, turning their backs on the isolation of rural farm life. Could the British institutions that formed the backbone of the young Dominion withstand the test of the "frontier"? Clearly, the effort to direct young, single women and men to rural posts was not going to work. Such efforts were meeting with resistance, if only because young women, for example, refused to register for such domestic placements. Other solutions to unemployment were necessary. Perhaps, in fact, the problem was not simply one of over-supply.

In Canada, the experience of the war had profound implications for how social problems were to be discovered and characterized. As Marlene Shore has indicated, the war gave rise to "an almost militant nationalism" that was strongly influenced by the notion that "the great struggle would mark the birth of a new society."[5] If the goal was to forge a new society, by whom was this society to be populated? How were the problems of the old society to be resolved? What, moreover, were those problems? Heredity and the evolutionary ideas of Lamark and Spencer figured prominently in the thinking of many of the leading social practitioners considered here. So, too, did the ideas and ideals of scientific management and the methods of Taylorism. Efficiency and reconstruction were twin concepts applied to an ever-widening range of human activity and social relations.

Human society was understood to be driven by the same evolutionary forces that propelled all organisms. That is, the potential for development existed at the level of the single organism, as well as at the level of human society and culture. The object was to study and comprehend the interaction of natural forces on the one hand, and environmental forces on the other. The question was whether human behaviour answered to cultural or to biological forces as the fundamental motive for change. Orthodox eugenicists remained fixated on the argument that "feeble-mindedness" was the hereditary source of all social problems.[6] The ultimate solution posed by an orthodox reading of eugenics was not only distasteful but depressing, arguing as it did the futility of any human effort. What did appeal, however, was the knowledge and technology developed under the guise of mental hygiene. The roots of eugenic theory remained, but the technique, in particular that developed through the CNCMH, was the main instrument and focus of reform. Indeed, the 1920s marked an international movement in the development of knowledge and knowledge-practices about mental hygiene. Through the principles of mental hygiene, psychological knowledge was applied to problems of industry.[7]

At the same time as mental hygiene and psychology flourished, so did sociology. Sociologists sought to demonstrate that nature and culture were distinct processes which, while they interacted, could not be used to explain each other. This allowed human behaviour to be separated out as the province of culture, an act of professional defensiveness by which sociologists tried to "deprive their scientific cohorts [the biologists] of the right to explain human behaviour."[8] Cultural evolution was thus distinct from biological evolution, and sociology's place within the humanities was assured. Humans were separated from animals and therefore rescued from the dismal cul-de-sac of eugenics. The Chicago School was to make significant incursions into Canadian social and economic policy through the McGill Social Research project, as Marlene Shore has explored. Convinced that the Great War was the product of a massive "breakdown of social control," Shore explains, "many academics, especially social scientists, believed that the time had come for a kind of social engineering that had never before existed."[9]A significant focus of their ensuing research and social policy development work was the perceived problems of unemployment, immigration, assimilation, and industrial relations. A key figure in the McGill School project was Dr. Clarence Hincks of the CNCMH.[10]

In his study of the historical development and application of psychology to social institutions in England, Nikolas Rose demonstrates how the question of human subjectivity has figured centrally in the historical project of governmentality. Rose adopts Foucault's definition of governmentality as "the ensemble formed by the institutions, procedures, analyses and reflections, the calculations and tactics, that allow the exercise of this very specific albeit complex form of power, which has as its target population."[11] The project of governmentality is indelibly drawn toward the appropriation and direction of human subjectivity in a manner that implicates agency and seeks to deny the capacity for resistance. So, for example, Rose characterizes the ever-widening project of governmentality through the creation of new knowledges and through incursions into areas of human activity and agency, normalizing some identities while seeking to deny or neutralize others:

> Innovations in knowledge have thus been fundamental to the processes by which the human subject has entered into the webs of government. New languages have been invented for speaking about human subjectivity and its political pertinence, new conceptual systems have been formulated for calculating human capacities and conduct, and new devices have been constructed for inscribing and calibrating the human psyche and identifying its pathologies and normalities. These ways of knowing have made it possible to assemble 'human technologies': ensembles of forces, mechanisms and relationships that enable action from a centre of calculation — a government department, a manager's office, a war room — upon the subjective lives of men, women and children.[12]

The expanding project of governmentality asserted boundaries of citizenship on the basis of notions about individual worth and efficiency. These notions, in turn, were grounded in concepts/knowledges of social pathologies. Degeneracy and deficiency comprised the counter-balance to progress and efficiency. These, then, were the parameters according to which the new economy of the social was to be constructed.

Unemployment and the "Origins" of the Welfare State

Historians of the development of the Canadian welfare state have pointed out that nineteenth-century approaches to unemployment were rooted in the moral economy of the pre-industrial poor-law system. Constitutional debate and jurisdictional boundary disputes found convenient refuge in the poor law heritage, as the federal government repeatedly insisted that poverty and relief were local, community responsibilities. The inauguration of the welfare state apparatus would therefore depend on the ability of its proponents to overcome the obstinate position of a reluctant federal government hiding behind constitutional arguments. Dennis Guest's classic study of the development of social security in Canada illustrates the evolutionary approach to the "emergence of the welfare state" which informs much of the literature about unemployment and social welfare:

> Thus it was that while the need for health and welfare provisions on a nation-wide basis grew with Canada's increasing industrialisation, the responsibility for initiating and paying for these services was, by judicial interpretation, left firmly in the care of the provinces who lacked the necessary finances to carry out the responsibility.... The impasse that developed because of the incongruity between legislative responsibility and financial capability was one reason for the delay in the establishment of vital programs of social security in Canada.[13]

According to Guest, the principle of "less eligibility" guided the prevailing approach to poverty. Unemployment was seen to be a matter of incompetence and immorality, intemperance and laziness. "Generous assistance" would encourage such unfortunate individual attributes. Preferable was the punitive approach of the workhouse and the work test. It awaited enlightened notions of social justice to guide investigations into the causes of poverty and subsequently change this pre-industrial approach: "It was only when the causes of poverty began to be decisively redefined that a foundation for changes in the social security system was laid. These changes came about as a result of a host of socio-economic forces unleashed by industrialisation."[14]

Struthers' study of the origins of the *Unemployment Insurance Act* reveals a similar approach, one that locates the "emergence of the welfare state" in a model rooted in economic determinism on the one hand, and social control on the other: "As in other market societies during the nineteenth and twentieth century, Canadian attitudes toward the unemployed were overwhelmingly conditioned by the cultural imperatives of enforcing a work ethic."[15] According to this view, welfare state policy is linked to a positive process of modernization which invariably is seen to accompany industrial capitalism. The emergence of a national labour market brought with it the need for a consistent policy of regulation, including a system of social insurance to underwrite the costs of job loss. Struthers describes the deliberate policy implications of the debate between conservative rural re-population or "pioneer back-to-the-land" adherents and the progressive, forward-looking advocates of social insurance:

> Beneath the nostalgic rhetoric and fears of rural depopulation lay the sterner imperatives of a labour market that had to supply sufficient quantities of cheap unskilled labour to the agricultural and resource frontiers. At stake in the debate between proponents of "back-to-the-land" on the one hand and unemployment insurance or relief on the other was a controversy over the meaning of work.[16]

Like Guest, Struthers characterizes the unyielding pressure fiscally-challenged local governments were left to struggle with in the face of Ottawa's obfuscation as the rationale for restrictive relief-distribution policies. An enlightened central government awaited another day. In the meantime, "the financially beleaguered municipalities were unable to provide jobs and had to restrict direct relief to married men with families."[17]

Recent studies have built on these analyses while challenging their failure to address the historical experiences of women. Margaret Hobbs' detailed historical study of the gendered basis of the social and labour policies initiated and/or implemented during the 1930s Depression in Canada takes up the deliberate exclusion of women from wage labour in all but domestic work. As Hobbs indicates, the solution to male unemployment was female unemployment, principally that of married women. Notions about what constituted legitimate work and occupation were increasingly rooted in the politics of separate spheres and the politics of difference:

> [T]he federal government moved ... slowly and with great reluctance, towards establishing principles, mechanisms and policies that would constitute a public safety net to catch the unemployed victims of the economic collapse — victims that were presumed to be male in all but a limited number of cases.[18]

Certainly, the development of a welfare state apparatus in Canada was more than a project of establishing services for the "needy"; gendered notions of work were reified in social and economic policy.

At this point, I would like to turn to the 1916 Commission on Unemployment, to see how occupation and skill were taken up through the category of unemployment in a manner that reflected and transformed the social relations implicated by work, industry, and citizenship.

THE ONTARIO COMMISSION ON UNEMPLOYMENT, 1916

The Ontario Commission on Unemployment was appointed on December 22, 1914, in the midst of a depression that caused at least one in every ten working people to lose their job.[19] The Commission was principally concerned with investigating the extent of male unemployment. Investigators devoted much of their time debating the merits of recent innovations in labour market regulation introduced in England. The most novel features in the British system, also under review in the United States, were unemployment insurance and a labour exchange system. Here was an attempt to get at the structural causes of unemployment, in the recognition that scientific investigation called for more than the trite moralisms that had up to that point informed much of the commentary on the causes and nature of poverty. In the report's opening pages, investigators made it clear that their purpose was to acquire more precise knowledge of the causes of unemployment, leading to more effective methods of prevention. Even if the point was to investigate social-structural causes, however, the individual worker still managed to take centre stage:

> Personal causes have received, heretofore, a disproportionate amount of attention. Not that they are less involved in the solution sought for, but with an improved economic adjustment, and a more efficient industrial organisation, *personal deficiencies may be found to have less room for growth and greater opportunity for repair.*[20]

Commissioners strongly favoured a system that aligned labour policy more closely with economic development, one that involved government directly in the regulation of wages and the flow of labour generally. Throughout, measures were suggested that would regulate capital, particularly the system of private employment agencies that profited from frequently unscrupulous activities. All of the proposed measures were predicated on state involvement in the market for labour, asserting a national interest in a smooth, harmonious economic system that both protected the market interests of private industry and international trade, and characterized workers' interests as consumers as well as employees. Underpinning these principles was the presumed unity of interests between the individual and the nation: regulation of capital was in the national interest.

This was a significant departure from the conventional paradigm of laissez-faire individualism, and from the conservative approach to philanthropy and relief. Still, the Commissioners justified their proposals as the basis for an economic system that would achieve greater efficiency through improved knowledge and, above all, an improved capacity to identify and correct the problems obstructing optimum performance:

> It is not proposed to standardise inefficiency, but it is felt that the supply of labour available should not alone determine the share of its rewards. National well-being is inseparable from the generous recognition of working ability. Restrictions which lessen the output or reward of workers tend to lower general efficiency and impede national economic progress through which alone an increase in individual well-being is made possible.[21]

Nikolas Rose has observed how the system of labour exchanges set up and operated as state agencies, and as sites for governmentality, worked to shape the subjectivity of individual workers. As he explains, "[l]abour exchanges were, perhaps, the first technical solution to this linked problem of economy and subjectivity, aiming to establish not only a free market in labour for the genuine unemployed, but also to expose the industrial malingerer to deterrent sanction."[22] A similar phenomenon can be observed here, quite explicitly in fact, in the testimony of at least one witness who observed that "[t]he absence of Public Labour Bureaux is another cause of unemployment. These are permanently needed not only to register those out of work, but to classify them and discover their capacity."[23] Similarly, the Commission applied an inter-related approach, desiring a system that viewed the "labour market" as an entity in its own right, while elaborating a system by which the "unemployed" could be subject to identification, classification, and remedial action. The system in place in Germany was favourably received since it was seen to accomplish precisely these dual objectives: "They made it possible to secure accurate and up-to-date information on the condition of the labour market. Without the exchanges it would never have been possible to classify the unemployed for special and detailed treatment."[24] The Commission recommended a system of public employment offices, with separate agencies for men, women, "juveniles," and "unskilled" workers. At the level of market interaction, this apparatus would ensure the regular flow of labour supply and demand, the interruption of which, most agreed, was the primary source of structural unemployment.[25]

A different strategy was needed to come to grips with that other type of unemployment, caused by "personal deficiency." And it is here that one can begin to see the transformation of unemployment from the moral category inscribed in the Poor Laws apparatus into an arena for scientific efficiency management, heavily informed by the principles of mental hygiene. This point was made emphatically by Dr. R.W. Bruce Smith, Inspector of Hospitals and Charities for Ontario and a familiar figure in the mental hygiene circuit. Smith supported the proposed scheme of industrial farms for individuals picked up on vagrancy charges. While regretting the cessation of deportation proceedings with the start of the war, Smith suggested that the systematic incarceration of the vagrant "type" would at least improve conditions for "regular" workers:

> It is safe to say that more than fifty per cent. of the unemployed are economically sub-normal. The establishment of something on the lines of the Industrial Farms for these sub-normal people would materially strengthen the labour market.[26]

Women's unemployment was taken up in a manner that reflected the prescriptive view of appropriate paid labour forms for women. The Commission also substantially transformed how unemployment was read as a social pathology when applied to women workers. This reading in turn shaped women's subsequent access to state forms of regulation in the area of the "labour market" and state-led administrative responses to unemployment. Domestic labour was the preferred solution for women workers,[27] and it took on the same significance as did farm labour for men:[28] both gendered labour forms provided a remedial outlet for women and men who were in danger of slipping outside accepted social and economic relations of power.

Commissioners faced a fundamental contradiction in their assumptions about unemployment generally, and about the proposed remedies specifically. Throughout, investigators and many of the witnesses who testified explained the individual causes of unemployment in terms of individual deficiency. The overriding assumption was that the majority of "the unemployed" were "unskilled" workers, men and women. What is interesting is the proposed remedy for unemployment: the farm pool for men worked well. Farm labour, it was argued, did not require much skill or training. The women were another matter altogether. An unskilled domestic worker was deficient morally, financially, and socially. The point was to upgrade the status of domestic labour. Through certified training, domestic service could resume its alleged former status as a viable option for young women. Perhaps in the process they could be lured back into their proper place in society, away from the allurements of the city with all of its perils. One could hardly call for increased training in domestic work, for certificates and referral networks, while at the same time sending unskilled and possibly "deficient" girls into service.

The Commission dealt with unemployed men in a manner that rigidly separated personal deficiency from economic causes, using the category of vagrancy to distinguish the legitimate claims from the illegitimate. These "industrial malcontents" were best dealt with through an extended industrial prison farm system, one that would direct any man who applied for relief into a correctional system designed to teach useful skills and employability.[29] Such a systematic approach was to be preferred to the existing outdoor relief system, according to the Commissioners, because it reflected the latest techniques of scientific investigation, knowledge, and correction. No one would be able to slip through the relief system only to turn up at some other agency's door, or the police court in the neighbouring town. In this, investigators rejected the slackness of the existing system, one that perpetuated poverty by failing to identify and address its causes: "It is realised ... that no adequate remedy for the destitution which follows unemployment can be found in philanthropic endeavour. Employment problems, if they are to be solved at all, must be solved from within."[30]

Fortunately, the Toronto Neighbourhood Workers Association, under Peter Bryce's leadership, had taken steps to implement a more systematic approach to social work. The city's relief system had been carefully charted and divided — military-style — into separate divisions. All record-keeping had been regularized and all records centralized. In this way, unnecessary duplication was eliminated. The individual and family were opened up to more careful scrutiny and comprehensive intervention. Bryce was clearly pleased with the combined results of record centralization and consistent case-conferencing among each division's team of social workers:

> An intimate knowledge of all the facts of the case under consideration is desirable, imperative in fact, if one is to intelligently help the family seeking assistance .... Our hands have been greatly strengthened in this respect by our extensive knowledge of each family, acquired through long and intimate association with the district.[31]

According to H.C. Hudson of the Ontario Office, Employment Services of Canada, there were three classes of unemployed. The job of the employment office was to categorize each applicant according to the correct classification, and ensure that subsequent actions addressed the problem accordingly. These classes were, first, those who were "conscientiously seeking work"; second, those who "owing to some physical or mental disability are unemployable" and should, therefore, be segregated from the general population through the intervention of the appropriate social agency; and third, the most troublesome class of "those who follow the line of least industrial resistance and who take advantage of the generosity of the community."[32] It is clear, however, from Hudson's comments that the unemployment problem was mainly an issue of male vagrancy. This is where official discourse continued to concentrate its attention — namely, at the level of vagrancy, indolence, and the morally deleterious effects of direct relief. Also evident, however, are the first tentative incursions of mental hygienists into the terrain of industrial hygiene, industrial relations, and labour policy.

"THE SPECIAL UNEMPLOYMENT PROBLEMS OF WOMEN"

The women's representative on the Commission was Marjorie MacMurchy, a leading figure in the movement to professionalize "social work." MacMurchy went on to become secretary to the Canadian Reconstruction Association (CRA), in charge of the Women's Department. The CRA was mainly an employer organization, charged with the task of achieving "efficiency in production"[33] through the implementation of techniques including the application of mental hygiene practices in industrial settings.

Commissioners had to admit that women represented a large and growing percentage of the work force. However, they were quite reluctant to condone women's apparent preference for the freedoms offered through a regular day job to the confinement of live-in domestic service.[34] Women worked in a variety of economic sectors, particularly manufacturing, retail, and clerical. In fact, it is likely that the more strategic importance of women in the labour force was not lost on investigators or witnesses. As recent studies have indicated, women's lower wage was critical to the business strategy pursued by employers. Like the Minimum Wage Boards that followed, the Commissioners were unlikely to rock the boat to the point of challenging the power and the right of employers to draw on women as a source of low-waged, non-unionized labour.[35]

Commissioners acknowledged that the "important position in paid employments now occupied by women is imperfectly appreciated." Women were in the work force and were likely to remain, and for this reason "the provisions recommended for improving conditions for men apply equally, in many cases, to women workers."[36] The principal investigators, however, studiously avoided acknowledging the impact of international trade, foreign-held debt, seasonal industries, and fluctuations in market conditions on the demand for women's labour. This form of analysis was reserved for working men, in effect shaping the understanding of occupational study, vocational training, and remedial state intervention in the market for labour. For women, the point was not so much the *lack* of work as it was the prevalence and character of jobs in which women predominated. Skill was a central organizing category in this gendered analysis of work, occupation, and unemployment, as was personal deficiency. And both were organized through notions of race, culture, nationality, and ethnicity.

The commissioners were clear about where they preferred to find employment for women when they declared that the well and properly trained home-worker need "never to be unemployed." If she was, however, then no clearer evidence was needed to predict her capacity as a mother. An unemployed home-worker was clearly no candidate for motherhood. Here, then, were the boundaries that framed women's relationship to the market economy as a waged worker. This was a difficult, if not impossible, identity to escape: "if they are not skilled workers in paid work outside, they cannot be skilled in their own employment at home."[37] Obedience to social forms in waged work extended to those of property as well, in the form of a prescriptive admonition to follow the appropriate path to become a suitably disciplined class of workers. Therefore, "factory girls" who were "indifferent" to their work and station were characterized as unlikely candidates for their future vocation as mothers. Such rebellious female youth refused to show the obedience and discipline expected of the working girl. Their refusal to conform was only self-defeating, of course, since factory girls who showed "a disrespect for property and material" ultimately brought "disrespect on the factory girl as a class."[38]

The investigation of women's unemployment concentrated on, and carefully linked, assumptions about occupation, skill, and vocational aptitude. Based on work that, at this time, was well ahead of similar employment-based research in Canada,[39] MacMurchy drew extensively on the work of her colleagues in the United States to formulate recommendations for the Canadian context, specifically the Philadelphia employer association of 40 "larger and more progressive employing concerns" including General Electric, formed for "the discussion of regularization and other human and efficiency problems in employment."[40] According to this organization's research, approximately 90 per cent of all unemployment "which makes men and women suffer and which demoralises and degrades them can be eliminated by proper organisation within our factory walls."[41]

The Commission recommended that private industry become more systematic in its personnel practices, in particular by establishing a separate "employment department" within the company. As an early example of "personnel management," the employment department combined the principles of assessment and psychological testing, case management, vocational and aptitude testing, and training. Better still, such careful management at the firm level, by enhancing the efficiency goals of the industry, furthered the objectives of national efficiency, measured as improved productivity. Employment departments really were the most sensible plan, and MacMurchy made sure the point was made repeatedly in her occupational studies of women's employment.

Six women's occupations were selected for special study: the house worker, factory worker, saleswoman, stenographer, trained nurse, and "women who work by the day." Investigators listed training needs, demands on health, employment conditions and levels, and the nationality of the women found to be exclusively engaged in those occupations. It is perhaps not surprising that the occupation that drew the greatest criticism was that of the "women who work by the day." In tasks, such women came closest to domestic workers. The job involved washing, ironing, scrubbing and cleaning, emptying ashes and charring. What differentiated this work from domestic service was not, however, the amount of dirt involved, but rather the "instability" of this irregular form of employment. Of course, it is also possible to understand the absence of a regular employer-employee relationship as the greater freedom to come and go at will. Certainly factory girls were singled out for the same charge, dubbed "occupational wanderers" as they irresponsibly drifted from "pillar to post," from one job dipping chocolates to another forming boxes, roaming from factory to factory just as they pleased.

If young working women were neglected and left to their own devices during times of leisure, they were most certainly neglected through education and industry. It was more than time that the vocational training needs of young women were attended to. The industrial unrest among men was attributed to the "dehumanising and depersonalising effects of modern industry." Perhaps this was now generally accepted. And if so, the case was even more pressing for women, given that "neither educational, social nor industrial institution nor tradition has arisen giving to the young girl worker, any vocational guidance, any preliminary industrial training, any preparatory general education." The answer, then, was to "correlate the job and the girl," to give her the tools she needed in the form of vocational training to help her unravel "the intricate maze of tangled threads from which her little woof is woven."[42]

Based on a study conducted by the Bureau of Women in Industry in New York State, the problem of occupational drifting was redefined as a problem of skill. The study compared the rate of turnover on the basis of age, department, and skill and then compared the results between men and women. There was not much variance in each of these areas, with one notable exception: the turnover rate was highest among the least skilled workers. After that, it was highest among women doing the least skilled work. This was the central ambiguity in the puzzle: just what was the relation between skill and employment stability?

For working-class women engaged in allegedly "unskilled" work generally, but more particularly for the women day-workers, the charge of deficiency was closely linked to notions about skill, which was itself becoming an index of personal, industrial, and ultimately social efficiency. What is most interesting here are the convolutions through which the investigators had to pass in order to make the case against the "women who work by the day." Such labour was irregular, based on an employment contract apparently bound by task, not by time. There was no primary employer-employee relationship. Women, it was assumed, engaged in this labour not through aspirations to vocation or career but simply because they needed the money. This was acknowledged through the assertion that these women were mostly married with children, or were widowed or deserted.[43] That is, they were engaged in waged labour as a result of the failure of their primary occupation as mother and wife. Many of these women were registered with the Toronto Women's Patriotic League and at the day nursery operated through the league. The League had been set up to administer the system of mothers' pensions locally.[44] The majority of these women were from Ireland and Scotland. They had, additionally, been subject to examination by the practitioners at the Toronto Psychiatric Clinic, the principal research organ of the CNCMH. It is likely that this arrangement had been established because of the League's function as the administrative agency for distributing pensions.

The Commission reserved its clearest terms for women in this occupational group. They experienced the greatest problem with unemployment (although it is unclear how the incidence of unemployment could have been measured for a group whose jobs were so irregular). Further, the question of training for this occupation was given short shrift, with the observation that "few of the workers can be described as highly efficient or even as efficient." And finally, most damning of all, these women were held to exemplify all that was wrong with the "economic sub-normals" who were plaguing industry and holding back the objectives of national efficiency:

> A considerable number of women who appeared to be not normal mentally applied for work at the Women's Patriotic League .... It is apparent from this report, and from other evidence secured during the present investigation, that the matter of providing care for mentally unfit persons is a question of urgency.[45]

Control of the "national" pool of labour would require a greater capacity to direct the international movement of people. One section of the Commission's report was devoted to the question of immigration. Here, observations and recommendations echoed those made by mental hygienists and others engaged in scientific social work. Recommendations targeted the operation of private immigration agents operating overseas in connection with transportation companies, encouraging a steady stream of immigrants drawn by false and misleading advertisements to certain failure. These were the individuals who ended up drawn into the underside of the cities, adding to the defective stock. According to the Commission, "in the problem of immigration is involved that of unemployment. The one cannot be solved apart from the other."[46] In addition to supporting calls for compulsory medical examination at the port of departure, and increased regulatory control on the operation of steamship companies with their immigration promotion schemes, Commissioners proposed an ambitious program of population control that encompassed the Empire as one unified, integrated administrative unit, bound by a common political, racial and imperial destiny:

> For this purpose and for the general purposes of inter-Imperial migration and land settlement the United Kingdom and the Dominions should be viewed as a single whole. It should be possible, effectively to unite the Imperial and Dominion Governments in a policy which will keep the movement of population more and more within the Empire and check the drain of population to foreign countries and so conserve British manhood for the development of British territory and the support and defence of British institutions against future contingencies.[47]

Social Reconstruction and the New Industrial Citizenship

Having established the close connection between immigration and unemployment, it was no small step to developing a solution to satisfy concerns raised in both areas. At the top of the list stood medical and psychiatric inspection. The CNCMH, through C.K. Clarke and C.M. Hincks, led the charge on this question, but that alone would not resolve the matter. It was also important to ensure that the Dominion of Canada's interests were not trampled over by the dictates of the Empire, particularly given the postwar priorities of population distribution and control.

In its report to the Social Service Council of Canada in 1919, the Committee on Immigration and Colonization warned of the need for the federal government to state the country's position on the "question of East Indian immigration ... in no ambiguous terms"[48] specifically in the wake of the conclusion of negotiations working out the terms of the peace Treaty of Versailles. The position was that no persons from East India would be welcome in Canada.[49] Similarly, the committee warned of the need to be ever watchful against dumping, since all nations would be looking to "transplant their surplus female population to those countries where the relative numbers of the sexes are more nearly equal."[50] Vigilance was required in particular to avoid the incursions of throngs of potentially "defective" women. The problem was not their immorality, necessarily, although that was certainly cause for concern. Rather, the economic and occupational incompetence that was the consequence of degeneracy would lead to unemployment, and from there invariably "relief by the only vile alley that seems still open – these are the usual corners along the street of shame."[51]

Fortunately, according to the Committee, agreement had been secured through Order-in-Council to tighten up Clause 38 (c) of the *Immigration Act*, adding literacy as a new requirement for entry, and empowering the Governor-in-Council to

> ... prohibit for a stated period, or permanently, the landing in Canada, or the landing at any specified port of entry in Canada, of immigrants belonging to any race deemed unsuited to the climate or requirements of Canada, or of immigrants of any specific class, occupation or character.[52]

These changes were greeted favourably by the editors of *Social Welfare*, who made it clear that "Canada is determined to set a high standard for her citizenship, and to enforce rigorously all legislation tending to the creation and maintenance of that standard."[53]

Dr. Samuel Zane Batten, from the Philadelphia project, spoke for many when he asserted that scientific education and scientific management would lead the way to prepare employees for citizenship in industry. But, he warned,

> ... we might as well face the fact that a large proportion of the people are not efficient workers. They are not efficient as economic units. What I believe we should work for as social workers, always and everywhere, as the preparation for full democracy, is to create in the minds of the people efficiency, preparation for faithful, effective work as industrial citizens .... In other words, the manager from this time forward holds some responsibility for his worker, and he must do everything that lies in this power to prepare himself for effective service, for citizenship and industry, as democracy recognises its responsibility to prepare people for citizenship in the State.[54]

Conclusion

The Social Service Department at the University of Toronto announced that it was ready to launch a new course for the fall term in September 1919. The course, to be offered afternoons and evenings in order to draw as many students as possible, would provide full training in "Employment Management." The course outline, reproduced in full, was as follows:

1. Personnel Management. Principles and Practice; including methods of securing, selecting, promoting and transferring employees, trade tests and earning scales, job analysis and personnel specifications, organisation and work of a personnel office, labour turnover and its reduction.

2. Industrial Psychology. The application to business of modern psychology, ways of learning and of teaching business processes, intelligence tests and their application to industry, influences making for harmony or disharmony, co-operation or antagonism within industry.

3. Economic Principles and Methods involved in 1 and 2. Causes which have brought about the present economic situation, wage determination (various plans), labour problems and proposed solutions, labour organisations, labour laws, etc.[55]

The promise of such a course, offered to the widest possible audience in private industry, was being demonstrated daily through the activities of the Department of Soldiers' Civil Re-Establishment. Norman Burnette, director of the department's Ontario Vocational Branch, pointed out that his service made it possible for society to "reclaim" 90.2 per cent of disabled soldiers through the careful work of the Vocational Psychologist working in concert with the psychiatrist.[56] Assessment of aptitude and capacity, along with physical rehabilitation, could go a long way toward reclaiming the individual whose "capacity to work" was impaired. The key to understanding this new therapeutic approach lay in understanding that occupation was central to an individual's identity. Occupation was not, as too many thought, merely "diversional":

> With the mentally afflicted, much of what has been said concerning the physically disabled, is equally applicable. We have the same broad classification, those who are totally incapacitated, and whose lives, therefore, must be brightened by occupation, those who are amenable to cure by occupation, and those whose lives can be made useful and productive by education in occupations fitted to their capabilities, even though their lives must be lived under institutional care.[57]

A comprehensive system of employment and vocational study, firmly rooted in the principles of mental hygiene, would open up the weaknesses of the current industrial system to full view. At that time, it would be possible to weed out the "inefficients" who were otherwise permitted to flourish under the indifference of free market industrialism. This issue was particularly relevant when applied to women industrial workers. Young girls and women were permitted to drift in and out of industry without any proper guidance. Inefficiency was, paradoxically, encouraged by industrial development, as the following commentator tried to explain: "The development of machinery has favoured their employment and given them earning power — the larger the plant, the higher their wages and the greater the possibility of their permanent employment."[58] The work of the Employment Department would therefore include a comprehensive analysis of the requirements of each job; careful selection of applicants; comprehensive training of new hands; systematization of promotions; investigation of causes for leaving; and regularization of employment.[59]

The era of postwar reconstruction included a strong bid for industrial peace. Motivated in part by the fear of political organizing among the left in the labour movement, social practitioners took on the task of reorganizing relations in industry according to the principles of mental hygiene. If unemployment was the spectre to be averted, the objective had to be a careful mapping of the labour supply itself, to search out the defects before their deficiency was manifested in the social pathology of "unemployment."

The administrative proposals included in the Commission's final report widened the capacity for scrutiny of the individual who worked for pay. Measures to increase the regulatory capacity of the state and of private industry over the market for labour in fact mapped out the boundaries of a "national labour market," at the same time as waged work/workers were organized and assessed on the basis of skill, occupation, and alleged employment capacity. These categories were themselves heavily informed by and, in turn, informed notions of gender and of citizenship.

Notes

1. Editor, "Immigration of British Women Workers to Canada," *Social Welfare* 1, 1 (October 1918): 19.
2. For a description of social, familial, and economic conditions faced by women during the period, see Veronica Strong-Boag, *The New Day Recalled: Lives of Girls and Women in English Canada, 1919-39* (Toronto: Penguin, 1988).
3. Editorial, *Social Welfare* 1, 4 (January 1919): 77-78. Emphasis in original.
4. See, for example, Dennis Guest, *The Emergence of Social Security in Canada* (Vancouver: University of British Columbia Press, 1980).
5. Marlene Shore, *The Science of Social Redemption: McGill, the Chicago School and the Origins of Social Research in Canada* (Toronto: University of Toronto Press, 1987), 29.
6. For an examination of the research and social policy agenda of the leadership of the mental hygiene movement associated with the Toronto Psychiatric Clinic and the Canadian National Committee for Mental Hygiene, see my "The 'Incorrigible', the 'Bad', and the 'Immoral': Toronto's 'Factory Girls' and the Work of The Toronto Psychiatric Clinic," in *Law, Society and the State: Essays in Modern Legal History*, ed. Louis Knafla and Susan Binnie (Toronto: University of Toronto Press, 1995).
7. For an analysis of the discovery of the "maladjusted worker" in England during this period, see Nikolas Rose, *Governing the Soul: The Shaping of the Private Self* (New York: Routledge, 1989), 5.
8. Rose, *Governing the Soul*, 115.
9. Rose, *Governing the Soul*, 202-03.
10. See Ian Dowbiggin, *Keeping America Sane: Psychiatry and Eugenics in the United States and Canada 1880-1940* (Ithaca: Cornell University Press, 1997); John D. Griffin, *In Search of Sanity: A Chronicle of the Canadian Mental Health Association, 1918-1988* (London ON: Third Eye Books, 1989).
11. Rose, *Governing the Soul*, 5.
12. Rose, *Governing the Soul*, 8.
13. Guest, *The Emergence of Social Security in Canada*, 7.
14. Guest, *The Emergence of Social Security in Canada*, 38.
15. James Struthers, *No Fault of Their Own: Unemployment and the Canadian Welfare State, 1914-1941* (Toronto: University of Toronto Press, 1989), 6.
16. Struthers, *No Fault of Their Own*, 210.
17. Struthers, *No Fault of Their Own*, 37.

18. Margaret Hobbs, "Gendering Work and Welfare: Women's Relationship to Wage-Work and Social Policy During the Great Depression," Ph.D Thesis, University of Toronto, 1995, 226.

19. Carolyn Strange, *Toronto's Girl Problem: The Perils and Pleasures of the City, 1880-1930* (Toronto: University of Toronto Press, 1995), 47.

20. Ontario, *Report of the Ontario Commission on Unemployment* (Toronto, 1916), 11. Emphasis added. Hereafter Commission.

21. Commission, 15.

22. Rose, *Governing the Soul*, 63.

23. Commission, 204.

24. Commission, 130.

25. See, for example, Struthers' analysis of contemporary interpretations of the causes of unemployment. Progressive historians like Struthers, of course, see unemployment as endemic to industrial capitalism. For an attempt to assess the level of systemic unemployment, principally among men, during the nineteenth century using census data, see Peter Baskerville and Eric Sager, "The First National Unemployment Survey: Unemployment and the Canadian Census of 1891," *Labour/Le Travail*, 23 (1989): 171-78.

26. Commission, 250.

27. See Hobbs, "Gendering Work and Welfare," for a general discussion of prevailing assumptions about women and unemployment. See also Strange, *Toronto's Girl Problem*, who demonstrates how this remedy was consistently suggested in major government studies of female employment during the decades 1880-1930.

28. In all of the primary and secondary literature consulted for this chapter, the agricultural economy is treated as though it were a sponge soaking up excess male industrial "unskilled" labour. In fact, the relationship between the agricultural economy (and the "male" agricultural wage) and the industrial/manufacturing economy has informed much economic and labour policy and historical analysis. Although beyond the range of this review chapter, this is an area of analysis I intend to pursue, consulting in particular the work of Canadian economists and economic historians including Harold Innis, Arthur Lower, Hugh Easterbrook, and V.C. Fowke's classic study of the "'wheat economy." In addition, the work of these men would provide an interesting contrast to the work of feminists like Marjorie Cohen, Joy Parr, and Bettina Bradbury.

29. Commission, 13.

30. Commission, 15.

31. Commission, 299. For an intriguing analysis of the regulatory impact of welfare state forms on social forms, agency, and subjectivities available through "the family" see Jacques Donzelot, *The Policing of Families* (New York: Random House, 1979).

32. H.C. Hudson, "Mobilising to Reduce Unemployment," *Social Welfare* 4, 11 (1922): 243.

33. Editorial, *Social Welfare* 1, 4 (1919): 76.

34. Strange, *Toronto's Girl Problem*.

35. For a discussion of the development of labour policies in Western Canada, including the operation of the Minimum Wage Boards there, see Bob Russell, "A Fair or A Minimum Wage? Women Workers, the State, and the Origins of Wage Regulation in Western Canada," *Labour/Le Travail* 28 (1991): 59-88.

36. Commission, 13.

37. Commission, 64.

38. Commission, 171.

39. More formal investigations and research following this particular line of inquiry appear to have begun in earnest in the 1920s. Backing from industry, led principally by funding granted by the Rockefeller Foundation, provided the impetus. McGill University and the University of Toronto both fostered research programs, in close collaboration with the CNCMH. For a discussion of the McGill School, see Shore, *The Science of Social Redemption*.

40. Commission, 35.

41. Commission, 35.

42. "Some Aspects of Women in Industry," *Social Welfare* 3, 10-11 (1921): 282.

43. Commission, 189.
44. The League was likely a chapter of the Canadian Patriotic Fund, formed at the start of the war to provide material aid to families of soldiers overseas. See Margaret McCallum, "Keeping Women in Their Place: The Minimum Wage in Canada, 1910-25," *Labour/Le Travail* 17 (1986): 29-56.
45. Commission, "Eighty-One Country Positions: An Analysis of Cases of Unemployed Women Sent to Country Positions," 193.
46. Commission, 50.
47. Commission, 51.
48. "Report of the Committee on Immigration and Colonisation," *Social Welfare* 1, 5 (1919): 110.
49. See Barbara Roberts, *Whence They Came: Deportation from Canada, 1900-1935* (Ottawa: University of Ottawa Press, 1988).
50. "Report of the Committee on Immigration and Colonisation," 110.
51. "Report of the Committee on Immigration and Colonisation," 111.
52. "Report of the Committee on Immigration and Colonisation," 111. The domicile requirement was increased from 3 years to 5 years as the minimum period required to establish residency for citizenship. In the prohibited class, those identified as "mental defectives" or found "at any time previous" to have been "insane" were excluded. The clause had been amended from "within the last five years."
53. "1919 Amendments to Immigration Act," *Social Welfare* 1, 8 (1919): 209.
54. Dr. Samuel Zane Batten, "Industrial Reconstruction. The Student's Point of View," *Social Welfare* 1, 7 (April 1919): 164.
55. "Notes and News," *Canadian Journal of Mental Hygiene* 1, 3 (1920): 266.
56. Norman Burnette, "Invalid Occupation as a Guide to the Vocational Fitness of the Handicapped," *CJMH* 1, 3 (1920): 227.
57. Burnette, "Invalid Occupation," 230.
58. "Some Aspects of Women in Industry," *Social Welfare* 8, 10-11 (1921), 282.
59. "Why Do Women Leave Their Jobs?" *Social Welfare* 3, 12 (1921): 290.

chapter eight

INDISPENSABLE BUT NOT A CITIZEN
The Housewife in the Great Depression

Denyse Baillargeon
Translated by Yvonne M. Klein

Introduction

In an article published in 1975, the historian Terry Copp, after describing the difficult conditions that the Montréal working class endured during the Great Depression, concluded, "One of the great mysteries of the depression decade is the reason for the relatively low level of social unrest ... that these conditions produced."[1] It is true that, despite especially high rates of unemployment, the 1930s did not see any extraordinary incidence of working-class mobilization. Leaving aside the On to Ottawa Trek that was staged by young single men who were inmates in the Bennett government's labour camps, it must be said that mass demonstrations were extremely few and that protests by the unemployed did not seriously threaten the foundations of the liberal economy or the capitalist social order.[2] Addressing himself to the task of elucidating this mystery, Copp attributes the relatively stable social climate first to the fact that only a minority of wage-earners, which he estimates at twenty per cent, were profoundly affected by the Depression, and second to the decrease in the cost of living which would have more than made up for reductions in wages. As a result, "many working-class families were, in fact, better off during the 1930's than they had been in the 1920's."[3] In essence, Copp suggests that the times were not "hard" enough to provoke revolt.

Copp may be correct, but the arguments he advances are certainly not sufficient to explain a phenomenon such as this. In the years since Copp wrote this article, a number of feminist historians have made the point that the economic indicators he cites to explain the weak level of social protest actually turn out to be quite imperfect instruments for evaluating working-class standards of living. Hence it would be risky to draw conclusions from these indicators concerning the revolutionary potential of such social conditions. Indeed, if we consider under-employment, small business and shop bankruptcies, and the extraordinary length of time that certain groups of labourers were without work, especially in the building trades, we might just as easily conclude that the Depression generated a measure of poverty and of economic, social, and psychological insecurity much greater than that revealed by official statistics. Wages were not, however, the sole resource upon which families depended for their support. From the beginning of industrialization, working-class families had employed a range of survival tactics that were based as much on the labour of women in the home as on that of male breadwinners and of children.[4] The responsibilities undertaken by women within the home were indispensable even during "prosperous" times such as the 1920s; they turned out to be even more crucial during the Depression when government relief measures were far from making up for losses in wages.[5] For this reason, these women are unquestionably one of the key elements we must take into account if we are to understand properly the weakness of social protest in the period compared with the economic collapse that characterizes it.

More recently, several feminist historians have also observed that the Great Depression has appeared, both at the time and in retrospect, as an essentially "masculine" crisis, as a crisis of masculinity, in fact, because it undermined the breadwinner status that constituted the foundation of male power and identity.[6] All the same, the aid programs, home relief, and public works established by the nascent Canadian welfare state operated to support the prerogatives of the male heads of the household, as married women, seen as the economic dependants of their husbands, could not avail themselves of such relief programs directly.[7] The intervention of the Canadian government may have been reluctant and largely inadequate, but it did confirm the privileged access men had to a source of income, a proof of both their independence and their status as citizens. In so doing, state policies simultaneously consolidated patriarchal family structures and encouraged men to remain faithful to their role as breadwinner.[8] Housewives, excluded as they were from the job market and subordinate to the man of the house, were not regarded as citizens of the developing welfare state even if, implicitly, the state recognized women's contribution to family maintenance.[9] In fact, relief payments were as a rule largely contingent on good housekeeping, which state representatives checked up on through home visits to recipients; likewise, the allocation of tracts of land to aspiring "pioneers" in the "colonization areas" depended upon the ability of their wives to adapt to a life on the farm.[10] Thus the state expected women to make a specific contribution to their families' welfare as a complement to whatever public assistance it might extend. Governmental measures and the unpaid labour of women in the home combined to cushion the worst effects of the Depression not only on the economic scheme, but also on patriarchal social and family organization. Placed under severe strain in the public marketplace, the bases of masculine identity were thus preserved in the domestic sphere, which probably contributed to calming any rebellious urges on the part of married workers and fathers.

On the basis of thirty interviews undertaken among francophone women from Montréal,[11] in this chapter I will examine the dynamics of gender relationships and the contribution made by women to the survival of workers' families during the Great Depression. In the 1920s or at the beginning of the 1930s, these women, from poor backgrounds, married labourers, white-collar workers or small businessmen who, for the most part, would suffer from periods of joblessness or underemployment.[12] This "feminine" take on the economic crisis will bring to light the dependence of both society and the state upon these "non-citizens," providing an excellent example of the interrelation between the public and private spheres as well as of the ways in which social policies and private welfare activities are articulated. The latter rely, in particular, on the failure to acknowledge the citizenship of housewives in the same way as that of men.

The Gender of Work

When women married, it was understood that they would quit work in order to take care of the house and the children, while their husbands would work outside the home to earn the money needed for the household. The ideology of separate spheres was so entrenched that this gendered division of labour seemed to spring from immutable natural law, and so the question would never even arise as a topic of discussion between engaged couples. Almost by instinct, these women knew that the male identity depended on the ability of the husband to "support" his wife and they were perfectly aware of the social prohibitions against paid work for married women. As one respondent said, "Married women weren't allowed to work in those days. My husband did not marry me for me to support him.... Men had their pride. They didn't want their wives working" (I23).[13]

Though the breadwinner/homemaker model was rigid, it could allow certain accommodations. In fact, almost two-thirds of these women worked for a salary or wages even before their husbands fell victim to unemployment or cuts in pay due to the Depression.[14] In reality, at the time of their marriage, only five of the husbands earned more than twenty-five dollars a week, the level that could be termed a decent salary; more than half were earning less than twenty dollars a week and a few were making less than ten dollars. According to the figures of the federal Department of Labour, it would require $20.18 a week in Québec merely to cover the costs of food, heating, light, and rent, these outlays representing approximately 65% of the expenses needed by a family of five.[15] From all the evidence, the image of the homemaker wholly dependent on the male wage and exclusively dedicated to housework and child care represented a virtually unattainable ideal for the majority of these poor working-class households. In the absence of a genuine "family wage," family survival depended by necessity on intensive domestic production and the extremely close management of the household budget, to which were often added the earnings from paid work of the mother of the family.

Unable to make ends meet, especially after the birth of their first children, several of these women sought sources of supplementary income. Five of them worked at jobs outside the home for brief periods; the others worked at home in one or more paid capacities, sometimes several at a time, in addition to carrying out their household responsibilities. They did sewing, knitting or took in laundry, they took care of boarders, they worked as domestics, managed a small business, sold home-made baking — all ways of transforming their "feminine" expertise into hard cash. While the amounts they were able to earn from these activities varied considerably — depending on how much they charged and on the customers who used their services (if they were working for themselves, for example), or on the amount of work they did for their employers in a given week — this monetary contribution on the part of women might represent a considerable part of the household income: "We didn't have enough money. I used to smock baby clothes. Then I had my boarder who gave me six bucks a week. That helped a little, my husband was making ten dollars a week" (I13). Without always representing such a large proportion of the total family income, the money these women earned in their "spare time," as they put it, often made the difference between living below or just a little above the poverty line. It also allowed them to avoid going into debt: "It didn't pay a helluva lot, but it was only that it gave me a little something at the end of the week. ... When [my husband] didn't have enough, then I was the one who paid, I would put it toward the rent or to buying clothes for the kids. ... It meant that we stayed out of debt" (I17).

If male salaries were largely inadequate before the Depression, the financial situation of the majority of families deteriorated even further during the 1930s.

Unemployment, underemployment, and pay cuts affected the great majority of heads of households, forcing more than half of them to fall back on relief payments. This circumstance did not, however, lead to a major disruption in attitudes, limited by the patriarchal social norms in force, toward the financial contribution of wives to the family economy. Thus only two women became the principal support of their families while their husbands were unemployed. On the other hand, nine of the men lost their jobs for periods ranging from several months to several years without there being any question of their wives' looking for work. Full-time homemakers since the day they married, they pointed to various obstacles to explain this paradox, such as the number of children at home, the impossibility of finding work, even work at home, but also, and perhaps chief of all, the opposition of their husbands. "I would have liked to go to work," one of them maintained, "but [my husband] didn't want me to. Anyway, the children were too little, I couldn't leave them. In those days, you didn't leave your babies with someone else" (I20).

For this woman, as for several others, having young children seemed to present a major barrier to her entry into the job market, even if the father, who was unemployed, would have been available to take care of them.[16] Mothering was so profoundly identified with femininity that it seemed unthinkable that it could become a male responsibility. Most of these women also asserted that there was no employment to be had, even if they had not actually looked for work, or that jobs were strictly reserved for men, a discourse that was an article of faith during the Depression.[17] As one woman mentioned, "There wasn't any more work for girls than there was for men in those days. ... And I'd never had a job,[18] let me tell you I'd have had a lot of trouble finding work too" (I19). Another declared: "Married women did not have the right to go to work.... There was too much unemployment — they would rather hire heads of families" (I6).

Underneath these arguments, one detects a strong reluctance, as much from the women as from their husbands, against bringing about a reversal in roles that would be incompatible with defined and accepted social norms[19] — indeed, in these instances, the sexual division of labour was integrated in so rigid a manner that it precluded any possibility of redefining, even briefly, how responsibilities were shared within the home. The opposition of a husband resolved to preserve his dominant status was probably the determining factor in most cases, but, as Margaret Hobbs suggests, some of these full-time homemakers perhaps were fearful that if they were to stand in for the male breadwinner, they might encourage their husbands to lose interest in their family obligations.[20] In this connection, moreover, the women were anxious to stress that it was the husband's assignment to apply for government aid, a chore they were happy to leave to him: "It wasn't me who would have gone — I would have starved to death before going to ask for home relief. ... He knew perfectly well that he was the man of the family — it was up to him to go see them. It wasn't up to me" (I19). In this very special circumstance, where it was a question of publicly admitting an inability to take care of his family, having breadwinner status was nothing to envy. The men who had this experience suffered a profound assault on their masculine dignity and came out of it feeling humiliated. Nevertheless, remitting aid to the head of the family left power relationships within the family intact. Those wives who were economically dependent on husbands who refused to shoulder their responsibility to provide for their families, perhaps because they drank or gambled for example, had to stand by while the resources necessary for their survival and that of their children were continually squandered: "The dole was given in the husband's name, not the wife's. So that meant that he went to collect it and if he spent it, then you had nothing. It happened a lot — he went to get the relief money and when he came home, he didn't have a penny left" (I22).[21]

The women who had engaged in one or several paid occupations at home before their husbands lost their jobs continued and even augmented their work as far as was possible.[22] But none of them imagined replacing the work they did in the home with an outside job, which, by their own admission, their husbands would never have stood for: "During the Depression, I took in sewing to bring in some money. I was a big help to my husband — he did the best he could and so did I," one of them remarked. But when she was asked if she had thought about looking for a paying job, she answered, "My husband would never have let me, not at all" (I22). Just like the men whose wives made no financial contribution to the household before they were unemployed, those who agreed to their wife's working at home for pay would never have put up with her finding a job outside the home. This reversal of roles would have been a direct threat to their superior position as man of the house and would have represented too stern a blow to their pride, which had already been sufficiently shaken by their failure to fulfil this role adequately.

Just as the wives did not attempt to take over their husbands' place as breadwinner, the men were not prompted to participate more fully in the housework because their unemployment gave them more time on their hands, even if they already were in the habit of doing certain chores, like going to the store or washing the floors. Undeniably, the majority of the women considered the house their domain and they themselves did not ask for any additional help. To ask for help was the same as admitting that they were not able to carry out their part of the husband-wife contract, and that would bring their own femininity into question: "We didn't ask them to help us — as far as we were concerned, it was our work. We said, 'We don't want to have them in our pots and pans.' We were the ones who looked after that" (I29). Many others agreed: "When you're married you each have your own job" (I7). Additionally, a number of these men spent most of their time outside the house. Some of them were employed for short periods on public works projects or were doing various kinds of odd jobs,[23] but others stayed away regularly, claiming to look for work. In this way, they could escape the "female" universe in which they had difficulty situating themselves and which could seem to threaten them — constant immersion in the world of women could be seen as yet another attack on their already shaky male identity, weakened as it was by their being out of work.[24] The women themselves preferred their husbands to get out of the house, as they found their unaccustomed presence rather annoying or even a bit abnormal, since men did not belong in the domestic space: "Oh, sometimes, I'd really get fed up. I used to think, this is not his place. A man's place is to go to work, not to hang around the house" (I19). Even if the wives sometimes expressed impatience at having their husbands underfoot, they rarely complained about it to them. Part of their wifely role was to maintain their husbands' morale and preserve their self-respect; they fulfilled this by not seeking to become the principal breadwinner and by avoiding reminding the men of their failure to provide properly for the family. Some of these women insisted that their husbands had also tried to cheer them up. It is certainly possible that some of these men had kept their feelings of insecurity or desperation to themselves in order to preserve their image as a protector able to cope with any situation. Still, one of the few men who did participate in part of the interview with his wife acknowledged that he had often cried in secret.

Making Ends Meet

According to a tradition that was deeply rooted in the working class in Québec as well as elsewhere, it was most often the wife who was responsible for managing the family budget. As several feminist historians have observed, giving over the pay envelope to the wife, far from representing a real delegation of power, allowed the men to avoid the trial of having to manage on insufficient wages (a reality that called their status as breadwinner into question) without having to go so far as to renounce the definite privileges which that status conveyed.[25] Most of the men in fact kept back a certain amount for their own expenses or expected that there would be something left over for them if they said they needed it. For their part, the women were explicitly aware that they were managing money earned by someone else and clearly felt that it was not theirs by right. Their economic dependence thus induced women to get by on the amount available without complaining about not having enough money, which in turn contributed to maintaining the myth that their husbands continued to be adequate providers.

Despite the additional amounts that women's paid work provided, their families' income was still generally very low because these extras most often added to only the lowest of wages. Making ends meet represented a daunting challenge confronting most of these women. To respond to it, they committed themselves to an extremely strict set of priorities to which they made every effort to conform, no matter what. At the top of the list came the irreducible expenses like electricity and rent, seen as "debts" that they made a point of honour to pay regularly. The remainder of the money went for food, for wood or coal for the stove, and, in last place, clothing, transportation, and insurance, if there were a few pennies left. Very few among them were able to save anything at all. Households that had succeeded in accumulating any savings had to nibble away at them before resigning themselves to signing on for the dole.

Checking prices, buying only what was strictly necessary, wasting nothing, and not going into debt were watchwords that recurred constantly in their oral testimonies: "I never wasted anything" (I1); "You had to really know not to buy anything you didn't need. We didn't waste a thing" (I26). What they got in return for this dedication was the most intense household labour, with a bare minimum of domestic appliances and in housing conditions that were often substandard. On their coal or wood stoves, which were also the only source of heat, they cooked every meal, from soup to dessert, not to mention pickles, jams, and jellies. Those who had learned how to sew made most of the clothing, at least for the children, often out of old clothes they altered to fit. Most of them sewed the household linen — sheets, tablecloths, dishcloths, bedspreads, and curtains. As well, most of these women had a sewing machine, if only to repair rips and tears. This purchase, more advantageous because it represented a source of savings, often came before a washing machine, and it seems that the majority delayed until the second or third child appeared before buying one of these. Despite the absence of this convenience, very few of the women patronized commercial laundries and none used their services on a regular basis. What this meant was that for some significant time almost all the women did the washing on a washboard in a laundry sink or bathtub, if there was one in the flat.

The amounts that the women could spend on rent, between twelve and eighteen dollars a month, restricted them to substandard accommodations, that is, to flats that were poorly lit, badly insulated, with softwood floors that were difficult to keep clean, and sometimes infested with rats and cock-roaches.[26] All these lodgings were connected to the municipal water mains and had electricity, but rarely were they supplied with gas; less than half of the women interviewed had always lived in quarters that were equipped with a bathtub and almost none of them could afford to buy or rent a hot-water heater. Their inadequate incomes often meant that these families had to make do with accommodations that were too small, even if it meant sac-rificing the living room in order to make an extra bedroom. Some of the chil-dren might have to sleep in the kitchen or in the hallway on a folding bed that was put up and taken down daily.

This brief sketch reveals that, for these women, managing the family expenses proved to be an almost obsessive concern, while housework repre-sented a trying, physically exhausting obligation that they had to carry out in difficult circumstances, without always having the household conveniences they needed to do it. Faced with the consequences of unemployment and shortened work weeks, they had very little room to manoeuvre, considering what they were already providing for their families. Indeed, their domestic production encompassed such a range of products and services that, when the Depression hit, it was difficult for them to add new tasks to those that they were already doing. But since they were already consuming no more than necessary, reductions in wages and, even more, the low level of state assistance obliged them to reduce their expenditures in vulnerable areas, which translated into an increase in and intensification of their workload and ever greater deprivation, which they were often the first to experience.

Buying the least possible was already one of the habitual consumer strate-gies of these housewives. Particularly when it came to food, however, they often found it hard to cut back on quantities. Therefore, the housewives sought new ways to economize by purchasing lower quality goods and by procuring their groceries in new ways. For instance, some of the women began to buy their meat directly from the abattoir rather than from the local grocery, which permitted them to obtain greater quantities at the same price though they had to travel longer distances to get there. It was also possible to get cut-price meat by buying it late on a Saturday evening, just before the stores closed;[27] a number of grocers who did not have refrigeration preferred to get rid of their stock rather than risk losing their merchandise by storing it until Monday morning. Some of the women would get fruits and vegeta-bles that were on sale or even being given away because they were wilted or beginning to rot, even if it meant taking a little more time to prepare them: "It was a lot of work to make them all right to eat. Sometimes they were starting to go. But if you picked out what was edible ..." (I5). Just one of the respondents tried several times to make bread, but, as she pointed out, it was a long and complicated process, not to mention that her inexperience made it more likely that there would be waste. It was cheaper to go directly to the bakery at the end of the day: "We would go there at four o'clock in the afternoon when the bread runs came back. We could fill up a whole pillowcase with bread for twenty-five cents. You'd see everybody there — I would see them on the corner, they all had a pillowcase folded up under their arm or some of them had bags ..." (I20).

Preparing the same amount of food with fewer means and from inferior quality products required a good pinch of ingenuity to create appetizing meals. Sausage, minced meat, spaghetti, and noodles appeared very often on the table, prepared in every imaginable way. Dishes in sauce, made with a base of flour and water, were also an economical solution, since they generally did not contain meat: "I made potatoes and white sauce, eggs and white sauce, beans and white sauce, and tinned salmon and white sauce. We ate a lot of paste!" (I25).[28] Desserts were skipped altogether or consisted of "broken biscuits" sold cheaply in bulk or made from recipes that did not ask for expensive ingredients, like the famous "pouding chômeur" (literally, unemployed pudding, poor man's pudding).

Despite all of these strategies, some of the informants and even their husbands simply had to deprive themselves of food so their children could eat: "I would make a stew, as we called it. ... I would make it out of spaghetti and whatever stuff was the cheapest and the most nourishing. But that doesn't mean we were well fed. ... All it meant is that we had something to eat and even then sometimes we had to leave it all for the children" (I27). One couple often made do with macaroni and butter and sugar spread on bread, while another informant admitted that she had often eaten sugared bread dampened under the faucet. Another explained, "We often ate mustard sandwiches ... before the next cheque would come. When we got to the last stretch, we had a little jar of mustard and a few slices of bread and we would say, we're going to have to be happy with that — what do you want, there isn't anything else. ... My mother-in-law would come and take my little girl. As long as I knew my little girl would have something to eat, it was all right, I knew we'd get by" (I19).

During spells of unemployment, buying clothing was the first thing to go. Women, whose wardrobes were already strictly limited, were the most likely to pass up new garments in favour of devoting whatever resources were available to clothing for their growing children or for their husbands who had to go out of the house more often. One of them recalled that during the

Depression she had only two dresses to her back: "I only had two dresses — wash the dress, iron the dress. Two days later — wash the dress, iron the dress. ... Me, who hates to iron!" (I26). Some respondents patronized the outlets run by the Salvation Army or St. Vincent de Paul, while others, who had never previously done any sewing, had to resign themselves to learning how: "That's when I learned to sew because I used to buy ready-made clothes for my kids in the beginning but later on, I couldn't. ... You had to make new clothes out of old ones. Everybody gave me clothes — I'd take them apart and make them up for the kids. I didn't have a machine — I'd go to my mother's to use hers" (I12).

Half of the families also moved, sometimes several times, into ever cheaper housing, which meant smaller, less comfortable, and less well-equipped accommodations.[29] Women were thus forced to give up what little comfort and convenience they had enjoyed. If the whole family suffered from the deterioration in their housing conditions, it was the women, for whom the house represented both their workplace and their living space, who were the most affected. For women, moving to new accommodations represented an increase in their work as well. Not only did they have to find the new flat and pack and unpack the family's belongings, but they also had to clean it from top to bottom and, if they had the money, repaint or repaper, run up new curtains, and the like.

The Depression likewise deprived a number of these women of their customary amenities, for a number of reasons. One of them, for example, did the laundry for several months in the bathtub because she did not have the money to get her machine fixed: "I had a wooden agitator with a handle in the side and the wringer was broken, which meant I had to do the wash in the bathtub. And it was only something that cost thirty-nine cents. I did the laundry for I think five or six months in the bathtub like that" (I27). Others avoided using their electrical appliances, especially the iron or the washing machine, in order to save on electricity. Those who had their lights cut off because of unpaid bills reported doing some of their chores in the evening, when they could reconnect illegally without worrying about inspectors from the company coming by, but this seriously complicated their housework schedule.[30] Finally, two of the women went back to live in the countryside because their husbands were not able to find jobs and could not reconcile themselves to going on the dole. Without electricity or running water, they had to give up their washing machines and other electric appliances and return to making a good number of items at home, like bread and soap, that they had previously bought. These two women had already experienced this kind of life, which made it easier for them to adapt to their new situation. All the same, it represented a net loss in the standard of their working conditions.

In short, even though these women were already doing practically everything they already could to balance their budgets and could only with great difficulty do more, the Depression nevertheless meant an increase in the burden of their household tasks, since they had to accomplish them with less money, less space, and fewer conveniences. Without any extra help from their husbands, they had to shoulder the additional labour occasioned by loss of income all by themselves and they were generally the first to leave the table hungry or to manage without decent clothing. The unequal distribution of resources within the home, already a present reality for these families before the Depression, was only heightened in the absence of a wage.[31]

Motherhood

More than other Canadians, Québécoises at the beginning of the century were the target of religious and medical pronouncements that exhorted them to have children in order to insure the future of the "race."[32] This pro-birth rhetoric, reinforced by legal prohibitions on birth-control devices and by the notion of "conjugal duty," which presumed the husband's unlimited and unconditional access to his wife's body, varied by not a single syllable during the Depression. For women starting their families in this period, the intransigence of the Church, which could impose individual control over their behaviour through the agency of the confessional, meant they had but two choices: they could either live in the perpetual anxiety of "getting caught" or employ "artificial contraception" and experience a profound sense of guilt.

From their wedding day, these women deeply desired to have a baby, since motherhood represented one of the fundamental elements of their feminine identity. As one of them said, "Life was having children" (I24). The daily responsibilities of taking care of them and raising them did, however, become a heavy load to carry, especially when money was short. Repeated pregnancies represented a considerable burden for women whose strength was being sapped at the same time that they had to undertake greater toil. If her husband lost his job, she would spend her pregnancy in conditions that were worse for her own health and that of the child she was carrying, as she would not be eating properly or receiving adequate medical supervision. From the strictly monetary point of view, the arrival of another child might turn out to be simply a catastrophe. The doctor's fees alone for a delivery amounted to at least ten dollars, an astronomical sum in view of the fact that this was the equivalent of a week's wages for the poorest worker. Then there would be another mouth to feed at a time when there wasn't enough money as it was. A birth represented such a drain on the family finances that *Assistance maternelle* of Montréal, a female philanthropy founded in 1912 with the aim of offering material aid and free medical care to poor mothers, was rapidly overwhelmed by the demand: whereas in the 1920s it helped an average of 800 women a year, in the 1930s it aided between 3,000 and 4,000 expectant mothers annually.[33]

After the birth of two or three children, a number of these women wished to space out their pregnancies and, despite the fulminations of the Church, fifteen of the couples[34] did indeed take steps to prevent conception. The economic situation certainly played a considerable role in their desire to limit the size of their families, but it should be noted that economic difficulties were not the only motivation underlying this decision and did not always lead to the use of contraception. In fact, if the majority of couples using birth control did rely on home relief for a greater or lesser period of time or suffered from cuts in income, the women also offered other reasons to justify their choice, like the workload involved in a large family and the desire to pay enough attention to each of the children and bring them up properly: "I told the good Lord to send me children, but that I did not want them to suffer afterwards. Large families always have problems. Someone is always overlooked in a big family, even if it isn't meant. ... I said, I'd rather have a small family and be able to give them what they need. It was their education that I was thinking about for later" (I16).

On the other hand, other couples, equally affected by serious financial problems, never imagined the possibility of limiting the size of their families. One of the women, who was pregnant sixteen times and bore eleven children although her husband rarely worked and drank up a portion of what he did earn, stated, "I thought that's the way it always was, since I came from a big family" (I22). Another said, "There wasn't anything, you never heard of anything that would prevent a baby. ... You'd often think, if I only had something. ... Some had ways that they talked about, but I only learned about them later" (I3), while a third woman maintained, "Birth control was out of the question. It was the law of the Church. You had to have babies" (I29).

Ignorance of contraceptive practices and the internalization of religious values could therefore lead to an almost fatalistic acceptance of successive pregnancies, despite precarious economic circumstances. But more often than not, it was those couples whose relationships were the most hierarchical, where the husband's authority was the most heavily felt, and where all discussion between husband and wife was absent who were the least likely to control their fertility. In view of the contraceptive means available — condom, withdrawal, and the rhythm method[35] — the women could not manage without the agreement and cooperation of their husbands. It was the men who had all the freedom to decide how and how often sexual relations would take place and they could easily decide not to worry about any possible consequences. Women who had not sought to limit their families and who were confronted with particularly trying economic conditions spent their pregnancies in anxiety and dread lest they not be able to provide sufficiently for their babies: "He was working up until 1933. ... After that there wasn't any more construction. And the little ones kept coming every year. That was really hard. They have to eat, eh? But when the man isn't working ..." (I12).

On the other hand, given the religious climate of the period, women who did turn to contraception had guilt and reproach to deal with. Even when they were convinced of the logic of their decision, most of the women who limited the size of their families felt they were in the wrong in breaking the rules of the Church and continued to confess their sin, at the risk of being refused absolution, something that happened to more than one of them: "Oh, yes, madame, I was refused absolution, yes, indeed, that happened to me. I didn't repent because I was using my head. In my opinion, the priests were there to inform us, but they weren't there to raise our kids. And in those days, it wasn't easy. ... You know, women always felt guilty because in those days ... when you went to the retreat ... we had one evening in the week about it, you were going to go straight to hell. ... When you came away, you were shook up, let me tell you" (I16). Even if it was the men who actually employed the contraceptive, it was the women who were condemned by the Church. Men seemed to have a much more elastic conscience and, in order to be left in peace, did not hesitate simply to hide the facts from their confessor. One husband recommended that, if his wife wanted absolution, she not tell "what we do in our own bed" (I6). Another felt fully justified in limiting the size of his family in the light of his income: "My husband said, I'm the one who earns the money. It doesn't make sense to live like the animals, neither better or worse" (I5). Used to enjoying a large measure of autonomy and to exercising both their free will and their authority, men easily convinced themselves that they were well within their rights, especially as their earning capacity was objectively demonstrable.

For women, more children certainly meant more work, more worries, and greater risks to their own health, but the Church and patriarchal society had taught them that their needs and even their lives counted for little in the scheme of things: "It was cruel when you went to confession. It was not a small thing to say that you had used birth control. ... The priests would scold us. ... We would tell them, 'The doctor said that I mustn't have any more children.' They didn't care — the baby would live even if the mother died. That's all they had to say to us. It wasn't right" (I5). Whether or not these couples used contraception, their histories reveal that motherhood for these women represented more a source of anxiety than of joy.

Help From the Family

Even with increased household production and a decision to limit the number of children, most of these families, especially those who lived for a number of years on the dole, could not have coped without the support of their relatives. Mutual aid within families did not of course occur simply in times of economic crisis; rather, it was a common occurrence necessitated by poverty.[36] But what stands out in the histories is the differences in the help provided depending on economic circumstances. In ordinary times, for example, services most commonly rendered would include baby-sitting during a lying-in or an illness, and the exchanging or giving of clothing, but we can also observe the very frequent practice of sharing certain implements of work, like a sewing or washing machine or the use of the telephone. The tendency of relatives to settle in the same neighbourhood or even in the same street facilitated these exchanges.

An effect of the Depression was the enlargement of the range of services rendered by relatives. Gifts of meals or foodstuffs and fuel increased, as did gifts and loans of money and of shelter for the young couple: "Oh, they helped me a lot because they brought me lots of vegetables from the country. I had a sister who was married to a farmer and that meant she could bring me lots of vegetables. ... We would go over to my mother's, sometimes for weeks at a time. ... If we didn't go, she'd send someone over to us. ... She'd say, 'Come over, I want some company. ...' Then I'd do a lot of little things while we were there ... like sewing, knitting. I made a lot of things when I was at my mother's. ... We were lucky to always have my mother-in-law. ... If we didn't have enough to eat, we would go and eat at her house, and that was that. ... My mother-in-law would come for my little girl. ... Sometimes she'd keep her for three or four days" (I19).

All these kinds of help obviously went beyond the framework of customary exchanges, and some of the women who benefitted from them felt decidedly dependent on their families: "It was my mother who had me under her wing. Mama would send over food to eat — we didn't have anything to eat — he was out of work" (I27). Another remarked, "I didn't like it very much. If I had been on my own, that's OK, but there was my husband and my little boy ..." (I9). Even if it came from very close relatives, these women still felt as humiliated to be on the receiving end of this sort of assistance — which exposed not merely their extreme poverty but also their husband's failure to provide for his family's needs — as they did to turn to the state for aid, something which the majority of couples viewed only as a last, and shameful, resort.[37] The ideal of financial autonomy, a measure of respectability, was a value so deeply rooted in the majority of these couples that one of them even hid the fact that they were on the dole from those closest to him.

This case is, however, exceptional. In fact, more often than not, the immediate family played an essential role in supporting those of its members who were afflicted with unemployment. In theory, the state granted aid only to those without work who absolutely lacked any resources and who could not turn to their families for help. In practice, families contributed in many ways to supply those needs that the meagre relief allowances granted to the unemployed could not provide for, especially in regard to clothing, food, and shelter. The amounts dispensed as aid were so inadequate that any hope of surviving on them, not, at least, without going seriously into debt, was an illusion. After having exhausted their own resources and every tactic for cutting down on their spending, these couples then turned to their own families. The Depression thus intensified the importance of the traditional networks of mutual aid that depended on the commitment of women relations. The contribution made by the work of female relatives, most particularly mothers and mothers-in-law, was just as essential as governmental aid to maintaining a minimum standard of living for the families who were helped. In short, it was all of these women, and not merely those wives whose husbands were out of work, who bore the brunt of the effects of the Depression.

Conclusion

Unlike their masculine counterparts, working-class women were not unemployed during the 1930s as their families counted more than ever on their labour, their dedication, their self-sacrifice, and their ingenuity in order to survive. Of course the contribution they made to supporting the family did not prevent a decline in the standard of living of their households, but the domestic labour of the wives of unemployed men, together with that of the women of the extended family and state welfare payments, meant the difference between poverty and abject destitution and made it possible to cope with material conditions of existence that would otherwise have been viewed as intolerable. In fact, women's private welfare efforts represented an essential complement to meagre public assistance. Women thus acted as an important social stabilizing factor during this troubled period in Canadian history, even though the women themselves were not considered full-fledged citizens. Montreal housewives of the 1930s held only partial political citizenship since they did not have the right to vote in provincial elections. Unlike other Canadian women, they were still deprived of their societal rights by reason of their maternal function, whereas the Bill concerning needy mothers would not be finally adopted until 1937. Both the Church and the criminal code prohibited them, at least in theory, from controlling their reproduction. According to the civil code, they were subject to the authority of the head of the house and excluded in fact, if not in law, from the job market. They were thus denied full legal competence, self-determination, and economic independence, the bases of male citizenship. Seen as dependent on a male provider, it was only thus that women had access to state support, because, except for rare exceptions, they could not claim the role of head of the family on which rested the social rights that were conferred on men at the beginning of the Depression. Established as a way of preserving the patriarchal structure of both society and the family order, the economic dependence of women, which was at the core of their non-citizenship, nevertheless camouflaged the interdependence of the family and of society on the work they did, which was unpaid and disregarded. Hidden from the eyes of their contemporaries and from history, their domestic endeavours were crucial all the same to softening the impact of the Depression on the family structure. In the end, it is probably no accident that social protest arose primarily among young single men with no family connections.

Notes

1. Terry Copp, "The Montreal Working-class in Prosperity and Depression," *Canadian Issues 1* (1975): 8.
2. See Andrée Lévesque, *Virage à gauche interdit. Les communistes, les socialistes et leurs ennemis au Québec, 1929-1939* (Montréal: Boréal, 1984) for an appraisal of social conflict in Québec and especially in Montréal.
3. Copp, "The Montreal Working-class," 8.
4. Bettina Bradbury, *Working Families: Age, Gender and Daily Survival in Industrializing Montreal* (Toronto: McClelland & Stewart, 1993).
5. The scale of allowances fixed by the city of Montréal was set at $36.88 a month in summer and $39.48 in winter, the amounts allotted to cover the costs of food, fuel, rent, and clothing for five persons. These sums constituted barely half the minimum considered necessary by the federal Minister of Labour. See Leonard C. Marsh, *Canadians In and Out of*

Work: A Survey of Economic Classes and Their Relations to the Labor Market (Toronto: Oxford University Press, 1940), 193.

6. Ruth Roach Pierson, "Gender and the Unemployment Debate in Canada, 1930-1940," *Labour/Le Travail* 25 (1990): 77-105; Margaret Hobbs, "Rethinking Antifeminism in the 1930s: Gender Crisis or Workplace Justice? A Response to Alice Kessler-Harris," *Gender and History* 5, 1 (1993): 4-15; Cynthia R. Comacchio, *The Infinite Bonds of Family: Domesticity in Canada, 1840-1950* (Toronto: University of Toronto Press, 1999), 124.

7. This was the case except in certain narrowly-defined circumstances. On the topic of aid programs adopted during the Depression, see James Struthers, *No Fault of Their Own: Unemployment and the Canadian Welfare State 1914-1941* (Toronto: University of Toronto Press, 1983).

8. In its report for 1935, the Society for the Protection of Women and Children of Montréal stated: "During the past five years, 'failure to provide' and its companion offence 'desertion' by the male parent has progressively and markedly decreased." The report attributed this decrease (of 33%) to the lack of work and to the distribution of welfare that kept families together. In contrast, in 1946, the same association recorded an increase of 48% in cases of desertion and failure to provide in comparison with the preceding year and concluded: "We can look for an upswing in these figures, because it has always been our experience, proved by records, that with the return of economic prosperity, desertions, the number of which always tapers off in periods of financial depression, increase markedly." (ANC, MG28I129, Society for the Protection of Women and Children 2 Minutes and 6 Minutes, 1947-1950).

9. On women as citizens and the specific mode of their integration into the state, see Carole Pateman, "The Patriarchal Welfare State," in *Feminism: The Public and the Private*, ed. Joan B. Landes (Oxford and New York: Oxford University Press, 1998), 241-76 and Sylvia Walby, "Is Citizenship Gendered?" *Sociology* 28 (1994): 379-95.

10. Denyse Baillargeon, *Making Do: Women, Family, and Home in Montreal During the Great Depression*, trans. Yvonne Klein (Waterloo, ON: Wilfrid Laurier University Press, 1999).

11. For summary biographies of these women, see Baillargeon, *Making Do*.

12. Thirteen married between 1919 and 1928, five in 1929, ten between 1930 and 1932, and two in 1933 and 1934. Twenty-six of the spouses were either manual or non-manual workers. One was unemployed at the time of his marriage and had rarely had a job, while the three remaining owned small businesses (a barber shop, a snack bar, two taxi cabs). We must make it very clear that the status of owner did not mean that they enjoyed a standard of living necessarily higher than that of those working for others, since the Depression forced two of them to sell up before bankruptcy. Of the other twenty-six, only four neither lost work nor suffered from salary cuts during the period. Four had their work week shortened by one or more days and three others, though working the same hours, had their wages cut by as much as 20%. Seven were without a steady job for more than three years, six for a period of between one and two years, and the remaining one for only a few months. Two other participants in the survey had to turn to the St. Vincent de Paul Society for help or to home relief because their husbands refused to support them. In all, fifteen of the couples received assistance of some sort and two chose to go back to the land as a way to cope.

13. The quotation is taken from interview number 23. Hereafter, references to interviews will be indicated by an upper-case I followed by the interview number.

14. Only three of them looked for a way to make money specifically because their husbands were partly or wholly out of work. Veronica Strong-Boag likewise notes that married English Canadian women often had to earn money to make up for the shortfall of the principal breadwinner in the period between the two world wars. "The incorporation of paid work into domestic routines appeared relatively commonplace in both the 1920's and 1930's, a good index of how tough times were not restricted to the Great Depression" [Veronica Strong-Boag, *The New Day Recalled: Lives of Girls and Women in English Canada, 1919-1939* (Toronto: Copp Clark Pitman, 1988), 125].

15. Québec, *Annuaire statistique*, 1930 and 1934, 400 and 426; Canada, ministère du Travail, *La Gazette du Travail*, février 1933, 249.

16. The women who did work outside the home had a maximum of two children and someone other than the husband took care of them, even when he had the free time to do it.

17. On this topic, see Hobbs, "Rethinking Antifeminism in the 1930s."

18. In fact, this informant had taught for a year before getting married, but she did not seem to consider this a real job.

19. On the impossibility of reversing roles during the Depression, see Mirra Komarovsky, *The Unemployed Man and His Family* (New York: Arno, 1971) and Ruth Milkman, "Women's Work and Economic Crisis: Some Lessons of the Great Depression," *Review of Radical Political Economics* 8 (1976): 85.

20. Hobbs, "Rethinking Antifeminism in the 1930s," 9.

21. In fact, article 23 of the Montreal Unemployment Commission regulations stipulated that "If the husband drinks or gambles away his aid cheque, then the registrar should immediately be informed. He will see to it a new registration is made in the spouse's name or that of another responsible person or Society that can replace the head of the family...." This article does not seem to have been widely circulated, and, in any event, in order to get benefits paid in her own name, this woman would have had to challenge openly her husband's prerogatives and authority, something which seemed impossible to her [Montréal, Commission du chômage, *Renseignements à l'usage des chômeurs nécessiteux et des propriétaires* (Montréal: n.p., n.d.), 6].

22. Which it was not always. During hard times, even professional dressmakers lost some of their private clientele, for example.

23. Before turning to the state for aid, or even while on the dole, six of the men tried hard to support their families by undertaking various sorts of work. Digging out a cellar with a shovel, washing walls and ceilings, shovelling snow in the fashionable districts of the city, reselling breads and cakes bought directly from a commercial bakery at the end of the day when the unsold merchandise was returned, peddling the remainders of blocks of ice or bootlegging alcohol which the man made in his shed (and hid in the baby carriage for delivery!), and opening a little "restaurant" at home were some of the notable stopgaps to which the men, newly unemployed, turned in order to find new sources of income.

24. Hobbs, "Rethinking Antifeminism in the 1930s," 8.

25. Meg Luxton, *More Than a Labour of Love: Three Generations of Women's Work in the Home* (Toronto: The Women's Press, 1980), 161-99; Strong-Boag, *New Day*, 133-44; Elizabeth Roberts, *A Woman's Place: An Oral History of Working-Class Women, 1850-1940* (Oxford: Basil Blackwell, 1984), 125-68; Pat Ayers and Jan Lambertz, "Marriage Relations, Money, and Domestic Violence in Working-Class Liverpool 1919-39," in *Labour and Love: Women's Experience of Home and Family, 1840-1940*, ed. Jane Lewis (Oxford: Basil Blackwell, 1986), 195-219.

26. An equipped six-room flat cost from twenty-five to forty dollars a month in January 1929 and from eighteen to thirty-three dollars in January 1933. A six-room flat without modern conveniences, or only partially equipped, cost between sixteen and twenty-five dollars a month in 1929 and between fifteen and eighteen dollars in 1933 (Canada, ministère du Travail, *La Gazette du Travail*, février 1929, 256 and février 1933, 257).

27. In this period, most shops stayed open until 11:00 on Saturday night.

28. White sauce was made of water and flour, also used to make wallpaper paste.

29. The number of removals in Montréal was in fact on the rise throughout the initial years of the Depression: 54,000 in 1930, 55,000 in 1931, 65,000 in 1932, and almost 82,000 in 1933, according to figures supplied by Montreal Light, Heat and Power (*La Patrie* 17 avril 1931, 3 and 17 avril 1933, 3). Moreover, the economic situation meant that the majority of families were looking for low-cost housing. This is why the best flats remained vacant while there was overpopulation in older housing. In this connection, see Marc Choko, *Les crises du logement à Montréal* (Montréal: Éditions Saint-Martin, 1980), 109. I must mention, however, that two of the couples in the study were able to buy property thanks to the rock-bottom prices of certain houses that were being sold for back taxes. On the other hand, a third couple, who had bought a house due to a little inheritance just before the Depression hit, were forced out of it when their unemployed tenants could not pay the rent. In fact, it appears that the Depression more often generated the sort of situation that discouraged

property buying, since only 11.5% were homeowners in 1941 compared with 15% ten years earlier (Canada, *Recensement du Canada, 1931 and 1941,* V, 989 and XI, 98, cited in Choko, *Les crises du logement à Montréal,* 114).

30. It should be recalled that Montreal Light, Heat and Power enjoyed a virtual monopoly in the Montréal region, which permitted it to maintain high rates and to disconnect with impunity clients who failed to pay their bills. According to Robert Rumilly, more than 20,000 families were cut off from electricity in the depths of the Depression [cited in Claude Larivière, *Crise économique et contrôle social: le cas de Montréal, 1929-1937* (Montréal: Éditions Saint-Martin, 1977), 175].

31. The unequal distribution of resources in poor households has been noted on numerous occasions by feminist historians and sociologists. In this regard, see the works listed in note 25 as well as Ruth Lister, "Women, Economic Dependency and Citizenship," *Journal of Social Policy* 19, 4 (1990): 445-67.

32. There have been a number of studies of this discourse. See Andrée Lévesque, *La norme et les déviantes. Des femmes au Québec pendant l'entre-deux-guerres* (Montréal: Éditions du Remue-ménage, 1989).

33. *Assistance maternelle* provided a layette, bed linen, food, and fuel, and sometimes even furniture. It also paid for the costs of the delivery and for a month's supply of milk following the birth [Denyse Baillargeon, "L'Assistance maternelle de Montréal: Un exemple de marginalisation des bénévoles dans le domaine des soins aux accouchées," *Dynamis, International Journal of History of Science and Medicine,* Special number, *Mujeres y salud. Prácticas y saberes/Women and Health* 19 (1999): 379-400].

34. That is, a little over half the fertile couples, as two of the thirty in the study had no children.

35. Three of the couples using contraception employed condoms, eight engaged in withdrawal, and four used the rhythm method ("Ogino-Knauss"). The first two methods seem to have been the most frequently employed throughout Canada [Angus McLaren and Arlene Tigar McLaren, *The Bedroom and the State: The Changing Practices and Politics of Contraception and Abortion in Canada, 1880-1980* (Toronto: McClelland and Stewart, 1986), 22].

36. In this connection, see Andrée Fortin, *Histoires de familles et de réseaux. La sociabilité au Québec d'hier à demain* (Montréal: Éditions Saint-Martin, 1987); Marc-Adélard Tremblay, "La crise économique des années trente et la qualité de vie chez les montréalais d'ascendance française," Académie des sciences morales et politiques, *Travaux et Communications 3, Progrès Techniques et qualité de vie* (Montréal: Bellarmin, 1977): 149-65.

37. Recent studies reveal similar attitudes. See Lister, "Women, Economic Dependency and Citizenship."

chapter nine

TIME, SWIMMING POOLS, AND CITIZENSHIP
The Emergence of Leisure Rights in Mid-Twentieth-Century Canada

Shirley Tillotson

Most of Canada's provincial governments began in the 1930s to put into law a new understanding of leisure as a universal citizen right. First came legislation that redefined the normal hours of paid work, then provincial acts providing for annual holidays. With the national standards set in the *Canada Labour Code* in 1965, the process was largely complete. This body of employment law, which was also in effect "leisure law," arose from social science research and labour activism, as well as from the electoral calculations of politicians and from responses to market forces. A related development that shared most of these origins was the creation in the 1930s, 1940s, and 1950s of provincial public recreation services. In these two dimensions of state involvement in leisure, both new rights to leisure and new obligations in its use took shape.

In this chapter, I trace this history by examining, in sequence, the origins of leisure law and both the origins and the implementation of public recreation programs. I will argue that, in this story, we can see the interplay of both liberal and democratic ideas of citizenship in mid-twentieth-century Canada, and the increasing influence of democratic ideology in public culture. Both the liberal and democratic traditions include a notion of universal citizen rights.[1] The distinctive feature of liberal citizenship, however, is that the individual is the bearer of rights. By contrast, democratic ideas of citizenship are defined by the notion that the state must be responsible to "the people," defined more or less inclusively and collectively. As critics of the liberal tradition have argued, it is quite possible, in liberal terms, for whole categories of people in a society to be non-citizens if they are deemed not to meet the standard that defines individuality. In other words, if they are different from the canonical individual of the liberal tradition, their difference disqualifies them from citizen status. In these terms, so-called "universal" citizen rights may be held by only a minority of the population. The democratic tradition counts as citizens those to whom the state owes a duty of service and accountability, accomplished by one means or another. In the West, this tradition intermingles historically not only with liberalism, but also variously with republicanism or socialism. In relation to liberalism, its most common partner in twentieth-century Canada, democratic ideology weighs in favour of enlarging the scope of citizenship and against the exclusions that liberalism entails. The influence of democratic ideas is apparent when the practices of public life work to reduce the significance of the differences that, in liberal terms, demarcate the citizen from the non-citizen.

In the history of leisure rights, I will suggest, those differences included class, gender, and race, but also (and less commonly recognized) rurality, and the pattern of change over the period I discuss (1930 to 1965) is that public policy reflected less and less the use of these grounds to limit or confer leisure rights. The key concept underpinning this change was the emergence of a right to health, understood as being both individual and social. The notion of a right to health formed a point of contact between liberal and democratic conceptions of leisure rights and a basis for consensus. Ideals of social health — democratically inclusive standards of citizen responsibility, entitlement, and participation — were crucial in warranting governments to guarantee leisure time for an increasing proportion of paid workers and, by the end of the period, to provide services for the use of leisure time for unpaid as well as paid workers, women as well as men, and rural as well as urban folk. Only race, or racialized identities, persisted as a category of exclusion in the public dimensions of leisure, in part because members of some communities were prevented from assuming or were unwilling to assume a sufficiently individualized form of citizenship.

Hours of Work

In the twentieth century, the international debates about the need for leisure time and services began by addressing the length of the working day and the length of the week and moved later to the provision of vacations with pay and public recreation facilities. Evidence had been accumulating since the 1890s that reducing industrial workers' daily shifts from 12 hours to 10 or even from nine hours to eight actually increased daily output. In Salford, England, in Jena, Germany, and in Liège, France, modern social science experiments recorded results that, by the 1920s, literally became textbook cases of the productivity benefits of shorter days. Perhaps the most widely publicized exercise based in this new model of labour was the British government's reduction of munitions workers' hours in World War I. In the desperate context of war production, where 12-hour shifts could certainly have been imposed, the introduction of the shorter, 10-hour shift showed how persuasive was the case that workers with more leisure could make more shells. Shorter hours meant workers with better health and greater alertness, less time lost to illness and injury, and employees willing to work at a higher level of intensity.[2]

In the United States, studies by the National Industrial Conference Board on American war industries confirmed these results and provided part of the evidence that economists drew upon to argue, throughout the 1920s, that long hours did not pay.[3] Although socialist elements in labour and reform contended, outside the efficiency discourse, that long hours limited wage earners' political freedoms and stunted their family lives, they shared with progressive management experts and more conservative unionists the aim of preserving or improving workers' health.[4] In 1919, the salience of the shorter hours issue was clearly indicated when it headed the list of urgent, necessary improvements in the "Labour" section of the Treaty of Versailles. And, correspondingly, the first Convention adopted by the International Labour Organization (ILO), which was formed by that treaty, was one that declared an eight-hour day and a six-day week to be an international standard for conditions of industrial work.[5]

The 1930s saw the Canadian parliament take up the question of shorter hours, responding, as did US governments, to concerns about unemployment. In 1935, the House of Commons debated an *Eight Hours Bill*, which was part of the package of social welfare legislation known as R.B. Bennett's "New Deal." It shared the fate of the entire package when, after the defeat of Bennett's Conservatives by Mackenzie King's Liberals in the autumn of 1935, it was referred to the Supreme Court and was found to exceed the constitutional jurisdiction of the Dominion parliament. Provincial governments had already begun to legislate in this area and were increasingly doing so in the 1930s (see Table 9.1). While a full understanding of the forces that produced hours of work laws would require a close examination of the nine diverse provincial cases, the debate over the federal law provides a means to see an array of the views about work, leisure, and citizen rights that were current in the policy context of the 1930s.

table 9.1 • Chronology Of The Introduction Of Employment Law With Respect To Paid Vacations And Limits On Hours Of Work, 1916-1970

(*The textual footnotes provide brief, general descriptions of the provisions in the first statute in each jurisdiction.*)

YEAR	JURISDICTION	HOURS OF WORK	ANNUAL VACATIONS WITH PAY
1916	Man.	Fair Wage Act[a]	
1933	Quebec	Limiting of Working Hours Act[b]	
1934	B.C.	Hours of Work Act[c]	
1935	N.S.	Limitation of Hours of Labour Act[a]	
1936	Alberta	Hours of Work Act[d]	
1937	Sask.	Industrial Standards Act[a]	
1938	N.B.	Industrial Relations Act[a]	
1943	Alberta		Labour Welfare Act[a]
1944	Sask.		Annual Holidays Act[e]
1944	Ontario		Hours of Labour — Holidays with Pay Act[f]
1946	B.C.		Annual Holidays Act[g]
1946	Quebec		Minimum Wage Act[h]
1947	Nfld.	Labour (Minimum Wage) Act[a]	
1954	N.B.		Vacation Pay Act[i]
1958	Canada		Annual Vacations with Pay Act[j]
1958	N.S.		Vacation Pay Act[h]
1965	Canada	Canada Labour Code[k]	Canada Labour Code[e]
1967	PEI		Vacations with Pay Act[g]
1969	Nfld.		Annual Vacations with Pay Act[e]
1970	PEI	Labour Act[l]	

Sources: Canada, Department of Labour, Legislative Branch, *Provincial Labour Standards* and *Labour Standards in Canada*, various years; *Newfoundland Statutes*, 1947, c.31.

Notes:

a. Rulings by boards of adjustment or similar bodies, permissive, industry by industry.

b. No maximum hours per week, minimum hours are 33 hours/week in a six-day week, maximums set by industry through regulations to the Act.

c. Six-day week.

d. Female maximum eight hours/six days, male maximum nine hours/six days.

e. Two weeks' paid holidays per year.

f. Eight hours/day, 48 hours/week maximum and one week's paid holiday per year.

g. One week's paid holiday per year.

h. One week's paid holiday per year after one year's continuous service with one employer.

i. Uses a stamp system and applies only to workers in construction and mining.

j. For employees subject to federal labour jurisdiction: one week's paid holiday per year after one year, two weeks after two years.

k. For employees subject to federal labour jurisdiction: eight hours/day, 40 hours/week, maximum of eight hours' overtime.

l. Minimum wage section introduces a definition of overtime that applies to both male and female workers (48 hours/week) in some occupations with exemptions for seasonal workers and different standards for women and men. This statute replaced the female-only minimum wage legislation passed in 1961.

The parliament that debated the *Eight Hours Bill* in March 1935 was a remarkably diverse one ideologically. It included the usual array of wealthy lawyers and other conservative opponents of regulation.[6] As well, there were spokesmen for a kind of rural conservatism, who spoke, not for the free hand of the market, but for protection of traditional rural industries.[7] The parliament's advocates of social change and government intervention included the vestiges of the National Progressive party, MPs such as agrarian populists Agnes MacPhail and E.J. Garland. Affording their distinctive brands of principled eloquence were socialists Angus MacInnis and J.S. Woodsworth. They had an odd ally in a Toronto ex-mayor, T.L. Church, whom Kenneth McNaught labels a "Tory democrat."[8] Playing an especially prominent part in the Eight Hours debate was craft unionist Humphrey Mitchell, who had been elected as an independent in Hamilton East in 1930 and who was destined to become a King Liberal and minister of labour during World War II.[9] The 17th Parliament represented the mainstream of Canadian political ideology at one of its broader moments.

Four themes in the parliamentary debate illuminate the conceptions of work, leisure, and citizenship current in this formative period of Canada's national welfare state. Together these themes point to the relentlessly utilitarian ways in which leisure appeared as a public issue. The first theme is the absence in the 1935 debate of positive assertions of leisure's intrinsic value. The central issue for this debate was not whether workers deserved more leisure, but rather whether setting maximum hours of work would serve to distribute more widely the fewer hours of paid employment that the depressed economy was generating.[10] The unemployment crisis was the occasion for the crafting of this bill, and questions of whether the bill was adequate, or necessary at all, or sufficiently inclusive of all classes of workers all touched on its capacity to distribute work equitably. Some of the parliamentarians claimed that the eight-hour day already existed for most employees and that therefore the bill would create no new work. The socialists agreed and called for a six-hour maximum so as to create new jobs. MPs with links to the steel industry acknowledged that an eight-hour maximum would require blast furnace operations to be staffed with three shifts rather than the normal two, 12-hour ones. They did not dispute the bill's potential for job creation, but they did not care for having to increase their payrolls. The Minister of Labour claimed that (approximately) 35 per cent of some undefined category of workers would be "affected," although he was careful not to make concrete claims about job creation.[11]

In all of this, the arguments that had been made by the shorter-hours movements of the eighteenth and nineteenth centuries (with their republican and socialist roots) were missing. No one seemed to think that it was pertinent to say that workers needed leisure time so as to be active in clubs and unions and political parties.[12] Sharing work, not enlarging leisure, was the point. Agnes MacPhail's remark that she, herself, was "lazy" enough to wish for a four-hour day rather than the MP's more usual 14-hour one, was only partially in jest.[13] The notion of leisure as laziness was implicated in the debate's earnest focus on a fairer distribution of the burden of "enforced leisure" — unemployment — by a redistribution of the hours of work.[14] In this context, the right to work, not the right to enjoy leisure, was the element of citizenship at issue.

A second theme of the debate indicates, not just disregard of the right to leisure, but even, in some quarters, active resistance to it. Many of the participants in the debate spoke on behalf of rural manufacturing industries — sawmilling, fruit and vegetable processing, fish canneries, cheese factories, and creameries. They spoke of how schedules of work were set by weather, by tides, by water levels, by the workings of bacteria. They mistrusted the Labour Minister's assurances that their constituents in these industries would be allowed to employ labour in shifts set, not by the clock of modern industrial time, but by the demands of the task. Their remarks show that the pattern of leisure time that the *Eight Hours Bill* was meant to guarantee was foreign to rural Canada.

To be sure, the unrelenting work of a farm family's struggle to survive was deplored as a disadvantage of rural life, implying that some greater access to leisure was considered desirable. But the rural perception that work schedules were set by nature was an article of common sense, not easily shaken. When J.S. Woodsworth suggested that farm workers might one day have eight-hour shifts, if farm commodity prices were higher, he earned only derision, even from his ally, MacPhail. She suggested that farmers and their wives might enjoy more leisure over a lifetime if "everyone" were granted pensions at age 60, but otherwise, she indicated, farmers had no interest in shorter hours.[15]

In the third and fourth themes of the debate, however, the outlines of a case for a positive right to leisure began to be visible. These intertwined themes were the humanitarian significance of shorter hours and the importance of fairness in regulating hours of work. The preamble of the *Eight Hours Bill* referred to the language of the Treaty of Versailles, which committed its signatories to attempt to ensure "fair and humane conditions of labour for men, women, and children." The treaty and the bill further specified "the supreme importance" of the "physical, moral and intellectual well-being" of "industrial wage-earners."[16] But because the International Labour Organization had left to signatories the task of determining where to locate

the boundaries between industrial, commercial, and agricultural labour, parliamentarians had plenty of room to debate which workers should be covered by the bill, and, in the process, to articulate what kinds of humanitarian benefits were conferred by leisure and what fairness meant.

One of the main categories of labour discussed in the debate was hotel
and restaurant workers. When Humphrey Mitchell argued that the employment of these workers should be regulated by the bill, he was urging a standard of fairness among employers and, as a related humanitarian benefit, the
preservation of a culturally defined standard of living. A revealing exchange
on these themes took place between Mitchell and Wilson Mills, a Liberal and
a farmer. Mills defended the need for long hours, saying that employers of
"white labour" had to exact these hours to compete with restaurants run by
"Chinese." Mitchell's retort was a logically and factually flawed racist one,
but one clearly meant to appeal to common cultural touchstones: our civilization (the western) is a better one than China's, as is evident by our greater
prosperity, he said; we have achieved that prosperity without accepting their
lower labour standards; their lower standards give them an unfair competitive advantage; and so we need labour legislation to deprive them of their
competitive advantage. For white restaurant owners to "take boys off the
farm and make them work twelve hours a day for $9 a week" was thus a
sign that unfair competition had forced white employers into exploitive practices like those of the "foreigner."[17] The state had to legislate protections for
men's leisure time, as it already had for some women workers, so as to protect the standards of western civilization. In the language of "civilizations" on
which Mitchell drew, British civilization was often identified with the
Greeks, where "Greek civilization" implied a belief that leisure was both the
condition for and a concomitant of health and citizenship.[18]

Other arguments that were offered on the inclusiveness question illumi-
nated a consensus between employers and workers on a key humanitarian
benefit: physical health. Independent member Allan Neill took a leading role
in arguing for the exemption of fish plants from the regulation of hours. In
making his argument that these plants were an exception to the rule, he first
established his credibility by showing that he understood the reasonable arguments for the bill. He had seen British Columbia's eight-hours law in operation, and he understood its benefits. Employers had had to hire more workers, to be sure, but they "get more work in shorter hours," as well as better
work and fewer accidents.[19] Similarly, when Nova Scotian steel manufacturer
Thomas Cantley conceded the benefits of shorter hours, he pointed to lower
accident rates and associated productivity improvements. And when he
nonetheless insisted that his industry needed 12-hour shifts, he claimed that

automation had made the steelworker's job little more than machine tending, so that in even a long shift there was "practically nothing to do." These shifts, moreover, took place in "scrupulously clean, bright, and comfortable" rooms, so that the work was, he implied, really not much of a strain.[20]

Although both Neill and Cantley had reasons to oppose the bill, their way of presenting their case showed that the contribution that shorter hours made to workers' health had become a point of common sense. E.J. Garland also relied on this consensus when he argued for the inclusion of restaurant and hotel workers. Because they were often young people, he said, they should work shorter hours so that their health would not be harmed at their start in life.[21] When these ideologically diverse parliamentarians linked shorter hours, efficiency, and health, they spoke in terms that were also used in labour circles.[22] This robust consensus around the association of health, leisure, and efficiency would ground the right to leisure, described as a measure of civilization and the good life, when this right was later explicitly asserted in the 1940s and 1950s.

Finally, the debate about the scope of the bill raised the question of fairness among workers. If some workers were entitled to relief from long hours, why not all? In other words, was leisure truly a universal citizen right? MacPhail drew a verbal picture of the pitiable farm family, barely surviving by dint of constant toil, and warned that shortening urban workers' hours would only heighten the existing "disequilibrium between the country and the city." If the government was going to "care for the health and welfare of the people," as T.L. Church declared it should, then MacPhail wanted the means adopted to be ones that served all of the people.[23] MacInnis's response to the farmer arguments was to deliver a sermon on the social nature of production and distribution, to exhort farmers to remember that they shared in a common economy and to realize that bettering conditions for the urban worker would also benefit country people.[24]

From a more straightforward egalitarian position, Humphrey Mitchell spoke to the disparity between the working conditions of unorganized workers and union members. For him, government's role in legislating maximum hours was to protect those, such as restaurant and hotel workers, who (he thought) were very likely unorganizable, but who deserved the same basic rights as the organized.[25] William Duff, a Nova Scotian fish merchant and Liberal, also excoriated the bill's unequal coverage of the labour force: "If we can pass a national law to cover everyone, I am for that law; but I do not believe in stepbairns in the family. Everyone should be treated alike." Duff had suspicions about the state's regulating labour at all, and his proclaimed support for a fair national law was probably specious.[26] But the terms of his criticism indicated a small-l liberal criterion for social legislation: that it treat similarly-situated citizens in identical ways. If a right to leisure time was to be enacted, all of the critics of the Conservatives' Eight Hours Bill wanted that right to be universal, at least for participants in the formal economy. No one in this eight-hours debate (excepting possibly Agnes MacPhail, in her suggestion of universal pensions) enlarged the category of citizens covered by "universal" entitlements to include housewives. The differences between housewives' work (its familial context, its absence from the labour market) and work as these parliamentarians imagined it apparently justified (following the liberal tradition) the exclusion of housewives from leisure rights.

By 1956, twenty-one years after this debate, all of the Canadian provinces except PEI had followed the lead of Manitoba, Québec, and British Columbia and had enacted hours of work legislation (see Table 9.1). Various anomalies in the adoption of these laws deserve to be explained by means of systematic study of provincial politics. Why was Ontario later than Québec in legislating shorter hours, given the similarity of their economies? If the economic importance of rural commodity production might explain the later adoption of leisure laws in most of Atlantic Canada, why was Nova Scotia relatively quick off the mark with legislation in 1935? Either partisan politics or, more broadly, political cultures must have played a part in support for regulating hours of work, given the fact that the rural prairie provinces took the lead in this area of law.

Annual Vacations with Pay

The ideology of the shorter-hours debate in the 1930s had a momentum that carried on into the 1940s, in the war years and after, as provision for annual vacations and public recreation services enlarged the body of provincial and federal leisure law. Three features of the shorter-hours debate persisted in later policy discourse. First and most central was the rationale for leisure as a means of health. Second, the principle of universality was reiterated and also acquired more complex content. Third, the association of leisure with a standard of civilization (re-stated as a standard of living and a democratic way of life) remained as a touchstone for promoters of leisure policy.[27] Left behind in the Depression was the work-sharing rationale for time off from labour; it was supplanted in later decades by positive arguments for leisure rights.

Like shorter hours, annual vacations with pay had been part of organized labour's legislative program for years in advance of their adoption in law: the Trades and Labour Congress of Canada (TLCC) added "Holidays with Pay" to its "Platform of Principles" in 1931. In 1936, standards for paid vacations were the subject of an ILO Convention.[28] In the 1920s, many salaried workers, and the middle class more generally, had come to expect time off with pay as part of their employment contract, but by 1937 neither welfare capitalism nor collective bargaining had managed to spread this entitlement very widely among wage earners.[29] The National Employment Commission report of that year showed that only 22 per cent of the 7,725 firms it had surveyed provided paid vacations to wage-earners, whereas, among salaried employees, 66 per cent vacationed every year at the company's expense.[30] A new study in 1939 showed a marked expansion in private industry's provision of this benefit, with a quarter of all the plans that covered wage-earners being newly introduced in 1937 and 1938.[31] In 1938, organized labour's *Canadian Congress Journal* celebrated these developments, reiterating that holidays made workers "fitter" and gave them "a brighter outlook on life," while improving efficiency and lowering production costs.[32]

Journalists and politicians in the late 1930s through to the late 1950s echoed and helped sustain the consensus that paid holidays were an important health measure and an element of a civilized way of life. While thus drawing on themes from the shorter-hours campaign, they also innovatively linked these to universality in social rights. A 1939 editorial in the Toronto *Daily Star* illustrates these associated ideas:

> The habit of taking an annual vacation is becoming increasingly widespread among wage-earners. It is due largely to the constant education of the public as to the importance to health of rest and recreation. An annual holiday which extends to one or more weeks is also symbolic of the change that is taking place in standards of living. The employed workman who can afford an annual vacation enjoys a standard of life which is above the bare subsistence line; it is a standard which approaches a comfort and cultural level.[33]

The editorialist went on to acknowledge that wage-earners could not afford to forego earnings: hence the need for paid vacations. If all members of society were to share a common culture, there would have to be material support for workers' leisure. In making its case for this reform, the editorial noted that only "white collar" workers had "as a rule enjoyed this privilege [of paid vacations]," thus suggesting that manual workers, still the defining element of the industrial working class, suffered relative disadvantage. To argue for a universal standard of living with respect to leisure, therefore, was to make a claim for class equality. Class equality arguments also joined the health and civilization themes in a 1941 editorial in the Hamilton *Spectator*, celebrating that city's extension of paid vacations to its civic Works Department staff. According to the somewhat optimistic editorialist, this measure showed that "the good things of democracy" were being "shared equally," and "the lines of class distinction" had ceased to find "intelligent support." Remarkably, the editorialist even claimed that "kindly women" were giving their servants paid holidays in this more democratic world.[34] Later, in 1957, as the national parliament debated an annual paid vacations bill, T.S. Barnett, a CCF MP from Vancouver Island, would refer to the need to give industrial workers the same right to paid holidays as was normally enjoyed by people in "other fields of activity."[35] In that same debate, Stanley Knowles explicitly affirmed that annual paid vacations should be considered a "right," equally enjoyed by "those who do this nation's work."[36] The legislative trend from 1943 onward suggested that, whether or not they endorsed class equality, most Canadian governments saw good electoral sense in enacting legislation that universalized the practice of annual paid vacations for workers in the formal economy (see Table 9.1). Those whose work was unpaid remained outside this framework of legislated rights.[37]

Public Recreation Services

In the same period that saw the consolidation of paid workers' rights to shorter hours and annual vacations, the public interest in leisure rights was also manifested in state-financed recreation services. The first of these was British Columbia's Pro-Rec program, created in 1934. Later, the *National Physical Fitness Act* of 1943 provided funds that helped prompt all of the other provinces except Québec to create or expand programs in the late 1940s and 1950s.[38] In this emerging dimension of the regime of leisure law, health and civilization rationales recurred, linked in new ways to the international issues of the Cold War. The universality theme was elaborated in terms that transcended the labour-market definitions of work and leisure, to include affirmation of the leisure rights of citizens who had been mostly or entirely absent in the themes of the hours of work debates. Rural people such as farmers and fishers, as well as housewives and children, and not just industrial or urban workers, were included when public recreation programs were framed to provide for "all the people."[39]

The importance of health in the rationale for publicly-funded recreation is immediately evident in the origins and institutional offspring of the *National Physical Fitness Act* of 1943. That *Act* was a direct product of the planning for social health insurance.[40] The advocates of the *Fitness Act* successfully argued that, if the state was to secure its citizens against the financial risks of ill health, then it had an interest in promoting good health. They also pointed out that governments had an interest in fostering a healthy military force and that raising the manpower for such a force had been hampered by Canadian men's low standard of health. Armed forces recruiters had rejected between 16 and 33 per cent of applicants for basic training during World War II.[41] Drawing the connection between recreation services and the public interest, Ian Mackenzie, minister of Pensions and National Health, said that such services would make Canadian men better suited for war and for work. And, he added, women and children who were more physically active would enjoy improved "intellectual and social morale."[42] When the *National Physical Fitness Act* was passed, it established the Physical Fitness Division within the Health section of Mackenzie's department.

In the ideological work undertaken by the Physical Fitness Division, the health benefits of leisure were redescribed in the language of universal rights. Moreover, the right to leisure was coupled with a right to services in support of wholesome recreation. In the Physical Fitness Division's 1947 training film called *Fit For Tomorrow*, community services — recreation facilities, trained leaders, organized activities — counted among the "opportunities for a healthy, happy way of life" to which all Canadians had a right.[43] Recreation programs would produce healthy citizens who would have "what it takes to do our daily work, have plenty left over for activities in our leisure time, and still have a reserve for emergencies." The authority of the newly formed World Health Organization was cited in support of recreation, as the film's narrator intoned: "The right to health is a fundamental right of every human being, regardless of race, creed, politics, economic or social condition." The "fundamental freedoms" would be protected only when people were healthy. Over footage of men and women, girls and boys bicycling, singing, doing gymnastics, skiing, and square dancing (among many other activities), the film linked the possibility of world peace to the spreading international practice of state-funded recreation programs and to the "calm, clear-thinking minds, in healthy bodies" that such programs would produce.[44]

"Total fitness" was the name that recreationists of the 1940s gave this model of health, and it included a notion of social well-being, not just individual vitality. In *Fit For Tomorrow* this social dimension of the ideal was voiced-over footage of mixed-sex, mixed-age (but all white) groups engaged in serious and merry meetings, as well as pan shots of a disused school building and a barn, and action shots of a mainly female group (some young, some older) labouring together to paint a room in a hall. After noting the passage of legislation to support recreation, the narrator went on to insist that the state does not act without society:

> [I]t is through the efforts of the people within the community that positive action for better use of leisure hours comes about. They form community councils, work out organized recreation programs. Schools and rural halls become their headquarters. Then, with the program firmly established, unused buildings are made over to pro-vide extra facilities.

In the remaining footage of the film, which shows people engaged in recreational pursuits, Canadians were represented uniformly as white (with some darker-skinned, apparently southern European boys and girls appear-ing only in a cautionary sequence depicting idle youth, prone to crime). But young, old, and middle-aged were depicted, and combined with the pre-dictable shots of men woodworking and women knitting was footage of girls playing softball and practising archery and of boys standing at easels, wield-ing artists' brushes. Implied was the ideal that neither age nor sex should exclude people from the full array of community leisure programs. Co-oper-ative endeavour, among sociologically diverse citizens and between govern-ment and "community," was part of the model of a socially integrated (although apparently all-white) democracy that recreation theorists, policy makers, and program directors sought to foster in the new programs of the postwar period. Recreation, they hoped, would counter narrow sociological exclusivity, bringing together people across class, generational, and gender lines in ways that would encourage personal growth and social integration.[45] Total fitness was a norm for both society and selfhood, a vision of a "civi-lization," the democratic way of life.

This vision of a social democracy existed in the context of Cold War con-cerns about European-style totalitarianism, and so had to be modified to accord with liberal values. This perspective was apparent in the ILO in 1954, in the response of the Canadian government to a resolution that urged the governments of member nations to provide "methods of assisting workers to derive maximum benefit from their annual holidays with pay." Such meth-ods included additional holiday accommodations and facilities. The Canadian government representative abstained, on the grounds that publicly funded holiday facilities and the other measures proposed (including an institution as innocuous as travel information services) constituted an intru-sion on Canadian workers' freedom. He said, "our people should be free of suggestion as to how they shall relax, what they shall do and where they shall go on holidays."[46] Leisure was a realm of freedom, in which individuals' opportunity for unfettered choice was fully exercised. Identities could be more flexible in play, and, both in leisure activities and in the organization of recreation programs, people could make use of capacities that their work did not allow them to express.

In public recreation programs, then, liberals contended that "modern" recreation should abandon the prescriptive, normative mode that was associated with the turn-of-the-century playgrounds movement and with services sponsored by churches or by social welfare institutions. Recreation programs should not seek to solve social problems but merely to open up channels into which would flow the normal healthy tastes of ordinary people for leisure activities. Rather than only "selling" recreation to taxpayers as a means, for example, of preventing youth crime or working class drunkenness, advocates of a publicly funded program should paint a picture of enjoyment as a right possessed by all citizens. In this view, state-financed agencies served merely to equalize access and, non-directively, to facilitate communities' natural inclination to organize services. In this way, public recreation would enable communities to tailor recreation services to locally distinctive tastes and needs. In the process, both individual health and social well-being would be enhanced, but there would be no illiberal intervention by the state into the normatively private choices of healthy adults' personal leisure choices. The risk of totalitarian social control would be avoided. All the people would be served, without being forced into a collective mold.

This liberal ideal of non-directive service to freely-choosing individuals proved difficult to implement in the face of existing beliefs and practices. The therapeutic tradition in recreation theory had considerable common sense purchase. For example, men's service clubs, church groups, and women's community organizations provided many of the volunteers who staffed the recreation committees that were mandated by provincial recreation legislation in Ontario. Volunteers from these groups were accustomed to providing services for children and youth, designed to foster good values and self-discipline and to prevent children from becoming morally or physically weak. Recreation directors imbued with a liberal universalist ideology of leisure entitlement had to persuade these volunteers that it was worthwhile to organize leisure pursuits for their adult fellow citizens, whose characters were presumably already formed and whose spare time needs were already catered to by the market or by private associations. Why have a government-subsidized agency to organize craft classes or square dancing nights when adults could find amusement at the movies or in their own clubs and coteries?

The answer from the liberal-minded advocates of universal rights in recreation was twofold. One was that many adults, and not just children, were poorly served by the market. Low-income people were less able, for example, to afford to build their own swimming pools or to pay the fees for tennis or golf clubs. Well-to-do people with interests in the less commercial forms of film or music or drama might have difficulty, in all but the largest cities, in getting access to these or finding others with similar tastes. Mothers of young children might find themselves socially isolated and unable to find time for themselves or discretionary income of their own. Least well served by the market generally were rural communities. While the automobile had effectively brought city and country closer together by the 1950s, country people still lacked access to the array of sports facilities, movie theatres, and meeting places that cities offered. In Ontario, the 1919 *Community Halls Act* had been an attempt to provide some sort of recreation infrastructure in the countryside.[47] But even where halls existed, there was still the challenge of providing programming, which was deemed to require trained leadership. And other kinds of facilities, such as playing fields with night lighting or arenas to house hockey games and other entertainments, were in short supply. In Ontario (and in other provinces, too), public recreation programs promised to help meet these rural needs.[48]

Rural municipalities were nearly half of the first 96 communities organized under Ontario's Physical Fitness and Recreation regulations between 1945 and 1948. Over the subsequent nine years, 178 more communities joined the public recreation movement, and 85 per cent of these were rural.[49] Participation in public recreation brought to places like Dunnville, Lucknow, and Manitoulin Island benefits such as a subsidy to hire trained recreation directors or advice on raising funds and facilities planning or volunteer training in puppetry or weaving or amateur theatre. In Nova Scotia, the provincial recreation authority left Halifax and Dartmouth and Sydney largely to their own devices and concentrated on the rest of the province.[50] They helped rural organizations such as the Federation of Agriculture to organize leadership training schools in which learning how to organize recreation held equal place with farm marketing sessions.[51] In rural elementary schools, provincial advisors showed teachers new games and dances and craft activities to get them away from the past practice of treating only the quasi-military Strathcona drill exercises as part of the school curriculum.[52] For rural people or others ill-served by the market, the public agency could enlarge opportunities, whether by providing information, by helping to organize activity groups, or by providing funds.

In addition to compensating for gaps in commercial leisure provision, the other reason to offer publicly-funded services to adults was that, by engaging in volunteer organization of recreation, adults came to understand and feel a part of community democracy. If their own recreation needs, and not just children's needs, were among the concerns of the program, they would be more willing to invest time and energy in the work of organization. And unlike private hobby groups or sports clubs, municipally organized activities for adults would bring together people from a cross-section of the community and help to produce a democratically inclusive public culture. But in Ontario, at least, the optimism evident from 1945 to 1950 about recreation's potential for fostering a deeper, broader democracy faded by the late 1950s. It had become clear that a male group of professional recreation directors exercised *de facto* leadership, and that municipal recreation councils were not as inclusive of both sexes as the images in "Fit for Tomorrow" had suggested.

While the related patterns of professionalization and male dominance were clear, it is more difficult to judge whether recreation organizations were inclusive and egalitarian across class lines. Promoting class equality was not one of the public recreation movement's explicit goals in the same way that volunteer involvement or more widespread participation by women and girls was. But in a local study of Brantford I have shown that a class differentiation emerged between a middle-class recreation commission, with decisive policy-making authority, and a more predominantly working-class network of community committees, who were permitted to advise and protest, but who were not allowed, on key spending matters, to decide. The recreation movement's ideology of community democracy was a liberal one: it endorsed the participation of society's less powerful strata, but it had little to say about how to counteract the material interests or persistent cultural values that reproduced within the recreation movement the social hierarchies of postwar Canadian society.

If transcending class cleavages and levelling gender hierarchies proved difficult for public recreation, the obstacles to making services inclusive of all races and religions seem to have been even more formidable. Obstacles were presented both by the cultural mainstream and by minority communities. Racial mixing in recreation remained controversial in postwar Canada. For example, Blacks continued to encounter the race bars or segregation that had limited their access in the past to movie theatres and dance halls, skating rinks, and taverns.[53] Jews, too, as a racialized religious minority, faced exclusion from some kinds of leisure facilities, such as clubs, beaches, and camps.[54] In response, such communities often developed their own privately financed facilities and programming.[55] These arrangements served important interests for these communities. Private recreation services were arguably a necessary condition of true leisure for racially marked people if, as Spelman has explained, there is a kind of emotional work toward social reproduction of race that is exacted from people in minority racial positions.[56] And private recreation services for minorities also provided job opportunities for people who were excluded from recreation leadership roles that were reserved in general for white Christians.[57] In light of these interests, minority communities had reason to feel ambivalent about integrated public recreation services.

But public provision was supposedly open to all.[58] And the staff of public recreation departments made some efforts to work toward this democratic goal. Sometimes, in the immediate postwar years, public recreationists contributed to programming for African Canadians in the halls and organizations that they had made for themselves.[59] A recreation director from one urban Ontario program during this period recalled happily that their program had managed to get Protestants and Catholics together in one hall.[60] And recreationists in Ontario lobbied successfully, late in the 1950s and in the early 1960s, to have "Indian" reservations treated as municipalities for the purposes of recreation grants, so that these mainly rural communities, with little access to commercial entertainments, could claim the recreation funding available only through the channel of municipal government.[61] But public recreation's ideology of social inclusion was neither fully implemented nor always welcome. In Québec in the 1950s, for example, the Catholic Church sought to ensure the protection of the faithful from the "naturalistic and materialistic" influences of Protestant English Canada by refusing to accept subsidies under the *National Physical Fitness Act* for the province's many parish playground committees.[62] Socially integrated recreation services in effect competed with other, private agencies that helped some communities to sustain valued group identities and enjoy leisure space that was at least somewhat free from racialized social relations. And, in liberal terms, protecting leisure time with private, non-state spaces for the enjoyment of particular identities was entirely understandable.

Conclusion: Leisure and Participatory Citizenship

Although some liberal values thus had helped to limit the achievement of a normatively healthy standard of social integration, the right to leisure time (a right rooted in a liberal standard of non-discrimination) began, in the 1950s, to help involve some workers more fully in citizenship. In postwar Canada, more time off the job was giving the relatively well-paid wage-earners in unionized workplaces the time to participate in the life of their community. B.C. labour leader Lloyd Whalen made the connections explicit in a 1955 speech to a Labour-Social Work conference: "'We have fought for and gained increased leisure,' he said. 'And therefore, just as we believe we have a moral duty to give part of our income to voluntary agencies, so must we also be prepared to give of that increased leisure.'"[63] In a 1956 speech, Canadian Labour Congress officer Donald MacDonald also celebrated the consequences of shorter hours for working-class citizenship, and underscored its significance for class equality:

> As [a] consequence of shorter hours, greater security and improved social and economic status, which, in turn, are the result of Labour organization, the worker in these latter years is in a position to occupy himself with affairs of general interest. … [D]uring the time he was prevented from active participation in the affairs of society, activity and leadership in these affairs went by default or pre-emption to those who could afford to devote time, money and effort to them — mainly business and professional people, and those in public life. Today, that pattern is changing.[64]

As I have shown elsewhere, this rhetoric was matched in the 1950s by the emergence in the labour movement of community services committees, whose members joined the social leadership of their cities and towns, serving both as representatives of a labour perspective and as disinterested citizens.[65] The success of campaigns for wage-earners' formal rights to leisure, the creation of publicly-funded recreation services, and the labour movement's increased involvement in cross-class community organizations were all markers of an incipient democratization of Canadian society and government over the period from 1930 to 1960. A class of people once excluded from social leadership both by the material conditions of their lives and by ideological disparagement of their abilities came to have the time to be citizens. Social workers, unionists, and some politicians celebrated this change as a sign of social health.[66]

The ideal of social health could only be realized when labour standards for hours of work changed. Employment law was an important development in the material conditions that made the right to leisure in some way real. So, too, were the recreation centres, playing fields, provincial parks, and other recreation services that provincial funding helped provide in Ontario in the 1950s, and in the rest of Canada to varying degrees and on different chronologies then and later.[67] But because democratic public culture depends on material conditions, the diverse circumstances of people's lives limited (and continue to limit) the impact of rights and services that are meant to be universally enjoyed.

Promoters of citizen participation today who are blind to the social complexity of material constraints are as likely to fall short of their goals as Ontario's public recreationists did in the 1950s. Today, many people find that lack of leisure is a barrier to their ability to be involved in the life of their communities in any way other than through work. Some Canadians must carry a load of multiple jobs because low wages make it impossible for them to meet their needs on the income earned in a 40-hour week.[68] Others face a struggle over spare time within their families, as couples in two-earner families try to negotiate fairly the competing demands of paid work and unpaid domestic labour.[69] For professionals, managers, or the self-employed, the regulation of hours by employment law is not an option.[70] In these and other contexts, both social health and individual well-being continue to be at stake as we strive to make the right to leisure a reality. While such struggles may be experienced as individual or family ones, the history of leisure law and public provision for recreation should remind us that these are also questions for collective reflection, organized action, and even, sometimes, government intervention.

Notes

1. The characterizations of liberal and democratic traditions and critical perspectives on liberalism in this paragraph draw on the following work: Janet Ajzenstat and Peter J. Smith, *Canada's Origins: Liberal, Tory, or Republican?* (Ottawa: Carleton University Press, 1995), 1-11; Samuel Bowles and Herbert Gintis, *Democracy and Capitalism: Property, Community, and the Contradictions of Modern Social Thought* (New York: Basic Books, 1987), 123-24; Jürgen Habermas, *Legitimation Crisis*, trans. Thomas McCarthy (Boston: Beacon Press, 1973), 123-24; C.B. Macpherson, *The Real World of Democracy* (Toronto: Canadian Broadcasting Corporation, 1965), 1-11; Ian McKay, "The Liberal Order Framework: A Prospectus for a Reconnaissance of Canadian History," *Canadian Historical Review* 81, 4 (2000), 623-32, 640-44; Carole Pateman, "The Fraternal Social Contract," in *The Disorder of Women: Democracy, Feminism and Political Theory* (Cambridge: Polity Press, 1989), 39-41; Sherene Razack, *Canadian Feminism and the Law* (Toronto: Second Story Press, 1991), 11-18; Iris Marion Young, *Justice and the Politics of Difference* (Princeton, NJ: Princeton University Press, 1990), 91-95.
2. John G. Jenkins, *Psychology in Business and Industry: An Introduction to Psychotechnology* (New York: John Wiley and Sons, 1935), 176-77; Elton Mayo, *The Human Problems of an Industrial Civilization* (New York: Macmillan, 1933), 1-4; Charles S. Myers, ed., *Industrial Psychology* (London: Thornton Butterworth, 1929), 68-70.
3. David Roediger and Philip Foner, *Our Own Time : A History of American Labor and the Working Day* (London: Verso, 1989) 127-31, 235-36, 349-50.

4. Frank C. Gallant, "The Human Machine vs. The Industrial Machine in Industry," *Canadian Congress Journal* (September 1939): 31-32; Trades and Labor Congress of Canada (TLCC), *Report of the Proceedings of the 47th Annual Convention*, resolutions 44 and 50 (1931), 126-27; Roediger and Foner, 178, 182-83, 234.

5. International Labour Organization. *The International Labour Organization: the First Decade* (London: George Allen & Unwin, 1931), 27-29, 103, 106.

6. Intervenors in this debate who fit this description include Ambrose Bury, K.C. (Conservative, Edmonton East), John F. White (Conservative, London), Col. Thomas Cantley, LL.D. (Conservative, Pictou), and Charles Dickie (Conservative, Nanaimo). *Canadian Parliamentary Guide* (hereafter *CPG*), *1935*, ed. A.L. Normandin, (Ottawa: Le Syndicat des oeuvres sociales, 1935), 150-51, 234, 153, 159-60.

7. In their number we can count Col. Henry Mullins (Conservative, Marquette), William Duff (Liberal, Antigonish-Guysborough), Peter Veniot (Liberal, Gloucester), Louis Parent (Liberal, Terrebonne), Thomas Thompson (Conservative, Lanark), and Allan Neill (Independent, Comox-Alberni). *CPG*, *1935*, 203, 161, 232-33, 205-06, 230, 205.

8. Kenneth McNaught, *A Prophet in Politics: A Biography of J.S. Woodsworth* (Toronto: University of Toronto Press, 1959), 158, 177-78, 217, 232.

9. *CPG 1935*, 201-02.

10. Canada, House of Commons, *Debates* (hereafter *Debates*), 1935, 1591 and 1574-97, 1667-85 passim.

11. *Debates*, 1935, 1580.

12. Bryan D. Palmer, *A Culture in Conflict* (Montreal: McGill-Queen's University Press, 1979), 126-27, 134; Roediger and Foner, 7-8, 13-14.

13. *Debates*, 1935, 1676.

14. The notion of "enforced leisure" or "enforced idleness" as something other than genuine leisure was used in the Depression as one way of calling attention to the human costs of unemployment. See, for example, TLCC, *Proceedings* (1931), 126; "Mobilized Charity," *Halifax Mail-Star*, 18 October 1933, 4; William R. Cook, *Organizing the Community's Resources for Use of Leisure Time* (Ottawa: Canadian Welfare Council, 1938), 3; Martin H. Neumeyer and Esther S. Neumeyer, *Leisure and Recreation* (New York: A.S. Barnes and Company, 1936), 21.

15. *Debates*, 1935, 1676.

16. *Debates*, 1935, 1587.

17. *Debates*, 1935, 1585-86.

18. Thomas Goodale and Geoffrey Godbey, *The Evolution of Leisure: Historical and Philosophical Perspectives* (State College, PA: Venture Publishing, 1988), 18-24, 27-28.

19. *Debates*, 1935, 1590.

20. *Debates*, 1935, 1581-82.

21. *Debates*, 1935, 1581.

22. Frank Gallant, "The Human Machine vs. The Industrial Machine in Industry," *Canadian Congress Journal*, (September 1939): 31-32.

23. *Debates*, 1935, 1668, 1676. Québec MP Louis Parent also raised the concern about differential benefits to urban workers and employees in rural industries (1582).

24. *Debates*, 1935, 1680-81.

25. *Debates*, 1935, 1580-81.

26. *Debates*, 1935, 1583-84.

27. A 1948 article celebrating the five-day week in Australia brought out the health and standard-of-living rationales (Anne Dupree, "Australia's Prosperity With 40-Hour Week," *Saturday Night*, 1 May 1948, 12). The emphasis in policy making on need for rural services and the arguments for universality will be demonstrated in the following discussion.

28. *Labour Gazette* 36 (1936): 616.

29. For American data on the differential rates of annual holidays between the salaried and the hourly wage-earners, or working class and middle class, see Cindy S. Aron, *Working to Play: A History of Vacations in the United States* (New York: Oxford University Press, 1999), 203; Daniel T. Rodgers, *The Work Ethic in Industrial America, 1850-1920* (Chicago: University of Chicago Press, 1978), 106.

30. National Employment Commission, *Report on Phases of Employment Conditions in Canadian Industry* (Ottawa: King's Printer, 1937), 53, cited in Margaret McCallum, "Corporate Welfarism in Canada, 1919-1939," *Canadian Historical Review* 71, 1 (1990): 68.
31. *Labour Gazette* 39 (1939): 886.
32. "Holidays with Pay," *Canadian Congress Journal* 17, 3 (1938): 11.
33. Quoted in "Holidays with Pay," *Canadian Congress Journal* 18, 9 (1939): 23.
34. Quoted in "Vacations with Pay," *Canadian Congress Journal* 20, 7 (1941): 21.
35. *Debates*, 1957, 929.
36. *Debates*, 1957, 525.
37. Further research might uncover whether, at any stage of the policy process, decision-makers in Canada actively considered state-financed holidays for unpaid workers such as mothers of young children. A provision of this sort was actually adopted in New Zealand in 1937. The *Physical Welfare and Recreation Act* passed in that year allowed for "holiday bursaries for mothers of large families" (National Archives of Canada, RG 29, Records of the Department of Health and Welfare, vol. 2008, file R433, draft article for *Global Report*). In this measure, the New Zealand government was apparently following in the steps of private welfare agencies, which in Canada and the United States and presumably in New Zealand, sometimes included mothers with the children who were provided with vacations at "fresh air camps."
38. Elsie Marie McFarland, *The Development of Public Recreation in Canada* (Ottawa: Canadian Parks and Recreation Association, 1970), 51-60.
39. The expression "all the people" was a shibboleth of postwar recreation organizations. One example of its use is in the title of a National Film Board film that the Physical Fitness Division of the Department of Health and Welfare used as an example of successful community organization (National Archives of Canada, Reference no. 147740). "When All the People Play," produced in 1948, told the story of the public recreation program in Annapolis Royal, Nova Scotia.
40. Canada, House of Commons, *Special Committee on Social Security, Minutes of Proceedings and Evidence*, 1943, 32.
41. Gail Pogue and Bryce Taylor, *History of Provincial Government Services of the Youth and Recreation Branch (Part I: 1940-1950), Recreation Review, Supplement Number 1*, (November 1972): 5.
42. *Debates*, 1946, 2796-97; *Special Committee on Social Security*, 1943, 34.
43. National Archives of Canada, audio-visual division, Reference no. 147739.
44. The countries listed in the film were "China, Britain, the United States, Sweden, Russia, and others."
45. The following argument about the greater universality of services and their value for community organization is based on my book, *The Public at Play: Gender and the Politics of Recreation in Post-War Ontario* (Toronto: University of Toronto Press, 2000). Supplementary evidence has been added where noted, and the sources of direct quotations are also cited.
46. *Labour Gazette*, 54 (1954), 1128-29.
47. *Statutes of Ontario* 1919, c. 55.
48. McFarland, *The Development of Public* Recreation, 50, 53, 55-56, 59.
49. Department of Education, "Report of the Minister," in Ontario, *Sessional Papers*, 1951-59. "Rural areas" means here either municipalities of fewer than 4,000 inhabitants or counties or townships.
50. Annual reports of the Nova Scotia Department of Public Health and later the Department of Education. These reports and the Department of Education scrapbooks provide the basis for the descriptions of the Physical Fitness Division's geographic range of service.
51. Nova Scotia, *Journals of the House of Assembly*, 1950, part II, Appendix 17, *Report of the Department of Public Health*, 228-29; Charles Topshee, "The Hants Folk School," *Journal of Education* 20 (1949): 39-42.
52. Interview with Dorothy Walker, 1989. Ms. Walker was one of the Nova Scotia Physical Fitness Division's longest-serving members in the 1940s and 1950s.

53. Robin W. Winks, *The Blacks in Canada: A History*, 2nd ed. (Montreal: McGill-Queen's, 1997), 420-22; James W. St. G. Walker, *"Race," Rights and the Law in the Supreme Court of Canada* (Waterloo, ON: Wilfrid Laurier University, 1997), 146-47.

54. In 1959, a Canadian journalist reported that discrimination against Jews in leisure facilities and activities remained one of the most persistent kinds: Phyllis Lee Peterson, "The Jew in Canada: Where Does He Stand Today?" *Maclean's Magazine*, 24 October 1959, 22, 62. A particular example of that kind of discrimination is provided by the experience of politician Joe Salzburg, who was unable to rent vacation property on Toronto Island because of anti-semitism [Ruth A. Frager, *Sweatshop Strife* (Toronto: University of Toronto Press, 1992) photo caption, n.p].

55. Two of Canada's community centres for Black Canadians were created in Montreal and Toronto. Their mix of clubs, choirs, craft classes, social recreation, and family services are described in Isabel Lebourdais, "Canada's First Community House for Negroes...," *Saturday Night*, 25 July 1942, 4-5 and D.P. Sykes, "Earlier Negro Centre," *Saturday Night*, 22 August 1942, 2. Two of the summer camps for Jewish children that served the Montreal area are described in Gerald Allan Cohen, *If You're an Egalitarian, How Come You're So Rich?* (Cambridge, MA: Harvard University Press, 2000), 30-33.

56. Elizabeth V. Spelman, "'Race' and the Labor of Identity," in *Race and Philosophy*, ed. Susan E. Babbitt and Sue Campbell (Ithaca, NY: Cornell University Press, 1999), 207-11.

57. Evidence of such exclusion may be found in Archives of Ontario, RG 65, Records of the Ministry of Tourism and Information, Recreation in Ontario collection, series B1, box 20, file 655, application for approval of recreation director appointment, 26 February 1957; memo from Field Supervisor to District Representative, 17 April 1957 and memo from CPB Director to Deputy Minister of Education, 27 April 1957.

58. National Archives of Canada, MG 28 I 10, Canadian Council on Social Development, file Recreation, Public-Private, Relationships 1947-1957, "Relationship Between Public and Private Services in the Recreation Field." Paper given by Murray G. Ross to the Canadian Conference on Social Work, 11 June 1948.

59. Nova Scotia Archives and Record Management, RG 8, Records of the Department of Education, volume 269, scrapbook, "Adult Group Attends Course," clipping, *Mail-Star*, 7 May 1952 [describes NSAACP event in the historically African-Nova-Scotian community of Upper Hammonds Plains, with leadership by a recreationist and an adult educator from the Department of Education]; Archives of Ontario, RG 65, Records of the Ministry of Tourism and Information, Recreation in Ontario collection, series A9, box 15, file 382, "Centre Director Resigns, Takes Huntsville Post," clipping, *Chatham Daily News*, 23 August 1955 [refers to the municipal recreation director's commitment to serving the Black community in Chatham].

60. Tillotson, *The Public at Play*, 114.

61. Archives of Ontario, RG 65, Records of the Ministry of Tourism and Information, Recreation in Ontario collection, series B3, box 23, file 857, Report of Staff Conference, 29 May 1960, 9; series A9, box 16, file 456, interview transcript, 16, and file 407, interview transcript, 6-7. In northern Ontario, this money was accompanied by the help of non-Native civil servants which, in the sensible view of one northern recreation director, meant that it was an exercise in cultural imposition (series A9, box 16, file 450, interview transcript, 4-5). How the money was used may have varied around the province. After about five years, programs conducted under this funding arrangement foundered on the federal-provincial jurisdictional issue in Native affairs (series A9, box 16, file 442, interview transcript, 10-11).

62. For a description of these committees, les Oeuvres des terrains de jeu (OTJ), their provincial federation in 1946 as the Confédération otéjiste provinciale, and the constitutional position they represented, see Roger Levasseur, *Loisir et culture au Québec* (Montreal: Les Éditions du Boréal Express, 1982), 58-62, 68.

63. National Archives of Canada, MG 28 I 10, Canadian Council on Social Development, volume 77, file 564, newspaper clipping, *Vancouver Sun*, 28 January 1955. The file also contains a pamphlet reprinting Whalen's speech.

64. "Labour Participation in Community Chests," *Canadian Labour* 1, 7 (1956): 17-18.
65. " 'When our membership awakens'": Welfare Work and Canadian Union Activism, 1950-1965," *Labour Le/Travail* 40 (1997): 144-46; "Class and Community in Canadian Welfare Work, 1933-1960," *Journal of Canadian Studies* 32, 1 (1997): 79-83.
66. Tillotson, "Class and Community," 77-78; Tillotson, "When our membership awakens," 163-67. I would suggest that the elements of the leadership of the Ontario CCF who supported a greater role for labour in the CCF should be taken as examples of politicians who welcomed the broader involvement in social activism of working-class people as evidence of a more democratic society. For a summary of attitudes about labour held by Ontario's CCF leaders, see Dan Azoulay, *Keeping the Dream Alive: The Survival of the Ontario CCF/NDP, 1950-63* (Montreal: McGill-Queen's University Press, 1997), 234-35.
67. Hilmi Ibrahim, *Leisure and Society: a Comparative Approach* (Dubuque: Wm. C. Brown, 1991), 156-57; McFarland, *The Development of Public Recreation*, 68-70.
68. Statistics Canada, Household Surveys Division, *Labour Force Update: Hours of Work* (Ottawa: Minister of Industry, 1997), 3, 32-34.
69. Meg Luxton, "'Time for Myself: Women's Work and the 'Fight for Shorter Hours,'" in *Feminism and Political Economy*, ed. Heather Jon Maroney and Meg Luxton (Toronto: Methuen, 1987), 174-77.
70. *Labour Force Update: Hours of Work*, 26-27; Joe Polito, "Flextime and Parenthood," letter to the editor, *Globe and Mail*, 20 September 2000.

PART IV

PEDAGOGIES OF BELONGING AND EXCLUSION

chapter ten

"THE GOOD CITIZEN"
Masculinity and Citizenship at Frontier College, 1899-1933

Lorna R. McLean

By the turn of the twentieth century, frontiersmen, as they were known, pop-ulated parts of Northern Ontario working in lumbering, construction, min-ing, and railway camps. In the lumber industry alone, the remote and sparsely populated settlements in Northern Ontario housed over 40,000 men.[1] During the summer, they slept, socialized, and ate in rudimentary tents provided by employers. Sweltering heat, persistent black flies, and mosquitoes added fur-ther misery to daily labours. Other workers housed in bunkhouses at winter camps were confined at the end of working days in roughly built structures averaging 30 to 52 feet. When full, these buildings accommodated from 80 to over 100 men. In winter, large stoves provided the heat, and when the men returned from work, clothes were hung to dry along lengthy rafters. The combined odours of sweat left a heavy, rancid smell in these enclosed spaces and contributed to the spread of illnesses.[2] Physical deprivations and the monotony of camp life were alleviated by occasional gambling and drinking.

Improving the daily working conditions and future employment oppor-tunities of frontiersmen became the overriding ambition of Reverend Alfred Fitzpatrick when he founded the Canadian Reading Camp in Northern Ontario in 1899. (See Figure 10.1) Drawing on the influence and ideas of George Grant, his mentor at Queen's University, and the ideology of the Social Gospel movement, Fitzpatrick established a series of camp libraries to provide labourers at work sites with reading material and a tent for leisure hours. Fitzpatrick's efforts marked the beginning of what would later become Frontier College, a non-denominational pan-Canadian organization devoted to teaching literacy.[3] What began in 1899 as a series of small reading libraries and incorporated 20 years later as Frontier College, evolved by 2000 into an organization of literacy tutor training programs with 5,000 student literacy volunteers from over 50 universities and colleges across Canada. As in the beginning, volunteers currently teach in isolated areas that now extend to penitentiaries and to Native and Inuit communities and serve farm workers and other labourers, handicapped people, and immigrants; volunteers also offer peer tutoring in various cities.

figure 10.1

Alfred Fitzpatrick.

SIMPSON BROS. / NATIONAL ARCHIVES OF CANADA / C-056817. REPRODUCED BY PERMISSION.

It was the ability of Frontier College to survive and thrive, from its rudimentary origins in a small reading tent with a handful of volunteers to a national organization of over 10,000, that drew me to the extensive archives of this uniquely Canadian organization. As I began my research I was intrigued to discover how this Association, unlike other organizations that emerged from the Social Gospel movement, thrived and expanded while still maintaining its original nineteenth-century ideal. In this chapter I examine how the College made the successful transformation from a religiously based Reading Camp Association to a secular college by investigating the early history of the College up to 1933, when its founder Fitzpatrick resigned. To do so, I outline how the College forged an organizational structure based on four key features: leadership, pedagogical innovation, marketing, and student needs. Throughout the tenure of his leadership, Fitzpatrick and his administration skillfully balanced the interests of potentially conflicting and diverse donors such as church groups, businessmen, labour organizations, and the provincial Ministry of Education. Equally important, the Association established a unique teaching and working model to meet the needs of the institution, teachers, and students. But it was the response of the Association/College to the major demographic changes in the early 1900s that shaped the College's future direction and ultimately fostered its success. The resulting shift in clientele from a predominately Canadian/Anglo/Celtic based population to "foreign born," combined with a restructuring of curriculum, facilitated the transition from a sectarian-based Reading Camp to a modern, independent College.

With the exception of several excellent, focused articles and illustrated institutional histories, there are few published studies that examine this unique Canadian institution.[4] Furthermore, none of the research that probes this predominantly adult male college (at least until the mid-twentieth century) has explored the way in which meanings of masculinity shaped the College's pedagogical culture. To do so, I analyze the language and images of manliness that infused the curriculum and the photographic and printed material related to Canadian citizenship. By studying language and images we can begin to understand the way in which particular forms of masculinity were attached to early twentieth-century ideals of citizenship among a select immigrant population. Here then, this study of masculinity shifts the lens to examine the histories of male subjects who themselves were "othered."[5] Moreover, we can identify the ways in which these constructions of masculinity and pedagogical innovation, political ideals and immigrant culture served to further the overall aims of the College as it evolved into an innovative educational model.

From Travelling Library to Classroom, 1899-1909

The principles of the nineteenth- and early twentieth-century Social Gospel movement formed the basis for the original ideology of the early Reading Camps.[6] In response to unsettling economic changes and the perceived deteriorating social conditions caused by industrialization, urbanization, and immigration, a range of private philanthropic associations emerged. While many unions and reformers organized in urban areas, little in the way of organized labour or associational aid was offered in rural or isolated frontiers until Alfred Fitzpatrick began the Reading Camp Association in 1899. It was here, in the Canadian hinterland of mines, lumber camps and railway construction gangs, that the Association and later the College found its pedagogical and ideological niche (see Figure 10.2).

Fitzpatrick's earlier career as a Presbyterian minister and student of social gospel under the tutelage of Queen's University principal George Grant informed the religious basis that underlay the Camp's mission. Fitzpatrick had seen first-hand the severe working conditions of lumberers during his years serving as a missionary with the American Presbyterian church in the

California redwood lumber camps. One of his brothers had died in the western lumber camps, and after a lengthy absence Fitzpatrick hoped to reunite with his other brother who also worked as a lumberer. A fortuitous reunion between siblings may have been the inspiration that convinced Fitzpatrick to return to Canada and later serve as a parish minister in an area where he visited lumber camps. Thus began Fitzpatrick's ambition to educate the labouring adult, following the tenets of the social gospel model of education for achieving reform.[7]

figure 10.2

Interior of old-time bunkhouse common on Frontier Works during the period 1890-1925.

NATIONAL ARCHIVES OF CANADA / C-038620. REPRODUCED BY PERMISSION.

The social gospel of the early twentieth century covered a range of themes, but one of its dominant strands focused on achieving personal development through studying culture and religion. In George Grant's view, the notion of "practical Christianity" emphasized both the pragmatic and social role of religion.[8] According to Brian McKillop, this objective of following Christian principles to become the ideal man was "propelled by a social passion for doing good."[9] In its application this meant reading selected literature to promote morality. As one instructor explained in one of the early Camp Annual Reports, "[t]o a person with a sense of delicacy and modesty it is refreshing and gratifying to note how good reading matter stifles, or at least reduces, profane and filthy jesting."[10]

The Reading Camp reflected this ideal in its motto of "Entertainment and Culture for Manual Labourers and Manual Training for Teachers."[11] The rhetoric of personal improvement came chiefly from the selection of books provided by the Ministry of Education and through private donations. Collected books, mostly British, ranged from Charles Dickens to Sir Walter Scott, featured stories of male virtue, moral tales, and quest narratives[12] and evoked the influence of noted British educationalist Matthew Arnold and his emphasis on character building. As one Camp supporter described the constructive influence of moral literature on a man, success depends on books that "tend to elevate the moral and religious character of the men."[13] "Good clean reading," as Fitzpatrick observed, among the "nearly a quarter of a million sturdy Canadians [who] must live six, eight, ten months a year in camp, [is].... to get some good entertainment without sacrificing manhood...."[14]

Gender relations were a key component of this approach. As a quote from the popular novelist Ralph Connor in the 1901 Annual Report illustrates, men were "'fighting out that eternal fight for manhood, strong, clean, God-conquered.'"[15] This quotation reflects a wider trend observed by McKillop in upper-level education in the early twentieth century that "the culture of manliness occurred at a time when genteel culture was in the process of being feminized with the sentimentalism of the liberal arts increasingly equated with feminine attributes."[16] The informal moral code of the day, which combined manly ideals with Christian conversion (what McKillop describes as "a complementary inversion of the way in which the 'Christian soldiers' of the period were 'marching as to war'"), reflects the influences of muscular Christianity on masculine attributes.[17] But there was more to this manly code than religion and education. By 1907-08 the Camp's Report observed how church and state owe a duty to the men in the camp that they may be saved for "Christ and for Canada, to manhood and to citizenship."[18]

This final comment reminds us of another ideology linked to social gospel that boded well for the initial direction of the Camp project and for the future development of the College: that of imperialism and citizenship. While the former emphasized ties to Britain, the latter, as we shall see, was linked to the discourse on nationhood and called for the Canadianization of new immigrants. Expressions of practical Christianity sought to establish the social relevance of religion, partly to draw the working man back into church. Such a mission, as seen by Grant and other supporters of the social gospel, was at the heart of imperialism and was made clear in the readings and publications of the Camp.[19]

Indeed, publications became an important vehicle for promoting the ideals of the Association and for marketing and fundraising. Fitzpatrick utilized the Camp's and, later, the College's Annual Reports to provide a critical link among supporters by uniting the interests of donor agencies with the objectives of the Camp. In the early years he began to write and publish booklets that resembled sermons on topics related to Camp activities and needs. For example, in his 1905 treatise on "The Education of the Frontier Labourer," he appealed to the moral and social justice sentiments of church-going

Canadians to support the Camp's work: "What these socially, intellectually and morally buried [workers] need is not charity, but social justice."[20]

As well, the Reports frequently printed the testimonials of various supporters to underscore the Camp's success. As one lumber agent stated in his letter in 1902,

> I think it is not too much to say that the health of our camp has improved, the sleeping camp being less crowded in the evenings, and Sundays, and there has been less jumping (to other lumber camps) and fewer visits to the saloons. More men have written to their friends, and, in general, the moral tone of the camp has been raised.[21]

In another instance, the Annual Report included a letter from W. H. Drummond announcing the resolution of the Toronto Conference of the Methodist Church that endorsed the establishment of reading rooms that were "largely preventative of dissipation, gambling, drinking, and Sabbath-breaking."[22] Nonetheless, despite the Camp's creative endeavours, funding became a perennial problem as Fitzpatrick and his administration sought to win the support of both public and private agencies. In particular, writing as Secretary of the Camp Association, Fitzpatrick reminded the provincial government of its civic responsibility to improve conditions in the Camp and to contribute to the education of the workers for no other reason than because of the enormous economic benefits the government received from frontier work.[23]

In addition to Annual Reports and promotional material, Fitzpatrick further demonstrated his effectiveness as a leader in his use of the media to promote the project, garner support, and acquire materials for the Camp. His success is demonstrated in the enthusiastic response of a *Globe* reader to one such editorial: "I am heartily in sympathy with the aims there suggested, and will take pleasure in devoting [sic] a half dozen copies of my little work on 'The Trees and Shrubs of Ontario,' if you will accept the gift."[24] The use of pictures in newspapers and testimonials in Annual Reports further promoted the goals of the Association. One such Report included an excerpt from a clerk, M.J. Shea, on the reading room at Booth and Gordon's Camp No. 1: "Mr. Jas. McCool has put up the following rules and he sees that they are observed: 1) No card playing; 2) No spitting on the floor; (3) No loud talking etc."[25]

During these years, the culture of pedagogy altered from a passive approach of reading, leisure, and entertainment to an active, instructive classroom. The Camp grew rapidly, and by 1903 it had expanded to 24 reading tents.[26] From its early years, it created and maintained innovative teaching styles oriented to adult learning. In 1903, throughout the 24 reading rooms, "instructors/librarians" were available to assist the men in selecting and signing out material and to offer guidance with reading and writing in the evenings and on Sundays. However, it soon became evident that if the Camp was going to have instructors to teach the workers, it needed more funds. The program, as Fitzpatrick reported in a letter in 1903 to the ministry, was "at a standstill."[27]

The solution came, as the story goes, in 1902, when one of the Camp leaders, Angus Gray, grew tired of waiting for the workers to return to camp and began working alongside them.[28] Thus began the innovative teacher/labourer concept. This concept not only appealed to the worker by enabling a closer rapport and respect to develop between the teacher and student, but it also benefitted the Reading Camp Association because the teachers earned a daily wage paid by the lumber, mining or railway construction employers, not by the Reading Camp. Most notably, this adjustment to Camp practice represented a significant departure from the passive role of "librarian" to the more active one of "teacher." This change was further reflected in 1905 in Fitzpatrick's new title, Superintendent of Camp Education, and in his annual publications of sermon-like pamphlets promoting the work of the Camp.[29]

Another important Camp development also occurred during this time. The Association followed the movement of workers to the west and, by 1906, as superintendent, Fitzpatrick oversaw 27 instructors from various colleges and universities in Saskatchewan and Manitoba. A year later, additional reading rooms were established in Alberta, British Columbia, and Manitoba. This expanded network of Camps was reflected in its publication "Canada's Frontiersmen."[30] But the wider educational net not only included other regions and a western profile; as we shall see, the shift in Canadian demographics at the same time had a profound influence on the ethnicity of the workers.

The early 1900s marked the beginning of a large influx of immigrants to Canada.[31] Furthermore, for the first time in Canadian history, a large percentage of the immigrant population was from non-English speaking countries. In 1891 the foreign-born population accounted for 13.3 per cent of the total population, but the overwhelming majority were from the United Kingdom (76 per cent). During the next 30 years, British immigration continued to dominate, but Canada witnessed a dramatic increase in the number of immigrants born in other European countries, most notably eastern and southern Europe.[32] As one instructor and later principal of the College Edmund Bradwin signalled in a 1907 article,

These foreign born are becoming a fast increasing element of Canada's population, and a primary duty of the state in the next decades will be to aid, by all means possible, the assimilating of these into our national life. Toward this end the reading camp instructor is by no means an inconsiderable force.[33]

With this directive, the Reading Camp initiated what would later become one of its main platforms: assimilating the "foreigner" through education.

The changing nature of the workforce affected the Camp in two important ways: it intensified the emphasis on patriotism and introduced instruction in English as a second language. The Camp did not abandon its earlier ideals, but rather it took on a new focus, as seen in the way the teaching of patriotism embedded notions of masculinity and social gospel ideals. By 1907, Annual Reports regularly tracked the nationalities of "foreign men" attending classes. For example, one instructor reported on the attendance of the "mixed bunch" of sixteen "foreigners" in "his class comprised of Turks, Finns, Swedes, Bulgarians and Italians."[34] Another reported, "On Sunday night I talk to the men on different subjects and try to show them a pure life is the best life."[35] The gendered vision of nationhood had a class dimension as well, illustrated in the following passages selected from the poem "The Strangers Within Our Gates," quoted in its entirety in the Camp's Report: "Oh, these builders of the nations, They are men — I tell you — men! ... Lawless, these our peace endanger ... But we'll teach them to be true, First and last Canadians ... We can make them high in station: We can make them gentlemen."[36]

Lessons in English as a second language led to a greater emphasis on basic elementary subjects such as reading, writing, grammar, spelling, and, for some, geography and history. The Camp's unflagging belief in adult literacy drew on the rhetoric of earlier social gospel teachings that adults could ennoble and improve their minds through education. Thus by 1907, 25 university men worked as labourers by day and instructors in the evenings and on weekends teaching a wide range of workers.[37] This innovative approach established a rapport with the workers, either foreign or native, and enhanced learning. As one teacher noted, "The experience is unspeakably better than the student missionary gets. ... We rub shoulders with the men, understand their problems, and learn to sympathize with their point of view. Besides, they are more interested in what one has to say."[38]

For workers attending classes, learning English yielded both social and economic benefits. Botska Penskoff, a former blacksmith who knew little English, felt that learning the language would help him in his business after leaving the camp.[39] Another Polish man was able to get a position as section foreman after learning to read and write in night school.[40] Equally important, attending classes challenged prior ethnic stereotyping among some instructors and workers. As one instructor wrote, after teaching a "gang of ninety-five Italians and from thirty five to fifty English and French speaking men,"

> Italians ... came to the car regularly to take lessons on arithmetic, writing and reading. ... twelve who came regularly and got along with the work rapidly, much to the surprise of the English spectators, who thought their (Italians) stronghold was the shovel and nothing higher. Their chief aim being, however, to learn English and figures well enough to fit them for the position of interpreters and foremen.[41]

Yet another instructor remarked, based on the "remarkable" progress that some of the students had made, that his "ideas concerning the foreigner have certainly been changed."[42]

Transition Years, 1909-1919

The shape of the College during these years was influenced by several factors: the burgeoning immigrant population, World War I, and the perceived threat of external political influences on Canadian society. In studying this period of transition we can observe the ways in which the changing pedagogical culture nurtured this new population that included a large proportion of "foreign" labourers. Assimilation was key to integrating other nationalities into the Canadian way. Annual Reports during these years demonstrate how the mission of the College focused on building a unique educational model that provided institutional support to further this objective of assimilation. In building this structure, Fitzpatrick and the College drew on notions of muscular Christianity and the role of manual labourers in the project of nation-building.

The 1910s marked a critical period in the Camp's evolution. Examining three key areas of the pedagogical culture — the organizational structure, curriculum, and the expansion of Camps — demonstrates the way in which the Reading Camp Association changed direction from being an itinerant cultural and entertainment Camp to being an educational institution. In so doing I highlight the internal ideological shift from a social stabilizing agency ensuring that the "culture of civilization" would aid men, to the more political aim of guiding workers as citizens to contribute to the betterment of the

Dominion. Canada's resource-based economy depended on frontier camps and would therefore rely on frontier labour for the decades ahead.

In 1913, the Camp's change in direction was marked when its unofficial name became "The Frontier College." The inclusion of a patron, The Duke of Connaught, and a list of officers who made up the Camp's executive (nine directors, and five regional camp school inspectors), further signalled the shift to an educational institution. All the while, Fitzpatrick maintained his key influence as Superintendent of Camp Education. As he declared, the task of "educationalists for the next ten years is to devise ways and means of taking the school and college to the Frontier"[43] By 1914, Camps were established in all provinces but Prince Edward Island, with approximately 70 reading camps and night schools.[44]

The ideology of the Camp drew on the earlier tradition of imperialism fused with notions of nation-building. To quote the Camp's patron, the Duke of Connaught, "[t]he greatest duty that devolves upon Canadians is to make Canadians of those who are coming to Canada's shores from other lands, and to see that they are loyal to the British Crown."[45] This emphasis on fostering British ways was often combined with contemporary fears of revolutionary politics among Eastern European immigrants. For instance, the 13th Annual Report noted that Canadians were awakening to the fact that to maintain the "well-being and security of this Dominion and maintain a worthy place within the Empire, we must with urgency proceed with the task of Canadianizing the foreigners within our shores, and bring them into intelligent harmony with our Canadian and British Ideals."[46]

All the while, the Camp had not abandoned teaching Anglo-Celtic workers, but by 1914 it was devoting "special energy" to educating the foreigners. As Fitzpatrick noted in his report, "[i]n a few years they [the foreigners] will have the votes, and it is imperative in the interests of the Empire and Canada that they should intelligently understand the privileges and duties of citizenship in a free democracy"[47] (see Figure 10.3). In 1917, for example, the curriculum reflected these ambitions. Fitzpatrick wrote a handbook for teaching new Canadians. It contained a series of lessons in English "for the help and guidance of foreigners in Canada who are struggling toward naturalization and full citizenship."[48] The book was to be used to teach English as a second language, but, clearly, making Canadian citizens was imbedded in the text. Separate chapters were devoted to topics on Canadian government, social structures, and the economy.[49] In promoting the Camp's philosophy across the growing network of facilities, Fitzpatrick wrote a series of 17 booklets between 1900 and 1919.[50]

figure 10.3

D.L. McDougall giving a lesson in civics to a class of Scandinavians at Mond Nickel Co.'s Mine near Larchwood, Ontario, 1913.

NATIONAL ARCHIVES OF CANADA / PA–061772. REPRODUCED BY PERMISSION.

In his Annual Reports and published articles, Fitzpatrick also sought to reassure Canadians of the College's commitment to patriotic war work by ensuring the successful integration of foreigners willing to assume their rightful place in the democratic process.[51] This intent is clearly articulated in a 1917 article, "The Diffusion of Education": "Each man seeking the vote should be required to have a working knowledge of a minimum number of English words and an insight into the government of Canada, in federal, provincial and municipal affairs before being granted full citizenship in the country."[52]

Instructors were integral to the Camp's educational initiative. In recognition of the ideals of Christian masculinity and citizenship in the program, the Annual Report of 1914 noted that 60 to 75 Christian young male instructors "demonstrate what it really means to be a Canadian" by carrying on "the process of assimilation."[53] In highlighting the innovative labourer/teacher approach, the Report underscored the effectiveness of the "personal contact" of the instructors.[54] In addition to instructors' toiling amongst their students, class distinctions were further blurred by the symbols of manly attire worn by the instructors who donned the "rough dress" to win workers "to themselves and their cause." Bradwin, who joined in 1904 and became an inspector of reading camp instructors in 1907, was himself a part of Christian masculinity. As he noted in his published thesis on the Reading Camp, "[f]ew men physically are so splendidly endowed as the workers in frontier camps. They have not only the masculinity that can endure privation, but the courage to confront physical dangers."[55]

So by 1919 the Camp, now officially incorporated under the name Frontier College, had completed the transition from a travelling library to an educational institution. Throughout the 1920s, the College continued to consolidate these earlier administrative and pedagogical initiatives and, as we shall see, moved to the forefront of national agencies responsible for "Canadianizing immigrants." This latter trend played a pivotal role in the transformation and survival of the organization. Moreover, as I argue, the College's ultimate success resulted, in part, from fusing the mandates of the College, "education for citizenship" and "Canadianizing the immigrant," during a critical period in Canadian history. This alignment of state and College objectives facilitated the College's transition into a modern organization.

Consolidating the College, 1919-1933

Efforts to assimilate "foreigners" (as they were called) took a more urgent turn at the end of the war as immigrants continued to arrive from countries facing social and political unrest. Also, as Donald Avery notes in his study of immigrant workers, the legacy of the Winnipeg General Strike produced a spirited national debate on Canada's immigration policy.[56] Some Canadians feared that, if immigrants were not educated, their political and social ideas could fuel the spread of revolutionary actions in Canada.[57] As the Member of Parliament for Brandon, Manitoba declared in 1919, "[n]ot only have we not had any real Canadian policy of immigration, but we have had no national educational conception adequate for the assimilation of the foreigners brought into our country. The alien is very largely what we have not made him."[58]

Further ominous warnings persisted, as evidenced in the newspaper report of a speech delivered in the House of Commons by Mr. W.A. Buchanan, MP for Lethbridge, Alberta: "... people [from Central Europe] who refuse to govern themselves according to British standards of living, and who try to perpetuate separate radicalism in Canada rather than have their children educated in the English-speaking public schools are rightly regarded as a menace to Western Canada."[59] Similar sentiments echoed in other newspaper reports. Another article illustrates the more general appeal of assimilation. Under the banner headline "Foreigners to be Made Good Canadian Citizens by Proper Instruction," a leading proponent and instructor of a course designed to train specialized teachers for "Canadianization" decried the contemporary ad hoc, sentimental attempts to assimilate the foreigner, asserting that the "time is ripe for a more stable method of educating the adult foreigner." Moreover, he warned that "[p]eople have not recognized that teaching English to foreigners is a special kind of work, but they must realize that this is an essential part of Canada's national life, and that these newcomers must be assimilated or they will preponderate in her civilization."[60] Jurisdictional disputes over the education and integration of immigrants into

Canadian society resulted in few government initiatives, and more frequently led to the funding of private institutions.[61] Hence, Frontier College became one of several non-governmental institutions that responded to calls for a national program to educate the foreigner.[62] Indeed, many of the same supporters who had endorsed the Reading Camp Association's initial moral and religious platform now favoured calls for education to foster assimilation to head off potential unrest.

As seen in the press reports, the appeal of assimilation through education partly eased public concerns. Fitzpatrick and his colleagues attempted to assuage these fears and promote the national work of the College. His publication "The Instructor and the Red" featured the College's "school of citizenship." Instructors, as he declared, "stand for firm Canadianism ... . They do a national work, not only in Canadianizing foreigners, but also in diffusing education generally."[63] The symbol of the College was clearly stated in its new slogan, "A National Asset, and a National Necessity."[64]

Many new immigrants sought work in frontier camps across the country. According to the College's profile of workers in 1921, the breakdown of nationalities shows that almost half of the workers were from Eastern European countries.[65] College classes reflected similar trends throughout the 1920s. Of a total sample of 3,005 workers between 1924 and 1928, the majority originated from eastern and southern Europe. Therefore, in 1921 under the sub-title "Coming of Age," Frontier College declared its intention to "educate and citizenize the immigrant" as one of three objectives, and Canadianization emerged as one the four main pillars of the College.[66] An examination of the representations of masculinity and citizenship throughout the 1920s, focussing on language, symbols, and images, allows us to identify how gender was imbricated in the rhetoric and ideals of a loyal citizen. In particular, we see how class-based constructions of the family man were held up to immigrant workers. The significance of family values was doubly important because of the single and relatively youthful adult-male culture that predominated in the work camps.[67]

The 200-page *Handbook for New Canadians*, written by Fitzpatrick and published in 1919, attempted to standardize the College's curriculum across the country. In this reader, citizenship teachings were encoded in a variety of themes through vignettes and text designed to offer instructors a methodology and textual material to be used for classroom teachings. Among the numerous examples, one of the most predominant discourses dealt with the domestic realm. In this area, the rhetoric of citizenship focused on three main areas: the male breadwinner, family values, and industry. As head of the household, a family man was responsible for providing for his wife and children. One vignette that depicted a manual labourer working on the streets had the caption, "he saves money for his wife and children from Russia."[68] As with many of the other images in the book, the virtues of a respectable manual labourer, such as honesty and cleanliness, were a constant feature among the illustrations. Another vignette of "The Workman's Family" featured a picture of two well-dressed young girls with the accompanying first-person narrative describing how, at the end of a day of work, "I can go home to my wife and little family. ... I want them to get a good schooling."[69] Women rarely appeared in the photos, and when they did they were confined to supportive domestic roles, as wives and mothers making the family's lunch or beautifying their home by gardening.

The virtues of the respectable working man as a good citizen were not just about manliness and citizenship; one discourse informed the other as seen in the poem "ARE YOU A GOOD CITIZEN?" that was published in the *Handbook* under a picture of working men.

> The good citizen –
> Loves God
> Loves his own family
> Loves Canada
> Loves the Empire
> Helps his neighbour
> Protects women and children
> Is truthful
> Is just
> Is honest
> Is brave
> Works hard.
> Does his work well
> Keeps his promise
> Keeps his body clean
> Is every inch a man.[70]

This rhetorical poem speaks to another theme of the *Handbook* that stressed the benefits of citizenship through industry in both urban and rural settings. One man's testimonial recounted how difficult it was to clear the land, but given the manly qualities of perseverance and hard work, "I will succeed."[71] In the photo illustrating this text the husband appears well dressed and prosperous and is pictured beside his immaculately groomed wife and another female adult, possibly his mother or mother-in-law. Along with the three children they are all posed in front of a large, well maintained home. As suggested in these written and pictorial images, in decidedly male terms using masculine imagery, men could aspire to provide middle-class lifestyles for their families. Elsewhere in the book, within sections devoted to leisure time activities, images included dining at fancy restaurants and attending theatre. Notably, assimilation served to promote both the material and cultural traits of a middle-class family within a predominantly working-class milieu. At the same time, holding out such ideals aided in promoting stability and security among immigrants and helped ensure that the much-needed workers would remain in Canada.[72] The incorporation of masculinity into models of citizenship that combined the role of breadwinner and patriarch helped to create and endorse a new set of masculine ideals that formed a part of modern Canada.

During the 1920s and early 1930s, the College's Annual Reports increasingly included images of College classes and instructors' reports to document pedagogical endeavours. More than anything else the College projected an unfailing belief in the power of education to foster social change. To provide a fuller understanding of how the College infused masculine imagery and citizenship within its pedagogical culture, a sampling of the type of photo that dominated the pages of the Reports appears in Figure 10.4.

figure 10.4

Excerpt from
Frontier College
publicity flyer,
ca. 1928.

NATIONAL ARCHIVES
OF CANADA / PA-148987.
REPRODUCED BY PERMISSION.

Notably, the focus of the text and illustration relates to aspects of citizenship education. Unlike earlier pictures showing men seated in a formal classroom, here we have a large group of men appearing mostly in relaxed poses. This informal photograph features workers who share similar masculine characteristics of industry and persistence, characteristics compatible with citizenship. Despite a hard day of labour the men's poses are strong, the physical stance determined, with staring eyes meeting the camera head on, feet solidly planted on the ground, squared shoulders upright. But overall the workers appear relaxed and, surprisingly, without their identification as Europeans in the captions, their general demeanour could be mistaken for that of respectable Anglo-Celtic men.

The placement of what appears to be a university graduation picture of the instructor beside the workers is particularly striking and requires further comment. In 1922 the College managed to secure a Charter enabling it to set up an extra-mural degree program. Throughout the 1920s, the government tried to convince the College to withdraw this section from its Charter, but Fitzpatrick launched what became "the fight of his life" to retain the College's degree-granting authority.[73] In the end, however, the government withheld the College's funding and by 1932 forced it to cancel the program. Hence, the instructors' academic standing as seen in these pages was an important component of the College's efforts to establish its credibility as a viable teaching institution.

Finally, the juxtaposition of the picture of the instructor and the workers reminds us of another important aspect of masculinity and citizenship. If the instructors were depicted as middle-class men with all the authority and status of the well-educated, good citizens, then what of the positioning of the other, marginal male group? These contrasting images serve to remind us of the existence of different masculinities and their significance when we study immigrant, working class men who themselves were "othered."

In assuming this emphasis on citizenship, I do not want the reader to conclude that Fitzpatrick or Frontier College ever abandoned the goal of improving working conditions and educating the worker. Indeed, the evidence supports the finding that the leaders and the instructors pursued this direction, alongside other plans, because they believed during the 1920s and 1930s, as they had in the early days when they first set up Camps and distributed reading material, that their mission was first and foremost to benefit the workers. Moreover, this study hints that the ideology of assimilation may have either indirectly or directly tempered the degree of tensions associated with the arrival and settlement of immigrants deemed "assimilable" into Canadian society. More ominously, however, my research also suggests that this ideology, which perhaps filtered some of the anti-foreign bias toward "suitable subjects for assimilation," in turn reinforced the bias and discrimination directed toward those racial and ethnic groups deemed unassimilable under early twentieth-century constructions of the citizen.

In sum, neither the college nor its leaders were simply opportunistic, nor were the workers mere pawns in a grand assimilation scheme. Clearly, as indicated in the letters that frontiersmen wrote about their experience at the College, many seized upon this opportunity to learn English, study arithmetic, advance job opportunities, and ease their integration into Canadian society.[74] And, as we see in the following testimonial by F. Sokal, a Ukrainian immigrant attending Frontier College in the early 1930s, schooling, in his view, was mutually beneficial for both student and teacher:

A Worker's Recommendation

Mr. Sokal Camp 2 to Frontier College

I am Fred Sokal working on Camp IE2 and I attend school at night time. My teacher was Mr. Fred Ongley. Mr. Ongley is a very good man and teacher for me. He teach me to read and to writes and lots words which I need in Canada. I thank him ever so much. And we need more such men same kind of Canada. I wish him the best education.[75]

Conclusion

The work of Fitzpatrick and the College pioneered and promoted key innovative pedagogical practices in modern-day Canada. First, it recognized the importance of education for adults regardless of wealth and helped to promote adult education in Canada. Second, the College became an early advocate of distance education and promoted the philosophy of taking education to people rather than expecting students to move to the College. Third, the College maintained the ideal that learning did not occur simply by reading books, but also in applying theory to real-life situations. Fourth, the College was, I suspect, among the first in Canada to develop a program to teach English as a Second Language. Finally, Fitzpatrick and his colleagues were tireless promoters of universal education. Although we often think of lifelong learning as a late twentieth-century phenomenon, in fact Fitzpatrick and the College saw it as a late nineteenth-century project.

Ramsey Cook states that the social gospel movement led to secularization because the reformers started to do something that other organizations did better.[76] As we have seen, Frontier College developed the capacity to teach literacy and remain relevant in a world that values education. Overall, the principle of education as a means to reform endured despite the changing nature of frontier societies, from morality to citizenship, from Social Gospel Association to Frontier College. The apparent lack of women in this study does not mean that gender was not part of the debate. The trumpeting of the patriarchal family and masculine identities of citizenship were brought together in this era to define who was part of the body politic in a way that excluded women from political life.[77] If this analysis of citizenship represents a wider view of citizenship education in Canada, then further study may help to explain why the men sitting on the Supreme Court of Canada in 1928 determined that women were not persons and therefore not eligible for appointment to the Canadian Senate.

Finally, the irony of this project of citizenship is that it offered these men the opportunity to become citizens of Canada, to share in the rights and privileges of a democratic country, with its common notion of fairness and equity as a basis for human rights. At the same time, however, we have seen how this common notion of Canadian was infused with Anglo-Celtic ideals and images of which these foreigners were not, and many could not ever be, a part. One wonders to what extent the assimilationist vision of Canadian citizens served to inspire the immigrants' own sense of cultural identification and pride in a country not fully their own, and how their isolation may in turn have contributed to subsequent enthusiasm for ethnic and racial identification in post-modern Canada.

Notes

I want to thank Dianne Dodd for sharing her unpublished paper on Frontier College with me; Michael Piva, Joan Sangster, members of the research group, Institute of Canadian Studies, University of Ottawa and the editors of the collection for their thoughtful comments on this chapter; and Colla MacDonald for her insights on organizational structures.

1. For a lengthy treatment of this topic, see Ian Radforth, *Bushworkers and Bosses in Northern Ontario, 1900-1980* (Toronto: University of Toronto Press, 1987).

2. Alfred Fitzpatrick, *The University in Overalls* (Toronto, 1923), 4-7.

3. James H. Morrison, *A Pictorial History of Frontier College Camps and Classrooms* (Toronto: The Frontier College Press, 1989), 3.

4. In addition to those cited above see, Edmund Bradwin, *The Bunkhouse Man* (New York: AMS Press Inc., 1968 reprint, originally printed in 1928); Larry Krotz, with Eica Martin and Philip Fernandez, compilers, *Frontier College Letters* (Toronto: Frontier College Press, 1999); George L. Cook with Marjorie Robinson, "'The Fight of My Life': Alfred Fitzpatrick and Frontier College's Extramural Degree for Working People," *Histoire sociale/Social History* XXIII 45 (May 1990): 81-112.

5. Franca Iacovetta, "Defending Honour, Demanding Respect," in *Gendered Pasts: Historical Essays in Femininity and Masculinity in Canada*, ed. Kathryn McPherson, Cecilia Morgan and Nancy M. Forestell (Toronto: Oxford University Press, 1999), 199-222.

6. Morrison, *A Pictorial History*, 7-8.

7. Morrison, *A Pictorial History*, 5-8.

8. Carl Berger, *The Sense of Power: Studies in the Ideas of Canadian Imperialism* (Toronto: University of Toronto Press, 1970), 31.

9. A.B. McKillop, *Matters of the Mind: The University in Ontario, 1791-1951* (Toronto: University of Toronto Press, 1994), 217-19.

10. Archives of Ontario (hereafter AO), RG 2, MS 5634, Eighth Annual Report of the Reading Camp Association, 1907-1908, 25, G.C. Speer's Report.

11. AO, RG 2, MS 5634, Sixth Annual Report, Reading Camp Association, 1906-1907.

12. AO, RG 2, MS 5634, Ontario Traveling Library, Case Y, Catalogue of Books, 1904.

13. AO, RG 2, MS 5634, Letter from R.A. O'Connor, St. Peter's Cathedral, Peterborough, ON, to A. Fitzpatrick, 12 Oct. 1900.

14. AO, RG 2, MS 5634, Eighth Annual Report of the Reading Camp Association, 1907-1908, 5.

15. National Archives of Canada (hereafter NAC), MG 28, I 124, Vol. 107, Reading Camp Annual Reports, 1901, Ralph Connor, in Preface to "Black Rock."

16. McKillop, *Matters of the Mind*, 244. On the influence of femininity on religion, see Susan Curtis, "The Son of Man and God the Father: The Social Gospel and Victorian Masculinity," in *Meanings for Manhood: Constructions of Masculinity in Victorian America*, eds. Mark C. Carnes and Clyde Griffen (Chicago and London: The University of Chicago Press, 1990), 67-78.

17. McKillop, *Matters of the Mind*, 243.

18. AO, RG 2, MS 5634, Eighth Annual Report of the Reading Camp Association, 1907-1908, 17. On the emphasis on Christ in the new masculinity see Curtis, "The Son of Man and God the Father."

19. Berger, *The Sense of Power*, 31.

20. AO, RG 2, MS 5634, Seventh Annual Report of the Reading Camp Association, 1906-1907, 4.

21. NAC, MG 28, I 24, Vol. 107, Library Extension in Ontario ... Reading Camps and Club Houses, Second Annual Report Canadian Reading Camp Movement, 1901-02. Letter from R. Jackson to Mr. Alfred Fitzpatrick, 15 Feb. 1902, 30-31.

22. Ibid. Resolution of Toronto Conference of Methodist Church 1901, W.H. Drummond to Mr. Alfred Fitzpatrick, 1901, 40-41.

23. NAC, MG 28, I 24, Vol. 107, Library Extension in Ontario ... Reading Camps and Club Houses, Second Annual Report Canadian Reading Camp Movement, 1901-02, "Home Education Extension," 8.

24. NAC, MG 28, I 24, Vol. 107, Library Extension in Ontario ... Reading Camps and Club Houses, Second Annual Report Canadian Reading Camp Movement, 1901-02, letter from W.H. Muldrew, 31 Aug. 1901, 40.

25. NAC, MG 28, I 24, Vol. 107, Library Extension in Ontario ... Reading Camps and Club Houses, Second Annual Report Canadian Reading Camp Movement, 1901-02, Letter from M.J. Shea to Alfred Fitzpatrick, 30 Dec. 1901, 36.

26. Morrison, *A Pictorial History*, 9.

27. AO, RG 2, MS 5634, letter from Alfred Fitzpatrick to Hon. Mr. Harcourt, Minister of Education, 29 June 1903.

28. Dianne Dodd, "Frontier College," Historic Sites and Monuments Board of Canada Agenda Paper, (Unpublished paper, nd) 3.

29. See, for example, Fitzpatrick's 1906 brief on "The Education of The Frontier Labourer," AO, RG 2, MS 5634.

30. NAC, MG 28, I 28, Vol. 107, Eighth Annual Report of the Reading Camp Association, 1907-1908.

31. Donald Avery, *Reluctant Host: Canada's Response to Immigrant Workers, 1896-1994* (Toronto: McClelland and Stewart, 1995). See also Ninette Kelley and Michael Trebilcock, *The Making of the Mosaic: A History of Canadian Immigration Policy* (Toronto: University of Toronto Press, 1998).

32. Avery, *Reluctant Host*, 22-26.

33. NAC, MG 28, I 124, Vol. 107, Camp Education with the Seventh Annual Report of Reading Camp Association, 1906-07, E. Bradwin, "The Reading Camp and the Foreign Navy," 23.

34. AO, RG 2, MS 5634, Canada's Frontiersmen with Eighth Annual Report of the Reading Camp Association, 1907-1908, "Extract from Letter of Instructor Dwight Gray," 14.

35. Ibid, "Letter of Instructor A.M. Shook," 19.

36. AO, RG 2, MS 5634, Canada's Frontiersmen with Eighth Annual Report of the Reading Camp Association, 1907-1908, "The Strangers Within Our Gates," 35.

37. AO, RG 2, MS 5634, Canada's Frontiersmen with Eighth Annual Report of the Reading Camp Association, 1907-1908, 9.

38. AO, RG 2, MS 5634, A. Fitzpatrick, "The Education of the Frontier Labourer," Extract from Instructor's Letters, 15 March 1905, 20.

39. AO, RG 2, MS 5634, Canada's Frontiersmen with Eighth Annual Report of the Reading Camp Association, 1907-1908, "Report of H. Waters," 30-31.

40. AO, RG 2, MS 5634, Canada's Frontiersmen with Eighth Annual Report of the Reading Camp Association, 1907-1908, "G.C. Speer's Report," 24-25.

41. AO, RG 2, RG 2 MS 5634, Reading Camp Association 1906-07, Annual Report, 11. Letter from A.J. Keeley to A. Fitzpatrick.

42. AO, RG 2, MS 5634, Canada's Frontiersmen with Eighth Annual Report of the Reading Camp Association, 1907-1908, "Letter of Instructor T. Richards," 17.

43. NAC, MG 28, I 124, Vol. 107, Twelfth Annual Report, 1913, 1.

44. NAC, MG 28, I 124, Vol. 107, Thirteenth Annual Report, 1914, 7.

45. NAC, MG 28, I 124, Vol. 107, Thirteenth Annual Report, 1914, 2.

46. NAC, MG 28, I 124, Vol. 107, Thirteenth Annual Report, 1914, 2-3.

47. NAC, MG 28, I 124, Vol. 107, Thirteenth Annual Report, 1914, 4.

48. NAC, MG 28, I 124, Vol. 107, "The Diffusion of Education," with the Seventeenth Annual Report of the Reading Camp Association, 9.

49. The book appears to have been reissued in 1919 as *Handbook for New Canadians* (Toronto: The Ryerson Press, 1919).

50. Fitzpatrick, "Introduction," in *Handbook for New Canadians*.

51. NAC, MG 28, I 124, Vol. 107, Thirteenth Annual Report, 1914, 2-7.

52. NAC, MG 28, I 124, Vol. 107, "The Diffusion of Education," with Seventeenth Annual Report of the Reading Camp Association, 1917, 9.

53. NAC, MG 28, I 124, Vol. 107, Thirteenth Annual Report, 1914, 5. On the role of education and the assimilation of immigrants in Canada, see J.T.M. Anderson, *The Education of the New Canadian: A Treatise on Canada's Greatest Educational Problem* (Toronto and London: J.M. Dent and Sons Ltd. 1918); James S. Woodsworth, *Strangers Within Our Gates* (Toronto: University of Toronto Press 1972, c1909).

54. NAC, MG 28, I 124, Vol. 107, Thirteenth Annual Report, 1914, 5.

55. Bradwin, *The Bunkhouse Man*, 291.

56. Avery, *Reluctant Host*, 79-80.

57. See Avery, *Reluctant Host*. For contemporary accounts see Anderson, *The Education of the New Canadian*; Woodsworth, *Strangers Within our Gates*.

58. Canada, House of Commons, *Debates*, 1918, 1003. (See reference on the same page to assimilation and Anglo-Saxon ideals.)

59. *Ottawa Citizen*, 6 May 1919, 16.

60. *The Globe*, 22 April 1921, 13, 15.

61. Avery, *Reluctant Host*, 235.

62. For example, YMCA, church groups, and settlement houses.

63. NAC, MG 28, I 124, Vol. 107, "The Instructor and The Red," with Nineteenth Annual Report of the Frontier College, 1919, 1, 3.

64. Undated Frontier College advertisements located in files at the NAC. From the information in the reports, I have assumed that they were published in the 1920s.

65. NAC, MG 28, I 124, Vol. 107, "The Frontier College: Coming of Age," Annual Report, 1921.

66. The other objectives were welfare, instruction, and leadership. See NAC, MG 28, I 124, Vol. 107, "The Frontier College, Coming of Age," Annual Report, 1921, 3, 11.

67. Of the workers attending school between 1924 and 1928, two-thirds were under the age of thirty.

68. Fitzpatrick, *Handbook*, 41.
69. Fitzpatrick, *Handbook*, 52.
70. Fitzpatrick, *Handbook*, 34.
71. Fitzpatrick, *Handbook*, 76.
72. Avery notes that prior to 1930 there was a slow rate of citizenship applications among certain groups of immigrant workers. *Reluctant Host*, 12.
73. Cook with Robinson, "'The Fight of My Life.'"
74. Instructors often assisted workers in applying for their naturalization papers and in preparing for citizenship tests.
75. Annual Report, 1934 cited in Morrison, *A Pictorial History*, 169.
76. Ramsay Cook, *The Regenerators: Social Criticism in Late Victorian English Canada* (Toronto: University of Toronto Press, 1985), 6.
77. For an analysis of gender politics in Ontario in an earlier period, see Cecilia Morgan, "Good Men Must Unite," in *Gendered Pasts*, ed. McPherson, Morgan and Forestell, 12-28.

chapter eleven

EDUCATION FOR MOTHERHOOD
Creating Modern Mothers and Model Citizens[1]

Katherine Arnup

> The duty of bringing up children does not belong to the state, but rather to the mothers, and whatever we do we must not be too ready to relieve them of their responsibility. The state can, however, do much to see that the rights of the children are not ignored and that the mothers have the opportunity given them of learning how best to rear their children.
>
> Charles A. Hodgetts (1921)[2]

The image of the family as a "haven in a heartless world"[3] has persisted ever since industrialization led to a separation of the public and private spheres in the late eighteenth and early nineteenth centuries. Yet, over the course of the twentieth century, the home was increasingly "invaded" as doctors, psychologists, and a host of other child-rearing experts attempted to create and enforce new standards of child rearing. Charged with the responsibility for producing and protecting the future citizens of the nation, mothers found themselves subject to "heightened public scrutiny."[4] Through child-care books and pamphlets, newspaper columns, and home visits by nurses, mothers were bombarded with detailed instructions on every aspect of pregnancy and infant and child care. Experts promised that careful adherence to their instructions would produce healthy, well-disciplined children, future citizens for the modern, scientific age.

Child-care experts prescribed not only rules of infant and child care but also an ideology of the family and of appropriate gender roles within it. Measured against the new standards of modern mothering — standards that took for granted a middle-class, Anglo-Saxon family model with a male breadwinner and full-time home-maker — many mothers found themselves wanting. Yet motherhood was a responsibility they could not evade, for their status as citizens depended upon their role as mothers. They were to be the "mothers of the race," producing the new industrial and clerical workforce, the politicians, physicians, and leaders. Motherhood, and their role in defending the home front, had earned women the vote; in the postwar period, it would be their activities in the home that would test their mettle as citizens.

In this chapter I analyse the emergence of "modern" motherhood during the early decades of the twentieth century and examine the impact of this development on women's participation in both the public and private spheres. I will begin by examining the demographic and political context of early twentieth-century Canada, as concerns over national health took on crisis proportions. Responding to this crisis with modern scientific techniques and advice, physicians assumed an increasingly dominant role as overseers of the nation's health. In this capacity, they became the intermediaries between women and the state, dictating and ensuring the proper implementation of the rules of scientific child care. I will examine the key elements of this advice, considering its impact on women's experiences of motherhood. Finally, I will analyse the limitations that their role as "mothers of the race" placed on women's capacity to participate as full citizens.

"The Century of Canada"

Canada emerged from World War I as "a nation transformed." In 1918, it appeared that the twentieth century might indeed, to use Sir Wilfrid Laurier's phrase, be "the Century of Canada." As countless Canadian historians have observed, the modern nation of Canada was forged on the battlefields of Europe. For the first time in its brief history, Canada had participated in the international conflict in its own right, thereby earning the right to be a signatory to the Treaty of Versailles and to send a representative to the League of Nations. That participation came, of course, at a huge cost. Over 60,000 Canadians lost their lives, and countless others returned home with profound mental and physical disabilities. Families were fragmented, and thousands of mothers were left to raise children on their own, with little financial aid.

In addition to the suffering and destruction it caused, World War I both revealed and exacerbated existing social problems. During the late nineteenth and early twentieth centuries, high rates of immigration, rapid urbanization in areas completely lacking in sanitation and health facilities, and widespread urban poverty had led to tremendous social and health problems. The carnage of the Great War, coupled with the postwar problems of high unemployment, high inflation, and anti-labour wartime legislation, led to widespread labour unrest, culminating in the Winnipeg General Strike of 1919. Many observers, shocked by widespread evidence of "social decay" at home and revolution and Bolshevism overseas, expressed concerns about just what sort of century it was that Canada had inherited.

Foremost among these concerns was the issue of national health. Recruitment for military service during the war had dramatically revealed the poor health of Canadian men: 68 per cent of the applicants for enlistment were rejected as unfit.[5] That fact, compounded by the staggering losses of the Great War and the Spanish influenza epidemic, the steadily declining birth rate among the "native-born" population, and high rates of immigration prior to the war, led to widespread fears of "race suicide."[6] Without drastic measures, many reformers and government officials believed that the future of the nation — the white Imperial Nation — was at stake.

Infants and young children appeared to be especially at risk. Despite some improvement in the health of the general population as a result of developments in medical technology and sanitation and discoveries in bacteriology and immunology, infant mortality rates continued to rise. In 1901, in Toronto, for example, 160 of every one thousand babies died before reaching the age of one.[7] Montreal claimed the highest infant mortality rate in North America, as one in every three babies died before reaching its first birthday.[8] Cities across the country recorded similarly grim statistics. Infant mortality had of course long been a fact of life, a regrettable if efficient means of ensuring the survival of the fittest. By the early twentieth century, however, attitudes toward population and national health had changed. Nations could no longer afford to squander their future citizens in the grim display of the "slaughter of the innocents." Instead, doctors and politicians came to believe that infant mortality must be curbed.[9]

Preventing infant mortality was essential because babies and children held the key to national strength. As Dr. Helen MacMurchy,[10] first chief of the federal Division of Child Welfare, explained, "We are only now discovering that Empires and States are built up of babies. Cities are dependent for their continuance on babies. Armies are recruited only if and when we have cared for our babies."[11] Children came to be seen as a "national asset," one that had to be preserved and protected at all costs. To preserve this valuable resource, government officials established infant welfare commissions, wrote scientific reports, set up government agencies, and deployed hundreds of public health nurses to wage a war on infant mortality. While experts acknowledged that many factors, including poverty, overcrowding, and malnutrition, contributed to the problem of infant mortality, in looking for solutions they focussed almost exclusively upon mothers. As MacMurchy argued, "*It is through the mother that infant mortality can be prevented.*"[12]

There were, of course, excellent reasons for this focus on mothers. As Cynthia Comacchio has argued, "babies could not be approached, much less saved, except through their mothers." Not only were children entirely dependent upon their parents for their physical survival, but attempting to bypass parents through direct intervention into the family (to remove children from troubled homes, for example) held a political danger as well: "To focus directly on the child would have meant implementing the kind of extraordinary measures that the reformers labelled 'bolshevism.'"[13] In light of the fears engendered by the Russian Revolution, measures requiring direct intervention into the family were ones that neither state officials nor reformers were prepared to entertain. As Comacchio notes, "Child welfare advocates never interpreted the rhetoric of 'child as national asset' to mean that the state was to have direct responsibility for the health of children. Rather, it meant that there was a new obligation to make mothers more responsible to the state."[14]

To ensure that women willingly accepted their responsibility, motherhood was elevated to the status of a national duty. To combat the alarmingly low national birth rate, women — especially Anglo-Saxon middle-class women — were exhorted to take up the challenge of motherhood. As Mariana Valverde has argued, "Women did not merely have babies: they reproduced 'the race.' Women did not merely have just enough babies or too much sex: through their childbearing they either helped or hindered the forward march of (Anglo-Saxon) civilization."[15] Although women were "naturally" equipped for pregnancy and childbirth, they were sadly lacking in the skills and knowledge that motherhood required. Maternal instincts were no longer sufficient for the modern age. Reflecting the views of the broader social reform movement, infant welfare experts advocated a model of "scientific motherhood," a motherhood that captured the "efficiency, progress, and modernity" of twentieth-century Canada.[16]

Most women were, in fact, willing participants in the campaign against infant mortality. As Jill Vickers recently argued, "Nationalist women of British descent were required to perform two functions — have children, because of the scarcity of the British population, and participate actively in nation-building. Their public activism had to be consistent with their maternal role."[17] On the political front, Canada's maternal feminists had struggled for decades for women's enfranchisement, arguing that women's maternal role made them ideally suited for a role in the public sphere. Women would be the nation's housekeepers, sweeping government of corruption and the streets and offices of the nation of immorality.[18]

The war provided the ideal opportunity for women to demonstrate their capacity to fulfill this new role. Through their participation on the home front, caring for their families while their husbands fought overseas, running voluntary organizations, and, to a limited extent, operating factories, women were deemed to be worthy of the ultimate reward of citizenship: the vote. While numerous factors, including the need to create an electorate favourable to conscription, led to women's enfranchisement at this time, it was women's wartime service that was used to justify granting women the franchise in 1918. Thus, for women, access to citizenship was granted not in recognition of their participation as equal players in the public sphere. Rather, citizenship was grounded in their role as mothers, a role they could fulfill with equal ease in the private and the public spheres.

It was not only maternal feminists but mothers themselves who embraced the emerging ideology of motherhood. High rates of maternal and infant mortality led many women to fear for their own lives and for those of their children. As Maureen O'Neil has noted in a recent article on women and citizenship, "For most women, having babies and looking after them have until very recently overshadowed everything else. Not only did these responsibilities take up most of their lifetime — no matter what other work they did in addition — for centuries it took their lives."[19]

Finally, women were anxious to make a contribution to Canada's century. Unmarried women would be nurses and teachers, social workers, and volunteers. For married women, motherhood was their vocation. Motherhood in the home and in the national arena was an important role that only women could fulfill. Thus mothers, like their sisters in the women's movement, were active and willing participants in the campaign to educate mothers. Hence educating women for motherhood became the theme of infant and child welfare work in Canada during the first half of the twentieth century. Through films, radio talks, lectures, clinics, and home visits by public health nurses, and through the production of pamphlets and booklets at a staggering rate, experts sought to teach women the skills of scientific motherhood. Mothers would be trained to preserve the most valuable national asset: the child.

Mounting an Educational Campaign

While new mothers today may well feel inundated by advice literature, the volume of advice literature produced during the 1920s was truly staggering. Between March 1921 and March 1922, for example, a total of 365,503 child welfare publications were distributed by the federal Department of Health's Division of Child Welfare alone.[20] When compared with the total female population of child-bearing age of 2,142,000, that represents more than one piece of literature for every six women in Canada.[21] During its 12-year life span, 800,000 copies of *The Canadian Mother's Book* were distributed, a figure that represents nearly one copy for every four live births in Canada between 1921 and 1932.[22] The federal Division of Child Welfare was only one of several branches of government producing advice literature during this period.[23] In fact, all levels of government as well as non-profit agencies, individual authors, and even baby-food companies produced booklets, pamphlets, and texts on child rearing.[24]

As I have noted, this advice was not forced upon women; on the contrary, they actively sought it out. Throughout the period under consideration in this chapter, publications on infant and prenatal care were in high demand. As MacMurchy was to remark, "No one will ever convince the Division of Child Welfare that mothers do not want to learn. Thousands of mothers' letters are on file to prove the contrary."[25] Women (and their husbands, friends, mothers, and sisters) wrote to all levels of government requesting copies of the publications. In addition, publications were distributed by public health nurses and were available in doctors' offices, in registration offices, through magazines, and in department stores and supermarkets.

Why *did* women turn to experts for advice on prenatal and infant care? As traditional female support networks broke down with the exodus from the family farm, new mothers found themselves alone on what must have often appeared to be alien terrain. The decline in family size, which had begun in the late nineteenth century, also meant that women lacked the experience in caring for young children that had traditionally accompanied life in a large family. While fertility rates declined first among the urban middle classes in English Canada, that trend gradually spread throughout the rest of the Canadian population. As a result, twentieth-century mothers increasingly found themselves in the position that one author has termed "double jeopardy — they have no one to teach them and no previous experience."[26]

Not only were women essentially alone in an alien world, but it was an often terrifying place. The fears engendered by infant mortality and morbidity, coupled with an acute shortage of medical care for rural and poor women, led many mothers to seek advice from child-rearing experts. Information about the latest scientific discoveries, ranging from immunization to the importance of vitamins, was available only from a doctor, public health nurse, or other child-care expert. Not surprisingly, then, many women turned to their family physician or to the nurse at the local baby clinic for information on the most up-to-date views on child care.

Dramatic changes in medical wisdom and ideas about infant care meant that few women could turn to their own mothers for help — even if their mothers were geographically accessible. This problem was greatly compounded by the systematic attack on traditional methods of child rearing that began in the early decades of the twentieth century and has continued to the present day. Authors of advice literature repeatedly urged mothers not to "try out fancy theories learned over the back fence,"[27] encouraging instead an almost religious adherence to the doctor's advice. Reinforcing the doctor's emerging role as expert advisor, a typical passage warned readers, "Be sure to tell [your doctor] all that you have observed and follow his instructions minutely. Avoid the advice of neighbours or relatives and accept that which you pay for getting."[28]

New mothers were frequently warned of the dangers of seeking advice and assistance from their own mothers. Referring to a popular advice manual written by Dr. L. Emmett Holt, a physician, a 1923 publication reminded its readers, "A 'Holt' in the hand is worth more than two grandmothers in the bush."[29] Thirty years later, author June Callwood referred to grandmothers as "a species doctors feel are the natural enemies of modern science,"[30] an assessment based on interviews she had conducted with physicians. The message in the advice literature was clear: modern mothers consulted experts, not their hopelessly old-fashioned mothers. Such counsel would have contributed to the physical isolation that many mothers were already experiencing.

The shift in the location of childbirth from home to hospital may also have contributed to women's reliance on expert advice. In marked contrast to a home birth, where a woman made the transition to motherhood surrounded by family and friends in a familiar setting, a hospital birth offered the new mother efficient baby nurses who took command of the care and feeding of the baby. While the quality of care the baby received may have been above reproach, many women found that the combination of hospital procedures and being in a foreign environment left them feeling alienated from their newborns.

In the face of high rates of infant and child mortality, mothers feared for their children's well-being. Child-rearing experts warned mothers that failure to adhere to their prescriptions could result in serious illness or even death, an outcome that would be blamed almost entirely on the mother. They were not being abandoned, however, for the medical profession was there, as expert counsel, advisor, and judge of maternal behaviour.

MEDICALIZING MOTHERHOOD

Throughout this period, one of the most significant developments was the increasing medicalization of motherhood. All aspects of maternity, including pregnancy, childbirth, and infant and child care, were subject to heightened medical attention. This began long before the baby arrived. As one author advised, "The mother should, on the slightest suspicion of pregnancy, consult the best physician available, put herself under his direction and be guided by his advice."[31] Texts prescribed a new role for physicians as the mediators between mothers and the state. While mothers were ultimately "responsible to the state,"[32] it was physicians — through prenatal visits, ongoing medical supervision following childbirth, and regular "checkups" — who would ensure women's compliance.

Although experts offered a variety of instructions concerning prenatal care, including the importance of diet, sleep, and freedom from worry, the single most important (and most oft-repeated) "order" was to consult the doctor. "If there is anything wrong with you at all ... ask the Doctor about it at once," MacMurchy advised, reassuring the mother that "there is always something the Doctor can do to make you better. That is what a Doctor is for."[33] Such a promise could only be fulfilled, of course, if the doctor's orders were strictly observed. Therefore, MacMurchy admonished women to "[d]o *what the doctor tells you.*"[34]

Women were to derive their daily instructions from advice literature, but they were to consult their doctors to ensure that they were implementing these rules in exactly the right way. It was a partnership that suited both government officials and the medical profession. By entrusting the care of mothers and infants to physicians, state officials could avoid making significant investments in services and health care. For their part, physicians, through the supervision of prenatal care and childbirth, could be assured of a point of entry to families' future medical care, thereby expanding their sphere of practice.[35]

The physician's role was to continue long after the period of confinement, as his terrain extended into matters of infant and child care ranging from breastfeeding and weaning to habit formation and temper tantrums. Indeed, by the 1930s a significant proportion of the doctor's time was taken up with care of the "normal child"[36] rather than with the treatment of disease. In light of both the volume and the detailed nature of the infant- and child-care advice, it is not surprising that such visits might take up so much of the physician's time.

SCIENTIFIC CHILD CARE

The way to protect child health was through the implementation of what was termed scientific child care. At issue was not only national health, but also the needs of the modern industrial workplace. As Cynthia Comacchio explains, if mothers

> became scientific managers of the household, they could run their homes like the ideal modern factory. They could minimize inefficiency and waste at their source by improving the health of their children through scientific child care methods. And once physical welfare was assured in infancy, they could manage and train their children all along the path to healthy, productive, and efficient adulthood.[37]

Thus, during the 1920s and 1930s, child-rearing experts attempted to transform the rearing of infants and young children from an affective, tradition-based relationship into a scientifically controlled and managed experiment. Whether they were successful is not at issue here. That they did seek to promote a radically different style of child rearing — a style that broke with traditions previously passed from generation to generation — is clearly reflected in the advice literature.[38] Child rearing booklets in the 1920s and 1930s advocated regimentation and regularity in all dimensions of the child's development in an endeavour apparently to help mothers to turn their babies into what noted pediatrician Alan Brown approvingly termed "little machines."

The key to scientific child rearing was the establishment of fixed times for every activity. From the minute the baby arrived home from the hospital (and indeed from the moment he or she was born) a rigid timetable was to be set up. Charts indicating the correct time for feeding, sleeping, elimination, bathing, and even sunbathing were included in almost every pamphlet. Everything was to take place "by the clock." Only then would the baby learn what was expected of him. MacMurchy explained the importance of this regimen as follows: "Keep Right to the Time-Table. It gives the baby a good start in life, with good habits of eating, sleeping, bathing, toilet and recreation. Watch him Live and Thrive. Regular habits are Best for the Baby."[39]

It is perhaps not surprising that in an era inspired by the ideas of Frederick W. Taylor in the workplace, experts should attempt to apply scientific management to the home. The rigidity with which the concept was applied to babies, however, is rather alarming. The process of child training had to begin early, for, as a Toronto publication advised, "It is in the first few days that the baby's habits are formed. He is born without habits, and it is just as easy to form good ones as bad ones. He should be fed regularly, should be made comfortable and left in his bed to sleep."[40] The authors stressed that the task of ensuring the development of good habits rested "largely with the mother or attendant."[41] In the 1933 edition of *The Baby*, the authors delineated the lines of responsibility more sharply:

> The responsibility for the formation of habits of conduct in the child of normal mentality rests entirely with the parents, both parents sharing equally in this responsibility. Neither the primary school, the playground, nor the Sunday school can be anything but contributing factors.[42]

While the author of this passage referred to "parents," it was clearly mothers who were responsible for habit training and formation.

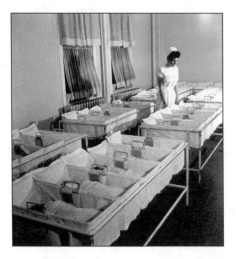

figure 11.1

Nursery in the Ottawa Civic Hospital, 1946.

FRANK ROYAL / NFB / NATIONAL ARCHIVES OF CANADA / PA-190433.

There can be no doubt that the infant, once properly trained, was a much easier charge for the caregiver to manage. If training went as directed, the child would be predictable, well-behaved, and even-tempered, requiring fewer diapers, fewer feedings, and more sleep. Mothers were given licence to leave an obstreperous youngster to cry, knowing it was "for its own good." At face value, perhaps, the scientific child-rearing advice may have benefitted both mother and child. But two questions remain unanswered: Did mothers follow this advice? And, if they did, what effect did it have on their experience of motherhood? It is to these issues that I will now turn.

Following the Rules

Did mothers try to implement the advice they received? Did they appreciate the efforts of child-rearing experts? What happened to those women who, for whatever reasons, failed to implement the advice? The answer to these questions will always to some degree remain speculative. In my larger work on this issue, I turned to three sources to assess maternal responses: the records of the health-care professionals, mothers' letters to child-rearing experts, and interviews with mothers.[43] I will draw briefly upon these sources in the following discussion.

First, did women comply with the experts' advice? One sector that considered this question at length was the nursing profession.[44] In contrast to doctors, who rarely commented on this issue, assuming perhaps that their dictates would be followed without question, nurses did attempt to assess mothers' response to their advice. Records of the nursing profession suggest that nurses received a warm reception from most sectors of the population. The author of the following 1923 article in *Canadian Nurse* described women's ready acceptance of the nurses' counsel:

> The effect of this constant teaching has been well seen during the past summer. The rate of mortality from summer diarrhoea among these babies this year has been only one-fourth the rate from the disease in the city on a whole. Many mothers have said, "Yes, baby began to get sick last week, but I did just what the nurse said and he got all right by the next day."[45]

Surveys of participants in prenatal classes in Toronto during the 1940s indicated an equally positive response to the teachings of public health nurses. In a report based on one such survey, the author noted that, "with very few exceptions, the comments on the value of the classes, educationally and practically, were enthusiastic." One mother was quoted as saying that "classes helped more than all baby books could do." Another indicated that she had "enjoyed motherhood so much more because of knowledge given in classes."[46]

Maternal education, through well-baby clinics, home visits, and mothers' classes, provided an ideal opportunity to introduce immigrant mothers to the most up-to-date "Canadian ways." In her recent book, historian Julia Grant argues that education served as a powerful mechanism for Americanizing new immigrants:

> During the late nineteenth and early twentieth centuries, Americanization campaigns were conducted by middle-class, largely Protestant reformers to usher immigrants into mainstream society by teaching them the English language and American principles of citizenship. The reformers also strove to disseminate American "family values" to ensure the acculturation of seemingly unassimilable southeast European immigrants.[47]

Grant notes that "[a] special rhetoric evolved in the education of immigrant mothers that linked the adoption of American child-rearing methods to citizenship."[48] Similar efforts to Canadianize immigrant mothers were an important component of the infant and child welfare movements in Canada during the early decades of this century. Indeed, Anglo-Canadian women, working as nurses, social workers, and teachers, were often in the vanguard of these initiatives. As Jill Vickers has noted, "many married women working as volunteers in women-led organizations, and unmarried women working as teachers, social workers, settlement workers, nurses, missionaries, journalists, even a few women doctors, lawyers and magistrates — supported the goals of nation-building."[49]

Public health nurses played a key role in teaching "Canadian ways" to new immigrants. In urban areas, health departments hired nurses who were able to speak to immigrant mothers in their own language. For example, in an effort to reach its growing population of immigrants, Toronto's Department of Public Health appointed Matilda Simone, an Italian-speaking nurse, in 1914. The following year, a Russian-born nurse who also spoke German, Ukrainian, Polish, and Latvian, was hired. The appointment in 1920 of a nurse to work with Macedonian immigrants completed the roster of "language nurses."[50] In addition, the Department began translating its prenatal and infant care literature into Italian and Yiddish. When Nurse Simone resigned in 1921, however, the department chose not to replace her. The author of a 1945 history of public health nursing in Toronto explained the decision as follows: "It was beginning to be realized ... that the appointment of nurses to serve our non-English-speaking population was not altogether wise and that instead every effort should be made to have these people use the language of the Country."[51]

Whether they could speak the language of immigrant mothers or not, public health nurses faced other barriers in their efforts to persuade immigrant mothers to adopt the methods of scientific child rearing.[52] As Marion Royce explains,

Language was not the only barrier .... Equally formidable were the fears and forebodings of the immigrant mothers. Far from their native soil, they were baffled by the nurses' unfamiliar ways of infant care. They insisted, for instance, that a child should not be bundled into layers of clothing that the mothers thought essential to its comfort.

While Royce notes that the nurses' "new-fangled" methods were unfamiliar to Canadian-born mothers as well, she suggests that those women more readily accepted the nurses' advice. "So radical a departure from traditional ways was less acceptable to perplexed immigrant mothers who misunderstood and often resented the nurse's interference even if the infant might be more comfortable." Royce concludes, however, that while the nurses were "outsiders in an immigrant community," nonetheless "they were there, calling and to be called in case of need, and over the years mutual respect often blossomed in friendship."[53]

figure 11.2

Nurse Beatrice Kitchen of St. Luke's Mission Hospital holding Quaga while Soudlo, the baby's mother, prepares powdered milk formula, 1946.

GEORGE HUNTER / NFB / NATIONAL ARCHIVES OF CANADA / PA-166452.

It is likely that first-time mothers may have been particularly receptive to the nurses' advice. Discussing expectant mothers' unwillingness to attend prenatal classes, the author of a 1930 article in the *Canadian Nurse* lamented,

The older and more experienced prenatal case has consistently been found to develop a still more *independent* attitude towards offers of clinical help or advice during this very important period, and in many cases the result of her *indifference* works to the detriment of both mother and child.[54]

Elsewhere, public health nurses commented on the receptiveness of first-time mothers, finding them subject to neither the "independent attitude" nor the "indifference" exhibited by mothers who already had older children. The interviews conducted by Denyse Baillargeon provide an interesting insight into this issue. Several of Baillargeon's informants "remarked that it became too difficult to get to clinics after the second or third child. 'But after that, the third one, I didn't go to the Gouttes de Lait anymore. I had to take all three of them with me.'" Other mothers complained about the fact that the clinics were filled with babies with "colds, with whooping cough,"[55] dangers many mothers would have wisely sought to avoid.

Testimony of mothers, found in letters and interviews, provides an almost uniformly positive image of expert advice.[56] Virtually all of the mothers I interviewed talked about the help they had received from advice literature.[57] One mother, who used Dr. Goldbloom's book throughout the 1930s, referred to his book as "a tower of strength."[58] Another mother, the wife of an obstetrician, used Dr. Spock's *Baby and Child Care* throughout her child-rearing years. "He was a great comfort in those days," she recalled. When other child-rearing experts were lecturing her with "all the 'you shoulds,'" Dr. Spock reassured her that "it's O.K. to ... follow your instincts."[59]

Mothers' letters to authors of child-rearing literature expressed tremendous gratitude for the help they provided.[60] Almost without exception, mothers indicated that they had followed the advice and that the result had been better health for their children. The following are typical responses: "I found the last book a great help in raising my baby. She is a fine healthy girl today thanks to you." Another mother commented: "When my baby was born the Victorian Nurse gave me your first book covering the first year of a child's life which I found so valuable. I went by it as for change of food, sleeping habits, etc. and I really don't know just what I'd have done without it."[61]

Many letters expressed a feeling of closeness with the authors of advice manuals. A Québec mother told the United States Children's Bureau in 1921, "Much I would like to know you, as your [sic] just like a mother to me, as I'm an orphan." "Words can not express what I feel for you in my heart," she continued. "I can only write that I thank you infinitely for your kindness towards helping me with my baby."[62] Another woman, living on an Alberta homestead, "miles from a telephone and many more miles from a doctor or any dependable person of whom I could ask advice," expressed her gratitude for the pre-natal and post-natal letters. "They have been just like letters from a very dear and trusted friend and I miss looking forward to their arrival."[63]

Radio broadcasts, such as the ones conducted by Dr. Allan Roy Dafoe, doctor of the Dionne quintuplets, appear to have played a similar role for women living far from friends and family. One listener, who lived in the mountains near Boulder, Colorado, told Dr. Dafoe, "I have no one to advise me on the care of my three babies, and surely do appreciate your help."[64] Another mother reported, "I never miss your broadcasts and believe I've learned more from them than from all the advice given by friends and relatives."[65]

How are we to interpret this evidence? On the face of it, at least, it suggests that many women welcomed child-rearing advice, finding it helpful in dealing with the daunting tasks of motherhood. We must question, however, whether official records provide us with the complete picture. The vast majority of letters received by the Division of Child Welfare, for example, were destroyed.[66] While a much larger number of letters to the Canadian Council on Child and Family Welfare remain intact, they nonetheless represent only a portion of the total volume of mail received by the Council. Whether these glowing letters were indeed "typical" is impossible to determine, since we do not have the entire volume of correspondence upon which to draw. Furthermore, mothers who did not have a successful outcome to their pregnancies, or whose children died early in life, would have been unlikely to bring this information to the attention of child-rearing experts. Advice literature laid responsibility for children's health and well-being squarely in mothers' laps. If something went wrong, mothers had only themselves to blame. It would seem unlikely that such mothers would voluntarily come forward to admit their failure.

Nonetheless, the letters do represent eloquent testimony of the isolation of new motherhood and the desperate need many mothers felt for information and help, especially given the responsibility they bore and the relative lack of material support they received. Living on homesteads, far from neighbours and family, without medical attention or help, many Canadian women undoubtedly appreciated the information and even companionship that the advice pamphlets provided. Even after World War II, as electrification, telephones, and improved roads began to break down rural isolation, motherhood remained a lonely experience. The breakdown of extended family networks, the geographic mobility of nuclear families, and the physical isolation of nuclear family units within suburban developments meant that mothers continued to spend long periods of time alone with their children.

Women not only appreciated the companionship that advice literature provided, but many attributed the successful outcome of their pregnancies and the health and well-being of their children to the advice they had received from child-rearing experts. Does the historical evidence support their view? Statistics of infant and maternal mortality and morbidity rates clearly indicate that, over the course of the twentieth century, *all* of these rates declined significantly. By mid-century, the risks associated with child-birth had been dramatically reduced and mothers and children were enjoying longer, healthier lives. The issue of whether we can attribute improvements in maternal and child health to changes in health-care services and the widespread availability of prenatal and child care advice remains hotly debated by historians. While some historians[67] attribute these improved rates to the increase in physician-attended, hospital births, and changing child-rearing practices, others dispute these conclusions, arguing that improvements in nutrition and antiseptic conditions as well as the discovery of antibiotics were the key factors in improved maternal and infant health.[68]

While elements of the expert advice may have had a positive effect on children's health, much of the advice has now been partially and, in some cases, entirely disproved. In the area of childbirth, for example, mothers during the interwar years were ordered to remain in bed for ten to fourteen days following delivery. While some women may have welcomed the rest such an order provided,[69] others found themselves extremely weak as a result of the inactivity. By the time they were finally permitted to rise from their beds, their muscles had weakened to such an extent that they required special exercises to regain proper muscle tone. Other standard hospital practices made the transition to new motherhood difficult. Rigid scheduling, coupled with the routine use of supplementary feedings until the mother's milk came in, may, in fact, have rendered breastfeeding almost impossible. While most doctors officially recommended breastfeeding as the safest, most effective method of infant feeding, many of the specific details of their infant feeding advice would also have made breastfeeding difficult. Failing to recognize the value of colostrum, many hospitals concluded that it was not useful to make a newborn "struggle on an empty breast," and as a result they delayed the start of breastfeeding until as late as the fourth day.

Many of the other regimens of child care imposed similar hardships on the lives of infants and young children. The use of soapsticks and anal suppositories, advocated during the interwar years to encourage "regularity," had fallen into disfavour by the 1940s, as experts began to recognize the dangers of such procedures. Strict schedules and the practice of letting the baby "cry it out" had also fallen into disfavour by the postwar years. Nonetheless, countless babies suffered through such harsh regimes, as their mothers ignored their inclinations to comfort a crying baby in the interests of maintaining the all-important routine. The evidence suggests that even if it did occur to women to question the efficacy of such routines, it would have required considerable self-confidence to challenge the canons of medical science.

What did the shifts in child-rearing advice mean for mothers who found themselves in the middle of their child-rearing years when the shift from scientific child rearing to permissiveness took place? One such mother described her experience this way:

> I was serving a new vegetable to the boys. Suddenly I realized that I expected Peter, the oldest, to clean his plate. Daniel, the middle one, didn't have to eat it but he had to taste it. And little Billy, as far as I was concerned, could do whatever he wanted.[70]

Although she was able to view her dilemma with humour, many women found it difficult to make sense of the conflicting messages contained in the advice literature. Women whose child-rearing years often stretched out over twenty years or more undoubtedly found themselves struggling to keep pace with the changes in methodology and philosophy advocated by child-care experts.

Maternal confusion may, in fact, be a logical consequence of expert advice itself. While mothers often sought expert advice in order to bolster their self-confidence, the advice rarely had the desired effect. The reason may lie in the disjuncture between the experts' expressed desire to increase parents' confidence and their own need to establish themselves as experts.[71] If experts succeeded in raising parents' self-confidence to the level of self-sufficiency, they might in fact render themselves obsolete. This may account for the apparent contradiction between Spock's opening words of advice to parents to "trust yourself. You know more than you think you do," and the fact that the first edition of his book was 502 pages long and the second, 627 pages long.[72]

Advice literature engendered not only confusion in its readers, but also feelings of guilt. Authors frequently castigated mothers for adhering to "old-fashioned" practices. In the 1950s, for example, mothers were warned of the serious long-term psychological problems caused by early toilet training, force feeding, and rigid scheduling — all procedures advocated in the literature of the interwar years. By the late 1940s, women were accused of being inflexible, and of paying too much attention to schedules and rules and not enough to the baby's needs. While an astute reader might have been able to recognize that the blame lay with the experts and not with herself, the fear of having caused their children serious, long-term problems led increasing numbers of middle-class mothers to turn to child psychologists in search of help for the children they had supposedly damaged.

Perhaps the greatest problem for mothers lay in the disjuncture between the requirements of the advice and the reality of their own lives. Readers of advice literature were frequently inundated with detailed descriptions of the physical requirements of infants and young children, ranging from an elaborate layette to a separate nursery and bedroom for the new arrival. While the standards demanded by Helen MacMurchy were less elaborate than many, they were clearly beyond the reach of the average Canadian family. In one publication, for example, MacMurchy remarked, almost in an off-handed manner: "You are not living in a flat are you? A flat is not a good place for a baby."[73] Elsewhere she consoled: "You haven't a bath-room? Never mind, you can do without until you can get it," adding parenthetically, "(get it as soon as you can)."[74] No such sympathy was offered for the mother who needed to share a bed with her new baby. MacMurchy ordered the mother, "Never let the baby sleep with anybody!"[75] How was a mother to feel if she could not provide her baby with a room of its own, if poverty and inadequate heat led the family to share a bed with the baby in order to keep warm in winter? MacMurchy and other authors of advice literature warned that she might kill her child. But what choice did she have? Evidence suggests that many families were forced to share rooms and even beds, for lack of space.

figure 11.3

A Victorian Order nurse showing a woman how to bathe a baby, 1946.

FRANK ROYAL / NFB / NATIONAL ARCHIVES OF CANADA / PA-190432.

The inability to meet the expectations established by advice manuals undoubtedly caused worry and anxiety for many women. Yet, ironically, one of the strongest warnings encountered in the literature concerns the dangers of worry. Time and time again, the mother was exhorted to "cheer up."[76] In the 1923 publication, *How to Take Care of the Mother*, MacMurchy warned that "mother must not be hurried, worried, driven or oppressed. Worry is one of the greatest enemies of health and happiness."[77] But how were women to avoid worrying? For many women, deprived of their husband's income because he was unemployed or even dead, supplying their families with the basic necessities of life was a tremendous struggle. How was a mother-to-be to avoid worrying when she could scarcely afford to feed the children she already had? As one mother noted in a letter to Prime Minister R.B. Bennett, "The worry of all these things is driving me mad."[78] Another woman, a widow with four children, wrote, "I have been fighting against worry untill I feel as I am going to break down completely."[79]

One of the most eloquent descriptions of the contradiction between expert advice and the reality of women's lives appeared in an anonymous 1933 article entitled "I am a Canadian mother," published in *Chatelaine*. In an ironic tone that echoed the rhetoric of the infant welfare movement, the author wrote,

> The most noble calling in the world is mine. My country realizes that my children are its greatest asset. My country knows that the wisdom and intelligence I exercise now in teaching and training my children contribute much to their usefulness but a few years hence, and that the foods used in body-building now decide whether they shall become a burden or an asset. My country knows this and spends time and money to send out useful information to mothers within its borders. *I am a Canadian mother and the recipient of more free advice than any other mortal on earth.*

Despite all the "free advice," however, this woman's children were "starving and cold." While they had bread, they were unable to afford meat, milk, vegetables, or fruit on the meagre relief payments they received. "The honour and glory we read about are all a myth," she concluded. "Who wants to starve and freeze for honour and glory?"[80]

It was not only during the Depression that advice literature set standards which many mothers were unable to meet. Throughout this literature, authors assumed that women embraced motherhood as a full-time occupation. By the postwar era, this assumption, fuelled by the findings of Bowlby's research on maternal deprivation, had taken on the force of a dictum. Mothers were warned against working in the paid labour force and, indeed, Spock urged women to postpone taking a vacation or a new job until after the child had passed what he described as the fearful two-year-old stage. Coupled with the requirements of demand feeding, these postwar theories made the mother a virtual prisoner in her own home, unable to go out even to shop, lest the baby need to nurse or the two-year-old suffer "separation anxiety."

In contrast to the assumptions of the literature, many mothers bore considerable responsibilities in addition to demands of baby and child care. Caring for elderly and dying relatives, taking in boarders and laundry, managing the household economy — all of these responsibilities would have made the demands of 24-hour-a-day motherhood virtually impossible to meet. Furthermore, the increase in the labour-force participation rates of women with young children, particularly during the 1950s, suggests that many women were forced to disregard the prohibitions against full-time employment in order to provide for their families.[81]

Conclusion

Although women discovered a new-found status as "mothers of the nation" during the early decades of the twentieth century, they enjoyed neither autonomy nor self-determination in this role. They did not set the rules, nor did they determine their capacity to live up to them. Rather, their maternal behaviour was closely monitored by physicians and other child-rearing experts. Measured against middle-class standards, many mothers — poor women, single mothers, working women — found themselves judged as defective. As I have demonstrated in this article, the rules advocated by child-rearing experts were almost impossible to follow. It was easy for mothers to fail and, for many, impossible to succeed, despite their best efforts. Mothers alone were held responsible for the outcome of their child-rearing efforts. And in the balance hung their status as citizens, for this status was contingent upon their performance as mothers.

The focus on maternal responsibility adopted by child-care experts had significant implications for the maternal and child welfare policies of the first half of the twentieth century. Supported by medical and psychological evidence of the importance of the maternal-child connection, policy-makers could reject measures of direct state intervention that might have helped mothers to care for their children better. State support for child-care centres, for example, was virtually non-existent throughout this period, with the exception of the limited provision of Wartime Day Nurseries in Ontario and Québec during World War II. No significant efforts were made to socialize the tasks of child rearing, either through day-care centres, baby-sitting co-operatives, or play schools. Infants and pre-school children remained the sole responsibility of their mothers; those women who failed in this "national duty" — poor women, single parents, working mothers — had only themselves to blame. They had let down the nation; they were unfit to be mothers.

Faced with a virtual flood of advice literature advocating an Anglo-Saxon, middle-class model of family life, mothers did their best to measure up to the new standards of modern scientific motherhood. While the evidence suggests that some women did rebel, rejecting the advice as wrong-headed, impractical, or merely irrelevant, countless others struggled to make sense of the dictates, to do their best for their children, in a society that, despite the lip-service paid to the citizens of the future, provided very little concrete help for its mothers and children.

For some women, the advice books, pamphlets, radio broadcasts and magazine articles represented a friendly voice in an otherwise lonely world. The advice literature provided information about the tasks of child rearing that had become, for many women, frightening, alien chores. Such information and help was purchased at a significant cost, however, for, as Veronica Strong-Boag has noted, "in exchange, ... women had to surrender power over themselves and their offspring. It was an authority they would not easily recover, however much their faith in experts proved misplaced."[82]

Notes

1. I wish to acknowledge the support of the Social Sciences and Humanities Research Council of Canada for research upon which this article is based. Portions of this chapter have appeared in "Educating Mothers: Government Advice for Women in the Inter-War Years," in *Delivering Motherhood: Maternal Ideologies and Practices in the 19th and 20th Centuries*, ed. Katherine Arnup, Andrée Lévesque, and Ruth Roach Pierson (London: Routledge, 1990), 190-210; and *Education for Motherhood: Advice for Mothers in Twentieth-Century Canada* (Toronto: University of Toronto Press, 1994).
2. Charles A. Hodgetts, Chief of the Division of Statistics and Publicity, "Statistics and Publicity in Child Welfare Work," *Public Health Journal* 12 (1921): 107.
3. Christopher Lasch, *Haven in a Heartless World: The Family Besieged* (New York: Basic Books, 1977).
4. Beth Light and Joy Parr, "Managing the Family," chapter 4 in *Canadian Women on the Move, 1867-1920* (Toronto: New Hogtown Press and the Ontario Institute for Studies in Education, 1983), 154.
5. Cynthia R. Comacchio, *Nations Are Built of Babies: Saving Ontario's Mothers and Children, 1900-1940* (Montreal: McGill-Queen's University Press, 1998), 56. Similar concerns had emerged in Britain earlier in the century, when as many as one-third of the possible recruits for the Boer War had to be rejected as unfit for military service. This provided shocking evidence, in Anna Davin's words, of "the poor health of the working class in Britain, from which were drawn both soldiers and sailors to defend the empire, and workers to produce goods with which to dominate the world economically." Britain's poor showing in that war had further "dramatized fears of national inadequacy." Anna Davin, "Imperialism and Motherhood," *History Workshop Journal* 5 (1978): 12.

6. See Angus McLaren and Arlene Tigar McLaren, *The Bedroom and the State* (Toronto: McClelland and Stewart, 1986), and Angus McLaren, *Our Own Master Race: Eugenics in Canada* (Toronto: McClelland and Stewart, 1990).

7. Michael Piva, *The Condition of the Working Class in Toronto – 1900-1921* (Ottawa: University of Ottawa Press, 1979), 114. In her first report on Infant Mortality, Helen MacMurchy noted that the rate for the province of Ontario in 1898 stood at 128.22 deaths under one year per 1000 live births and in 1907 at 150.06 per 1000 live births. Helen MacMurchy, *Infant Mortality: A Special Report* (Toronto: King's Printer, 1910).

8. In his study of Montreal, Terry Copp states that, "Between 1897 and 1911, approximately one out of three babies died before reaching the age of twelve months. As late as 1926, the rate was still 14 per cent, a figure almost double the average for New York or Toronto." Terry Copp, *The Anatomy of Poverty* (Toronto: McClelland and Stewart Ltd., 1983), 93. The authors of the exhibit "Mother and Child" (Ontario Science Centre, 11 December 1986 to 30 April 1987) claimed that Montreal's infant mortality was the highest in the Western World.

9. Helen MacMurchy argued that "[a]t least 50 per cent, and probably 60 per cent, or even 80 per cent, of Infant Mortality, is preventable." MacMurchy, *Infant Mortality*, 18. To determine the best means of preventing infant deaths, the government of Ontario commissioned Helen MacMurchy, later chief of the federal Division of Child Welfare, to conduct a study on infant mortality. Her reports, published in 1910, 1911, and 1912, helped to shape the infant welfare movement in Ontario and indeed throughout North America.

10. For a full discussion of her life and career, see Kathleen McConnachie, "Methodology in the Study of Women in History: A Case History of Helen MacMurchy, M.D.," *Ontario History* 75, 1 (March 1983).

11. MacMurchy, *Infant Mortality*, 3.

12. MacMurchy, *Infant Mortality*, 15, emphasis added.

13. Comacchio, *Nations Are Built of Babies*, 11.

14. Comacchio, *Nations Are Built of Babies*, 50.

15. Mariana Valverde, "'When the Mother of the Race is Free': Race, Reproduction, and Sexuality in First-Wave Feminism," in *Gender Conflicts*, ed. Franca Iacovetta and Mariana Valverde (Toronto: University of Toronto Press, 1992), 4.

16. See Comacchio, *Nations Are Built of Babies*, 9.

17. Jill Vickers, "Feminisms and Nationalisms in English Canada," *Journal of Canadian Studies* 35, 2 (Summer 2000): 135.

18. Numerous feminist organizations were formed in the late nineteenth and early twentieth centuries, e.g., the Women's Christian Temperance Union, formed in Ontario in 1874, to fight against alcohol and its effects on family life; and the National Council of Women of Canada, formed in 1893, with a focus on motherhood and infant and child welfare work. In one of its first initiatives, the National Council of Women established the Victorian Order of Nurses in 1897, primarily to work with mothers and infants. The women's reform movement also had close connections (and overlapping leadership and membership) with the broader social reform movements of the day.

19. Maureen O'Neil, "Citizenship and Social Change: Canadian Women's Struggle for Equality," in *Belonging: The Meaning and Future of Canadian Citizenship*, ed. William Kaplan (Montreal/Kingston: McGill-Queen's University Press, 1993), 315.

20. Canada, House of Commons, *Sessional Papers* (1923); Department of Health, Report of the Division of Child Welfare (March 1921 - March 1922), 37.

21. Population statistics are derived from F. H. Leacy, ed., *Historical Statistics of Canada* 2nd ed. (Ottawa: Statistics Canada, 1983), Series A78-93. I have included all women between the ages of 15 and 50 for the census year 1921.

22. Norah Lewis makes this observation in her unpublished paper, "'No Baby - No Nation': Mother Education, A Federal Concern - 1921 to 1979," presented at the Canadian History of Education Conference, Vancouver, Oct. 1983, 3.

23. In March 1917, the Ontario Board of Health (hereafter OBH) published *The Baby*. Within two years, nearly 25,000 copies of that pamphlet had been distributed to mothers across the province. Toronto's Division of Child Hygiene also prepared pamphlets on prenatal and infant care, which were available at no cost to the mothers and could be obtained at well-baby clinics or from the visiting public health nurse.

24. Equally dramatic figures were reported by the Canadian Council on Child and Family Welfare and various provincial and municipal divisions of child welfare. During the 1930s, for example, the Canadian Council on Child and Family Welfare reported distribution rates of hundreds of thousands of pieces of literature each year, e.g., 1933-34, 128,215 sets or partial sets of literature; 1934-35, 206,494; 1935-36, 232,343. National Archives of Canada, MG 28, I 10, vol. 66, file 010, "CWC Maternal and Child Hygiene 1935-39," Report of the Division on Maternal and Child Hygiene, 2.

25. Helen MacMurchy, "The Division of Child Welfare," *Canadian Journal of Public Health* 19 (1928): 517.

26. Beatrice B. Whiting, "Folk Wisdom and Child Rearing," *Merrill-Palmer Quarterly* 20, 1 (January 1974): 11.

27. Ernest Couture, *The Canadian Mother and Child* (Ottawa: Queen's Printer, 1940), 122.

28. Canadian Council on Child and Family Welfare, *Pre-School Letters* 9, 2 (Ottawa: Canadian Council on Child and Family Welfare, 1934).

29. Provincial Archives of Ontario, RG 10, Series 30-A-1, Box 3, file 3-3, *Bulletin of the Division of Maternal and Child Hygiene and Public Health Nursing* (February - March 1923), n.p. The "Holt in the hand" is a reference to L. Emmett Holt's child care manual, *The Care and Feeding of Children*, a popular child-care manual. Originally published in 1894, it had gone through twenty editions by 1943.

30. June Callwood, "What To Do After the Doctor Leaves," *Chatelaine* (May 1953): 33.

31. Ontario Board of Health (OBH), *The Baby* (1924), 4.

32. Comacchio, *Nations Are Built of Babies*, 239.

33. *Canadian Mother's Book* (1923), 11-12.

34. MacMurchy, How to Take Care of The Baby (Ottawa: King's Printer, 1922), 4, emphasis in the original.

35. Suzann Buckley, "Ladies or Midwives? Efforts to Reduce Infant and Maternal Mortality," in *A Not Unreasonable Claim: Women and Reform in Canada, 1880s - 1920s*, ed. Linda Kealey (Toronto: Women's Press, 1979), 131-50. In her article in the same collection, Veronica Strong-Boag notes that "Childbirth was often the occasion which initiated a doctor's association with a family and its illnesses." Strong-Boag, "Canada's Women Doctors: Feminism Constrained," 111-12.

36. Alan Brown, *The Normal Child: Its Care and Feeding* (Toronto: McClelland and Stewart, 1932), 223.

37. Comacchio, *Nations Are Built of Babies*, 10.

38. For a discussion of the work of the child-care professionals in the interwar years, see Veronica Strong-Boag, "Intruders in the Nursery: Childcare Professionals Reshape the Years One to Five, 1920-1940," in *Childhood and Family in Canadian History*, ed. Joy Parr (Toronto: McClelland and Stewart, 1982), 160-78.

39. MacMurchy, "How to Take Care of the Baby" (1923), 13.

40. Toronto Department of Public Health, "The Expectant Mother" (1931), 11.

41. OBH, *The Baby* (1920), 37.

42. OBH, *The Baby* (1933), 54.

43. Arnup, *Education for Motherhood*.

44. Nurses' observations are recorded in the *Canadian Nurse*, journal of the Canadian Nurses' Association, and in materials deposited in the City of Toronto and Province of Ontario Archives.

45. V.M. MacDonald, "Child Welfare Work in Montreal," *Canadian Nurse* 19 (1923): 663.

46. City of Toronto Archives (CTA), RG 11, F1, Box 1, file "Historical Material - Maternal and Child Health 1936-65," "Secretary's Report on prenatal education from September 1949 to July 1950," 4. Similar reports appeared throughout the period under consideration in this article.

47. Julia Grant, *Raising Baby by the Book: The Education of American Mothers* (New Haven: Yale University Press, 1998), 72.

48. Grant, *Raising Baby by the Book*, 73.

49. Jill Vickers, "Feminisms and Nationalisms in English Canada," *Journal of Canadian Studies* 35, 2 (Summer 2000): 135.

50. For information on the language nurses, as they were called, see Marion Royce, *Eunice Dyke: Health Care Pioneer* (Toronto: Dundurn Press, 1983), 63-66.

51. CTA, RG 11, F1, Box 4, "Health Department History, 1923-1945," typescript dated 8 Jan. 1945, Janet Neilson, "The History of Public Health Nursing in Toronto," 5.

52. Writing about the efforts to "Americanize" immigrant mothers in the US, Jane Brickman notes that "antithetical to social workers' desires to make motherhood scientific were the immigrant mothering customs of demand feeding, swaddling the new born, and the use of the pacifier." Jane Brickman, "Mother Love - Mother Death: Maternal and Infant Care: Social Class and the Role of the Government" (Ph.D. dissertation, City University of New York, 1978), 440. Brickman notes that all of these practices are now in vogue.

53. Royce, *Eunice Dyke*, 65-66. Dyke was the director of the Public Health Nursing Division of Toronto's Department of Public Health from 1911 to 1932. Although immigrant mothers, like their Canadian-born counterparts, may have welcomed a visit from the public health nurse, it is likely that many of them preferred to hold onto their traditional methods of infant and child care.

54. Blanch Emerson, "Child Welfare," *Canadian Nurse* 26 (1930): 199, emphasis mine.

55. Denyse Baillargeon, *Making Do: Women, Family and Home in Montreal During the Great Depression* (Waterloo: Wilfrid Laurier University Press, 1999), 82. The quotations are taken from informants E 20 and E 23. See also Chapter 8 of this volume.

56. For my research, I interviewed twelve mothers, six of whom had raised their children in the 1920s and 1930s, and six during the 1940s and 1950s.

57. In *The Politics of Motherhood*, Jane Lewis indicates that "none of the 83 working class women interviewed had read an infant care manual," chapter 2, note 119. My interviews turned up a different result. Five of the six working-class women I interviewed indicated that they had used baby books and child-care literature.

58. Winnie Weatherstone, interview by author, 23 Jan. 1986.

59. Eleanor Enkin, interview by author, 20 March 1986.

60. The volume of these letters is truly staggering. Both Molly Ladd-Taylor, *Raising a Baby the Government Way: Mothers' Letters to the Children's Bureau, 1915-32* (New Brunswick, NJ: Rutgers University Press, 1986) and Julia Grant, *Raising Baby by the Book*, rely extensively on mothers' letters to child-rearing experts.

61. NAC, MG 28, I 19, vol. 66, file 010 "CWC - Maternal and Child Hygiene Division 1940-43, Canadian Life Insurance Officers," Report of the Division on Maternal and Child Hygiene, Canadian Welfare Council, 1 April 1942 to 31 March 1943, 5-6.

62. Mrs. F. D., Québec. Letter to the US Children's Bureau, 18 Dec. 1921. Mrs. F. D. was originally from Minneapolis, but had moved to Québec with her husband. The letter was the only one from a Canadian included in Ladd-Taylor, *Raising a Baby the Government Way*, 110-11.

63. Mrs. W.E. Corbett, Maloy, Alberta, to Canadian Council on Child and Family Welfare, 28 Aug. 1935, NAC, RG 29, vol. 991, file 499-3-2, part 2.

64. Mrs. A.H. Etekella [spelling difficult to determine], to Dr. Allan Roy Dafoe, 29 Jan. 1937. Province of Ontario Archives, Dafoe Collection, MS 598, Series B-1, vol. 1.

65. Mrs. Robt. Averbeck, to Dr. Allan Roy Dafoe, 19 Jan. 1937, PAO, Dafoe Collection, MS 598, Series B-1, vol. 1.

66. I have been unable to determine what became of these letters. I do not wish to imply that a conspiracy of silence took place. Their disappearance is more likely the result of office house-keeping than a deliberate attempt to alter the historical record.

67. See Norah L. Lewis, "Reducing Maternal Mortality in British Columbia: An Educational Process," in *Not Just Pin Money*, ed. Barbara K. Latham and Roberta J. Pazdro (Victoria: Camosun College, 1984), 339-40, and the work of Neil Sutherland.

68. Catherine Lesley Biggs, "The Response to Maternal Mortality in Ontario, 1920 - 1940" (M.Sc. thesis, University of Toronto, 1983), 49. See also Jo Oppenheimer, "Childbirth in Ontario: The Transition from Home to Hospital in the Early Twentieth Century," in *Delivering Motherhood*, ed. Arnup, Lévesque, and Roach Pierson, 67; Suzann Buckley, "The Search for the Decline of Maternal Mortality: The Place of Hospital Records," in *Essays in the History of Canadian Medicine*, ed. Wendy Mitchinson and Janice Dickin McGinnis (Toronto: McClelland and Stewart, 1988), 161.

69. Cecilia Benoit notes that women enjoyed their stay at the Burgeo cottage hospital because it enabled them to get away from their household responsibilities for a few days. *Midwives in Passage* (St. John's: Institute of Social and Economic Research, 1991), 3. Meg Luxton made a similar observation in her 1980 study: "Whatever their opinions, women unanimously noted one major advantage that hospital births have over home births. It is socially acceptable for a woman giving birth to spend four or five days in hospital where she is not responsible for anything. Women considered their hospital stays as vacations or holidays." Luxton, *More than a Labour of Love* (Toronto: Women's Press, 1980), 100.

70. Mary Bolton, cited in Barbara Ehrenreich and Deirdre English, *For Her Own Good: 150 Years of the Experts' Advice to Women* (New York: Anchor Books, 1979), 214.

71. Alison Clarke-Stewart makes a similar argument in "Popular Primers for Parents," *American Psychologist* 33, 4 (April 1978): 368.

72. Spock, *Baby and Child Care* (1946), 3. The first edition (1946) was 482 pages long without the index and 502 pages long including the index. The second edition (1957) was 597 pages long without the index and 627 pages including the index.

73. MacMurchy, *The Canadian Mother's Book* (1933), 25.

74. MacMurchy, *How to Take Care of Mother* (1922), 7.

75. MacMurchy, *How to Take Care of the Baby* (1922), 10.

76. One example, among many, is the following advice from Helen MacMurchy. "Don't be down-hearted - there is no reason you should be. Don't be frightened. Cheer up. We are all standing by you." *The Canadian Mother's Book* (1923), 29.

77. MacMurchy, *How to Take Care of the Mother* (1923), 24.

78. Dorothy Franklin, Kent, Ontario, letter to R.B. Bennett, 15 Dec. 1931, in *The Wretched of Canada: Letters to R. B. Bennett 1930 - 1935*, ed. L. M. Grayson and Michael Bliss (Toronto: University of Toronto Press, 1971), 16.

79. Mrs. Rose Artimus, Calgary, letter to R.B. Bennett, 13 May 1935, in *The Wretched of Canada*, 145 (spelling retained as in original).

80. Anonymous, "I am a Canadian Mother," *Chatelaine* (April 1933): 18, emphasis mine.

81. While only 11.2 per cent of married women participated in the paid labour force in 1951, that number had increased to 22 per cent by 1961. Monica Boyd, "Changing Canadian Family Forms: Issues for Women," in *Reconstructing the Canadian Family: Feminist Perspectives*, ed. Nancy Mandell and Ann Duffy (Toronto: Butterworths, 1988), 92.

82. Veronica Strong-Boag, *The New Day Recalled: Lives of Girls and Women in English Canada, 1919-1939* (Toronto: Copp Clark Pitman, 1988), 150.

chapter twelve

CONSTRUCTING NORMAL CITIZENS
Sex Advice for Postwar Teens[1]

Mary Louise Adams

Introduction

In the years after World War II, "normality" was a primary marker of difference between individuals and between groups of people. In popular magazines and in prescriptive literature and films, young people were offered tools and strategies to use in the construction of themselves as normal sexual beings. In achieving this status they would exchange their conformity to rules and prevailing standards of behaviour for a position comfortably on the inside of the social body. Of course not all young people could meet the requirements of the label. Sexual normality was not simply about sex: normal was about being middle class; it was about whiteness and not being "ethnic"; it was about proper expressions of gender. As a concept, normality erased difference and limited the forms of sexual identity and expression available to young people. In the late 1940s and 1950s, the achievement of sexual normality was an unavoidable stage of the journey to responsible adulthood.

In postwar North America, sexual discourses were a conduit for fears and apprehensions about changes in the global balance of power, about the changing shape of the family, and about the effects of the war and the prosperity that followed it. In this chapter I argue that the symbolic positioning of teenagers as "the future" — as the citizens who would carry the nation through the 1950s — made them a likely target of interventions meant to maximize normality and therefore maximize stability and social order against the uncertainties of modern life. Sexuality was the basis of marriage and family life — that "psychological fortress ... [that] might ward off hazards of the age."[2] It was too important to be left to nature or circumstance.

In their attempts to "shape" teenagers into normal citizens, adults tried to assuage their own insecurities.

Attempts to shape teenagers into proper adults were certainly not unique to the post-World War II era. What is significant, however, is the way in which postwar efforts focused on sexuality as a requirement for the production of marriageable adults. In the 1940s and 1950s, adolescents were assumed by many to need sexual guidance before assuming their "inevitable" marital roles. The "new" companionate marriages that had evolved after World War I were meant to be held together by friendship and the sexual satisfaction of both husband and wife. Promoters of this "new" form of heterosexual partnership advocated education about sex for those on the verge of marriage, warning of the danger to marriage of sexual "deviations." By the postwar years, companionate marriage was no longer new or unusual. Still, it was assumed that young people, at ever-decreasing ages, needed to be prepared for it. The growing prominence of psychological notions about the fragile process of attaining sexual maturity meant that one could not be too careful or too concerned about the brides and grooms of the future: any child could turn into a deviant.

In the early years of the Cold War, writes legal historian Philip Girard, deviance from any number of mainstream norms "represented an independence of mind" that could not be tolerated.[3] Deviance, sexual or political, would preclude the homogenization that was seen to be central to Canada's strength as a nation. The conformity that is so often identified as a primary aspect of postwar social life was not simply a characteristic of increased consumerism or the centralization of popular culture and entertainment industries. It was also produced by an approach to citizenship that demanded a willingness to participate in social consensus, to adopt a shared set of behavioural standards and mores.

In this context, having a family became an important marker of social belonging, of conformity to prevailing standards. It was a sign of maturity and adulthood, of one's ability to take on responsibility. The social positions of mother/wife and father/husband defined individuals as contributors to their community and their country. As a psychiatrist argued in *Chatelaine*, the formation of families and the raising of children were, at root, a patriotic obligation. In becoming parents, men and women were "giving to the best of their ability."[4] Thus the nuclear family came to operate as a symbol of safety — not just on the individual level, but on the national level as well.

Whereas the primary focus of many earlier family discourses had been on women, motherhood, and the development of proper femininity,[5] postwar discourses about the family tended to show (and construct) most concern for the development of properly adjusted — normal — children. Sex-advice literature and films were meant to help make this task easier; they would help children develop into normal adults who would avoid the fate of those seen to be outside the family. Such people, from runaway youths to homosexuals, were anomalies. Hard to classify, they were often the objects of scorn or pity. Discourses about middle-class family life made available a variety of subject positions — parent, sexual being, responsible citizen, consumer — that were unavailable or were available in only limited ways to adults who were single. Families, narrowly defined — monogamous heterosexual marriages and the children produced within them — provided an important way of making sense of one's position in the postwar social structure.

Sex advice for teens appeared in inexpensive pocketbooks, in pamphlets, in magazine articles, and in educational films on love, dating, and sex. There are limits to using this type of prescriptive material for research purposes. Certainly it was not used by all young people, and it is difficult to determine who, in fact, did engage with it. One might also raise questions about the extent to which different groups of young people supported the ideas contained in the books, articles, and films about the distance between "advice" and "reality." But the possibility that young people did not subscribe to the information about sexuality and sexual behaviour they received from adults does not negate the role of that "advice" in constructing the normative standards by which teens were judged. Lesbian and gay literature is full of examples of individuals who have "acted" against normative standards while at the same time suffering emotionally because of them. Discursive constructions of good teenagers and bad teenagers, of healthy sexuality and immoral sexuality, may not have been the immediate determinants of teen behaviour, but they did influence the context of that behaviour and the meanings that would eventually be ascribed to it.

There was no explicitly Canadian popular discourse of teen advice. Canadians, expert and lay person alike, borrowed heavily from American work in this area. Canadian magazines published American authors and suggested the titles of American books to their readers. There was very little difference between what appeared in *Chatelaine*, for instance, and what was published in US pocketbooks. Marion Hilliard, who to my knowledge was the only Canadian to have published sex advice books in this period, used British and American publishers.

The books I refer to here are not to be confused with the marriage manuals that were popular in earlier decades and that continued to be published after the war. The "frankness" of the earlier volumes had no place in the primers for adulthood directed at postwar teens. For instance, the prime

Canadian example of the marriage manual, Rev. Alfred Henry Tyrer's *Sex, Marriage and Birth Control*, originally published in 1936, contained chapters on "Conception control," "Different positions for intercourse," "Temporary impotence" and "Venereal diseases."[6] Teen books, on the other hand, had chapter headings like "How to get — and keep — boys interested," "All about dating," and "Shy today and popular tomorrow." The new advice genre grew, in part, from changing social mores and the rise of self-regulatory discourses of personal development. It may also have reflected changes in marriage and dating patterns. In the 1950s, children were "dating" by the age of 12 or 13, and marrying around the age of 20, which gave them only 5 or 6 years to prepare — especially sexually — for what was assumed to be the eventuality of matrimony. Interwar marriage manuals had been written for young men and women; the 1950s advice books about sex were written for boys and girls who, despite impending marriages, were barely past childhood.

figure 12.1

Learning about menstruation. Still from the film, *Physical Aspects of Puberty*.

CRAWLEY FILMS / NATIONAL ARCHIVES OF CANADA / MISA 9508. REPRODUCED BY PERMISSION.

As with the advice books, postwar teens were also targeted by growing numbers of educational films. The films were more serious than the advice books, their tone set by the ever-present voice of a male narrator. Produced in Canada by the National Film Board and by private production houses such as Crawley Films in Ottawa for distribution by American textbook publishers, the films played before "captive" audiences in school classrooms, at youth groups, and, sometimes, on television. Perhaps because of this, their approach to content was more cautious than that followed by the advice authors. Whereas advice books were consumed privately, perhaps even secretly, films were viewed in public, sometimes in mixed groups of boys and girls. To those who thought sex education the responsibility of parents and not of the state, such materials were both ill-advised and dangerous.

Boards of education could face protest by offended parents and embarrassed teachers for using them. Given this, the restrained tone of the films was not surprising. It probably helped facilitate the securing of an audience.

It is in the films where one sees most easily the way teen advice was implicated in the construction of postwar middle-classness. These films flagged class in any number of ways, from simple matters such as the predominance of spotless and well-furnished two-storey houses, where children did not share bedrooms and where mothers were full-time homemakers (even if widowed), to the homogeneity of students in a classroom, to assumptions about dating, marriage, and future careers. *Joe and Roxy*, produced by the NFB, was the only one of the 37 films I considered that featured working-class teenagers: a girl living in an apartment with a mother who had been deserted by her husband; a boy whose father was a tradesman who tried to discourage his son from pursuing engineering. Among the sweater-set crowd, in the American-style soda shops that furnished many of the other films, *Joe and Roxy* would have been uncomfortably out of place.

In all of the films, all of the characters are white. None speak with accents or have "foreign"-sounding names. There is no mention of the way religious or cultural differences might affect one's popularity or one's ability to date or one's approach to marriage. Several films do suggest, however, the importance of marrying someone from a similar background. Overall, nothing disrupts the seamless representation of middle-class dominant culture. Certainly nothing suggests that the advice on growing up given in both the books and the films might not be useful to everyone.

The Straightness of Normality

There was a remarkable conformity among the different advice books and films about what constituted normality. While it was talked about as a unitary category, normality in these texts differed for boys and girls, teens and adults. And while it was presented as a self-evident descriptive, normality was constructed through a complex formation of professional and popular discourses, all of which were easily bent to serve moral ends. Biological and psychological discourses, which at times contradicted each other, were tucked comfortably alongside the most "unscientific" common sense. The end result of this eclectic approach was a peculiar mix of essentialist theory, moral coercion, and behaviouralist strategy that was all meant to inspire teens to "do the right thing."

At its most basic level, normality was grounded in notions of an inevitable, biologically-based attraction between males and females. Addressing young women, Ann Landers wrote in her 1963 book *Ann Landers Talks to Teenagers About Sex*, "Of course you would not be normal if you were able to keep your mind off the boys, completely. And no normal boy is able to keep his mind off girls completely either."[7] While heterosexual desire on its own was not enough to guarantee one's status as normal, it was essential. In the limited world of the teen manual, homosexuality marked the extreme outer edge of the abnormal. Homosexuality existed as that place in the books where discussions of abnormality were up front and explicit. It was a subject the more reticent films rarely touched.

In her 1960 book *Sex and the Adolescent*, journalist Maxine Davis wrote, "Human beings have always been frightened by phenomena which seem to be unnatural. For example, before they learned something about astronomy, they were terrified by the eclipse of the sun by the moon; they thought it was the end of the world. Today, the average healthy adult has a *comparable* aversion to homosexuality; he thinks it a dreadful incurable disease or an unnatural emotional deformity."[8] And while Davis claimed she wanted to allay these types of fears, homosexuality remained, in her text, something vastly remote from everyday life. Indeed, homosexuality was constructed as so outside the range of normal teen experience that it was presented in all of the books as an external threat. Homosexuals were other people — not, certainly, teens themselves. Thus, most of the information about homosexuality that found its way into these books was intended to help boys and girls to protect themselves from deviants.

In her often cited book, *Teen Days*, Frances Bruce Strain, a proponent of sex education in American schools, wrote, "Adults call these persons homosexuals. High-school students have their own names for them. One must know of them in order that they may be recognized and avoided."[9] Lester Kirkendall, another well-known American sex education expert, warned teens that they needed to know about homosexuals because young people were likely to encounter them as they began to venture afield from their homes. He claimed that homosexuals were most likely to be found in large cities and "around places where it is common for only men and boys, or girls and women, to gather."[10] He went on to explain how the careful teenager would be able to turn away the homosexual's advances. While Kirkendall and the other writers never explicitly explain how to tell the homosexual from someone who was normal, they did provide clues: first, homosexuals are male (lesbians are barely mentioned in the six books I'm referring to); second, homosexuals are adults. "True homosexuality," according to Davis, is "an unfortunate adult maladjustment."[11] As a product of failed, slowed or reversed sexual and emotional development, homosexuality is a condition that could not possibly be determined (or diagnosed) until the "transitional phase" of adolescence was completed. Of course the irony in this is that homosexuals were then considered by psychologists to be in an arrested state of adolescent development — they were seen as immature.[12]

Different writers had different explanations for the cause of a sexual aberration like same-sex desire. Strain said it might be due to the unavailability of the opposite sex at a crucial time of development, for instance, in the case of boarding schools. She also suggested other reasons related to poor family conditions or unpleasant early experiences.[13] The developmental focus on the causes of homosexuality made it possible for the broad range and occurrence of same-sex affections in teenagers' own lives to be corralled and put to good ideological use. In typical models of heterosexual development, there existed a secure place for same-sex attractions, or crushes. Advice writers described homosexual feelings or intimacies experienced by young people themselves as essential steps on the road to heterosexual normality. Most people, the writers claimed, go through some sort of homosexual "phase" at some point in their lives. Evelyn Duvall, who was recommended to Canadians in *Chatelaine* magazine, constructed a continuum of affectional and sexual ties that began with "same sex, same age" interests, passing through "same sex, older age" crushes on the way to "other sex, older age," before finally reaching the real thing, the "other sex, same age" stage of "love development."[14] In this model homosexual ties are seen as preparation or practice for heterosexual relationships.

Homo-erotic desire in this sense was not only normal but desirable. Nevertheless, it was important that this "not unusual part of growing up" did not expand into an active desire for physical contact — it was important to keep clear the boundaries between normal and abnormal. Should such transgressive feelings arise, the young person was advised to seek counselling to find out why his or her "emotional development [was] being delayed beyond what [was] considered normal."[15] The assumption was always that any same-sex sexual behaviour indicated a developmental stage that had been taken too far. Moreover, it was nothing a few new friends and some vigorous sports activity wouldn't put back on track.

These authors paid little attention to concerns that young people may have had about their own sexual identities, worries that they themselves might have been "a little queer." Ann Landers was the only writer to approach homosexuality from this angle and she talked only about boys, claiming that they accounted for 70 per cent of her mail on the subject. They are the ones, she wrote, who were "tortured with guilt and self-hatred ... terrified that someone may learn they aren't "like everyone else."[16] They were the ones who "yearn to be normal." Perhaps because of the letters she received, Landers was more willing than her colleagues to make a distinction (albeit an unhappy one) between homosexuality as a phase and homosexuality as a tragic future. While she believed sexual identities to be the result of a process of emotional development, she saw that process as relatively quick and finite. Thus Landers, unlike the other writers, thought that one could be an adolescent and a homosexual at the same time; homosexuality was not necessarily a phase. However she also claimed that cures were possible, although their chances of success were greater if "the homosexual seeks professional help in his early teens." But one wonders whether the young homosexual would have pursued such a course of action while everyone around him (or her, invisible though she was) was saying that homosexual feelings were a normal part of growing up. How was one to know the difference between homosexual desires that were "twisted and sick" and those that were preparing one for heterosexual matrimony? The negotiation of the normal/abnormal boundary could be very complicated.

Most of the advice writers claimed that they wanted to reduce people's fear of homosexuality, although they were clearly not interested in calming young people's personal fears about living homosexual lives. Instead, they focused on widespread social fears of homosexuals in the culture at large. It was widely believed in the 1950s, as it is by many today, that young people could be inducted into homosexuality by older homosexuals. In developmental theories of homosexuality, contact with an adult homosexual was one event that might send normal development astray. Davis wrote that if a young boy is seduced by an older man and "has repeated relationships with adult homosexuals, there is a serious risk that his originally normal instincts may eventually become permanently perverted."[17] Homosexuality, in this instance, is not something you perform or do, or something you are, it is something that might happen to you. This meant that, despite the "naturalness" of heterosexuality and the abnormality of homosexuality, young people were vulnerable to derailment from the straight path. As long as homosexuality was understood to be an external threat, notions of the "naturalness" and inevitability of heterosexuality were left unchallenged.

Normal Sex Needs Normal Gender

In teen advice books and films, the relationship between sexuality and gender was a fluctuating one. While postwar theories of homosexuality relied less on notions of gender inversion than earlier theories had,[18] theories of heterosexuality, by contrast, were heavily steeped in ideas about the proper fit between gender and sexuality. Whereas one could be a homosexual without feeling the inversion of gender, one could not be a successful heterosexual if one's gender was out of line.

Girls and boys who did not match prevailing images of masculinity and femininity — sissies and tomboys — were a challenge to the firmness of the boundary that separated abnormal from normal. But, surprisingly, not a single writer mentioned the possibility that these children might turn into homosexuals. Doing so might have given too much credence to theories that homosexuality was a biological condition, as Kinsey had tried to show, and not a perversion of normal instincts or evidence of relaxed moral standards. To succumb to biological arguments about the basis of "abnormalities" would have necessitated an admission of the futility of sex education and other regulatory measures as a prophylaxis against deviations from social norms. Such arguments would have put these writers out of business. So, in the few discussions of tomboys and sissies that appear in these texts, there is no mention that the improper alignment of gender might have non-heterosexual consequences. Instead we read merely of the difficulties that femmy boys and butch girls faced in the schoolyard. The hope was always that the "'minuses' of their sex"[19] could be rehabilitated. While homosexuality was thought to be the result of (failed) adolescent development, sissy-ness and tomboy-ness were presented as conditions that (successful) adolescent development could cure.

In the late 1940s, Kellogg's cereal company ran a regular ad in *Chatelaine* magazine that was formatted to look like a column by "psychologist Janet Power." A 1948 instalment was entitled "Barbara is a tomboy."[20] Psychologist Power (!) responded to a letter from Barbara's mother describing her daughter's habits and asking, "How can I make Barbara more feminine, yet not curb her high spirits?" Power suggested that Barbara's mother ignore "her tomboy antics" and instead praise Barbara "for everything feminine she happens to do." Barbara's mother was to encourage a closer relationship between Barbara and her sister, to take Barbara shopping, and to give both daughters more responsibility in the home. Eventually Barbara would calm down when she learned how proud it makes her mother: "Remember, stress CONSIDERATION OF OTHERS and GOOD MANNERS. At first Barbara will obey just to please you, but quiet, normal gentleness will soon become a habit with her. Show Barbara it's fun to be a DAUGHTER to you and FATHER — not a tomboy!"[21]

Femininity in this case is a matter of behaviour modification; it is not something one feels, but something one learns. Several versions of this approach were expressed in teen advice books and guidance films. The writers made clear that while young women have an inherent capacity for femininity — it is, after all, a "natural" product of their biological femaleness — they need instruction so their femininity will attain the proper shape:

> Most of what goes into making a woman act and behave and feel like a woman is learned as she grows up. ... Learning to enjoy boys as persons, to like men without being afraid of them on the one hand or being too overwhelmed by them on the other, learning to enjoy the fine arts and skills of being a real woman, with all the satisfactions and challenges that lie before women today — these are important, and they are for you to learn.[22]

But with questions around gender identity, as with other topics, there is a continual strain in these texts between "modern" psychological theories and "old-fashioned" explanations that draw on biology. Either set of theories could be easily adapted to meet the exigencies of moral discourses. That these two positions could, at times, be contradictory was a theoretical and narrative puzzle the advice writers left unsolved. In a 1942 book directed at parents and teachers, Frances Strain suggested that tomboys and sissies be referred to the family doctor to determine "the underlying physical basis" of "the problem." She also said that when such children enter adolescence and their hormones start up "either naturally or through medication, the minuses may both become pluses, delicate boys become virile and strong, stalwart girls become graceful and more feminine, ready to be to each other not pals but 'dates' and sweethearts."[23] Here, her advice differs from the behaviour training approach of the Kellogg's ad. But, four years later, in a book directed at young adolescents, Strain was caught between biological and psychological perspectives when she said that femininity in boys "is just on the surface. Given a chance, these boys swing back to normal." Should that not happen, or if it could not "because of individual make-up" they would just have to "live within the scope of their tastes and skills...."[24] They would have to "adjust": no need for hormonal remedies here. Whether the different exercise of biology in Strain's two books represents an updating of her theory or her attempts to be more upbeat with children than with adults, it is hard to say.

figure 12.2

Normal growth means normal gender. Still from the film, *Meaning of Adolescence.*

CRAWLEY FILMS / NATIONAL ARCHIVES OF CANADA / MISA 9984. REPRODUCED BY PERMISSION.

In most of the books and films, biology was presented as the source of things good while environmental and psychological/emotional factors were what turned good things into bad ones. This is very clear in Strain's later book, where she based her discussion of ideal genders on "nature":

> Boys are to be fathers and providers. They become broad of shoulder, long of limb, fleet of foot, stronger, tougher and more combative. The animal world gives plenty of evidence of male equipment for this task of winning a wife, protecting and caring for a family. The magnificent antlers of the bull moose and his roaring mating call up in the north woods has inspired many a dainty little doe and won her to him. The bull seal with his mighty tusks, the lion with his massive head and mane, the game cock and his spurs, all of these are Life's provisions for the male of the species.[25]

Unnatural gender types, like sissies and tomboys, were frequently said to be the fault of parents; a bad home life could turn one's "natural," normal constitution inside-out. Learning to maintain gender boundaries, to express the right kind of masculinity or the right kind of femininity, was partially a matter of giving shape to the kind of biological urges evident in the "animal world." As Evelyn Duvall wrote, "most young people have a strong urge to be normal...."[26] To do so, adolescents were to become the opposite halves of a heterosexual whole. Learning to date, then, was a means of building on biology, trying on heterosexuality, and fulfilling gender requirements. The reader of *On Becoming a Woman* learns that womanliness, for instance, is not something complete unto itself; it is something to be "practised" on men. To be a "truly feminine woman," according to Williams and Kane, a woman had to "really like men."[27] This didn't mean, however, that she joined them for games on the ball field. Girls needed to like boys in ways that would make them into dates, not into pals. Although there were many ways for boys and girls to be together, only one was evidence that nature was unfolding as it should.

Dating as Heterosexual Practice

If anything marks postwar ideologies about gender and sexuality and the relationship between the two categories, it's dating. Much has been written about dating as a fairly recent, North American institution. Beth Bailey, Ellen Rothman, and others have discussed the various historical factors that shaped the adoption of the "dating system" by young Americans.[28] In most of this writing, dating appears as a series of events or customs that change with the economic and social climate. But, as Karen Dubinsky has pointed out, these histories of courtship fail to look at dating as a key aspect of the institution-alization of heterosexuality.[29] Nor have they looked at the ways in which dating contributed to the construction of the teenager as a particular kind of sexual being, or how dating was as important for those who did not partic-ipate in it as it was for those who did.

By the 1950s, serial monogamy, via the institution of "going steady," had evolved as the preferred form of teenage dating. American historian Elaine May has written that this new form of dating reflected the larger search for security and stability during the Cold War.[30] But dating was more than a reflection of the larger economic and political circumstances; it was also a means of organizing social relations among youth. Peer-enforced standards of behaviour, encouraged by adults, brought the regulation of what was normal down to the level of young people themselves. As a public display of one's ability to fit in or not, "going steady" was a requirement of popularity that made obvious those who were not participating in its rituals. Serial mono-gamy, with its lack of spontaneity — its stability — made the unattached espe-cially visible. As a young woman says in Sylvia Fraser's autobiographical book about Hamilton, Ontario in the 1950s, "'It's better to stay home than to go with someone you don't like,' I assure her, knowing that I'm lying. All social life at Hamilton High is strictly two-by-two, as in Noah's Ark. Not to date is to be an object of scorn or pity."[31] Once on the outside of the coupled world, the chances of getting in were fewer than they might have been in the constantly changing social scene of the 1930s.

For all of the significance of going steady as a teenage institution, it was not, by any means, free of adult influence. While boys and girls could mark the boundaries of their social worlds in terms of who was with whom and who was alone, adults attempted to keep limits on the entire dating system, especially in terms of sexual expression and how interactions between boys and girls reflected contemporary ideologies about gender.

Adults in the postwar period, who would have been more familiar with the 1930s version of dating — where the number of different dates one had was a measure of one's popularity — were torn over whether or not teenagers should be encouraged to go steady. American marriage counsellor Clifford R. Adams, writing in *Chatelaine* in 1948, claimed that "courtship is much more wholesome and sincere than it was a few dozen years ago."[32] For him the trend toward serial monogamy was a sign of maturity and a stabilizing of moral standards that had been shaken by the war. Ten years later Dr. Marion Hilliard, a frequent contributor to *Chatelaine* on issues of sexuality, claimed disdainfully that going steady was little more than insurance for teens.[33] In going steady Hilliard saw a way for teens to express their conformity and to keep themselves ensconced in over-protected lives.

Writing for *Maclean's* in 1959, Sidney Katz showed a comparable lack of enthusiasm in an article called "Going steady: Is it ruining our teenagers?" Katz likened the practice to a social disease, claiming it had reached "epidemic proportions."[34] For him monogamous dating was a disturbing sign of the impact of postwar social welfare measures: "Children, evidently, have absorbed in concentrated form, the adult emphasis on security as evidenced by our own advocacy of health insurance, pensions and guaranteed annual wages. The teen-agers' premature conservatism and excessive desire to conform are also symptomatic of their search for security."[35] Katz saw teens as the inevitable product of too much prosperity. They were passive and lacked initiative. Why else would they be content to settle so early into staid and routine patterns of coupling? He also claimed that top kids in the social system did not succumb to social pressure to go steady, nor did immigrants. According to Katz, these two groups (which he constructs as internally cohesive and mutually exclusive) were more enterprising. Like other writers, it was Katz's contention that going steady was a "female device," developed by girls to achieve their own ends. Boys who participated in it willingly, he says, lacked masculinity.[36] They were not on the way to becoming normal men.

Other writers saw monogamous dating in a different light. For Williams and Kane it was good preparation for marriage.[37] And Frances Strain enthused about what she called the "dating pyramid," the road to marriage and the culmination of normal heterosexual development.[38] In her model, dating was practice for marriage, a useful way of training sexuality into a desired mode of expression, of normalizing it. Dating was the socially approved arena for young men and women to practise their masculinity and femininity on each other.

To the extent that it became institutionalized, with numerous ritual and structural intricacies, dating offered advice writers no end of opportunity to intervene in young lives. Dating, though the "natural'" expression of hetero-sexuality, was not something that just anyone could do properly; it had to be taught, and adults were more than happy to take on the job of teaching. As in the learning of masculinity and femininity, advice writers claimed no con-tradictions between their assertions that heterosexuality was "natural" and the assumption that it was an identity and a practice that had to be achieved: "Both girls and boys must learn how to be smooth in their dating. None of us is born with the attributes of being a good date.... Such learning can be fun, and it is important without question. On it hangs our feeling of being a successful member of one sex or another."[39] In this passage Evelyn Duvall is talking about grooming and being punctual and wearing the right clothes. But success as a dater, and as a young man or a young woman, was based on more weighty issues than these. Once one was in the dating system, one had to be able to stay there without "getting into trouble." Fear around the extent of sexual activity between daters was one topic on which the adults who were opposed to going steady agreed with those who were for it. But while the latter thought going steady was a way to control sex between teenagers, the former believed it encouraged dangerous intimacies.

Ann Landers wrote: "It is unrealistic to assume that healthy, red-blooded high school kids can be together day in and day out, month after month — sometimes year after year — and keep their physical urges under perfect con-trol."[40] Sex, she warned, was a "dangerous by-product of going steady." Marion Hilliard thought the same: "As a doctor I don't believe there is such a thing as a platonic relationship between a man and woman who are alone together a great deal."[41] A strong sex drive was seen to be normal (for boys and girls according to Hilliard), but a teenager needed to and could learn how to control it, because "Uncontrolled, this force can take over and direct you."[42] For those who agreed with Hilliard, sex education, like that found in the advice books, would give teenagers the moral grounding to stem their physical inclinations.

Some sources downplayed discussion of sex, perhaps because of a fear that too much sexual knowledge was itself a dangerous thing. Reading *Chatelaine's* regular column, "Teen Tempo," one could assume that the extent of teenage girls' concerns with sex stopped at whether or not to permit a goodnight kiss on the doorstep. Most dating how-to films, which were ostensibly presenting real teenage couples, managed to skip quickly over sex as an issue that might be of concern. In an American film called *Going Steady*, shown on a 1954 CBC talk show, *Youth Takes a Stand*, sex is introduced and dismissed in three short lines:

> Marie: Going steady? Yes, I guess I have been going steady.
> Mother: I hope Jeff doesn't feel he has the right to take liberties.
> Marie: Oh mother.[43]

The film was shown as part of a special episode on going steady. The conversation between Marie and her mother contains the only reference to sex in the entire program. A 1957 film, *How Much Affection?*, produced by Crawley Films of Ottawa for McGraw-Hill Books in New York, is unusual in that it dances around sex without actually having to say the word:

> Mary: Tonight the feeling between us kept getting stronger and stronger. And on the way home we stopped and parked. And then things seemed to happen, till we nearly — [Mary glances down at her dressing table, Mother stands by looking concerned, there is a long pause] — It was so close. Suddenly I realized what we were about to do. I asked Jeff to take me home. I guess he felt ashamed too. He said he was sorry, that it was his fault.
> Mother: Do you think it was his fault?
> Mary: Oh mother, I don't know what to think, I'm so mixed up. I don't even know if I want to go out with Jeff again.[44]

Mary and her mother have a talk about feeling "warm and affectionate" and about the times when "your physical urges fight against your reason." When Mary next runs into Jeff at school they apologize to each other. Later they see "poor Eileen" and her baby on the street. Her baby was born five months after a hasty marriage to Fred. Her face looks haggard. We are to assume Mary and Jeff learn from her "mistake."

Joe and Roxy, produced by the NFB, is the one film that shows working-class teenagers. Also produced in 1957, it is not quite as dramatic or explicit in its message as *How Much Affection?*, although it does include images of sexual behaviour.[45] We see a young couple hanging around the girl's house, unchaperoned, after school.[46] The boy fixes a broken toaster. They start to play tag. He chases her. He tackles her on the couch. They end up on the floor kissing. They stare into each other's eyes. He starts to feel uncomfortable and gets up to tidy up his repair job. When he comes back to the living room the two are shy with each other and sit apart on the couch. They talk about getting engaged. They start to rough-house but then they grow quiet. The narrator intervenes: "Moods change very swiftly at 17, gay and raucous and tender. An age of many moods and many doubts." Sex is there and not there at the same time.

These reticent portrayals of teenage sexuality were at odds with advice-book discussions of sex as powerful and "awe-inspiring." Teenagers were supposed to learn about sex as a wonderful natural urge, but then they were to ignore or control that urge until they were legally sanctioned to express it. People like Marion Hilliard assumed it was impossible; she frankly told girls not to trust themselves and to keep out of any situation where sex might occur.[47] Other writers thought the right information presented in the "right way" would prepare girls "to deal with the power [their] 'femaleness' places in [their] hands."[48]

In her book *Young, White and Miserable*, Wini Breines talked about the crazy-making contradictions that faced young American women in the 1950s. In a consumer culture that celebrated youth and sexuality it appeared there was a new openness to sex. Certainly postwar teenagers had plenty of opportunity to engage in sexual activity. The emphasis on co-ed activities at school and after, combined with the privacy that was inevitable for at least some part of almost every date, put heterosexual boys and girls in extremely close proximity to each other's sexuality. But, as Breines says, this openness and opportunity unfolded in the context of "prudish families and narrow, even cruel, sexual norms."[49] But unfold it did. In his 1953 study on women, Kinsey found that "very nearly 50 per cent of the females who were married by the age of twenty had had pre-marital coitus."[50] He also noted that the rates of pre-marital coitus for women had remained relatively constant, with only minor increases since 1930.[51] What was similarly surprising to his 1950s readers was Kinsey's claim that 90 per cent of all the women in his sample had engaged in pre-marital petting, while the figure rose to 100 per cent for those who subsequently married.[52]

In the face of widespread sexual behaviour among adolescents, advice writers continued their attempts to construct normal heterosexuality as a relatively non-sexual practice until marriage. Despite timid discussions about goodnight kisses and popular articles by learned women and men on the dangers of petting, teenagers did engage in a range of heterosexual sexual activity, although, as Breines says, it wasn't always pleasant or fun.[53]

When the social norm meant waiting until marriage, teenagers who engaged in sexual activity — girls especially though boys as well — played dangerously with their own social value and categorization. To meet their own needs and desires for sex as well as social requirements for at least the image of chastity, teenagers engaged in complicated negotiations around the categories of sexual activity. Can you kiss on the first date? The second? Sexual activity took place on a graduated scale that culminated in "going all the way." So long as a couple went up the scale in the proper order, at the proper stage of their dating relationship, the dating system could contain and sanction their intimacies. As an institution, going steady allowed both girls and boys to maintain their reputations while permitting them access to sex, in some cases even intercourse, so long as they didn't get caught. Pregnancy was an incontestable marker of having crossed the line between normal/moral/good and abnormal/immoral/bad. Even homosexuality was easier to hide.

Early marriage was the ultimate solution to teenage sexual behaviour. In the 1950s the average age of marriage dropped to 22 for Canadian women,[54] and not just because of "shotgun weddings." Marriage was a legitimate avenue of sexual expression for those young men and women who felt caught between the incitement to sex in the culture at large and the proscriptions against their own engagement in it. Early marriage was one way to bring changes in sexual behaviour into line with the established moral order. It could realign the boundary between abnormal and normal behaviour. It allowed sexually active young people to be reframed as responsible adults, as future parents, as citizens.

Conclusion

The ability to lay claim to a definition of normality was a crucial marker of postwar social belonging. To be marked as sexually "abnormal" in any way was to throw into question the possibility of achieving or maintaining status as an adult, as a "responsible citizen," as a valued contributor to the social whole. Normal sexuality, as constructed in postwar advice books, films, and magazines, was invariably the preserve of married, monogamous, adult heterosexual couples who produced children, and of the adolescent girls and boys who were preparing themselves to fit that model. That young people could "prepare for" or be prepared for normal sexuality is a central aspect of postwar sexual discourses. With the rise of developmental psychology, so-called normal sexuality was understood to be an emotional and psychic achievement. While this process played itself out on biological terrain, biology alone was not enough to guarantee one's normalness. Hence the tremendous impulse, expressed by many adults, to help shape teenage sexual development.

Teens were assumed to be works-in-progress, to be malleable and easily influenced — characteristics that many adults thought could facilitate teens turning into deviants or into model, sexually-responsible citizens. As a group, therefore, teens were often the targets of an "ideal" sexual knowledge intended to guide them toward maturity. Youth were portrayed in popular media and sex education materials as the "parents of the future," a formulation that brought teen sexual development to social prominence and aligned it with the development of the nation as a whole. Given this, it is not surprising that teenagers were frequently the ground over which the boundaries of normative sexuality were negotiated and reinforced.

As a category that could mark one's acceptability and cast one's future, normality had to be constantly fought for, despite ideological constructions of it as "natural." But while the classificatory power of normality had tremendous influence, it did not entirely determine the way people lived their lives, as Kinsey's figures suggested. As a discursive construction, normality was perhaps less responsible for shaping teenagers' daily activities than it was for curtailing the possible range of meanings that could be ascribed to them. Regardless of whether one felt normal or aspired to normality, it was always present as a standard by which one could judge oneself or be judged by others.[55] At times, the consequences of not measuring up were considerable. So-called abnormality was expressed at a terrible price, be it ostracism, incarceration or psychiatrization. Homosexuality, unusual expressions of gender identity, promiscuity, and pregnancy were all evidence of an unsuccessful struggle to keep firm boundaries between outside threats to one's own psycho-sexual development and internal, "natural" possibilities. As sexual beings in process, teenagers were assumed to be especially vulnerable. As the citizens who would carry the nation through the postwar period into the modern world, they were particularly singled out as targets for intervention by adults, because if they were normal, the future would be normal too.

Notes

1. This essay is a revised version of Chapter 5 in *The Trouble With Normal: PostWar Youth and the Making of Heterosexuality.* © University of Toronto Press 1997. Reprinted with permission of the publisher.

2. Elaine May, *Homeward Bound: American Families in the Cold War Era* (New York: Basic, 1988), 11.

3. Philip Girard, "From Subversion to Liberation: Homosexuals and the Immigration Act 1952-1977," *Canadian Journal of Law and Society* 2 (1987): 3.

4. Ruth MacLachlan Franks, "A Note to Brides: Don't Delay Parenthood," *Chatelaine* (May 1946): 29.

5. See, for example, Katherine Arnup, *Education for Motherhood* (Toronto: University of Toronto Press, 1994); Cynthia R. Comacchio, *Nations Are Built of Babies* (Montreal and Kingston: McGill-Queen's University Press, 1993).

6. Alfred Henry Tyrer, *Sex, Marriage and Birth Control* (Toronto: Marriage Welfare Bureau, 1943, originally published 1936).

7. Ann Landers, *Ann Landers Talks to Teenagers About Sex* (Englewood Cliffs, NJ: Prentice-Hall, 1963), 47.

8. Maxine Davis, *Sex and the Adolescent* (New York: Permabooks, 1960), 59, emphasis mine.

9. Frances Bruce Strain, *Teen Days: A Book for Boys and Girls* (New York: Appleton-Century-Crofts, 1946), 160

10. Lester A. Kirkendall, *Understanding Sex, Life Adjustment Booklet*, rev. ed. (Chicago: Science Research Associates, 1957, originally published 1947), 34.

11. Davis, *Sex and the Adolescent*, 63.

12. Barbara Ehrenreich, *The Hearts of Men: American Dreams and the Flight from Commitment* (New York: Anchor/Doubleday, 1983), 24.

13. Strain, *Teen Days*, 160.

14. Evelyn Millis Duvall, *Facts of Life and Love for Teenagers* (New York: Association Press, 1950, with copyright by the Young Men's Christian Association), 202-06.

15. Duvall, *Facts of Life and Love for Teenagers*, 274.

16. Landers, *Ann Landers Talks to Teenagers About Sex*, 81.

17. Davis, *Sex and the Adolescent*, 228.

18. Here I am thinking particularly of sexological writings like Havelock Ellis's *Studies in the Psychology of Sex* (New York: Random House, 1936), Volume I, part four, and Richard von Krafft-Ebing, *Psychopathia Sexualis* (New York: Paperback Library, 1965, original English translation, 1892). Radclyffe Hall's *The Well of Loneliness* also fits this model. An invert was, according to these writers, someone born with a bad match between their body and their felt gender. So Stephen, in *The Well of Loneliness*, felt she was very much a masculine soul living inside a feminine body.

19. Frances Bruce Strain, *Sex Guidance in Family Life Education: A Handbook for the Schools* (New York: Macmillan, 1942), 142.

20. *Chatelaine* (September 1948), 106.

21. *Chatelaine* (September 1948), 106, emphasis in original.

22. Duvall, *Facts of Life and Love for Teenagers*, 22.

23. Strain, *Sex Guidance in Family Life Education*, 144.

24. Strain, *Teen Days*, 81.

25. Strain, *Teen Days*, 75.

26. Duvall, *Facts of Life and Love for Teenagers*, 77.

27. Mary McGee Williams and Irene Kane, *On Becoming a Woman* (New York: Dell, 1958), 46, emphasis in original.

28. See Beth Bailey, *From Front Porch to Back Seat: Courtship in Twentieth-Century America* (Baltimore: Johns Hopkins University Press, 1988); Ellen S. Rothman, *Hands and Hearts: A History of Courtship in America* (New York: Basic Books, 1984); John D'Emilio and Estelle B. Freedman, *Intimate Matters: A History of Sexuality in America* (New York: Harper and Row, 1988).

29. Karen Dubinsky, *Improper Advances: Rape and Heterosexual Conflict in Ontario, 1880-1929* (Chicago: The University of Chicago Press, 1993), 114.

30. May, *Homeward Bound*, 101

31. Sylvia Fraser, *My Father's House: A Memoir of Incest and Healing* (Toronto: Doubleday, 1987), 71.

32. Clifford R. Adams, "Romance Isn't Easy," *Chatelaine* (September 1948): 4.

33. Marion Hilliard, "Can You Live Without Him?", *Chatelaine* (March 1958): 10-11.

34. Sidney Katz, "Going Steady: Is It Ruining Our Teen-agers?", *Maclean's* (January 1959): 9.

35. Katz, "Going Steady," 39.

36. Katz, "Going Steady," 38.

37. Williams and Kane, *On Becoming a Woman*, 46.

38. Strain, *Teen Days*, 130.

39. Duvall, *Facts of Life and Love for Teenagers*, 120.

40. Landers, *Ann Landers Talks to Teenagers About Sex*, 19.

41. Marion Hilliard, "Dr. Marion Hilliard Talks to Single Women," *Chatelaine* (February 1956): 48.

42. Williams and Kane, *On Becoming a Woman*, 29.

43. *Going Steady*, produced by Coronet Films, 1951.

44. *How Much Affection?*, produced by Crawley Films for McGraw-Hill Books, 1957.

45. A point obviously needs to be made here about the NFB's more "realistic" film compared to those produced for the American market.

46. *Joe and Roxy*, produced by the National Film Board of Canada as part of the Perspective Series, 1957. The fact that Roxy and Joe are home alone, while Roxy's mother is at work, was a relatively radical statement when US films were portraying mothers as forever baking, always home after school. In some American films, teens who brought friends over when their parents were out, let alone "boyfriends" or "girlfriends," were portrayed as misbehaving and risking punishment.

47. Marion Hilliard, "Dr. Marion Hilliard Helps Teen-age Girls Meet Their Biggest Problem," *Chatelaine* (October 1956): 100.

48. Williams and Kane, *On Becoming a Woman*, 28.

49. Wini Breines, *Young, White, and Miserable: Growing Up Female in the Fifties* (Boston: Beacon, 1992), 87.

50. Alfred Kinsey et al., *Sexual Behavior in the Human Female* (New York: Pocket Books, 1965), 287.

51. Kinsey et al., *Sexual Behavior in the Human Female*, 300.

52. Kinsey et al., *Sexual Behavior in the Human Female*, 233.

53. Breines, *Young, White and Miserable*, 115.

54. Alison Prentice, Paula Bourne, Gail Cuthbert Brandt, Beth Light, Wendy Mitchinson and Naomi Black, *Canadian Women: A History* (Toronto: Harcourt, Brace Jovanovich, 1988), 311.

55. Nikolas Rose, *Governing the Soul: The Shaping of the Private Self* (London: Routledge, 1990), 11.

chapter thirteen

BLACK NOVA SCOTIAN WOMEN'S SCHOOLING AND CITIZENSHIP
An Education of Violence

Bernice Moreau

"The most important manifestation of colour prejudice in Canadian history is in education"[1]

Introduction

Black women's[2] four-hundred-year quest for the adequate, formal education central to full social citizenship in North America has been shaped by an education of violence,[3] and their resistance to that violence. During slavery and segregation, African Canadians in Nova Scotia, and others in slave societies across the Western Hemisphere, were denied civil rights and the freedom to pursue formal education at all levels. Until the 1950s, formal education remained largely a privilege of the White society in Nova Scotia.[4] Blacks who were fortunate enough to receive formal education received an inadequate one either in segregated settings or under adverse conditions at schools for poor Whites. Black Nova Scotians resisted the mobilization of race, gender, and class relations, which functioned to deny them education and, by extension, full citizenship. Nova Scotia's *Education Act*, passed in 1953, reflects this history of resistance with its declaration that education would henceforth be "free for all." This elimination of the *de facto* school segregation by race signalled a significant milestone in educational freedom and full citizenship for Black Nova Scotians.[5]

The history of formal education and full citizenship of Black Nova Scotian women, as told by a group of Black women schooled in the early 1900s, is the focus of this chapter. I illustrate that Black women's need for adequate formal education as fully participating citizens was met with rejection until the early 1950s. The question of interest here is twofold: What is the educational and civic history of Black women in Nova Scotia (specifically those women schooled in the early 1900s), and what was their experience with educational violence in that province? I seek to address this two-part question through interviews with a group of Black women who received their early formal education in Nova Scotia during the early 1900s,[6] as well as a survey of selected secondary sources.

A Black Woman's Standpoint on the Margin: Resisting Oppression in Twentieth-Century Nova Scotia

The works of Patricia Hill Collins, Deborah King, and bell hooks offer an "Afrocentric" theoretical framework that informs this study.[7] These Black feminist scholars posit a self-defined standpoint of Black women that takes as its entry point the marginality of Black women, through their experience of racism, sexism, class domination, and other forms of oppression. It offers Black women a framework within which to conceptualize their social reality in light of their shared history as progeny of African slaves. Furthermore, it offers a collective interpretation and, thereby, a better framework for understanding the ways in which educational violence shaped the lives of generations of Black Canadian women. Their articulation of the experience of slavery, segregation, contemporary racism, and sexism, as expressed in educational, economic, and political oppression, offers important examples of accommodation and resistance. These Black Nova Scotian women, like their foremothers, were able to transform their designated isolated "barren margins" to "margin-centres" for their survival as a distinct group of people in Canada.

A practical example of this survival technique is evident in the way Black Nova Scotians dealt with their need for formal education and social recognition in the early 1900s. Throughout that era, educational reforms advocated compulsory education for all, although it was to be administered according to race. Although they were compelled by law to pay school taxes, Blacks were denied entrance to White schools in their own localities. One legislator cited "the known repugnance of whites to mix with [Blacks]" as justification for "shut[ting] them out of these [civil] benefits. ... [I]f they were to be taught at all," he added, "they must receive their rudiments of knowledge in separate and distinct establishments."[8] The ongoing struggle by Black Nova

Scotians to resist this educational deprivation is described by one of the women interviewed, who reported,

> When we in the community were able to gather enough money to have a schoolhouse it was built near the [Black] church. ...The school was never big enough and we never had enough seats for all the children. ...We had to search for a [Black] teacher for no Whites would teach us. ... The White schools were well built, had enough seats, teachers, books and other things. ...the government gave their own, but they never was willing to help us get a good education.[9]

Hill observes that "Black schooling in the Maritimes was ... poor, unsystematic and undependable. Black teachers did not always have much opportunity for training and were limited by their own experience in poorly equipped schools. ... The Bishop of Nova Scotia commented sadly [that] ... white residents of the province ... in general care so little for Blacks, that assistance cannot be obtained."[10] Throughout their history in Nova Scotia, Blacks accepted what little education was offered to them by benevolent Whites. At the same time, they made every effort to share among themselves the little education they had. In spite of their heroic efforts, they desperately lacked resources and trained teachers. Lucas White states that

> obtaining an education was especially difficult for early Blacks. ... There were those who had some education, whether self taught or learned at school, but for the most part, the majority were illiterate. Their marginal residential status contributed to the problems they faced in getting an education. Schools for Blacks were separate and not equal.[11]

Black feminist scholars argue that one objective for the government's organized illiteracy plan for Black women was to ensure a cheap labour force for domestic service for White families in that era. Maxine Tynes, one of Nova Scotia's Black educators and well-known poets, refers to Black women's domestic labours in White homes as being "in service." She describes "armies of Black women in the sea of domestic service, waiting for buses on prestigious street corners, carrying back bits and remnants of that other world. ... They were forced into the economic position and status of regimented cheap domestic labourers."[12]

The relegation of Black women to this menial labour placed them in the civic position of "outsiders within." As such, they were not regarded as genuine Canadians citizens. They were seldom permitted to acquire the knowledge and skills required for social respectability, educational advancement, economic progress, and the privilege of full civil rights. As one woman states,

> White folks believe that because we are coloured we must be poor and ignorant and they didn't care if we ever learned to read and write. I wanted to be a nurse, but in them days we were not accepted as nurses in the hospitals. We could only nurse sick White folks in their homes when I was in service.[13]

Collins' findings support the women's view of their situation. She claims that "recent [Black] scholarship has uncovered ... many African American women whose minds and talents have been suppressed by the pots and kettles [in White women's kitchens where they laboured], symbolic of Black women's subordination."[14]

In this seemingly hopeless situation, Black women's voices can be heard resisting the suppression of their minds: "Our souls are fired with the same love of liberty and independence with which your [White] souls are fired ... too much of your blood flows in our veins, too much of your color in our skins, for us not to possess your spirits."[15] Similarly, Black women in Nova Scotia in the early 1900s displayed this progressive spirit of freedom, and independence in their determination to resist social oppression, and thus influenced the course of their history. One instance is described by Hamilton:

> In 1917 the women of the African Baptist churches gathered together to establish a 'Ladies Auxiliary' which would take responsibility for the stimulation of the spiritual, social, educational, charitable and financial work of the local churches. ... These women gathered ... around a well [to strategize for action]. This gathering became known as "the Women at the Well" a symbol of resistance.[16]

The determination of these women to challenge the systemic, institutional, and individual oppression in that province strengthened the Black protests that were occurring across Canada at that time. Women like Mary Ann Shadd, editor of the *Fugitive*, a Black newspaper published in the late nineteenth century, inspired others.[17] In 1920, the Black Women's Convention was held in Halifax, the first of its kind in Canadian history.[18] These sociopolitical activities played a significant role in bringing about change in the civil and educational future of Black women in Nova Scotia.

Citizenship Denied: The Black Experience in Nova Scotia (1600-1800)

In his book *Belonging*, William Kaplan claims that citizenship means different things to different people and that "citizenship means more than the right to vote; more than the right to hold property; more than the right to move freely under the protection of the state; citizenship is the right to full partnership in the fortunes and in the future of the nation."[19] This was not a reality for Blacks in Nova Scotia in the first half of the twentieth century. Simms reminds us that, historically in Europe and European colonies, "it was generally accepted that not all people were granted full citizenship or even the same level of citizenship, ... slaves, foreigners and resident aliens were denied citizenship."[20] It would be easy to assume that the inferior social status of Blacks, first as slaves and later as resident aliens, which excluded them from equal rights with Whites, is now eradicated. On the contrary, as a Black woman in the academy I would dare say, from my personal experience and that of other women of colour, that this ideology of Black inferiority vis-à-vis White superiority continues to some extent throughout Canada's educational systems to this day.[21]

For the Black Nova Scotian women whom I interviewed, citizenship implied the positive recognition of their humanity, their femininity, and their racial difference. It also hinged on their freedom to pursue education, economic advancement, legal and civil rights, as well as the privileges and opportunities enjoyed by the White citizens of the province. The women all hoped that the service rendered by their ancestors in Nova Scotia as explorers, slaves, loyalists, Maroons,[22] refugees, and labourers, along with their resistance to White oppression, would result in the granting of educational freedom, economic advancement, legal and civil rights equivalent to those enjoyed by the White citizens of the province.

The presence of people of African descent in Nova Scotia began with the arrival of the first Black man, Mattieu de Coste, who arrived with the first Europeans to declare themselves citizens of Canada. De Coste lived and worked in Port Royal (later renamed Nova Scotia), Canada, as early as 1605. Although it can be assumed that de Coste had to be knowledgeable in some significant ways to be included on such a team of explorers, it is also unlikely that he was given equal rights with the White members on the team. While French explorers declared themselves Canadian citizens by right of their successful exploration and their unchallenged "discovery of the land," and the British claimed their rights through war agreements with France, de Coste was likely a "founding servant" among the "founding fathers" of Canada.[23]

Some time after claiming Canada for France, French colonists introduced a system of education for the lower classes. The objective of this benevolent educational initiative was not for the purpose of civility, but for servitude. Ralston argues that the real objective of the French elite class was "to make known our [French] name, power and authority, and to subject, submit and render obedient thereto all tribes [and races] of this land ... and by this means all others that are lawful to summon and to instruct."[24] This suggests that the education offered to the Mic-Macs, Blacks, and others was an education of violence, since its aim was not the advancement of these groups, but the entrenchment of their marginality.

Under the British rule of Nova Scotia in the early 1700s, "proper" education was the privilege of the elite. As a result, the educational system that was imported to Nova Scotia in the early 1700s was implemented specifically to prepare young males of influential White, Anglo-Saxon, Protestant families exclusively for positions of leadership in the colony.[25] Within the social, political, and economic environment of eighteenth-century Canada, White Canadians regarded the formal education of Blacks as not only wasteful, but positively dangerous. Pearleen Oliver states that Blacks "passed through an age when the theme song [of the White society] was, 'if you educate a Negro, you unfit him [her] for a slave.' And so illiteracy was another evil valiantly fought [by Blacks]."[26]

Any attempt to understand the educational and civil violence experienced by Black women in contemporary Nova Scotia must be done with the knowledge that the province is the home of Canada's oldest and largest group of indigenous Black people. In a former slave society, violence against Blacks in every area of life was an historically established societal norm.

Beginning in the early seventeenth century, Blacks who were brought to Nova Scotia as chattel slaves, loyalists, Maroons, and refugees were not accepted as citizens, but as labour power for the engines of economic advancement. The accounts of the women interviewed here reflect this history. Their limited educational, economic, and political progress and civil status sprang from the experience of their forebearers. A brief review of the history of Black Nova Scotian women's educational journey will help us to better understand the evolution of the education of violence that forced them, until recently, to be under-educated and only partial citizens.

In most cases, by the time slaves arrived for market in Nova Scotia, they were trained for their role. The slave traders' advertisements assured their buyers that the wills of the slaves were broken and their spirits transformed to the mentality of "beasts of burden." The administration of this type of education of violence was physically, mentally, and emotionally brutal. It was common practice for White slave masters to use guns, whips, trained dogs, ropes, and other destructive weapons as teaching aids in the learning process that took place on the job. Brizan found that "the distinctive African identity gave place to slave-type personalities; low self-esteem, self-hatred, inferiority complex, no cultural pride, contempt for others of one's kind, subservience, rejection of negroid features, and giving them the epithet of ugly. [Slavery] with its physical and psychological violence recreated the African in its own image."[27]

Fanon's vivid description of the devastating results of the education of violence experienced by early Africans gives us some idea of the determination of the master class in creating sub-humans from humans:

> ... I am talking of millions of men [and women] who have been skillfully injected with fear, inferiority, psychological complexities, trepidation, servility, despair, abasement ... they knew the farthest corner of the land of anguish....[28]

The objectives of the education of violence were transmitted intergenerationally from Black slaves through the Black Loyalists, who were the first large group of North American Blacks to be emancipated. Black Loyalists were brought to Nova Scotia by the British between 1776 and 1786. They were promised full citizenship, equal opportunity with Whites, land, social assistance, employment, formal education, and freedom of worship.[29]

Black Loyalists were replete with hope for a better life, but they soon found that although they were presumably emancipated they were still controlled indirectly by the "spirit" of the *Black Code*[30] pertaining to education and civil rights. According to Gates, the law declared

> ... that all and every person and persons, whatsoever, who shall hereafter teach or cause any slave or ex-slave to be taught to write or shall use or employ any slave as a scribe in any manner of writing whatsoever, hereafter taught to write [and read], every such person or persons shall, for every offense, forfeit the sum of one hundred pounds current money.[31]

While the *Black Code* was never adopted in Nova Scotia, segregation on the basis of race was a practical reality that confronted Nova Scotian Blacks even one hundred years later.

> [B]y 1876 all Black children were excluded from common schools. When petitions were circulated against this, the amendment allowed

for the admissions of Black children into the common schools if new
and separate schools for them did not exist in the given area. By the
revision of the *Educational Act* in 1918, inspectors still had the authority to recommend separate schools for the races.[32]

In some instances a few Black men were allowed very basic religious
training (which emphasized White supremacy) so as to encourage them to
teach other Blacks to be obedient and morally upright, thus protecting the
property and status quo of the Whites.[33] Needless to say, progressive-minded
Blacks were not prepared to accept the deception of the British government
and the hostility of the English colonialists and many migrated to West Africa
or the Caribbean.

By 1796, most of the disappointed Black Loyalists had left Nova Scotia and
were replaced with another group of cheap labourers, the militant Jamaican
Maroons. Unlike the groups before and after them, the Maroons were not
easily controlled or manipulated by threats of punishment, religion, morality,
education or denial of citizenship. Although they did assist in building the
fortifications of Citadel Hill, they generally displayed open warlike resistance
to any attempt by the government to enslave them. Consequently, the English
colonists were not successful in imposing on a large scale an education of
violence on this group.[34] By 1799 the Maroons demanded of the government
that they be sent to a British colony in Africa. Walker says of them, "the
Maroons had, after all, successfully resisted the White man; they represented
a kind of 'black power' which neither British arms nor Nova Scotian implor-
ings had been able to overcome."[35]

Black Women's Education in Nova Scotia (1800-1900)

In the early 1800s Nova Scotia desperately needed an economic boost to survive economic stagnation. On this occasion the British imported Black
refugees to relieve the severe shortage of labour in Nova Scotia. Although former slaves, trained for servitude, these refugees envisioned a better life now
that they were freed. Sadly, they remained social outcasts in Canada, their
position as former slaves exacerbated by acute poverty, sickness, illiteracy,
social rejection, and alienation.

In spite of their deplorable conditions, the refugees protested against government policies that denied them education, equal access to paid employment, and citizenship. On a few occasions their protestations were silenced
by societal hostility and political censure. One English politician accused

African refugees of being unproductive and non-progressive by nature. He justified his accusation by stating that they were "... slaves by habit and education, who no longer lived under the dread of the lash, their idea of freedom is idleness and they are therefore, quite incapable of industry."[36]

Beginning in 1820, almost every black settlement petitioned the government to establish schools for their children and themselves. One petition challenged the earlier characterization of refugees, stating that "without an education we and our children, will forever be destitute of the blessing which alone is calculated to promote our best interest."[37] Black Nova Scotians clearly recognized their own capacities for industry, education, and citizenship, but they lacked the freedom and opportunity to demonstrate their ability to perform and progress like Whites.

Canadian historical literature offers little information about the actual proceedings of the British parliament's emancipation proclamation of Black people in the British Empire. Hill, like several other writers, uncovered a brief statement that "the statute of 1833 abolishing slavery took effect August 1, 1834."[38] Apparently, the abolition of slavery was of little significance to White Canadian society since slavery by this time had declined and Blacks were seldom seen and rarely heard. It may be argued that, for most Black Nova Scotians, it was merely a statutory proclamation of the physical release of legal slaves from organized brutality. What was perhaps of more importance to the Blacks then was the lack of any legislated or socially organized plan for their acceptance and integration into Canadian society as full citizens. Instead, segregation immediately became more openly accepted by society and implicitly supported by government.

Therefore, segregation in Nova Scotia could be said to have been a strategy used to hinder any attempt by Blacks to become educated, respectable, and accepted citizens enjoying equal rights with Whites. Hill records the analytical protest of the imposed segregation made by one Black man who stated,

> Not because we are black, but because you [Whites] suppose us weak and ignorant, and because we are friendless and oppressed, therefore, you meanly give us additional kicks. You deny us the opportunities of improvement, and then reproach us with our degradation, Your horror of amalgamation is a lying pretence; "niggers" may shave you, cook for you, serve your tables, dress your fair ladies, and be your bedfellows ... so long we consent to be your slaves ... [then] you reproach us with our poverty ... [and our illiteracy].[39]

From this testimony we can conclude that the education of violence continued unabated, but was manifested in Nova Scotia in more subtle, innovative, and creative ways. Black women (and men) were now allowed to change their social status from the level of sub-humans to inferior humans and were renamed by Whites as the "coloured" race. This experience of segregation is told by the women whose voices we hear in this study.

Black Women's Accounts of Segregation, Resistance, and an Education of Violence

Between the late 1800s and early 1900s, several educational reforms took place in Nova Scotia. However, little was done to bring adequate education to Black communities or to ensure the inclusion of black females in the White educational system. Instead, their intelligence and ability to acquire knowledge were measured by colour, sex, and class codes that gave to Whites the highest level of intelligence, while Blacks and other non-White groups were labelled as lacking intelligence, industry, and initiative. In this hierarchy of intelligence, few if any Blacks could succeed.

In 1864 the pre-Confederation Nova Scotia government passed an *Education Act* stating that "all common schools shall be free to all children residing in the section to which they are established."[40] An 1865 addition to the *Act* made formal education for children from five to sixteen years compulsory. This was the beginning of the free school system for Whites and legally sanctioned educational discrimination against Black Nova Scotians. The *Education Act* divided the province into school sections to be controlled by a Board of Trustees. The 1865 amendment gave authority to the Council of Public Instructions to authorize separate departments under the same or separate roofs for students of different races and sexes. This was not possible outside of Halifax where the majority of Blacks were settled by government in scattered enclaves across the province. Because of this geographical segregation of Black settlements from White communities, there were no publicly funded schools built for Black students outside the city of Halifax.

All the *Education Acts* legislated between 1864 and 1952 formally required education for all children in the province while in practice perpetuating the segregation of education by geographical area. In most instances that meant that Black children were unschooled. Blacks continuously protested against the educational discrimination that they experienced. In April 1884, the *Halifax Morning Chronicle* published a heated debate involving several White politicians and Black leaders who were lobbying on the issue of unequal education. One White politician argued, in defense of segregation and inequality of education, that "laws were made for the greatest good of the greatest number, those being whites."[41]

Needless to say, Black Nova Scotians were not prepared to accept the government's decision to exclude their children and young people from the common schools. Boyd informs us that the people, led by their church leaders, created *ad hoc* educational committees to organize the lobbying of the government legislature against racially segregated common schools. One such "educational committee ...was organized to lobby against racially segregated schools, sanctioned by the Legislative Assembly of the Province of Nova Scotia, and to obtain re-admission of Black youth into the common schools ... to which the youth were entitled."[42] These petitions led to the admittance of some Black students into White common schools in poorer districts. But this was not without its problems: one woman describes the hostility and humiliation that they experienced when a few of them were finally admitted to poor White schools near their community. She recalls,

> The school I went to was White. They were forced to accept us coloured children because our parents paid school taxes and we were not allowed at White schools ...[43]

Another woman with visible anger remembers the hostility that Black children experienced at White schools. She said with great emotional pain,

> They treated us like animals when we tried to work anywhere else but in their homes ... coloured children were called nasty names and had horrible things done to us so as to keep us from going to their school and getting education. We had to keep them clean and they treated us like we were dirty.[44]

Most of the women who attended White schools remembered how White teachers used the socially-imposed illiteracy of Black parents to humiliate Black children in the presence of their White schoolmates. One woman in particular remembers,

> White teachers would not take a verbal excuse when I say that I was ill and was not able to complete my work. I had to bring a written note signed by one of my parents. Many Black parents could not write an excuse and those children were ridiculed in front of the whole class when they came without a written excuse. ... White

teachers knew that many Black [parents] could not read or write, but they demanded written excuses on purpose so as to discourage us from getting education.[45]

In the early 1900s the acquisition of formal education continued to be an ongoing struggle for Blacks in Nova Scotia mainly because of the colour of their skin. They suffered what may be termed "colour contusion" — a weapon employed to ridicule Black students and discourage them from seeking adequate education and citizenship. Colour was such an important issue for the women in the early 1900s since every aspect of their everyday lives was controlled by the colour of their skin. Colour lines were visible everywhere — notably in the educational policies and in the educational institutions. Walker observes that "by circumstances and public attitude, a colour line was drawn in Canada which affected the economic and social life of the blacks. ... Blacks were denied equal use of public schools in Nova Scotia and Ontario and the law recognized this division."[46]

In many instances, the government excluded Black children from common White schools in Nova Scotia while at the same time refusing to assist in the financing of post-primary education in poor Black communities. Most of the women indicated that because they were Black they were perceived as poor and illiterate, with only the capacity for domestic service. According to one woman,

> In the elementary schools they [White teachers] were willing to teach us because they were preparing us for service. ... We make better maids and nannies for their kitchens and bedrooms than for their offices. The trouble began we decided we didn't want to work in the White woman's kitchen. We want to do what they are free to do. We wanted to teach, we wanted to go to university, we wanted to be nurses, secretaries, clerks in stores and things like that.[47]

White society regarded any open resistance to these acts of colour contusion as presumptuous and confrontational. The colour contusion directed against Black women left an indelible mark on their lives. One of the women talked at length about the hostility that she and other Black children experienced at a poor White school near her community, identified by Whites as "nigger hill." She said of the teacher,

> Mrs. ----- was terrible. Today we would nickname her Hitler. She was just like Hitler. She was so cruel, hard and ugly to us as Hitler

was to the Jews. She would beat us for nothing with her big black strap. She had a corner where she sent us after the beating which she called black corner. When we got afraid that we forgot our poems or tables she would put us to stand on the dunce chair with a dunce cap on our heads. It was horrible for us. Many coloured children stopped school because her. She got rid of us fast from the White school.[48]

It was heart-breaking to see the pain that these women demonstrated after so many years. Colour contusion left scars that were transmitted from one generation of Black women to another. But still it was not only an education of violence that the women in the study inherited from their foremothers; they also were bequeathed the survival strategies of accommodation and resistance:

The coloured people kept quiet about not having the right kind of education and every thing else. We didn't like what was done to us and we sometimes said so. But we couldn't always fight to win them. We are coloured and no coloured could win in Nova Scotia ... we must never be as good as them. Then they could say that we are ignorant.[49]

These women may have been limited in formal knowledge, but they were wise in life's experiences and they knew how to survive without the validation that would flow from acceptance as full Canadian citizens.

One way in which the Black community showed its resistance to educational and civil oppression was by building schools to offer an educational experience to those who were not accepted at White schools. The interviewed women spoke freely about the apathetic attitude that most Whites exhibited toward the lack of adequate education for the Black community. One interviewee recalled,

Poor as we were we were made to build our own schools, hire our own teachers, and pay the teachers by community effort. All the schools were one room and the boys and girls were together. Our schoolteacher [a black young woman] did not get training for teaching. Our school was different in so many ways from the White schools because of colour prejudice and discrimination. White folks believed that because we are coloured we must be poor and ignorant. They didn't care if we ever learned to read and write.[50]

This woman's statement reveals how race, gender, and class relations, experienced as colour contusion, restricted Black Nova Scotians from accessing an adequate formal education. In her experience a good education and the freedom to use it would have altered her chances for meaningful employment and respectability in the community at large:

> We are coloured and so we must be poor. All kinds of barriers are set up to keep us from getting education and good jobs. White people made it very difficult for us to go to their schools, which were better than ours. Even when we struggled and got education we were not given meaningful jobs. I wanted to be a nurse but I was not allowed. We had no choice, most of us had to work in their homes as servants or teach in our own few schools where we had no money to buy school equipment like the White schools.[51]

The racist provincial government of the period used poverty and illiteracy as weapons of control over the Black community. It was common knowledge that Blacks received little or no help from the state for the promotion of adequate education, while many White communities were assisted in the establishment of schools. For example, Abucar found that, between the late 1800s and early 1900s, poverty and a limited knowledge base were insurmountable barriers for Blacks in the Preston Road School Section N.21. The community made an appeal to the provincial educational authority to cancel plans for higher school taxes. Instead of paying taxes that did not benefit them, they sought assistance to erect a school building for the community. The petition read, "Section N.21 has been unable under the operation of the *Free School Law* to build a good school house ... and any alterations by fees and subscription will be injurious to the cause of education."[52]

Clairmont and Magill, in their study of the Black community in Nova Scotia, also chronicled how several Black settlements were unable to provide formal education for their people. The authors refer to the reluctance of government officials, who controlled the educational budget and its distribution in the province, to assist Black communities in Lincolnville, in Guysborough County, to erect a school building. From 1890 to 1930 the community made several appeals to the government for assistance for a school. For almost 40 years, the community was without a school for its children. When the government finally decided to assist them in erecting a school building, the community was informed that it would have to provide the furniture, the teacher's salary, and the school supplies, thus defeating the whole effort.[53]

Similarly, Woodson found that Black communities had great difficulties in "financing Black education which had always being a problem [and] which became crucial during the depression years." "Racism," he concluded, "was not benign during the 1920s and 1930s."[54] In most cases, after the people had undergone great struggles to erect a schoolhouse in a Black community, they had to rely on their meagre resources for maintenance and supplies. One woman stated,

> It was the responsibility of the teacher [who in most cases was a young Black woman who lived on the margin of the White community and was given special permission by the inspector of schools to attend a White school for poor Whites] to find what she needed for the teaching and how to get what she wanted. ... They would not let her teach in their schools; she was coloured. She had to teach in a coloured school. She could go and get their old books, broken slates and other used materials from the White schools in the city. What they did not want is what we used.[55]

The Black teacher was forced to offer the children in her community a "recycled education," the results of which were and entrenchment of racism and sexism, along with semi-literacy, under-employment, class discrimination, criminal activities, and poor self-worth among Black youth. Yet most of the women admitted that while their schools were poorly equipped, with limited curriculum, no space and no opportunities for intellectual expansion, they still enjoyed school. There were so many children in the Black communities who wanted to go to school that school attendance had to be organized by the community.

Segregation, which was implemented to meet the demands of the emerging liberal-political ideology and capitalist economy, took little notice of the Black struggle for education and citizenship. They remained second-class citizens, illiterate, poor, underemployed, powerless and rejected. Black womanhood was held in particularly low esteem. In Nova Scotia, Black women turned to their sisterhood and the Black church for solace and strength.

The church, the first institution established by the early Blacks in Nova Scotia, played a unique role by providing stability and filling the needs of the Black community. It was the Black church that led the community in resistance against blatant racism in the denial of formal education and citizenship. According to one woman, "We lived seven miles from the nearest White government common school, but we were not allowed to go out of our school zone to a White school and there were no schools built in our school district. Our church was forced to provide us with some education."[56] Another woman gave an interesting view of her church in the context of the White-dominated society:

> The church is the one place where the White man has not tried to enter uninvited. It is the one place where we are not treated with scorn, where we are not insulted, called nasty names like we are nobodies. Our church is the only place where we are respected. We may be domestics, charwomen, wet nurses, janitors, cleaners or what have you in the White community in the week but on Sundays we are somebodies. We are recognized. We are wanted. In the White man's place we are coloured. We don't need no colouring in our church. We are sisters and brothers in the Lord. We are one in Christ.[57]

Throughout the history of Blacks in Nova Scotia, the church offered Black women the protection, the security, the self-worth, the knowledge, the solace, the courage and the strength to resist the educational and other types of violence that haunted their existence in Nova Scotia. The Black church, the vanguard in Black Nova Scotian struggle for educational and civic change, provided a forum within which resistance and self-preservation could flourish. The determination of Black church leaders played an important part in the decision of the provincial government to revisit its *Education Act*. In 1953, revisions to the *Act* created the following provision, headed "Schools to be free":

(1) All schools established or conducted under this Act are free schools.

(2) Subject to this Act and the regulations, *every person* over the age of five years and under the age of twenty-one years has the right to attend a school in the school section in which he resides.[58]

Conclusion

This brief study of the social history of Black women's struggle for schooling and full citizenship in Nova Scotia in the early 1900s reveals the intricate links between their experience of educational violence and that of their foremothers. The historical period that was investigated covered the receding shadows of slavery and the dawn of hope for educational and civic freedom. Legal segregation, a social policy implemented by the White judicial and political systems to destroy any possible integration that may have occurred for Blacks into the White social system, resulted in a nightmarish period of hostility expressed through colour lines, political and social rejection.

The educational transition for Black women from slavery to segregation and then to legal entitlement was a slow and arduous one. The journey, undermined by an education of violence, was paved with exploitation, rejection, racism, sexism, illiteracy, poverty, colour contusion, alienation, and numerous other forms of oppression. In the 1950s and early 1960s, with the emergence of the Black civil rights movement, Black Nova Scotians would finally make significant strides toward full social citizenship. In spite of these changes, the struggle goes on as the Black community heals itself of the past in order to be able to fully embrace its rights.

Notes

1. James Walker, *A History of Blacks in Canada* (Québec: Canadian Government Publishing Centre, 1980), 107.
2. I use the terms Black Nova Scotian, African Nova Scotian, and Black Canadian, interchangeably and also, for political reasons, I capitalize the word Black throughout the text.
3. An "education of violence" is a phrase that I have coined to capture the indoctrination, dehumanization, and defeminization imposed on African women by Europeans. Slavery followed by segregation and, more recently, race, gender, and class oppression, are regarded as systems of education of violence for Blacks.
4. William Pearly Oliver, "Cultural Progress of the Negro in Nova Scotia," *Dalhousie Review* 49 (June, 1943): 293-300.
5. Colin A. Thomson, *Born With a Call* (Nova Scotia: McCurdy Press, 1986), 9.
6. For more information on the research that informs this chapter, see Bernice Moreau, "Black Nova Scotian Women's Experience of Educational Violence in the Early 1900s: A Case of Colour Contusion," *Dalhousie Review* 77, 2 (Summer, 1997): 128-205.
7. Patricia Collins, *Black Feminist Thought: Knowledge, Consciousness and the Politics of Empowerment* (London: Harper, Collins Publishers, 1990); bell hooks, *Feminist Thought: From Margin to Center* (Boston, MA: South End Press, 1984); Deborah King, "Multiple Jeopardy, Multiple Consciousness: The Context of a Black Feminist Ideology," *Signs* 14, 1 (Autumn, 1980): 42-72.
8. Public Archives of Nova Scotia, *Statutes of Nova Scotia: Education Committee Report*, RG 5 Series R22 (1836), 36.
9. Interview (1990). Details concerning the collection of these oral histories can be found in Bernice Moreau, "Black Nova Scotian Women's Educational Experience 1900-1945: A Study in Race, Gender and Class Relations" (Ph.D. Dissertation, University of Toronto, 1996).
10. Daniel Hill, *The Freedom Seekers: Blacks in Early Canada* (Agincourt, ON: The Book Society of Canada, 1981), 161.
11. Lydia Lucas-White, "Blacks and Education in Nova Scotia: Implications for Social Work Education and Practice," *Social Work in Atlantic Canada* 1, 1 (1975): 37.
12. Maxine Tynes, "In Service," *Fireweed* 26 (Winter/Spring, 1988): 8-11.
13. Interview (1990).
14. Collins, *Black Feminist Thought*, 4.

15. *Maria W. Stewart, America's First Black Woman Political Writer*, ed. Marilyn Richardson (Bloomington: Indiana University Press, 1987), 40, cited in Collins, *Black Feminist Thought*, 4.

16. Sylvia Hamilton, "Our Mothers Grand and Great: Black Women of Nova Scotia," *Canadian Women Studies* 4, 2 (Winter, 1982): 35-36.

17. Daniel Hill, *The Freedom Seekers*, 187.

18. Hamilton, "Our Mothers Grand and Great," 35-36.

19. *Belonging: The Meaning and Future of Canadian Citizenship*, ed. William Kaplan (Montreal: McGill-Queens University Press, 1993), 21.

20. Glenda Simms, "Racism as a Barrier to Canadian Citizenship," in *Belonging: The Meaning and Future of Canadian Citizenship*, ed. William Kaplan (Montreal: McGill–Queen's University Press, 1993), 334.

21. Rashmi Luther, Elizabeth Whitmore and Bernice Moreau, *Seen but not Heard: Aboriginal Women and Women of Colour in the Academy* (Ottawa, ON: CRIAW, 2001).

22. As will be discussed below, the Maroons were a militant group descended from former slaves who arrived in Nova Scotia from Jamaica in the late eighteenth century.

23. Robin Winks, *The Blacks in Canada, A History* (Montreal: McGill–Queen's University Press, 1977).

24. Helen Ralson, "Religion, Public Policy and the Education of MicMac Indians of Nova Scotia, 1605-1872," A Paper presented at the Association for Sociology of Religion (San Francisco, 1978), 8.

25. Douglas Lawr and Robert Gidney, *Educating Canadians: A Documentary History of Public Education* (Toronto: Van Nostrand Reinhold, 1973).

26. Pearleen Oliver, *A Brief History of The Coloured Baptists in Nova Scotia 1782-1953* (Halifax: Cornwallis Baptist Church, 1953).

27. George Brizan, *Grenada, Island of Conflict, From Amerindians to the People's Revolution 1494-1979* (London: Books Limited, 1984), 85.

28. Franz Fanon, *The Wretched of the Earth* (New York: Grove Press, 1963), 12.

29. Walker, *A History of Blacks in Canada*, 28.

30. The *Black Code* comprised a number of punitive statutes, legislated by the white political and judicial systems, for controlling Blacks in the United States until the late 1800s.

31. Henry Gates Jr., "Writing 'Race' and the Difference It Makes," *Critical Inquiry* 12 (Autumn, 1985): 9.

32. Frances Henry, *Forgotten Canadians: The Blacks in Nova Scotia* (Montreal: Longman Ltd., 1973), 28.

33. Bridglal Pachai, *Beneath the Clouds of the Promised Land: The Survival of Nova Scotian Blacks 1600-1800* (Halifax: B.E.A. of Nova Scotia, 1987).

34. Walker, *A History of Blacks in Canada*, 36-39.

35. Walker, *A History of Blacks in Canada*, 36-37.

36. Walker, *A History of Blacks in Canada*, 42.

37. Walker, *A History of Blacks in Canada*, 43.

38. Hill, *The Freedom Seekers*, 182, 227.

39. Hill, *The Freedom Seekers*, 100.

40. Statutes of Nova Scotia, *Public Instructions* (1864), Ch.58.

41. Selina Pratt, *Black Education in Nova Scotia* (MA Thesis, Dalhousie University, 1972), 37.

42. Peter Evander McKerrow, *A Brief History of the Coloured Baptist of Nova Scotia 1783-1895*, ed. Frank Stanley Boyd Jr. (Halifax: Afro Nova Scotia Press, 1976), 36.

43. Interview (February 1990).

44. Interview (1990).

45. Interview (1990).

46. Walker, *A History of Blacks in Canada*, 107.

47. Interview (1990).

48. Interview (1990).

49. Interview (February 1990).

50. Interview (1990).

51. Interview (1990).

52. Mohammed Abucar, *Struggles for Development: The Black Communities of North and East Preston and Cherrybrook, Nova Scotia 1784-1987* (Dartmouth: McCurdy Printing Press, 1988), 45.

53. Don Clairmont and Dennis Magill, *Nova Scotian Blacks: An Historical and Structural Overview* (Halifax: IPA Dalhousie University, 1970).

54. Carter Woodson, *The Mis-Education of the Negro* (New York: AMS Press, 1977), 6-7.

55. Interview (1990).

56. Interview (1990).

57. Interview (1990).

58. *An Act to Amend and Consolidate Chap. 60 of the Revised Statutes, 1923, The Education Act,* SNS (1953) Chap. 4, S.2(1)(2).

PART V

THE BOUNDARIES OF CITIZENSHIP

chapter fourteen

THE CHILD – THE CITIZEN – THE NATION
The Rhetoric and Experience of Wardship in Early Twentieth-Century British Columbia[1]

Robert Adamoski

> The child of today is the citizen of tomorrow. In all phases of child welfare work this is a standard slogan and one which is ofttimes uttered with only a passing thought. And yet how much is embodied in these ... words. The child – the citizen – the nation.[2]

Throughout North America, at the close of the nineteenth century, there swept a radically new understanding of the role of the state in "rescuing" children in order to optimize their ability to become functioning citizens. This chapter examines the experiences of the first cohort of British Columbian children to experience public wardship. The data are drawn from an extensive study of the organizational records, correspondence, and case-files of the Protestant Vancouver Children's Aid Society.[3] The Society was established in 1901 under the *Children's Protection Act*,[4] which drew heavily on legislation passed ten years earlier in Ontario, where Canada's first Children's Aid Society had been founded.

Ostensibly, emergent Children's Aid Societies across Canada sought to save children threatened by urbanization, family-breakdown, and moral decline so that they might occupy positions as citizens of the Empire (and, later, of the young Canadian nation). Scholars examining the history and role of western welfare states have differed in their characterization of these programs. Some, influenced by Marshall's *Citizenship and Social Class*,[5] have posited a "warlike" relationship between social welfare rights and the free market. In these accounts, agencies like the Vancouver Children's Aid Society (VCAS) functioned to counteract the social inequalities resulting from the operation of capitalist economies.

The case files of the VCAS support this portrayal to some degree. Like the orphanages that preceded them, the Vancouver Children's Aid Society dealt primarily with children who had surviving parents, most from working-class backgrounds.[6] Often, where their social position allowed, these parents sought out the Society's assistance and attempted to negotiate the terms of its involvement with their families.[7] However, despite the fact that Children's Aid Societies offered an important resource to some working-class families, child rescuers did not anticipate a levelling of social relations in Canadian society. The records examined here suggest that it is more accurate to describe the philanthropic and social purity movements (of which child rescue was a part), as seeking "to establish a non-antagonistic capitalist class structure, not to erase class differences."[8]

The present study reveals that child rescuers operated with clear assumptions of how social class, race, and gender affected "the most desirable material, out of which to manufacture the best Canadian citizenship."[9] Early child rescuers, like J.J. Kelso and Charles South,[10] envisioned their project as the shepherding of the coming generation of Canadian citizens, and their policies and practices reflected and defined the class, gender, and racial parameters of the category.

"A natural aptitude for citizenship": Race, Ethnicity, and the Practice of Child Rescue

Throughout its early history, the VCAS, like many other child rescue organizations in North America, presented its work in terms of the cultivation of a new generation of citizens. Ideologically, this project drew upon the xenophobia of the era to constitute a population of "criminal" parents, whose regulation would not threaten the rights of upstanding Canadians to raise, discipline, and work their own children as they saw fit.[11]

Early Canadian child rescue societies joined many agencies in expressing dismay over "degeneration," which they regarded as the likely outcome of Canada's immigration policies at the turn of the century.[12] While many agitated for changes to Canadian immigration policies which would dam the "flood" of immigrants, others promoted the "Canadianization" of young immigrants and the coming generation of Canadian-born children.[13] One VCAS Board member noted that, although "it was a poor, short sighted policy to bring in adults of alien races of low ideals, who have no natural aptitude for citizenship, ... their children or children's children may make good citizens."[14] However, these comments also highlight the limits of this strategy. Some groups were deemed "non-assimilable" — inherently unworthy of the burdens and blessings of Canadian citizenship.

Of course, the question of what constituted the ideal Canadian citizen proved vexatious. The struggle to constitute a "Canadian" race that embodied the respect for authority, self-control, and self-regulation required of responsible citizens in a western democracy is reflected in Woodsworth's opening chapter, "Who are we?". "... There has not been sufficient time to develop a fixed Canadian type, but there is a certain definite *something* that at once unites us and distinguishes us from all the world besides. ..."[15] As Valverde describes, this "certain definite something" corresponded roughly to "Britishness, a peculiar mixture of social order and individual freedom, [which] functioned as a sign of both sexual and civic self-policing."[16]

Other ethnic and racial groups were ranked in relation to these ideal "Canadians," resulting in a hierarchy that was widely accepted but subject to little critical scrutiny. An influential example is found in Woodsworth's taxonomy, originally published in 1907, which evaluates immigrants according to his estimation of their aptitude for Canadian citizenship.[17] Ranking the groups from most to least assimilable, he discusses immigrants from the following assortment of geographic, ethnic, and racial groups: Great Britain, the United States, Scandinavia, Germany, France, Southeastern Europe, Austria-Hungary, the Balkans, the Hebrews, the Italians, the Levantine races, the Orientals, the Negro, and the Indian.[18] Children coming into the Society's care reflected ethnic backgrounds consistent with these notions. A large majority of the children in the present sample had at least one parent born in either Great Britain or Canada.[19] Among the cases sampled, only four involved children of Asian or African heritage.

The relationship between British Columbia's child rescue authorities and the Native communities of the province has drawn significant attention during the last four decades. During the first half of the twentieth century, federally funded residential schools explicitly sought to eliminate Native culture, language, and life-patterns in British Columbia.[20] Then, for several decades after World War II, child welfare practices in Canada pursued the assimilation of First Nations children through placement with non-Native families. This practice was promoted by a liberalized system of transfer payments through which the federal government encouraged provincial child protection agencies to assume responsibility for Native children.[21] For the period under study here, the Vancouver Children's Aid Society sought, in practice if not in explicit policy, to avoid involvement with Native families.

"They are Indians if they have been brought up as Indians": Child Rescue and Native Canadians

In his study of the formation of Australia's child welfare system, Robert Van Krieken notes the common-place colonial assumption that indigenous peoples who had not been "civilized" were, by definition, "inappropriate and improper" to function as parents.[22] More specifically, as non-citizens, indigenous peoples under colonial domination were incapable of aiding in the creation of a self-regulating citizenry.

figure 14.1

Charles John Wesley South, Secretary and Superintendent, Vancouver Children's Aid Society from 1901-1922.

CITY OF VANCOUVER ARCHIVES, PORT. P. 1141, N. 554. PHOTO TAKEN 1919. REPRODUCED BY PERMISSION.

In their published reports, correspondence, and case notes, officials of the VCAS frequently convey the belief that native families, in and of themselves, constituted an environment sufficiently threatening to their children to justify intervention. In the Society's first *Annual Report*, a curious summary of the year's "Work in Vancouver" enumerates the primary causes that brought children under the Society's care. The causes cited are "Drink" (11 cases), "Poverty" and "Orphans/Relinquished" (6 cases each), "Ill treatment" and "Delinquency" (2 cases each) and "Immorality" (a single case). Finally, one case is recorded simply as "Indian."[23]

The low regard in which British Columbia's child rescuers held Native families is a consistent feature of the documents uncovered in this study. However, in contrast to the logic that might be found in postwar discourse on child welfare policy, their response was limited to a condescending pity for the plight of young Native children and a concern for the moral effects of "the mingling of the races" on the Caucasian population.

One typical exchange involved two sisters of mixed race who, at the urging of local officials, were committed to the Superintendent of Neglected Children and promptly shipped to the Vancouver Children's Aid Society. As the children had a non-Native father, the Department of Indian Affairs denied responsibility for their care. In September 1921 and July 1922, Charles South, the secretary of the Society, expressed his disapproval in letters to the Superintendent's office, suggesting that an alternative system was in place to deal with Native children:

> I was very much surprised to hear from the Home that two Indian girls had been brought from the North. ... These girls were received in a most filthy condition, it being necessary to take the hair off their head, as it was so full of vermin.
>
> It was never intended that any Children's Aid Society should be a receptacle for Indian children.... These children ...are Indians if they have been brought up as Indians, but certainly they are not fit to be in our Home.[24]

Ignoring the Home doctor's opinion that the children presented no danger to the physical health of the other children in the Home, South clearly regarded them as a threat to its overwhelmingly Caucasian population.

Despite this reluctance to assume responsibility for children of Native heritage, South did intervene in some instances. The sample of 154 families spanning 1901-1930 uncovered ten families whose children were of Native heritage.[25] In each case, the families whose children became wards of the Society were inter-racial in composition. Generally, these families involved Native women living in long-term common-law relationships with Caucasian men (8/10 families).[26] All of the children of Native heritage studied here lived with their families in rural communities where the significant gender imbalance among immigrants and their daily interaction with indigenous peoples made mixed-race families much more common and mediated against some of the most blatant racist attitudes found in urban centres.[27]

In 1908, Charles South received correspondence from Reverend W.T. Rushbrook of St. John's Rectory, Port Essington, who was concerned about a young girl who had been committed to the Society's care some months previously:

> Some time ago while I was absent from town, judgement was given by which Elsie Timms of this town was handed over to the care of your association. Mrs. Timms was at the time living with a man

named Ben Moore an engineer somewhat unsteady, but making good money. I have since married the couple.

Now while the child is illegitimate, and the father has no legal claim, yet it is Mr. Moore's child and with the parents now man and wife, feel the loss of their only child very heavily. The mother has not recovered from the shock, and the father is utterly broken up. You *may have* done a little good to the child by its removal, but you are certainly *doing* a grievous injury to the parents....

I am informed that the chief reason of the child's removal was the state in which the parents were living (namely unmarried). This reason has now been removed.

May the parents get their child back again? ... Since it is a half breed child it certainly will never have a better home than the parents are able to give.[28]

South's reply appears calculated to shatter Reverend Rushbrook's portrayal of the Moores as a respectable working-class family. Without implying any form of physical or emotional maltreatment, South nonetheless cites the threats posed by the child's moral neglect:

... I regret to have to say that I take exception to some of your statements.

When I left with Elsie, Mrs. Timms was not suffering any shock from the action taken... Possibly the 'shock' you speak of arises from the drink rather than from any action I may have taken.

...The amount of good done to the child you are not in a position to judge and the child is to be considered before the parents who have lived in open immorality for so long. ... Mr. and Mrs. Moore must absolutely give up the drink before Elsie comes to them.[29]

The "open immorality" practised by Elsie's parents was widespread in the frontier communities of British Columbia. It took the form of non-sanctioned unions usually involving Caucasian men and Native women. As argued by Barman, these unions typically displayed many of the characteristics of fully sanctioned marriages with the exception that religious ceremonies were often not available.[30] Despite the prevalence of these long-term unions in non-urban regions of the province, men like South regarded them as strong indicators of a compromised morality.

The racial distinctions that shaped the Society's policies offer important insight into the struggles that surrounded the construction of Canadian citizenship in the early decades of the twentieth century. Charles South and other child rescuers clearly envisioned a relationship between the state and Native Canadians which differed radically from the state's relationship to men like themselves. Their fractionalized vision of citizenship was expressed organizationally in the Oriental Children's Home, the residential school system, and the Catholic and Protestant Children's Aid Societies, each of which dealt with what they regarded as fundamentally different problems of governance. Of course, race alone does not fully decode this emerging citizenship construct.

While South's correspondences repeatedly reflect his concern that children of Native descent presented a unique moral threat to the malleable Caucasian children in his charge, the threat that these children posed was not solely a function of their race. Gender also played a crucial role in structuring South's lexicon of morality, and young women "governed very materially by [their] Indian nature"[31] were common subjects of his concern. In what follows, I examine the experiences of a group of VCAS wards, emphasizing how gender shaped the threats that were deemed to confront them.

"I certainly have done my share of it": Gender, Labour, and the Experience of Wardship

When relying on the lens provided by the Society's case files, one must remain aware of the limitations of its aperture. For all its expansive rhetoric, the Vancouver Children's Aid Society actually dealt with a group of children who were dramatically circumscribed both racially (as described above) and in terms of social class. The wards who appear in the files differed in myriad respects, but were generally united by the working-class roles into which the Society envisioned them fitting. In this section I focus on the experiences of VCAS wards as a means of uncovering the gendered nature of the working-class citizenship for which they were prepared. While the wards' uniformity in terms of race and social class presents obstacles, the case files present a uniquely rich glimpse of the ideals that animated the formative experiences of these working-class boys and girls.

Although there was wide variety in the careers of the Society's wards, they spent on average less than one-third of their wardship in congregate care.[32] The remainder of their time was passed in what were variously termed "adoptive homes," "foster homes," "free homes," "indentures" or "wage homes." The case files of the Vancouver Children's Aid Society give us a fairly clear understanding of how class and gender structures informed the experiences of prospective male and female citizens in early twentieth-century British Columbia. The gendered nature of citizenship, and its impact on the experiences of wards, is most evident when we turn our attention to work, rather than adoptive placements.

figure 14.2

Children's Home, Wall Street. Operated by the Vancouver Children's Aid Society from 1907 through 1929.

CITY OF VANCOUVER ARCHIVES, BU. P. 383 #3 N. 330 #3. REPRODUCED BY PERMISSION.

Work placements were typically offered to children whose age, or other characteristics, left them unattractive to foster parents seeking adoption. Consistent with the philosophy of child-saving, there clearly was a note of charity in most requests — the implication being that the child would be treated kindly and trained appropriately. But matters such as schooling, provision of clothing, and other necessities clearly were secondary to the work at hand; this work, so long as it was appropriate to the age, gender, and class of the child, was deemed to be largely sufficient for his or her reclamation. A School Board Trustee who requested a 13-year-old boy wrote,

> I am enclosing an application for a boy as help on my small fruit farm, and general help round the place. ... On reading over the conditions, it does not seem feasible for them to be carried out completely in this case; ... If the boy is out working for his living and learning to take his place in life it would not be to his advantage or interest to be provided with everything until he is 21, besides being paid a fair wage...; As soon as he is earning enough to keep himself in clothes and necessities it is but right that he should realize these responsibilities.[33]

The independence, responsibility, and "manly" labour prescribed by this foster parent met with the approval of the Adoption Committee. It is likely unremarkable to point out that this foster child was to be occupied with work that fell strictly in line with the gendered division of labour characterizing most families during the era. However, the work upon which the Society and its foster parents relied to create appropriately gendered future citizens had important consequences for the experiences of wards in their placements.

One of the most striking impacts that the gendered division of labour had on the experiences of wards was geographical. The vast majority of male wards went to rural placements with the expectation that children of their class, gender, and race would benefit most from agricultural and horticultural work. As a result, only 15 per cent of boys remained in greater Vancouver for their first work placement. Instead, most went to major agricultural regions in the province.[34] Over 70 per cent of female wards, however, had their first work placement within the city — a fact that appeared to fly in the face of the rhetoric of rural redemption espoused by many child-savers.[35]

Foster parents interested in a work placement were required to enter into the same agreement as were prospective adoptive parents, agreeing to "act towards the child at all times with kindness and consideration," "provide the child with food, clothing, washing and necessities," "treat the child as a member of the family," "teach as far as possible habits of truthfulness, personal cleanliness, and industry" and "send the child to school as required by law." Foster parents were also expected to "write occasionally," especially in case of serious illness, death, desertion, dissatisfaction, or removal to another locality.[36]

The terms of these work placements often resulted in the Society assuming the role of mediator in disputes between wards and their employers. Drawing from the correspondence between foster parents, wards, and the Society, it is possible to examine very different roles within the family economies in which male and female wards were placed, and also their respective expectations. These, in turn, provide insight into both the Society's vision of the requirements of citizenship and wards' notions of what should reasonably be expected of them.[37]

Both boys and girls complained most often about being overworked. Over one-half of all wards advanced this complaint while installed in either an adoption or work placement. Generally, the Vancouver Children's Aid Society supported male wards in their complaints regarding work and reimbursement, but the Society's main preoccupation regarding male wards was the issue of truancy. Despite the protestations of the VCAS, both foster parents and wards consistently saw full-time labour as the most beneficial experience for boys of this class and racial background. One typical example involved a male ward who had been placed with a widower at age 13. Throughout the placement, South emphasized the importance of education to both the boy and his foster father, to little avail. Nonetheless, the child continued to keep South apprised of the "practical education" his foster father was providing:

> I have not been going to school now on account of Mr. Close's not beening able to do much he is trouble with the roomitthisim. ... I can drive horses, plough with a team of horses. I can mow hay. I can put hands to anything about the farm and do it.[38]

Three years later the same boy wrote,

> I am intending to leave Mr. Close soon and so I thought I would write an tell you. I have been with him now for 5 years. The first year I went to school prity steady and the next two I stayed home in the summer and the next two years I stayed home altogether and worked... I want to go and learn a trade of some kind.[39]

Male wards on work placements typically lived in standards quite different from those enjoyed by the children of their foster families and repeatedly expressed concerns regarding housing and clothing. Many boys spent the nights in outbuildings (barns, chicken coops, etc.) and one ward was left to sleep on the porch with a box for shelter. In some cases, community members and other government officials were moved to report the plight of male wards found destitute, apparently abandoned by their employers. In 1923, the Government Agent for Williams Lake wrote South to advise him of the plight of wards placed in the region:

> Charles gave his age as 15 years and advised that he had first been sent to Mr. H. then transferred to Mr. C. whom he left after a disagreement. Finally he worked for a Mr. F. until (one of his) horses was hurt. He then was without means or place of abode until the police took him in and cared for him...
>
> As I believe other boys have been sent to various persons in this district I would like to point out existing conditions and ask that caution be exercised in sending out such cases. ...It is to be regretted that in some cases motives in obtaining the services of boys are actuated by a desire for cheap and drudging labor.
>
> I have written you at length as the case of Charles J. very forcibly brought to mind the serious plight of a boy without home or employment. None of the persons he had worked for assumed any

responsibility for his care with the result that he was destitute and without a home during one of our winter months...[40]

As they were clearly regarded more as hired hands than as members of family, male wards were often treated with a great deal of suspicion by their employers. Complaints regarding theft (14 per cent of male wards) and untruthfulness (15 per cent of male wards) were common, and many wards were strictly denied access to the family home. One young boy had his foster placement terminated, apparently due to the uneasiness of his employers, as there were no allegations of theft:

> I cannot trust him with anything. We must lock [the] house when we go to milk the [cows.] If we leave the door unlocked [he] goes snooping from one room to the other. ... I cannot stand it anymore. I cuffed his ears twice ... but the next day we leave the house open he is snooping again...[41]

Comments of this type were common in the files examined. Although eager to accept strong working-class boys for farm labour, many foster parents were exceedingly wary and critical of the performance of these children. In the case cited above, the ward's subsequent placement with a rural farming family lasted 13 years. One could certainly interpret such a lengthy involvement as indicative of some mutual satisfaction, yet, in common with most files, the correspondences continued to show persistent ambivalence and dissatisfaction.

Male wards seldom voiced complaints about their exclusion from the family lives of their employers. Other researchers have found that "home" children often resented their status,[42] but case files of the VCAS seldom recorded any official complaints. Nonetheless, we can infer that many male wards did experience considerable despair:

> I am sorry to have to tell you that Vernon is dead. Was buried yesterday. Shot himself accidentally. ... [My wife] found him under some trees dead. ... When doctor and policeman came doctor said death was instantaneous. Bullet went through heart and out of back.
>
> ... They think he had sat down and was watching a squirrel in the tree beside him and had the gun between his legs and somehow it had gone off. I don't see how it happened as he was a very careful boy.
>
> [My wife] is very ill over it, we feel deeply grieved. He was such a fine boy and we thought as much or more of him than if he had

been our own. ... I would like to get another boy but will not find one like Vernon.[43]

Most boys apparently learned the "manly" traits of independence, self-reliance, and rational self-interest which their placements were, at least partially, intended to teach. While almost half of all wards eventually returned to their families, boys more often did so after securing their own occupation either with or without the aid of the Society. A Welsh boy who had found better paying work on his own initiative protested when asked to return to the placement arranged by the Society:

> ... As a matter of fact, I don't think much of the way they send boys to work here. They send me 50 miles from nowhere. I was dissatisfied, I asked if I could return, I was told to stay. I stayed as long as I could stand it and then I came here. Now that I have a good home, and good prospects, you ask of my return...[44]

It is important to mention one final means by which boys left the care of the Society. Among the present sample, eight male wards (over 7 per cent of cases with discharge information) died while under the guardianship of the VCAS. In comparison, only two female wards died while in care (1 per cent of valid cases). In part, the fact that male wards were perhaps seven times as likely as female wards to die in care reflects both the nature of their work and the often harsh physical conditions in which they lived. Other male wards, however, had their names enshrined on the "Honour Roll" that prominently occupied the back cover of Annual Reports during World War I. In 1922, the list included 23 boys who had been killed in action. One casualty was an Ontario ward whose foster parents had moved to British Columbia. After being notified in 1916, J.J. Kelso wrote to South. His letter reflected their shared vision of the centrality of military service to full male citizenship, especially for young, working-class males.[45]

> He is one of an increasing number whom we have saved from disaster and left upon a field of honor. While we cannot but regret the death of these lads, yet it is tinged with a certain sense of satisfaction that we have been able to kindle the fires of a better manhood than was probable at the time we made their first acquaintance.[46]

To South and Kelso, the deaths of boys like these represented the ultimate masculine expression of commitment to the State and its moral order.

Although each war-time death took its toll on South, he ultimately regarded each as a "hero lad," and assured himself that "they are amply blessed in the action they took and that they are rewarded for their great sacrifice."[47]

Whether they left heroically or merely drifted into independence along the trail of the labour market, most male wards appeared to accept and even to actively pursue the trappings of working-class male citizenship. Often they craved the independence and acquisitions that a good position offered them. Although their options were in some instances limited, their often stoic tolerance of difficult work and living conditions betrayed an expectation that hard work for a fair wage was their lot. Importantly, male wards benefitted from the congruence between this expectation and the expectations of the Society, for whom fair working conditions and minimal exploitation were major concerns.

The experiences of female wards were markedly different. While the expectation of hard work for a fair wage governed the Society's vision of working-class male placements, female wards who complained of being overworked or underpaid were typically regarded as unappreciative. The virtue of independence, so crucial to the future of wards as working-class, male citizens, was regarded as problematic when expressed by female wards, who were expected to remain dependent within their adopted families. Just as their mothers were often expected to couch their claims for assistance from nascent social service agencies in terms of their social position as mother or wife,[48] female wards were expected to remain compliant and self-effacing in their domestic role.

The relative rarity of Society complaints regarding the working conditions of female wards reflected the familiar "invisibility" of unpaid domestic labour. But if the ceaseless demands and monetary value of domestic labour were invisible to men like South, they were fully evident to the wards whose lives they shaped. Such a recognition is reflected in this letter from a 19-year-old ward whom South had branded ungrateful for leaving her "adoptive" family:

> ... As for helping those that helped me, I certainly have done my share of it. I have worked in the Hotel, washed and cooked and looked after a store and looked after Mrs. R. when she went on a big drunk for two months.
>
> And as for leaving school, I wanted to pass my entrance examination, but they took me out to work for them for nothing. If I wasn't there he would have to pay a woman twenty five dollars a month. So everything that I received from them, I think I well earned it.... I

don't see how he can send me out without giving me some money till I find work... .[49]

The primary concern voiced by the Society regarding girls in their care surrounded the issue of supervision. Female wards were often characterized by both the Society and foster parents as having proclivities toward sexual immorality, and both groups often linked this supposed trait to the tendency of girls to run from their placements. Supervision of these girls was of the utmost importance for the Society, as can be seen in the case of Elsie Timms, whose return to her newly solemnized parents in Port Essington had been so strongly protested by South. In 1918, ten years after their earlier correspondence, South wrote to Reverend Rushbrook announcing that the Adoption Committee had decided to return the child to her father if adequate supervision could be arranged. He wrote,

> ... Elsie can cook and wash, if she likes, as well as anyone, and she is learning many things that have been greatly to her advantage, but I am rather afraid that unless you personally keep a sort of supervision over, and interest yourself in this young girl, she will be easily lead astray.
>
> I may say to you confidentially that my experience is that when a girl has some Indian blood in her veins, it is very hard to control her when she reaches the age that this girl has.[50]

Unlike the male wards discussed above, the provision of shelter was seldom an issue for either the girls or the Society — as domestic servants, most girls were given quarters within the family home. While this feature of the gendered structure of labour had some benefits for female wards, it also undoubtedly contributed to the stifling sense of isolation that many experienced. While boys may only have been forcibly reminded of their status as hired hands during meals and in the evenings, girls were relentlessly confronted by the "superiority" of members of their foster-family.

Coupled with the ceaseless demands of housework and child care and their employers' reluctance to grant them unsupervised leave, female wards complained of isolation or loneliness in their placements far more often than did boys. One 13-year-old girl who had recently been placed with a family in Creston wrote to her sister still residing in the Children's Home:

> ... The girls and boys don't like me a bit here they talk about me and it is all lies that they do say anyhow. ... The girls slap me and the

boys kick me as if I was a stump ... and if I go to slap one of them they all will pile on me and the teacher doesn't care...

I asked Mr. South if I could come back and he said I couldn't so I have to stay here in this old place. It is far far far worse than when we were with Pa. I would rather be with Pa than stay here. Often I wish I were dead... .[51]

The rural placements that typified the experiences of male wards made it much more difficult to make contact with natural parents, siblings (both in and out of care), and extended family. This may partially explain the fact that female wards were far more successful in maintaining contact with their families while in care.[52] The qualitative data found in case records, however, suggest that it was not geography alone that contributed to this gender difference.

Continued familial contact appeared to be of greater importance to female wards, likely due to the greater sense of social isolation that characterized their work placements. One typical incident involved an 18-year-old ward who was living in Vernon in 1908. Evidently defiant, she first wrote to South protesting her social isolation and later wrote demanding to know where her younger brother had been placed:

> ... The next thing you know there will be trouble so just let me know why I don't get a letter from [my brother]. I never was satisfied with this place and I am less satisfied now. Just think I have been without hearing from him for a year and a half and you wonder why I am so saucy. If I ever had known we were going to be separated like we are and never hear anything more of one another. A person has some feeling for their family even though I am only a kid.[53]

Of course, control over contact with natural family members remained an important source of power for the Society, and South often displayed an understanding of his wards' craving for virtually any sense of familial belonging. When one "adoptive" parent wrote to South, distraught at her inability to keep her teenaged foster daughter from running away to the foster home where her brother was placed, he advised her to cast the child from her family:

> I am awfully sorry, for you have done so much for her, but it is no use, you must give her up, and I will deal with her as I see fit...
>
> The only thing is to make her feel that she is not your daughter, but a simple girl as she was before you adopted her.[54]

He then wrote to the girl in question,

> You are not now Minnie Wilson [her adopted name] as your foster mother has given you up for good. ... It is a poor return for what has been done for you. I hope you will not forget all the sacrifices that have been made for you, Minnie.[55]

These attempts to emotionally blackmail female wards into more compliant behaviour reflect a common theme in South's practices. Whether they were women upbraided as "unmotherly," or adolescents who deserved the respect accorded "someone's sister," working-class women encountering Charles South undoubtedly recognized that their position within the domestic sphere was, for him, the essential determinant of their standing.

As they reached late adolescence, many female wards began to rebel against their forced dependency within foster families. Primarily, they asserted their "independence" by fleeing wardship. Almost 85 per cent of female wards left the care of the Society before reaching the age of majority (set at 21 years under the Act[56]), many returning to their natural family (39 per cent). Another significant subset (25 per cent) simply lost contact with the VCAS. While many of these girls may have returned to their natural families, some were successful in establishing a degree of self-sufficiency away from both foster and natural families.

Often, however, isolation from their natural family and exclusion from the social life of their foster families and communities made marriage appear an attractive alternative for female wards. A relatively small proportion of wards were discharged from care when they married, but the contrast between male and female wards is quite striking. Of 155 female wards on whom information is available, 15 (or almost 10 per cent) left care in this manner. By contrast, only two of 113 males (under 2 per cent) married while they were wards. For most female wards, marriage represented an ideal avenue of escape from domestic service, even if it was realized infrequently. As Strong-Boag notes, the ideal of marriage constituted an important cultural symbol in the lives of Canadian girls and women during the inter-war years: "This fascination reflected the fact that most female Canadians not only expected to marry but took it for granted that marriage would provide satisfaction, security and purpose."[57] Although wards of the VCAS may have felt more keenly than most the pull toward the establishment of their own household, they were certainly not unique.

While many wards harboured visions of matrimonial rescue, those who began to put such plans into action attracted considerable resistance both from foster-parents and from Charles South. Faced regularly with such "threats" by female wards, South would caution them with what became threadbare tales of the perils of early marriage:

> A young girl that I knew very well married just about the age you are, against her parents' wish but who in just a few years had a family of very small children and who, because she had married before she was old enough, became insane. ... And everyone was afraid to have much to do with the children because they thought there was insanity on the mother's side.[58]

Nonetheless, it is clear that female wards — who entered marriages from a relatively disadvantaged social station — often found themselves in difficult circumstances. A 19-year-old former ward wrote to South requesting to board her own daughter at the Children's Home:

> This is my story since I have been married. Will left me two years this February without anything to eat and without any clothes and without any coal or wood. ... My baby was 6 months old when Will left me. ... Will never beat me or swore at me but he used to go to the hore houses + stay there for 2 or 3 days + baby and I would be starving. He used to get about $80 a month + we used to be without things all the time...
>
> I am having hard times. I am out working and have to keep my little girl in a home but it is not a very nice place. They don't keep her clean. I am getting $15 a month. I have to pay $8 of it for Maggie + buy her clothes.[59]

Given his familiarity with this former ward, South agreed to board her daughter, keeping her for five years until her mother was able to remarry.

Despite the often bleak outcomes of marriages entered into by female wards, many seemed to revel in taunting South with their notions of marriage and their worldly experience. In 1912, for example, a 16-year-old girl wrote repeatedly of her intentions to marry at her first opportunity:

> I am writing to tell you I have had many chances to get married so I am going to accept one so you won't be worried with me anymore. ... Sadie B. is married so I am going to get married too. I guess I must say good-bye to you. I remain, your girl who is going to get married, W.B.[60]

... Well Mr. South I have been asked many a time to get married. When I was in Vancouver I used to go out with a fellow and Mr. H. [foster father] thought I was at my *auntie's* but *no*. Anyway I know as much as any married woman ... so do you wonder why I want to be a wife?[61]

Like the male wards who often seemed to embrace their role as independent, working-class citizens, female wards often regarded marriage as the "obvious" solution to the isolation, dependency, and powerlessness that characterized their lives in domestic service. Although each group of wards suffered their own hardships and benefits, male wards were encouraged to value their own work as a key component of their lives as independent, working-class, male citizens. Female wards who brought attention to their exploitation were condemned for their unwomanly behaviour. Although many railed against it, female wards were systematically groomed to seek their satisfactions in things domestic and, essentially, to concede their own dependency.

Conclusion

The early history of what has become Canada's child welfare system highlights the complex effects that children's race, gender, and social status had on estimations of how best to prepare them to assume their appropriate station in Canadian society. More generally, this early component of the welfare state was never intended to ensure Canadian children a basic, universal level of social provision that would counteract the inequalities flowing from its capitalist economy and allow full and equal participation in Canadian society. In contrast to Marshall's claims, child rescue agencies did not envision a levelling of the "social edifice," but merely a raising of the floor level in the basement.[62] Certainly, children's aid societies (along with other early forms of public welfare) promised some benefit to those most disadvantaged by the market system; however, for many of the children whose experiences are documented here, "rescue" did not bring equality or independence. The stated goals of the Vancouver Children's Aid Society — the preservation and socialization of the child, the citizen, and the nation — explicitly functioned to differentiate between the bases of working-class male and female citizenship, and to exclude those deemed unworthy of full participation in Canadian society.

Notes

1. My thanks to Robert Menzies and Dorothy Chunn; Sue Baptie and Carol Haber of the City of Vancouver Archives; Barbara Jackson and Gillian Wallace of the Ministry of the Attorney-General; and Ross Dawson of the Ministry of Children and Families for their varied assistance to this research. An earlier version of this paper was presented at the B.C. Studies conference "Beyond Hope" at the University College of the Cariboo in Kamloops, B.C., May 2001. I would like to thank Dr. Robert Campbell for his comments on that draft.

2. City of Vancouver Archives, Add. Ms. 672, Vol. 129. N.a., "Twenty first Anniversary of the Children's Aid Society of British Columbia" (Vancouver: J.W. Gehrke Co. Ltd., n.d. [circa. 1922]).

3. Robert Adamoski, "Their Duties Towards the Children: Citizenship and the Practice of Child Welfare in Early Twentieth Century British Columbia" (PhD dissertation, Simon Fraser University, 1995). The study is based on a sample of 303 children from 154 families involved with the Society between 1901 and 1930.

4. *Statutes of British Columbia*, 1901, c.9.

5. Marshall proposes that, while the civil and political rights that developed prior to the end of the nineteenth century in western capitalist societies were aimed at "class-abatement," the social rights that characterized the twentieth century "imply an invasion of contract by status, the subordination of market price to social justice, the replacement of the free bargain by the declaration of rights." Thomas Marshall, *Citizenship and Social Class* (Cambridge: Cambridge University Press, 1950), 105. Widely-read Canadian contributions influenced by this perspective include Andrew Armitage, *Social Welfare in Canada: Ideals and Realities* (Toronto: McClelland and Stewart Limited, 1975); and Dennis Guest, *The Emergence of Social Security in Canada*, 2nd ed. (Vancouver: UBC Press, 1985).

6. Bettina Bradbury, "The Fragmented Family: Family Strategies in the Face of Death, Illness and Poverty, Montreal. 1860-1885," in *Childhood and Family in Canadian History*, ed. Joy Parr (Toronto: McClelland and Stewart, 1982); Mark Finnane, "Asylums, Families and the State," *History Workshop Journal* 20 (1985):134-48; Diane Purvey, "Alexandra Orphanage and Families in Crisis in Vancouver, 1892 to 1938," in *Dimensions of Childhood: Essays on the History of Children and Youth in Canada*, ed. Russell Smandych, Gordon Dodds and Alvin Esau (Winnipeg: University of Manitoba Legal Research Institute, 1992).

7. Adamoski, "Their Duties Towards the Children."

8. Marianna Valverde, *The Age of Light, Soap, and Water: Moral Reform in English Canada, 1885-1925* (Toronto: McClelland and Stewart, 1991), 29.

9. City of Vancouver Archives, Add. Mss. 672, Vol. 129, *Annual Report of the Vancouver Children's Aid Society*, 1911, 20-21. Hereafter, *Annual Report*.

10. J.J. Kelso was founder and long-time superintendent of Canada's first Children's Aid Society in Ontario. Charles John Wesley South was a founding member of the Vancouver Children's Aid Society, and served as its secretary, and *de facto* Superintendent of Neglected Children for the province, for over two decades.

11. See Robert Adamoski. "'Charity is one thing and the administration of Justice is another': Law and the Politics of Familial Regulation in Early Twentieth Century B.C.," to appear in *Regulating Lives: Historical Studies on the State, Society, the Individual and the Law*, ed. John McLaren, Robert Menzies and Dorothy E. Chunn (Vancouver: UBC Press, in press). In the United States context, see Bruce Bellingham, "The 'Unspeakable Blessing': Street Children, Reform Rhetoric and Misery in Early Industrial Capitalism," *Politics and Society* 12, 3 (1983): 310-15; Linda Gordon, *Heroes of Their Own Lives: The Politics and History of Family Violence* (New York: Viking Penguin, 1988), 27-37.

12. Angus McLaren, *Our Own Master Race: Eugenics in Canada, 1885-1945* (Toronto: McClelland & Stewart, 1990), 46-67.

13. McLaren, *Our Own Master Race*, 47.

14. *Annual Report*, 1911, 20-21.

15. James S. Woodsworth, *Strangers Within Our Gates or Coming Canadians*, new ed. (Toronto: University of Toronto Press, 1972 [1909]) 16.

16. Marianna Valverde, *The Age of Light, Soap, and Water*, 105.

17. Woodsworth, *Strangers Within Our Gates*.

18. See Valverde's discussion of the fictive construction of an Anglo-Canadian "race" and the hierarchical ordering of "others."

19. Approximately sixty per cent of the 303 children who comprised my sample had at least one parent who was from Great Britain or was a Canadian-born Caucasian. For a more detailed discussion of the ethnic background of VCAS wards, see Adamoski, "Their Duties Towards the Children."

20. See Elizabeth Furniss, *Victims of Benevolence: Discipline and Death at the Williams Lake Indian Residential School, 1891-1920* (Williams Lake, BC: Cariboo Tribal Council, 1992); Celia Haig-Brown, *Resistance and Renewal: Surviving the Indian Residential School* (Vancouver: Tilicum Library, 1988); Forrest LaViolette, *The Struggle for Survival: Indian Cultures and the Protestant Ethic in British Columbia* (Toronto: University of Toronto Press, 1973); John Sheridan Milloy, *A National Crime: The Canadian Government and the Residential School System* (Winnipeg: University of Manitoba Press, 1999); Paige Raibmon, "'A New Understanding of Things Indian': George H. Raley's Negotiation of the Residential School Experience" (Honours Thesis, University of British Columbia, 1994); J. Redford, "Attendance at Indian Residential Schools in British Columbia, 1890-1920," *B.C. Studies* 44 (1980): 41-56.

21. The discussion that follows highlights the importance of race in the construction of Canadian citizenship during the first three decades of the twentieth century. It is important to note, however, that a simple fiscal argument reinforced the VCAS's reluctance to become involved with native families. The main sources of public funding for the VCAS were provincial and municipal, while native Canadians fell under the jurisdiction of the federal Department of Indian Affairs.

22. Robert Van Krieken, *Children and The State: Social Control and the Formation of Australian Child Welfare* (Sydney: Allen and Unwin, 1992), 96.

23. *Annual Report*, 1902-03, 17.

24. CVA, Add. Ms. 672. Case number 3320. South to Acting Superintendent of Neglected Children, Brankin, 15 Sept. 1921. Volume numbers are omitted to preserve confidentiality. Case numbers are based on a coding key devised by the author. Persons obtaining permission to access the case-records of the Society may contact me for the key. Throughout this chapter, pseudonyms are used to refer to clients of the Vancouver Children's Aid Society.

25. Native families comprised 6 per cent of all families in the sample. Valverde, *The Age of Light, Soap and Water*, 108, cites statistics for 1901 suggesting that Native Canadians constituted 14 per cent of the province's population.

26. In two cases, children were apprehended from the custody of single "native" fathers.

27. Jean Barman, "What a Difference a Border Makes: Aboriginal Racial Intermixture in the Pacific Northwest," *Journal of the West* 38, 3 (1999): 14-20.

28. CVA, Add. Ms. 672. Case number 3530. Rev. W.T. Rushbrook to South, 22 Oct. 1908.

29. CVA, Add. Ms. 672. Case number 3530. South to Rev. W.T. Rushbrook, 9 Nov. 1908.

30. Barman, "What a Difference a Border Makes."

31. CVA, Add. Ms. 672. Case number 240101. South to Cowichan CAS, 13 Jan. 1919.

32. By dividing the average number of months spent in congregate care by the average total months in care, it can be estimated that boys spent, on average, 29 per cent of their wardships in congregate care while girls spent, on average, 25 per cent of their wardship in congregate care.

33. CVA, Add. Ms. 672. Case number 2519. Foster parent to South, 14 March 1921.

34. Specifically, 40 per cent of male wards had their first wage placement in the Fraser Valley, with another 30 per cent being equally divided between the Kootenays and the Chilcotin.

35. For further discussion of the redemptive qualities of agricultural work, see Stephen, chap. 7 in this volume.

36. CVA, Add. Ms. 672, "Agreement re: Foster Child".
37. The case files examined here are somewhat unique in that they consist primarily of original correspondence, rather than "distilled" "running-records." As such, they allow for an admittedly limited form of triangulation, which takes into account the perspectives of wards, foster parents, Society officials, and other parties. For a discussion of some of the limitations of case records as historical sources, see *Canadian Historical Review* 81 (June 2000): 266-93.
38. CVA, Add. Ms. 672. Case number 371001. Boy to South, 20 May 1908.
39. CVA, Add. Ms. 672. Case number 371001. Boy to South, 26 Feb. 1911.
40. CVA, Add. Ms. 672. Case number 2519. Government agent to South, 30 April 1923.
41. CVA, Add. Ms. 672. Case number 242801, Foster parent to South, 11 Oct. 1917.
42. Joy Parr, *Labouring Children: British Immigrant Apprentices to Canada, 1869-1924* (Montreal: McGill-Queen's University Press, 1980); *The Home Children: Their Personal Stories*, ed. Phyllis Harrison (Winnipeg: Watson and Dwyer, 1979); Margaret Barbalet, *Far From a Low Gutter Girl: The Forgotten World of State Wards: Australia 1887-1940* (Melbourne: Oxford University Press, 1983).
43. CVA, Add. Ms. 672. Case number 291402. Foster father to South, 1 Aug. 1921.
44. CVA, Add. Ms. 672. Case number 3517. Ward to South, n.d.
45. See Richard Titmuss, *Essays on the Welfare State*, 3rd ed. (London: Allen and Unwin, 1976).
46. CVA, Add. Ms. 672, Vol. 174. Kelso to South, 6 Nov. 1916.
47. *Annual Report*, 1922, 7.
48. Robert Adamoski, "Their Duties Towards the Children," 160-257.
49. CVA, Add. Ms. 672. Case number 3518. Girl to South, n.d.
50. CVA, Add. Ms. 672. Case number 3530. South to Rushbrook, 8 April 1918.
51. CVA, Add. Ms. 672. Case number 5010. Girl to sister, 23 May 1911.
52. Almost half of the female wards maintained contact with their parents while only slightly over one-third of male wards mentioned such contact.
53. CVA, Add. Ms. 672. Case number 2904. Girl to South, 21 June 1908.
54. CVA, Add. Ms. 672. Case number 242802. South to foster parent, 10 July 1922.
55. CVA, Add. Ms. 672. Case number 242802. South to girl, Sept. 1922.
56. *Children's Protection Act of British Columbia*, Statutes of British Columbia (1901), c. 9 s. 8(1).
57. Veronica Strong-Boag, *The New Day Recalled: Lives of Girls and Women in English Canada, 1919-1939* (Markham: Penguin Books, 1988), 81.
58. CVA, Add. Ms. 672. Case number 072401. South to girl, 26 Aug. 1912.
59. CVA, Add. Ms. 672. Case number 221701. Correspondence between girl and South, 12 Feb. 1915 and 30 Nov. 1916.
60. CVA, Add. Ms. 672. Case number 072401. Girl to South, 12 Aug. 1912.
61. CVA, Add. Ms. 672. Case number 072401. Girl to South, 18 Aug. 1912. Emphasis in original.
62. Thomas Marshall, *Citizenship and Social Class*, 107-08.

chapter fifteen

CREATING SOCIAL AND MORAL CITIZENS
Defining and Treating Delinquent Boys and Girls in English Canada, 1920-65

Joan Sangster

"The child is the most precious asset of the State."
Judge Hawley Mott, Toronto Juvenile Court, 1920.[1]

Judge Mott, like other legal and social leaders concerned with juvenile delinquency in twentieth-century Canada, understood that children were potential state assets, whose future role as model adult citizens rested precariously
on their upbringing, socialization, and ideological embrace of the norms of
law and order. They were, as many social commentators never failed to point
out, the key to Canada's future. Their education, not only in the school system, but through recreation, religion, and especially the family — deemed the
"bedrock" of the nation by one police chief[2] — was seen as an important
means of constructing future respectable and productive citizens. While
many educational endeavours focused on moulding values, the juvenile justice system was charged with *re*-moulding values, as children in conflict with
the law had indicated the temporary abandonment of certain cardinal rules
of youthful citizenship: a rejection of parental guidance and schooling, disregard for private property and social order, or rejection of moral and sexual
standards of decency, including participation in activities that were simply
off-limits to non-adults, such as drinking and sex. Delinquents, then, were
caught up in contradictory definitions of citizenship: *by virtue of* their youth
and their transgression of social norms, they were "outsiders" to full,
respectable citizenship, but *because of* their youth, they were seen simultaneously as potential, malleable "insiders" to a future citizenship.

From the late nineteenth century on, the state, the justice system, and an array of voluntary reformers, social work, medical, and educational experts expressed strong anxieties about the adult fate of children who had already run into conflict with the law. In this chapter, taking as my chronological focus the period between the end of World War I and 1960, I first examine the dominant definitions of delinquency in legal and social terminology, indicating how the process of definition was shaped by class relations, as well as social constructions of gender and, to a lesser extent, ethnicity and race. Second, I explore the strategies used to reconstruct delinquents into model future citizens, such as the increasing use of probation and counselling, the creation of alternative recreation and role models, and, the most punitive option, sentences to Training Schools. In the process, the dominant definitions of a "good" citizen are highlighted, as are the ways in which these hegemonic definitions reflected and reinforced social relations of gender and class inequality. Boys, it was assumed, should be re-moulded into *social citizens* with respect for democracy, law, and the work ethic, while girls needed protection, discipline, and self-control in order to become model *moral citizens*.[3] Because of the long time period covered, this chapter does not attempt a comprehensive survey of all anti-delinquency efforts in these decades. Rather, I have extracted specific examples of intense anxiety over, and solutions for, delinquency to highlight the changing — and unchanging — strategies used by the state and social experts to re-create model citizens.[4]

Citizenship and Delinquency in Twentieth-Century Canada

Many recent academic discussions of citizenship posed by mainstream scholars have emphasized the equation of citizenship with "rights, values and obligations."[5] Citizenship may engender debates about shared identity, political loyalty, or social entitlement, but liberal-minded writers often assume that a universal ideal of common rights and obligations prevails or, conversely, they lament the "divided loyalties" of many Canadians, sundered as they are by region, language, and culture.[6] Scholarship more cognizant and critical of the historical inequalities of citizenship may still focus on questions of identity,[7] while those authors schooled in political economy and socialist-feminist theories often address questions of hierarchical citizenship with attention to the structural dynamic of gender, race, and productive and reproductive class relations. As Jane Jenson and Susan Phillips point out, the state has long been engaged in the recognition of citizens and non-citizens in political, economic, and social life. Citizenship is not defined simply in relation to national borders, for there are also internal boundaries dividing citizens from non-citizens, first- from second-class citizens: "Citizenship establishes a system of inclusion and exclusion, defining boundaries and distinctions"[8] which may be formulated in law, or articulated through ideology and social practice. For instance, the work of feminist scholars exploring the immigration of domestic servants, the unequal social entitlement of women and men in the welfare state, or the patriarchal designations assigned by colonial laws to First Nations women, all provide concrete examples of the way in which citizenship was defined differently — and unequally — according to class, race, and gender.[9]

It is difficult to generalize about the definitions of and solutions for delinquency, as they did change over these four decades. However, it is significant that, even in periods when legal authorities and social commentators spoke of the need for collective, social solutions to youth crime, they never lost a fundamental belief in the necessity of transforming individual and familial "morality." Moreover, from the passage of the first federal *Juvenile Delinquents Act* in 1908 to the first major discussions about altering that *Act* in the early 1960s, there was always an ongoing social concern with delinquency expressed in the popular media and by professional experts, especially those involved in the juvenile justice system. This persistent preoccupation with youthful crime, transgression, and disobedience was quite understandable since delinquency underscored fundamental, enduring concerns of both the state and social elites with social reproduction and, more specifically, with the maintenance of gender roles, family forms, and social stability. Although other authors have implied that particular time periods — the 1950s for instance — witnessed "moral panics" about delinquency,[10] concerns about delinquency never disappeared over this entire period; nevertheless, certain social, economic, and political contexts could heighten public anxieties (sometimes about specific "problems," ranging from gangs to promiscuity) and certain social conditions might well temporarily escalate youthful rebellion and wrongdoing. As Eric Schneider suggests, the problem with stressing only the ever-recurring "moral panics" and social construction of delinquency is that this ignores structural conditions that may well lead to intensified alienation and law breaking, and it "also robs working-class adolescents of their one token of agency: their ability to cause trouble."[11]

Social attitudes and state policies concerning delinquency had deep roots in the late nineteenth century, when social elites in an expanding, urbanizing, and industrializing society initiated voluntary and state-sponsored efforts to re-educate and reform poor, neglected, and delinquent children. Their concerns focused initially on boys, whose public presence in the streets, as newsboys, beggars or simply "unrestrained" youth, raised fears of a future unproductive, criminal citizenry. One answer offered by Victorian reformers was the creation of a new child-saving bureaucracy, including organizations such as the Children's Aid Society; another was the construction of industrial schools where boys could be trained in useful work and re-educated in law-abiding, moral ways. By the turn of the century, industrial schools for girls were also commonplace, in some cases managed by philanthropic boards but increasingly placed either directly or indirectly under the purview of provincial governments.[12] Reform interests also gave rise to the first federal *Juvenile Delinquents Act* (JDA) in 1908, which built on existing laws but set out a new, comprehensive apparatus of juvenile justice. Until replaced by the *Young Offenders Act* in 1984, the JDA was a crucial cornerstone of youth justice, setting out legal definitions of delinquency, options for punishing and reforming youth, and the rules governing Juvenile Courts.

Yet the passage of this legal *magna carta* on delinquency did not halt public discussion of the "youth problem." During World War I, delinquency was attributed to the loss of paternal/male authority on the battlefront, and eugenic sympathizers — quite influential at the time — intensified their arguments for forced sterilization of the feeble-minded. whose "natural immorality" simply reproduced progeny inevitably headed for a life of delinquency, crime, and immorality.[13] As Cynthia Comacchio points out, the Roaring Twenties also saw an intense public debate about youthful licentiousness and abandon, as social commentators fretted that youth were "dancing themselves to perdition" in a society influenced by the materialism of mass culture and characterized by youthful disrespect for their elders.[14]

The Depression heightened these anxieties, especially for boys, since the economic crisis, unemployment, and the resulting "loss" of male family leadership supposedly pushed disenchanted male youth into despair and lawlessness. Girls, it was feared, were also likely to lose their moral way in economic bad times, falling into the trap of prostitution. Yet arrest statistics — perhaps a better indication of policing than actual delinquency — told a contradictory story during the Depression, never clearly indicating an ever-increasing youthful crime wave across the country. The number of juveniles in conflict with the law did rise temporarily with the onset of World War II, again indicating the importance of public anxiety, policing, and even demographic changes in shaping youth crime statistics.[15] The war brought with it another bout of public agonizing over the decay of the family and the rise of youth crime in a society supposedly characterized by materialism, loss of parental control with the absence of fathers, and inverted gender roles with the employment of mothers. These "jitters over juveniles" decreased by the end of the war, but then reappeared, dressed up in new forms, in the post-

World War II period, when a rising birth rate, fears for the patriarchal family in the Cold War, and new manifestations of delinquent rebellion created another wave of studies, journalistic reports, and institution building.[16]

Recurring themes in the popular discussions of delinquency over many decades were discernable. Acute material shifts (whether expansion or depression), supposed threats to the family and "traditional" gender roles, and periods of national mobilization or unrest were all used as the explanatory hook upon which to hang dissections of youth criminality. It is possible that, during periods of marked social change, youthful rejection of the generational authority or the law became particularly noticeable.[17] Moreover, delinquency took on different manifestations over these years: in the 1920s, drugs were a new concern; in the 1950s, gangs appeared to be increasing. Despite some important distinctions, however, delinquency never completely disappeared as a social issue from the public, reform or state agendas from the end of World War I until the 1960s.

Defining Delinquency: Youthful Outsiders

Adults with close links to the juvenile justice system, such as probation officers, psychiatrists, and penal workers, were one influential group involved in the definition of delinquency, and their pronouncements were endowed with considerable "scientific" and moral authority. Let us focus on the medical, social-science, and social-work experts who wrote about youthful criminality and its threat to the nation, for these experts not only played a crucial role in shaping the dominant understandings of delinquency, but also increasingly had an impact on the interpretation and operation of the law through their participation in the juvenile justice system.

While there were discernible differences between these groups of experts, at least two themes often re-appeared in expert writing about delinquency: on one hand, commentators stressed the individual (sometimes innate) pathologies and limitations that shaped delinquent behaviour, while on the other hand they stressed the social and environmental problems creating criminality, such as poverty, poor housing, and poor education. Often the individual and social overlapped, focusing on one faulty and blameworthy cause of delinquency: the inadequate family. Over time, there was alteration in the "scientific" paradigms utilized to explore delinquency. Until the end of the 1930s, hereditary or genetic justifications such as "feeble-mindedness" were entertained by some experts, but modern psychiatry and psychology, including Freudian and behaviourist theories, increasingly dominated.

In the World War II period, for instance, the Toronto Welfare Council released a study confidently declaring that delinquents were "made not born." As such, they could be un-made, through a combination of "child psychology, addressing the youth's lack of security and confidence," and by "social services" such as educational supports, healthy recreation and so on.[18] By the 1940s, a disease metaphor was consistently employed by those arguing for the reform of youth: delinquency, it was claimed, was just like a "physical illness, identifiable by certain symptoms in its incipient stages, but almost always treatable according to modern medical and social work methods."[19]

These definitions were, on the surface, "classless," and experts often maintained that any child who was mistreated, or who lacked proper supervision and parenting (or perhaps too strict parenting — parents walked a fine line between the two), was liable to end up in court. This was especially true in the post-World War II era when an individualized Freudian analysis of family "dysfunction" was extremely powerful. In reality, of course, children from Rosedale were seldom found sitting on the benches of the Toronto Juvenile Court, where reformers presumed they were more likely to encounter children from the city's East End. Expert writing revealed underlying suspicions that working-class and poor children were more likely to become delinquent, in part because of their inadequate living conditions, but also because of the poor parenting they received. If delinquency was a disease, said many experts, then it was also contagious, much like the measles, claiming its most numerous victims in urban spaces characterized by bad housing, transience, poverty, and a lack of social and individual self respect.[20] And, of course, working-class and poor children *were* more likely to end up in court: they were subject to more intense policing, they lived in "suspect" neighbourhoods, and their conditions of life — material deprivation, transience, marginality — led to more conflicts with the law.

Not only did experts believe that potential delinquents were likely to come from the urban underclass, they also revealed profoundly gendered notions of what constituted delinquency. One way of exploring this is to look at the narratives used by reformers to promote the reformation of boys and girls. During the inter-war period, for instance, Toronto Juvenile Court Probation Officers and social workers in Toronto's Big Sisters published vivid descriptions of typical cases in order to garner public support for their work. As Karen Tice argues, the social work "case record" was consciously employed as a means of "asserting professional expertise" and simultaneously as a "vital documentary source ... to arouse public sympathy" and champion social workers' "preferred solution to social ills."[21] In 1930, the Toronto Probation Officer (PO) wrote about the case of Billy, a "Ukrainian boy of nine years, and second youngest in a family of four children." His single mother, left to struggle financially after the father deserted, relied heavily on the earnings of the older teenaged children in the workforce. Billy's first court appearance, at age 7, occurred after he stole a wagon and dismantled it. A year later, he broke into an office, tore up the ledger book, and stole some lead pipe to re-sell. After being placed in the detention home for observation, and after a psychiatric exam, he went on probation, only to reappear in Court for steal-ing cigarettes from a truck. This time, his mother did not bother to come to his hearing (though she may have been working). Instead, noted the Officer critically, an unsupportive sister spoke, and made Billy's case even worse by complaining that he was "always stealing something, even her face powder." Again put on strict probation with his school now involved, Billy's prospects looked dim, but in the final part of the narrative, which often opened out into "redemption," Billy turned a moral corner. He was linked up with the Boys Club and a Sunday School, and these influences, along with his firm probationary guidance, created the possibility that he would escape a life of crime, despite the fact that the home remained a dubious moral influence.[22] Billy was now lauded for turning over to the police some money he found after a hold-up. He received a sled for Christmas from staff of the Court, and he quickly embraced the work ethic, earning some money by using it to haul beer. The staff were encouraged by his budding entrepreneurship even if they recommended more legitimate cargo in the future.

Although other typical cases (always boys) described by the PO assumed some variation, there were visible, common themes. Boys were often appre-hended for theft and vandalism, although gang membership and truancy were recurring concerns. The family's marginal economic status, location in a bad area or, occasionally, their immigrant status — which social workers feared created a generational clash of values — provided the framework for delinquency, although questionable, inadequate or neglectful parenting almost invariably appeared somewhere in the story. The boy delinquent was in danger of growing up rejecting the value of private property, avoiding the work ethic, engaging in vices such as smoking and alcohol, and lacking respect for duly constituted authority and the family.

Many of these themes were also apparent in the public stories of girl delinquents. Significantly, such narratives were far more difficult to locate, since research and writing about delinquency usually focused on the boy problem, not the girl problem. However, in the annual reports of the Big Sisters Association of Toronto, an organization committed to delinquency prevention, social workers offered up typical examples of their daily work. So compelling was one dramatic narrative of delinquent endangerment that it subsequently turned up in the Hamilton Big Sisters' public arsenal of "typical" cases as well, a veritable "urban myth" of delinquency.[23]

At one annual general meeting in Toronto the staff also "acted out" a play about a little sister, "Daisy," to make their dramatic point for their larger membership. Daisy came to the agency, said the Director, as a "sullen" girl, resentful of authority and headed for trouble. Handicapped because she came from a broken home and with an overly strict mother, Daisy inherited an irresponsible streak from her deserting father. She was choosing bad companions, would not attend Sunday School, lost interest in her studies, and, worst of all, sought out pleasure in "joyriding, dance halls and movies." Her "natural craving for pretty clothes" was a sign that she was using "extreme dress and make-up" to flirt with boys, providing a blatant threat to sexual purity and passive femininity. Luckily, after working with the Big Sisters, Daisy showed signs of common sense and subdued femininity: she found employment as a mother's helper, was buying practical clothes, and had gained a laudable familial role model in her Big Sister.[24]

While Daisy's initial downfall was attributed in part to truancy and financial irresponsibility (not working or spending money appropriately), the implied threat (or reality) of sexual promiscuity was also critical, and this was a common theme underlying the definition of delinquency for many girls throughout this period. Some girls were certainly involved in petty theft — probably far more than we know, since case workers taking notes on girls were more interested in sex than stealing — but fears about their inability to become responsible adults centred more on their runs from home, illegitimate pregnancies, and sexual promiscuity. Nor was this to change dramatically in the post-World War II era.[25]

During and after World War II, the popular CBC Citizens' Forum radio show featured a number of discussions on delinquency. Framed by the rhetorical question "Prisons or Playgrounds?", one show included interviews with a club of adult men volunteering with male youth in Winnipeg's north end. Delinquency, they told the radio-listening public, often brewed in the home environment of children, "especially when both parents were working and kids were left to themselves to run the streets." While "social factors" like poor housing were a problem, parents were also at fault for not "teaching [boys] good behaviour." Not surprisingly, the alternative offered to the "prison" was the "playground"; citizens needed to provide a "place for supervision and training while parents were away."[26]

Another Citizens' Forum asked a roundtable of Toronto-based experts about "Johnny Delinquent: Whose Responsibility?" Reflecting the emerging emphasis in child-rearing literature on cultivating creativity rather than mere discipline, the social work professor stressed that young boys need to be taught "democratic," not "autocratic," values and need to be treated with respect by adults. The PTA mother advocated more education for ignorant, incompetent parents; the educational expert wanted better-trained teachers and resources for the schools; and the juvenile-court judge suggested that both parents and society needed to take an active role in preventing delinquency. Despite the fact that issues such as poor housing were cited as key problems, and despite the PTA woman's admission that middle-class children were sent to boarding school while poorer children ended up in court, economic and social causes were stressed less than those emanating from "bad relationships," especially bad parenting. Confidently ignoring any earlier comments to the contrary, the moderator summed up the broadcast by saying that "the speakers have all said juvenile delinquency is a psychological problem, not an economic one."[27]

These radio programs reflected an increased emphasis in this later period on psychological explanations for delinquency and highlighted an ongoing contradiction in definitions of the concept. While claiming adamantly that any child from any family with bad personal relations could run into trouble, the experts then proceeded to offer examples that belied this image of classless delinquency. Moreover, their overwhelming use of male examples reinforced the expert preoccupation with masculine manifestations of delinquency. Indeed, an increasing preoccupation with gangs from the 1930s on, and especially in the post-World War II period, was another indication of the male-defined image of delinquency. Although some girls' involvement in gangs came into view by the 1950s, they were more often seen as molls and sexual appendages, not ringleaders. Boys' delinquencies were defined as more group-inspired and related to their aggressive acting out in ways that could be cured; in fact, they were almost accepted as rites of passage as boys "tested out their environment and rebelled against social norms."[28] Girls' delinquencies — though discussed less often — supposedly emanated from individual, emotional, and familial pathologies.[29]

Gangs sometimes also became a symbol of another anxiety: the equation of immigrant, especially non-Anglo families, with potential delinquencies. In public narratives promoting their work, reformers and Probation Officers might use examples of "foreign-born" or second-generation immigrant children — like Billy — to suggest that preventing and treating delinquents overlapped with a laudable project of "Canadianization." In reality, of course, those arrested in cities like Toronto were largely Canadian-born, and only a minority had non-Anglo parents. Although commentators in the earlier part of the century had sometimes linked race and ethnicity to criminality (and to lower intelligence),[30] by the late 1930s, as Marcus Klee argues, ethnicity was not a dominant explanation used for delinquency,[31] though there is no doubt that it remained a sub-text, used to explain either gang culture or girls' moral conflicts with their immigrant parents. Well into the 1950s, gangs were primarily feared as expressions of underclass masculine resentment and violence.[32] In contrast to the US, race remained less salient to the social construction of delinquency, at least until the 1970s and after, when it *was* increasingly linked to discussions of both immigrant cultures and Native youth dispossession.[33]

Both female and male delinquents were assumed to represent the more troublesome problems of the underclass, such as excessive drinking, other addictions or indolence. An inadequate, uncaring family, lacking either discipline or affection, was seen as the most blameworthy cause of their downfall. But even this familial maladjustment took on different forms for boys and girls: boys needed a firm, guiding hand and an understanding of democracy, law, and social order to develop into honest workers and *social citizens*. Girls, however, needed protection, discipline, and self-control to develop into *moral citizens*. These distinctions were also important to the efforts to reform young outsiders, making them into model adult citizens.

Solving Delinquency: Creating Model Citizens

The language of medical diagnosis and treatment used by modern social scientists, social workers, and medical practitioners to argue that delinquency could be effectively remedied, much like an illness, also implied that delinquency might be prevented — just as immunization was providing children with new protection against disease. As a result, the years after World War I saw the proliferation of voluntary, reform, and state-sponsored efforts to provide youth with the incentive and ability to grow up without falling into criminality. Efforts to identity the "pre-delinquent" and positively shape her or his values and conscience were sometimes created entirely by volunteer efforts such as the YWCA/YMCA or the churches, which offered wholesome recreation, religious instruction, and good role models for adolescents to emulate. Other pre-delinquency efforts began as volunteer ventures, but over time they became professionalized, hiring social workers to manage the clients and also utilizing state funding to bolster their fundraising. Big Brothers and Big Sisters, which emerged in a few large urban centres before World War I and spread to other areas in subsequent years, often fitted this model.

Across the country, Big Brothers and Big Sisters had distinct local organizations, goals, and projects, but their efforts often commonly encompassed the optimistic belief that delinquency could be cured with a combination of personal guidance (of a parental variety despite the sibling symbolism) and professional expertise. Some also became advocates for social reforms such as recreational facilities and better housing for the disadvantaged. Initially, many Big Sisters and Brothers were linked directly to the juvenile justice system, visiting the Juvenile Courts and offering probation services to children designated for counselling and aid by judges. As probation services were increasingly professionalized under the direct auspices of the Court, many Big Brothers and Sisters turned their attention to other projects for disadvantaged or troubled youth.

In Hamilton, for instance, the Big Sisters combined more traditional charity and the provision of material aid — dental care, camp payments, school books and scholarships, second-hand clothes, even family Christmas baskets — with the counselling of girls with "behaviour problems, [who are] the product of broken homes, poor social conditions, drunkenness and immorality."[34] Drawing on a sense of middle- and upper-class social responsibility, as well as maternal ideology, more affluent Big Sisters mentored their "little sisters," who were revealingly referred to in their early meetings as "the unfortunates." Their initial aims were couched unambiguously in the language of citizenship training: "we promote the welfare and uplift of ... girls before the Juvenile Court and others whose physical, mental and moral development have suffered. ... We enlist women to help girls become good citizens."[35]

Overlapping strategies characterized the Hamilton Big Sisters' efforts at creating new citizens. Professional casework and individual counselling by social workers were combined with attempts to alter girls' social surroundings, removing them from a home, helping them find a job, or placing them in a wholesome recreational experience; and, above all, "non-expert" maternal care was provided through the firm guidance, if not discipline, of volunteer Big Sisters.[36] Concern for the girls' future was often sparked by a shoplifting charge, a referral from the school system, or through calls from harried parents dealing with broken curfews and saucy daughters. While the girl's employment or educational future was often a consideration, her sexual, moral, and feminine character was always a central preoccupation. By providing a girl with the resources to build a new character — including respect for authority, self-respect, and confidence — Big Sisters consciously noted its role in reproducing future generations, for girls were also potential mothers: "we give opportunities where other changes cannot be made. ... guidance and understanding [have] helped girls accept their place in the community as worthwhile citizens — after all, these girls are the mothers of tomorrow."[37]

Their job, Big Sisters maintained, was different from that of Big Brothers: pre-delinquency was a gendered condition, largely because of a girl's endangered morality, something that could not be easily recouped: "you cannot exploit a girl without danger of a stigma. A boy who is reclaimed is a hero, not so the girl."[38] Nonetheless, the two organizations shared some ideals and strategies, as Big Brothers tried to combine character building through personal, paternal example with attempts to alter boys' social environment. Both organizations also focused their sights on aiding children in unstable or immoral families, with these "dysfunctional" families defined extremely loosely as simply "broken" (i.e., divorced, single-parent) or, more precisely, as violent, abusive, or impoverished.

In its early years, the Toronto Big Brothers claimed that 89 per cent of boys before the courts could be transformed into "good citizens," since the boys who were not "mentally or physically deficient" simply suffered from "energy plus." These over-energized "lads" needed respectable role models to befriend them, declared one promotional pamphlet, adding a wartime warning that "too many citizens of tomorrow are going wrong for lack for friendly guidance of the father" who is serving overseas.[39] Just over a decade later, as social anxieties concerning male delinquency intensified in the Depression, Toronto's Big Brothers shifted its focus, stressing the social causes of delinquency such as unemployment, poverty, slum housing conditions, and family problems, especially in working-class neighbourhoods. However, one solution was still to provide alternatives to petty crime in the form of healthy diversions and role models. As some Big Brother publications argued, drawing on psychological experts, gangs were not simply a sign of pathology, but a sign of growing boys' male bonding and budding masculinity: they offered deprived boys confidence, community, respect, and protection. "A boy without a gang," as a Big Brothers worker wrote, "is like a dog without a bone. ... Gang life is where a boy learns to become a man. It is his school of democracy. His first lessons in fair play and sacrifice are brought to him."[40] The challenge was to find alternative pastimes that fostered similar instincts without anti-social gang activities like bicycle and car theft.

By the early 1950s, studies of male gangs had proliferated, with middle-class investigators betraying an almost voyeuristic fascination with the contours of "underclass" boy life.[41] In one CBC Citizens' Forum broadcast, a Toronto teacher connected to Big Brothers, Clifford Pugh, relayed the results of his summer "undercover" infiltration of various levels of gangs (from the relatively harmless to the more menacing) of nine- to fourteen-year-olds. The listening audience was told that gangs were primarily involved in petty theft or minor vandalism, sometimes amounting only to "boyish pranks" like putting garbage in the street. The boys, he continued, were seeking stature and "recognition" but they could be satisfied with wholesome, diversionary recreation like swimming. A major reason for boys' anti-social behaviour, claimed Pugh, was that parents — in this case only bad mothers were noted — left them unattended and did not provide the companionship they needed. Still, his ultimate moral lesson also called for a broader social commitment: "our citizens' role is to clean up the slums, give these boys the activities they crave."[42] Indeed, the period after World War II, arguably stretching into the 1960s, reflected immense investment in recreation as a social panacea for moulding youth, as government task forces, citizens' recreation initiatives, and social workers all engaged in efforts to use recreation as a tool to create responsible, democratic values.[43]

If recreation and role models were two social solutions for turning pre-delinquents into model citizens, another key piece to the puzzle was the *Juvenile Delinquents Act* (*JDA*) itself, along with the Juvenile Courts that emerged from it. Because reformers and lawmakers perceived their job to be saving *potential* as well as real lawbreakers, they created an *Act* (and amended it over time) with extremely broad-ranging definitions of delinquency — encompassing everything from assault to breaking a local by-law to sexual immorality to truancy and disobedience. Theoretically, the young offender was to be treated "not as an offender but as one in a condition of delinquency and therefore requiring help, guidance and supervision."[44] Although treatment, not punishment, was the intended and rhetorical aim of the *JDA*, this "welfarist" emphasis was sometimes challenged by critics as too "soft," and it could also be contradicted in practice by the punitive treatment of some young offenders.

The *JDA* allowed judges and courts wide, discretionary sentencing powers, which increasingly became linked to technocratic, informal or "socialized" justice, that is, the use of non-legal experts such as probation officers and psychological and psychiatric experts to "diagnose, treat and rehabilitate deficient families."[45] Common strategies of socialized justice, such as probation, were devised by the courts to deal with both boys and girls, and there were some overlapping social concerns shaping the prosecution of delinquency. Offences against property (though boys were more likely to be engaged in break-and-enters or auto thefts, girls in minor thefts) and truancy were signs of potential future criminality for both sexes. In the case of truancy, it was feared that boys and girls who lacked the skills, values, and work ethic of school would never adopt the economic and psychological skills necessary to take their rightful place in a productive workforce and remain economically independent from state provision.

While social class, lack of education, and the presence of poverty were all seen as potential "markers" of a dubious future for boys and girls, there were also salient gender differences in the operation of juvenile justice. As Dorothy Chunn shows in a study of two urban courts, far more boys appeared in court, and for different reasons, than girls. The former were charged predominantly with property and public-order offences,[46] the latter with status and moral offences. Indeed, a 1924 amendment to the JDA forbidding "sexual immorality and other forms of vice" was designed — despite its gender-neutral language — to control supposedly promiscuous girls.[47] Boys' sexual misbehaviour might be noted as part of a package of concerns, while for girls sexuality often became *the* defining problem for probation officers and judges. Indeed, the very definition of sexual "deviance" was gendered: homosexual, violent or bestial acts were considered signs of boys' deviance, whereas for a girl, merely engaging in "too much" consensual heterosexual sex was the predominant sign of deviance and was usually enough to secure her a forced gynecological (and/or psychiatric) exam and to land her in court.

The ability of boys or girls to convince judges or court workers that they were on the road to reform rested not only on their actions and demeanour, but also on their family's social persona, especially their parents' embrace of good citizenship. Parents who were willing to move to new neighbourhoods, prove their own moral propriety and dedication to the work ethic, or plead their churchgoing and wholesome leisure activities were more likely to keep their children out of a training school. When two boys were arrested for breaking into a restaurant after a run from home, the Toronto Family Court agreed to probation rules involving a curfew, "keeping their rooms clean," and placing part of their part-time earnings (from employment with their father) in the bank. The father's claim that he was also assuring their school attendance and sending them to church, hockey, and summer camp was a sure sign for the court that these boys would not become repeaters.[48] Probation officers looked for signs of sobriety, sexual morality, and a willingness to work as they counselled and monitored delinquent girls and their families; indications of the mother's "immorality" were seen as especially problematic, the daughter being very likely to imitate the mother.[49]

Therefore, even if the letter of the JDA did not generally distinguish according to gender, its implementation, from formal court hearings to informal mediation, embraced and reproduced notions of sexual difference. As Chunn argues, in the eyes of the social and legal authorities, boys' and girls' future roles as model adult citizens shaped how they were treated in the court system.[50] While boys' misdemeanours were signs that they were not acquiring the appropriate discipline, morals, and habits — thrift, deferred gratification, respect for property — needed by worker/breadwinners, girls' misdeeds — sexual immorality, running away, and disrespect for the family — indicated that they would make less than ideal wives and mothers.

The differing treatment of girls and boys was also clearly expressed in the most punitive solution used to combat delinquency: sentences to industrial schools, later training schools, which, despite the educational nomenclature, were essentially correctional institutions.[51] A number of studies have revealed that girls were proportionately more likely to receive training-school sentences, even though their overall numbers in the juvenile justice system were far smaller than those of boys. From the founding of the Ontario Training School for Girls in 1933 to 1960, girls were more likely to be placed in a training school after no, or one, court appearance, in contrast to boys, who had more brushes with the law before this drastic measure was resorted to.[52] The reason for the propensity to harshly sentence girls related to the definitions of delinquency. Girls' delinquencies were perceived to be difficult to measure, survey, and regulate through informal probation as they could be "hidden" from view. Moreover, it was presumed that girls' more individual, emotional, and psychiatric problems, their runaway attempts, and especially their pathological promiscuity needed immediate and strong intervention as well as isolation from society.[53]

In sentencing girls and boys to training schools, judges offered up rationales that noted the importance of citizenship training for children seen to be at risk of becoming adult criminals or misfits. Explaining to one boy that he would be housed in a "cottage" with surrogate parents at training school, one judge told him that these parents would help him develop "habits of industry and fair play" so that he could become a model "social individual."[54] The Ontario Training School Board, an advisory body to the government, rarely lost an opportunity to make similar claims. In the boys' reform school, they wrote in 1950, boys were learning to be "good citizens of democratic society, with respect for authority and law, clean and polite ... aspiring to reach their educational limit."[55] Girls, too, were supposed to be industrious, clean, and polite; however, their sentencing lectures usually included admonitions not to throw away their virtue but to become moral citizens of the future. Explaining a training-school sentence to one girl, a judge noted that her promiscuous behaviour with "strange men" would endanger her *and* society: "this world needs good women more than ever before and there is nothing in the world that grows into good women except good girls."[56]

In their emphasis on training worker citizens for the future, girls' and boys' reform-school regimes did overlap. Both institutions stressed a program of very basic academic education of reading and writing, vocational training, and physical development, though girls were more likely to receive posture exercises and boys more outdoor, competitive games. Both stressed the desirability of "modern" penal practices, classifying and segregating children according to intelligence, ability, and behaviour, and both utilized an intricate system of rewards and punishments to re-shape children's characters. Boys and girls alike were encouraged to "understand their mistakes, gain insight into their problems so they can manage their own lives," and both were to be "polite, mannerly, clean and tidy."[57] Religious and moral instruction was part of the institutional cure for delinquency, with chaplains giving "classes in Christian citizenship,"[58] and there were attempts to gradually re-introduce youth to the outside world through community contacts and adult role models. While girls made tea for local middle-class women's clubs, boys worked as part-time golf caddies on a local course. Recreation involving team sports and cooperation was often encouraged, with the state-run Boys' Training School bringing in the local police and RCMP officers to run the annual games days, just to make sure the boys developed the requisite "appreciation" for duly constituted authority.[59] Investigations of the penal system, such as the 1938 Archambault Royal Commission, were concerned that boys' training schools find the right "blend of discipline, recreation," and physical work to produce adults with "respect for well-defined rules and competition," since this was the path to "self discipline, which is requisite in the formation of good citizens."[60]

Boys and girls were primarily educated for "respectable" working-class labour, in part because the state believed they should be self-sufficient as soon as possible, and in part because these working-class children were perceived to be best "fitted" intellectually for such work. A gendered division of labour, however, clearly defined this training. Especially in the inter-war period, girls were taught "a practical program of home management"[61] including cooking, sewing, and laundry work, preparing them either for work as servants or for their own homemaking roles. As domestic service increasingly declined as a viable employment option, girls were then placed as mothers' helpers, or channelled into factory, retail or clerical work. Homemaking, along with grooming, still remained an important part of the girls' education: inmates shared in the domestic labour needed to run the school as part of their character-building and life-skills exercises.

In contrast, the vocational program of the training school for boys in Bowmanville included carpentry shop, a shoe repair shop, horticultural training, barbering lessons, maintenance work, and later auto mechanics. By the 1950s, they were also taught some "life skills" such as cooking, but their future employment was assumed to be primarily manual and blue-collar.[62] Just as girls were placed out as "parolees" as domestic servants or child-minders, boys were placed out as agricultural workers on farms. This carried on a long tradition of placing working-class boys — orphans or delinquents — in "wholesome" rural settings in order to reconstruct their character, a strategy that ignored the fact that urban youth were unlikely later to make their living as farmers.[63]

The creation of self-sufficient, law-abiding worker citizens thus characterized the agendas of secular training-school efforts, whether they involved girls or boys. Nonetheless, these regimes still imagined distinct futures for boys and girls, just as their delinquencies were defined differently to begin with. For boys, work was associated with a life-long commitment to wage labour, while girls were assumed to need temporary vocational training until work within the home commanded their attention. Moreover, girls were also urged to develop more polite, passive, "feminine" personas, abandoning the tough, rambunctious, loud behaviour repeatedly lamented by their penal keepers. Girls' embrace of proper heterosexual norms, especially the renunciation of premarital sex, was also central to the remodelling of their conscience and character. As a consequence, marriage and motherhood were seen as one resolution to their delinquent endangerment. To penal workers and social workers, marriage spelled "sexual containment" (and perhaps male protection), and their reports could sometimes barely disguise their sighs of relief when girls married, even at an early age of seventeen: "it is the best thing that could have happened to her," commented one penal worker when a training-school girl married as soon as possible; "she is keeping house well now."[64] Presumably, sexual containment and embrace of her domestic future were signs that this young woman, once considered delinquent, was now on the path to adult, moral citizenship.

Conclusion

The solutions for delinquency, ranging from the surveillance of probation to the discipline of training schools, could be termed successes — that is, if one measures success by the rate of recidivism for youth offenders in these years, for the majority did not return to court repeatedly.[65] Since so many delinquencies were minor, some of them mere status offences that were not crimes in the adult world, this is hardly surprising. "Age," as some commentators point out, "is the best cure for delinquency."[66] Moreover, many young girls and boys who had some contact with the juvenile justice system never made their way into adult court for serious offences, though a minority, probably those who had the earliest and longest contact with state care and correctional institutions, did graduate to adult crime, precisely the progression that so many anti-delinquency crusaders feared.

Although the strategies and techniques developed to deal with delinquency were in one sense successful, they also revealed a troubling underside of the juvenile justice system. By extension, they exposed the construction of unequal social citizenship. The youthful outsiders who so worried social elites, the state, and many professionals dedicated to curing delinquency were not simply outsiders because they transgressed the law; they were perceived to be *potentially* delinquent and dangerous because they or their families were socially, economically, and sometimes racially marginalized to begin with. Also, young people coping with familial violence, poverty or social alienation did not have the same access to the social, economic or emotional resources that more secure and affluent children did. Yet solutions for their reformation were ultimately less cognizant of, and certainly less able to alter, these injuries and inequalities, and more concerned with the need for the inculcation of individual willpower, self-control, and morality. This was true of both sexes, but especially so for girls, who were often in trouble *because of* perceived lapses of individual sexual morality.

Since the definition and treatment of delinquency were shaped by poverty, alienation, and class relations, common strategies were employed to transform female and male troublemakers into adult citizens. In the case of both boys and girls, anti-delinquency efforts advocated optimistic blueprints for the alteration of the social conditions of life for children, but they often came to rest instead on more individualized solutions ranging from providing role models and counseling to surveillance and the inculcation of discipline. Despite an overlap between the treatment of boys and girls, gender differences were also significant, revealing very different understandings of the ideal adult citizen. The delinquent boy was to be remoulded into a *social citizen*, respectful of property, public order, democracy, and honest earning, while the girl in conflict with the law needed guidance to become a *moral citizen* whose wage labour and family life had also to encompass restrained heterosexuality, domestic monogamy, and honest motherhood.

Notes

1. City of Toronto Archives (CTA), RG 47, Box 135, Annual Report of the Toronto Juvenile Family Court, 1920.
2. CTA, Series 100, file 1350, Chief Draper, Annual Report for Toronto Police Board Commissioners: "the home creates the nation...the nation can rise no higher than its homes," 13 April 1944.
3. Since girls were often ignored in discussions during these decades, I have placed some emphasis on definitions of female delinquency. For the argument that criminology continues to marginalize and misinterpret girls, see Marge Reitsma-Street, "Justice for Canadian Girls: A 1990s Update," *Canadian Journal of Criminology* 41, 3 (1999): 346.
4. This approach therefore privileges an emphasis on regulation, intentionally leaving to another essay the important question of the responses of delinquents and their families to their re-socialization. While I draw on national sources to highlight the discourses defining delinquency, I use examples taken from the courts and training schools in Ontario.
5. *Belonging: The Meaning and Future of Citizenship*, ed. William Kaplan (Montreal: McGill-Queen's University Press, 1993), 21.
6. Desmond Morton, "Divided Loyalties, Divided Country?" in Belonging, ed. Kaplan.
7. For example, *Citizenship, Diversity and Pluralism: Canadian and Comparative Perspectives*, ed. Alan Cairns et al. (Montreal: McGill–Queen's University Press, 1999). While some research explores issues of social entitlement, approaches still tend to proceed from issues of identity or identity politics.
8. Jane Jenson and Susan Phillips, "Regime Shift: New Citizenship Practices in Canada," *International Journal of Canadian Studies* 14 (1996): 114.
9. Some examples include *Not One of the Family*, ed. Abigail Bakan and Daiva Stasiulus (Toronto: University of Toronto Press, 1997); Himani Bannerji, *The Dark Side of the Nation: Essays on Multiculturalism, Nationalism and Gender* (Toronto: Canadian Scholars Press, 2000); Margaret Little, *No Car, No Radio, No Liquor Permit: The Moral Regulation of Single Mothers in Ontario, 1920-97* (Toronto: Oxford University Press, 1998); Patricia Monture-Angus, *Thunder in my Soul: A Mohawk Woman Speaks* (Halifax: Fernwood, 1995); Teresa Nahanee, "Dancing with a Gorilla: Aboriginal Women, Justice and the Charter," in Canada, *Royal Commission on Aboriginal Peoples, Aboriginal Peoples and the Justice System* (Ottawa: Supply and Services, 1993), 359-82; Katharine Scott, "The Dilemma of Liberal Citizenship: Women and Social Assistance Reform in the 1990s," in *Feminism and Political Economy*, ed. Pat Armstrong and Patricia Connelly (Toronto: Canadian Scholars Press, 1999), 205-37.
10. Mary Louise Adams, *The Trouble with Normal: Postwar Youth and the Making of Heterosexuality* (Toronto: University of Toronto Press, 1997), 56.
11. Eric Schneider, *Vampires, Dragons and Egyptian Kings: Youth Gangs in Postwar New York* (Princeton: Princeton University Press, 1999), 51.
12. For some examples of late nineteenth- and early twentieth-century discussion, see Paul Bennett, "Taming 'Bad Boys' of the 'Dangerous Classes': Child Rescue and Restraint at the Victoria Industrial School, 1887-1935," *Histoire sociale/Social History* 21 (May 1988): 71-96; D. Owen Carrigan, *Juvenile Delinquency in Canada: A History* (Toronto: Irwin, 1998); Susan Houston, "The Waifs and Strays of a Victorian City: Juvenile Delinquents in Toronto," in *Childhood and Family in Canadian History*, ed. Joy Parr (Toronto: McClelland and Stewart, 1982); Dianne Matters, "The Boys Industrial School: Education for Juvenile Offenders," in *Schooling and Society in Twentieth Century British Columbia*, ed. J. Donald Wilson and David C. Jones (Calgary: Detselig Enterprises, 1980), 53-70; Indiana Matters, "Sinners or Sinned Against?: Historical Aspects of Female Juvenile Delinquency in British Columbia," in *Not Just Pin Money: Selected Essays on the History of Women's Work in British Columbia*, ed. Barbara Latham and Roberta Pazdro (Victoria: Camosun College, 1984), 265-77; Carolyn Strange, *Toronto's Girl Problem: The Perils and Pleasures of the City, 1880-1930* (Toronto: University of Toronto Press, 1995).

13. On World War I, see Carrigan, *Juvenile Delinquency in Canada*, 96. On eugenics, see Angus McLaren, *Our Own Master Race: Eugenics in Canada, 1885-1945* (Toronto: McClelland and Stewart, 1990); Theresa Richardson, *The Century of the Child: the Mental Hygiene Movement and Social Policy in the U.S. and Canada* (Albany: SUNY Press, 1989); Jennifer Stephen, "The 'Incorrigible,' the 'Bad,' the 'Immoral': Toronto's Factory Girls and the Work of the Toronto Psychiatric Clinic," in *Law, Society and the State: Essays in Modern Legal History*, ed. Louis Knafla and Susan Binnie (Toronto: University of Toronto Press, 1995), 405-42.

14. Cynthia Comacchio, "Dancing to Perdition: Adolescence and Leisure in Inter-war English Canada," *Journal of Canadian Studies* 32, 3 (Fall 1997): 5-35.

15. Jeffrey Keshen, "Wartime Jitters over Juveniles: Canada's Delinquency Scare and Its Consequences, 1939-45," in *Age of Contention: Readings in Canadian Social History, 1900-45*, ed. Jeffrey Keshen (Toronto: Harcourt Brace, 1997), 364-86.

16. Adams, *The Trouble with Normal*; Keshen, "Wartime Jitters over Juveniles," 364-86.

17. Comacchio, "Dancing to Perdition," 27.

18. Archives of Ontario (AO), RG 20-26-2 (Dept. of Reform Institutions), Container J 1, 'Juvenile Delinquency' Welfare Council of Toronto and District, "A Plan for the Reduction of Juvenile Delinquency in Toronto," 4-5, 18.

19. Ontario, *Annual Report of Ontario Training Schools* (hereafter *Annual Report*), Ontario Training School Advisory Board, 1959. See also Paul Tappan, "The Nature of Delinquency," in *Juvenile Delinquency: A Reader*, ed. Rose Giallonbardo (New York: Wiley and Sons, 1964), 9.

20. Canadian experts drew heavily on American studies that "mapped" delinquency by urban neighbourhood, such as Clifford Shaw and Henry McKay, *Juvenile Delinquency and Urban Areas* (Chicago: University of Chicago Press, 1942). For a Canadian example see Barbara Nease, "Measuring Juvenile Delinquency in Hamilton," *Canadian Journal of Corrections* 8 (1966): 133-45.

21. Karen Tice, *Tales of Wayward Girls and Immoral Women: Case Records and the Professionalization of Social Work* (Urbana: University of Illinois Press, 1998), 7.

22. CTA, *Annual Report of the Toronto Juvenile and Family Court, 1930*.

23. Hamilton Big Sisters Association (HBSA), the story of "Peggy" in the Hamilton newsletter of 1949, also found in the Toronto Annual Report of 1941.

24. HBSA, *Annual Report of the Toronto Big Sisters Association, 1933* (the Toronto reports were found within the Hamilton papers).

25. Joan Sangster, "Girls in Conflict with the Law: Exploring the Construction of Female 'Delinquency' in Ontario, 1940-60," *Canadian Journal of Women and the Law* 12, 1 (2000): 1-3.

26. National Archives of Canada (NAC), CBC Citizens' Forum, "Prisons or Playgrounds" #99076 (1949).

27. NAC, CBC Citizens' Forum, "Johnny Delinquent: Whose Responsibility?" #228543 (29 Oct. 1948).

28. Gloria Geller, "Streaming of Males and Females in the Juvenile Justice System" (PhD Thesis, University of Toronto, 1981), 74.

29. Anne Campbell, *Girl Delinquents* (Oxford: Basil Blackwell, 1981). On the invisibility of girls in delinquency studies at this time see Frances Heidensohn, *Women and Crime* (New York: New York University Press, 1985). Studies of the Toronto Juvenile Court done in the 1970s revealed striking continuities with these earlier decades as class relations and gender ideology remained central to the definition, policing, and sentencing of youth. See Geller, "Streaming of Male and Females," and Sherrie Barnhorst, "Female Delinquency and the Juvenile Justice System" (LL.M. thesis, Queen's University, 1980).

30. See for example, articles in the 1920s in the *Canadian Journal of Mental Hygiene*: E.K. Clarke, "Survey of the Toronto Public Schools," 2, 2 (1920): 182-85; and, on the "promiscuity" of feeble-minded girls, D.M. Le Bourdais, "Eugenical Sterilization in California," 4, 1 (1929): 7.

31. Marcus Klee, "Between the Scylla and Charybdis of Anarchy and Despotism: The State, Capital and the Working-Class in the Great Depression, Toronto, 1929-40" (PhD Thesis, Queen's University, 1998), 146.

32. Michael Young, "The History of Vancouver Youth Gangs, 1900-85" (MA Thesis, Simon Fraser University, 1993).

33. The increasing number of Native youth in conflict with the law after the 1950s and 1960s provided evidence that severe economic dislocation, social alienation, and racist denigration could provide catalysts for legal conflict and confrontation, although many of the early analyses of Native "criminality" relied more heavily on discussions of cultural dispossession and "backwardness," which themselves betrayed a deep-seated cultural racism. See Joan Sangster, "'She is Hostile to Our Ways': First Nations Girls Sentenced to the Ontario Training School for Girls, 1940-60," *Law and History Review* 20, 1 (Spring 2002): 59-96.

34. HBSA, Annual report file, 1936.

35. HBSA, Annual report file, 1936.

36. On overlapping strategies, including "non-expert" maternal discipline, see Kelly Hannah-Moffat, *Punishment in Disguise: Penal Governance and Federal Imprisonment of Women in Canada* (Toronto: University of Toronto Press, 2001), especially chapter 2. As probation workers, Big Sisters were supposed to monitor and report back on their little sisters for the Courts.

37. HBSA, Typescript, speech by D. Crawford, "What do Children Really Need?", n.d.

38. HBSA, Annual Reports file, 1921-22.

39. AO, Dept. of Labour, Deputy Minister's Subject Files, 7-12-0-9 (Industrial School boys were used as farm workers during the labour shortages of World War I).

40. NAC, Canadian Council on Social Development (CCSD) Papers, vol. 32, f. 151, Frank Sharpe, "What Good is a Gang?" His concerns echoed mental-hygiene specialists who declared that boy gangs had "positive aspects," such as aiding "independence". J.D. Ketchum, "Boys Gangs and Mental Hygiene," *Mental Health* 5, 1 (1930), 5.

41. Kenneth Rogers, *Street Gangs in Toronto: A Study of the Forgotten Boy* (Toronto: Ryerson Press, 1945).

42. NAC, CBC Citizens' Forum, "Meet the Gang," #29095 (1940s).

43. Adams, *The Trouble with Normal*; Shirley Tillotson, *The Public at Play: Gender and the Politics of Recreation in Post-War Ontario* (Toronto: University of Toronto Press, 1999).

44. The JDA did allow some provincial latitude in the age definition of delinquency. In some provinces teens came under the *Act* until they were 18, although in Ontario the age was 16. William L. Scott, *The Genesis of the Juvenile Delinquents Act* (Ottawa: Canadian Welfare Council, 1966), 9-10. See also Dorothy Chunn, *From Punishment to Doing Good: Family Courts and Socialized Justice in Ontario, 1880-1940* (Toronto: University of Toronto Press, 1992); Marge Reitsma-Street, "More Control than Care: A Critique of the Historical and Contemporary Laws for Delinquency and Neglect in Ontario," *Canadian Journal of Women and the Law* 3, 2 (1989-90): 510-30; Jean Trépanier, "Origins of the Juvenile Delinquents Act of 1908: Controlling Delinquency through Seeking Its Causes and through Youth Protection," in *Dimensions of Childhood: Essays on the History of Children and Youth*, ed. Russell Smandych, Gordon Dodds, and Alvin Esau (Winnipeg: Legal Research Institute, 1991): 205-32.

45. Dorothy Chunn, "Boys will be Men, Girls will be Mothers: The Legal Regulation of Childhood in Toronto and Vancouver," *Sociological Studies in Child Development* 3 (1990): 94.

46. This pattern was found in many other juvenile courts across the country. On Québec, see Tamara Myers, "The Voluntary Delinquent: Parents, Daughters, and the Montreal Juvenile Delinquents' Court in 1918," *Canadian Historical Review* 80, 2 (June 1999): 242-68.

47. Bruno Théorêt, "Régulation juridique pénale des mineures et discrimination à l'égard des filles: la clause de 1924 amendant la Loi sur les jeunes délinquants," *Canadian Journal of Women and the Law* 4 (1990-91): 539-55.

48. AO, York Domestic Relations Records, Box 1522, 1945-54. Anonymous case file. In the 1930s and 1940s, parents might also prove their disciplinarian virtues to the court by consenting to have their boys strapped as part of their punishment.

49. Sangster, "Girls in Conflict with the Law," 14.

50. Chunn, "Boys will be Men," 99.

51. Sometimes referred to as "reform schools," these institutions varied across the country, with some run by religious denominations (particularly the Catholic Church) and many managed by the state. Outside of Québec, almost all these institutions were inspected and at least partially funded by the state. The following examples are taken from annual reports and government records on the state-sponsored Ontario Training School for Boys in Bowmanville, founded in 1925, and the Ontario Training School for Girls in Galt, founded in 1933.

52. Figures taken from the category showing the number of times before the court for boys and girls sent to training school. *Annual Report, 1933-60.*

53. Gloria Geller's later study revealed similar assumptions: working-class boys were labelled dangerous because they were seeking "mastery of the world, discharging their aggression in theft, or vandalism," while girls' delinquency was the product of emotional disturbances requiring psychiatric aid, since their "out of control" sexual behaviour spelled rejection of proper gender roles. Of course, whether a girl was defined as neurotic needing therapy, or hopelessly delinquent needing the discipline of training school, depended also on her social class.

54. Judge quoted in *Child and Family Welfare*, 24 March 1946.

55. *Annual Report*, Report of the Training School Advisory Board, 1950.

56. AO, Ontario Training School for Girls (OTSG) case file 820, 1940s.

57. *Annual Report*, Report of Ontario Training School for Girls (OTSG, Galt), 1941 and Report of Training School for Boys (OTSB, Bowmanville), 1950.

58. *Annual Report*, Report of OTSG, 1955.

59. *Annual Report*, Report of OTSB, 1950.The RCMP were also brought into Bowmanville to offer "citizenship education" (1951).

60. *Report of the Royal Commission on the Penal System* (Archambault Commission), 1938, 192. Although the report ostensibly dealt with boys and girls training schools, in fact it was primarily concerned with juvenile male offenders.

61. *Annual Report*, Report of OTSG, 1938.

62. *Child and Family Welfare* 9, (March 1934): 46-49; *Annual Report*, Report of OTSB, 1948; 1950; 1955.

63. For example, in 1945, of 185 placed out to work, 96 were sent to farms. On earlier efforts, see Joy Parr, *Labouring Children: British Immigrant Apprentices to Canada, 1869-1924* (London: Croom Helm, 1980).

64. AO, OTSG case file G19, 1930s.

65. Between 1922 and 1945, the recidivism rate for major offences nationally ranged from 25 to 30 per cent. In the Toronto Family Court, the overall rate for delinquency was closer to 25 per cent. The majority of youth offenders do not become adult offenders.

66. Dorothy Chunn, "Boys Will be Men," 105.

chapter sixteen

SEX AND CITIZENSHIP
(Hetero)Sexual Offences, Law and "White" Settler Society in British Columbia, 1885-1940[1]

Dorothy E. Chunn

Suffice it to say that short of murder there is no crime ... more abhorrent than the forcible defilement of an innocent girl. In this case we have a young Scotch colonist, a type that we as Canadians have been ever ready to welcome to our shores, a child of that sturdy stock which has played such a noble part in the upbuilding of our young dominion, that race which has left indelibly its mark on our country's institutions, its history and its government. We as Canadians are proud of our country. ... We are proud that our women folk can go abroad unattended, secure in the chivalrous attitude of our citizens. Is that confidence to be shaken? What is to happen if the guilty are allowed to go unpunished? What then of the boasted freedom and safety of women folk, our mothers, wives, sisters, children?[2]

Introduction

Many writers have noted the common trends that characterize liberal states at particular points in time. During the late nineteenth and early twentieth centuries, for instance, Canada and other developing welfare states were clearly marked by a collective focus on moral regulation and social control that was manifested politically by moral and social purity movements and their "scientific" successors: social and mental hygiene movements.[3] Research and literature on this era in Canada and other western societies have revealed that, while not homogeneous, these movements were consumed with and united by a central concern with eugenics: a pervasive belief that social purity and health were dependent upon the moral, mental and physical fitness of individuals.[4] In turn, "fitness" became the basis for citizenship in the welfare state. Temperance, social hygiene, mental hygiene, "race" hygiene,[5] on one hand, and drunkenness, syphilis, feeblemindedness, "white slavery," on the other, became metaphors for and indicators of individual and social health and pathology respectively.[6] Moreover, conceptions of "fitness" were implicitly and explicitly linked to assumptions about gender, race, ethnicity, class, and sexual orientation. Indeed, the history of developing welfare states arguably is defined by debates and struggles about which categories of people in addition to propertied, white men would be accorded which citizenship rights.[7]

Regardless of their specific substantive concerns, moral and social reformers were preoccupied with the same questions: How can good citizens be (re)produced? How can the (re)productively fit be separated from the unfit? How can deviant but salvageable individuals be separated from the incorrigible and/or inherently unfit? During the late nineteenth century, reformers often advocated coercive strategies and initiatives to enforce their values among marginal populations. Law, and especially criminal law, was a primary institutional mechanism for patrolling and regulating the boundaries of "fitness."[8] Over time, however, persuasion and normalization received increasing emphasis as a means of facilitating self-regulation among the majority of the population and thereby effecting social control in developing welfare states. After World War I, institutional sites such as family and schools, as well as public education more generally, became more pivotal to the implementation of strategies for (re)producing good citizens that were aimed at "proper" socialization and internalization of dominant values and norms.[9] Coercive strategies themselves also were transformed as repression became intertwined with persuasion through the increasing reliance on the use of experts who employed non-legal knowledge and discourses not associated with the overt repression of "deviance."[10]

This latter development was clearly evident in criminal law, including the laws governing sexual offences, during the late nineteenth and early twentieth centuries in Canada.[11] Here as elsewhere, both purity reformers and hygienists linked women's fitness for citizenship — civil, political, social — to their reproductive potential: their (in)ability to be "mothers of the (white) race." Law was viewed as a means of protecting or salvaging that potential, or of identifying reproductively unsuitable women. Hence, it is not surprising that the (criminal) repression of "deviant" sex was a key demand of reform movements that were organized and gained strength during the 1890s. Reformers sparked a proliferation of new laws and the reform of existing ones that collectively criminalized almost all sexual relations outside marriage by the outbreak of war in 1914.[12] While the impetus for adopting a criminalization approach to "illegitimate" sex was explicitly moral, the increasing hegemony of "scientific" mental and social-hygiene movements during and after World War I had a marked impact on the operation of sexual-offence legislation. The administration of criminal justice increasingly involved not only legal agents but also non-legal, technocratic experts, such as medical doctors and social workers, who spoke the language of (positive) "science." Over time, the result was the (re)construction of law as a hybrid, organized around intersecting professional discourses and ideologies that marginalized or excluded lay voices, including those of complainants/victims, the accused, and other participants in the criminal process, rendering moralism invisible but leaving it intact.

Although purity and hygienist movements were ubiquitous in western liberal states during this period, it is important to consider the different contexts — both inter-state and intra-state — in which the same or similar ideas were promoted or influenced policies and practices.[13] In this chapter, I scrutinize the contribution of criminal law to the (re)production of healthy citizens and white settler society[14] in British Columbia during the late nineteenth and early twentieth centuries. More specifically, I examine the (re)construction and the effects of the criminal law governing sexual offences with respect to women complainants/victims,[15] doing so through an analysis of cases that went to a Grand Jury or were tried at the Criminal Assizes (i.e., the Supreme Court), held each spring and fall around the province between 1885 and 1940.[16] Data were collected from a variety of sources on 455 cases of seduction, abduction, rape, carnal knowledge, indecent assault (female), and incest.[17] This chapter is based primarily on preliminary hearing transcripts and other archival records containing, or related to, the testimony of medical "experts" and "lay" persons (i.e., the complainants/victims) in these cases.[18]

I begin with a brief discussion of the context in which concerns about citizenship and eugenics emerged in British Columbia. I then document how sexual-offence legislation operated to separate the (re)productively "fit" from "unfit" (young) women and girls. The analysis of the role of doctors at preliminary hearings indicates that medical professionals who testified for the state were increasingly central to the process of defining and responding to "bad" sex and thus to determinations of reproductive fitness. Not surprisingly, the examination of the role of complainants/victims at preliminary hearings in sexual-offences case reveals that they were expected to, and most often did, present their "lay" testimony within the parameters established by the legal and medical experts, thereby reinforcing the latter's accounts. I argue that, overall, the testimony provided by both the medico-legal professionals and the "lay" persons was key to establishing the (dis)reputability of complainants (and accused) in these cases and thus to differentiating between potentially fit citizens and the unsalvageable/unredeemable. Therefore, sexual-offence legislation effectively helped to create and enforce hegemonic conceptions of "fitness" that were the basis for citizenship in developing welfare states.

Eugenics and Citizenship in British Columbia

Most research on purity and hygiene movements in Canada, and indeed most socio-legal history of the late nineteenth and early twentieth centuries, is centred on the experiences of English-speaking Ontario. Arguably, however, one cannot simply extrapolate from developments in that province or elsewhere to British Columbia, since the ideas imported from these other jurisdictions were implemented in a very different context.[19] Adele Perry's point — that the "gender and racial character" of pre-Confederation British Columbia "challenged normative standards of nineteenth-century, Anglo-American social life" — is equally applicable to the province after 1871.[20] B.C. has a very short history of substantial, white settlement relative to eastern Canada.[21] Moreover, post-Confederation British Columbia was characterized by an accelerated pattern of "boom and bust" capitalist development based on primary extraction industries, which often employed single men, rather than by the creation of stable secondary industries and agricultural pursuits that are more conducive to settlement and family life. The question, then, is this: How did the gendered, racialized, sexualized, and class-based conceptions of what constituted "fitness" for citizenship, which came to dominate public culture in many developing welfare states, play out in the "West beyond the West"?

Citizenship assumed immediate importance for provincial authorities when British Columbia joined the Canadian Confederation in 1871. British residents of the province "shared a "charter ideology' ... of themselves as founding people and the others as immigrants,"[22] despite the fact that white settlement was concentrated primarily in Victoria and a few other enclaves such as New Westminster and Nanaimo.[23] In the province as a whole, 71 per cent of the approximately 36,000 people living in British Columbia were First Nation; 4.5 per cent were Asian; and only 24 per cent were British and Continental European.[24] Among the first decisions of the fledgling provincial government at the moment when political citizenship status became significant was the introduction of legislation to disenfranchise the Chinese and Aboriginal populations, who then comprised the majority of British Columbia's residents, even if they were British citizens.[25] Stripping Aboriginal peoples of political rights at the provincial level coincided with the introduction of federal control over First Nation peoples in B.C. under the *Indian Act* of 1868.[26]

Completion of the Canadian Pacific Railway in 1885 and incorporation of Vancouver as a city in 1886 prefaced attempts to transform the entire province of British Columbia into a white settler society. During the late nineteenth and early twentieth centuries, strategies aimed at recruiting white Anglo immigrants were implemented. Concomitantly, repressive strategies for "othering" non-Anglo racial and ethnic groups were put in place, including denial of entry to British Columbia, expulsion from the province, and segregation/containment within the province. Racism translated into law, and policy at all levels of government was central to these strategies.

Following their disenfranchisement, the Chinese and Aboriginal populations in British Columbia continued to be particular targets of exclusionary initiatives. For the former, the emphasis was on preventing reproduction through deportation of the (mentally) "unfit," barring the immigration of the wives and families of Chinese men who were living in Canada, prohibiting the employment of white women in Chinese businesses, and so on.[27] One conspicuous effect of these policies was the emergence of Chinatowns, otherwise known as "vice-towns," which were visible yet spatially contained and inhabited by "evil and inscrutable," "single" men who engaged in all manner of immorality, from gambling to drugs to "white slavery."[28] Analagous approaches to Aboriginal people were implemented, with intense effort concentrated on the "taming" of Aboriginal sexuality.[29] Sexual relations between Aboriginal women and white men and the resultant "mixed race" unions that had been the norm in the absence of marriageable white women became increasingly taboo and subject to legal regulation throughout the nineteenth century.[30] By the turn of the century, segregation on reserves and a system of residential and day schools aimed at the assimilation of First Nation children were in place.[31]

Provincial disenfranchisement of Chinese and Aboriginal peoples took effect in 1874 and was succeeded by a spate of legislation from the 1880s onward that included the successive disenfranchisement of other racialized populations, including Japanese (1895) and East Indian residents (1907). After World War I, authorities developed concerns about non-Anglo white populations, especially those viewed as politically threatening, one result of which was the disenfranchisement of Doukhobors and Mennonites in 1931.[32] Authorities also began to incarcerate Doukhobor men and women for civil disobedience and to apply the residential school "solution" to their children.[33] Despite protests and other forms of resistance,[34] none of these racial and ethnic minorities were re-enfranchised prior to the late 1940s. Successfully "othered," but arguably not conquered, they were marked as aliens who stood in stark contrast to the ideal white, Anglo citizen.

As racialized groups were being disenfranchised or denied the franchise, white working-class men and white women generally were moving in the opposite direction. With regard to the latter, part of the explanation for this reverse development is that white women remained a minority of the population in British Columbia until well into the twentieth century. Although 60 per cent of the province's population was British by 1901 and the ratio of women to men was fairly equal in Victoria by the 1890s, the ratio of non-Aboriginal women to men for the province as a whole did not reach parity until the 1950s.[35] Since white women were critical to the creation of a settler society in British Columbia, their cachet as "mothers of the race" arguably helped them in the quest for citizenship status. While they achieved full political status at the federal level only in 1920 and were not legally "persons" until 1929,[36] white women moved quite rapidly toward political and civil recognition at the local level after British Columbia entered Confederation. In 1873, non-Aboriginal women with property qualifications were accorded the right to vote in municipal affairs, a right that even extended to married women although it "did not include the right to hold office."[37] By 1900, women with property qualifications, or with husbands who met property qualifications, could run for election as school trustees.[38]

figure 16.1

Wedding Party, Ucluelet, BC, 1926.

BC ARCHIVES H-03676.
REPRODUCED BY PERMISSION.

Nonetheless, women in British Columbia did not succeed as quickly as white working-class men in their quest for citizenship status at the provincial level. Despite intense suffrage activities during the late nineteenth century, intransigent governments refused to act for thirty years. When the legislature finally extended the provincial franchise to qualified women in 1917,[39] the decision arguably was stimulated in part by the desire to entrench white settler society in British Columbia, as was the ensuing reform of domestic legislation. By the mid-1920s, B.C. had replaced domestic laws, which were more "antiquated" than those in virtually any other part of Canada, Great Britain, and the United States, with "cutting-edge" social legislation that gave married women new rights as wives and mothers within the family.[40]

It seems clear, however, that women did not qualify for citizenship simply by virtue of being white and meeting property qualifications. They also had to meet the criteria for social citizenship: mental, physical, and moral fitness. Those who failed to measure up — the "criminal," the mentally "defective" or deficient, the "morally delinquent" — often were segregated and subjected to indefinite detention in prisons, psychiatric hospitals, industrial schools, and other institutions.[41] Although racial and ethnic minority women were over-represented in such institutions, the majority of women inmates were white. Whiteness aside, only "fit" women could reproduce and sustain the ideal settler society.

It is the obsession with the purity of white women that runs through the sexual-offence cases analyzed for this chapter. The determination of whether the poor white women who constituted the majority of complainants/victims in these cases were worthy or capable of becoming "mothers of the race" was a central, albeit not always explicitly articulated, concern for all the legal and non-legal experts involved. In the next section, I look at the contribution of medical testimony to determinations of "whiteness" and purity in sexual-offence cases.

Doctors-in-Law

Even a cursory examination of the British Columbia cases reveals a clear trend with respect to the role of medical practitioners in sexual-offence cases from 1885 to 1940. Doctors increasingly provided testimony at preliminary hearings and their testimony became more and more detailed over time. Although most obvious in large, urban centres such as Vancouver, the incorporation of doctors into the court process was also well advanced in rural areas of the province by 1940. At the preliminary hearing stage, testimony came from state-affiliated doctors — police surgeons and doctors who worked in testing laboratories — as well as doctors who may have examined the victims/complainants at the request of family members. Defence counsel did not use their own medical experts, a factor that strongly influenced the way in which defence lawyers conducted cross-examinations at preliminary hearings.

It is instructive to note when medical testimony was introduced at preliminary hearings during this period and when it was not. Overall, most sexual-offence cases involved individuals from the same class, racial or ethnic background. Doctors were most often used as witnesses in cases with white accused and complainants/victims. In one sense this finding is not startling, since the majority of the cases in the study involved white people.[42] In another way, the finding is important because it stands in stark contrast to the lack of medical testimony in the form of depositions or at preliminary hearings in the majority of intra-Aboriginal cases. Part of the explanation for the latter is that Aboriginal accused were more likely to admit guilt at the hearing stage and Aboriginal complainants/victims probably had less access to personal physicians than did their white counterparts. However, the almost routine introduction of medical testimony at hearings involving white people also suggests that the "scientific" determination of sexual purity or impurity was most relevant in such cases; perhaps because, generally speaking, neither accused nor complainant/victim was automatically assumed to be "unfit."

A look at the use of medical testimony in inter-racial sexual-offence cases is illuminating as well. In most cases involving white accused and Aboriginal complainants/victims, no doctor submitted or gave evidence at the preliminary hearing. Although introduced more often in cases with a Chinese accused and white complainant/victim, medical testimony was not presented at preliminary hearings in the majority of such cases. Detailed medical testimony does seem to have been important in a bare majority of the few cases with an Aboriginal accused and a white complainant/victim, perhaps not so much to secure convictions as to legitimate very severe sentences.[43] Although race was not an absolute indicator of case outcomes, what my findings suggest is that "scientific" determination and corroboration of purity and impurity were not imperative in inter-racial cases because the fitness or unfitness of accused and complainants/victims was already assumed.[44]

When doctors did testify in court, what exactly did they do? Ostensibly, they provided "scientific," "factual" evidence about the condition of the complainant/victim at the time of examination or about the condition of her clothing (or sometimes that of the accused), which could be used to prove or disprove the legal guilt of the accused. That is to say, they gave ostensibly value-free, technocratic assessments of her physical, and sometimes emotional/mental, state and of any abnormalities such as stains on clothing.

In reality, however, doctors' assessments for the courts were replete with value-laden assumptions — about women and men, sex and sexuality — which rested on a submerged moralism. They presented ideologically-laced testimony that could be used to determine the guilt or innocence of the accused in two main ways. First, they reinforced the cultural and, to a certain degree, the legal definitions of "legitimate" and "illegitimate" sex that underpinned the laws of incest, rape, carnal knowledge, indecent assault, and seduction. "Good" sex was confined to relations between married partners; "bad" sex was the non-consensual, or fraudulently obtained consensual, penetration of woman by man. Second, doctors' testimony at preliminary hearings helped to establish the credibility or non-credibility — in short, the moral health or delinquency — of the complainant/victim (and, sometimes, the accused). Was she a "good" girl or a "bad" girl?

It is important to bear two things in mind, however: all of the legal and non-legal experts at the preliminary hearings in the sexual-offence cases I reviewed were men; and none seemed to be unaffected by dominant ideologies about family/sex/gender and about justice that were encapsulated in the sexual double standard and in androcentric conceptions of due process, respectively. Through their injection of non-legal knowledge and discourses into the existing legal frameworks, medical practitioners and other experts forged a critical alliance with state legal agents, particularly the police and prosecution. Doctors and other experts, lawyers, and judges all subscribed, in some degree, to patriarchal conceptions of "normal" and "deviant" sex/sexuality and "gender-blind" conceptions of criminal procedure. Therefore, a primary concern for *both* prosecution and defence in sexual-offence cases was the *negotiation* of meanings to be attached to medical and other expert testimony about the complainant/victim. The former most often tried to project an image of purity destroyed while the latter attempted to convey an image of consensual and even "victim-precipitated" sexual relations.

figure 16.2

Supreme Court of BC, Victoria, 1895.

BC ARCHIVES D-00808.
REPRODUCED BY PERMISSION.

REINFORCING CULTURAL AND LEGAL DEFINITIONS
OF SEXUAL OFFENCES

In British Columbia, doctor-witnesses gave oral testimony or submitted written reports that were introduced into evidence at preliminary hearings in sexual-offence cases. They routinely were asked to address, or themselves addressed, a number of standard questions, the answers to which were couched in medico-legal discourses: Where and when was the examination of the complainant/victim conducted? Was the hymen intact? If not, were there signs of recent penetration? If so, how much? Were there any signs of force and of resistance to force, such as injury or other physical marks? Was there evidence of disease, pregnancy or abortion? If so, when did these things occur? What was the outcome of tests conducted on the clothing of the complainant/victim and/or of the accused?

Taken as a whole, expert testimony arguably supported and reinforced dominant conceptions of sexual offences. Specifically, medical experts provided "scientific" information about whether the victim/complainant bore the internal and external marks of recent, forcible (non-consensual) heterosexual sex, or attempted sex, and if the complainant/victim had been a virgin at the time of the alleged assault. Their testimony consistently rested on the (hetero)sexist assumption that sexual assault was the unwanted (or fraudulently obtained) and *complete* penetration of a woman by a man. It is significant that although this was a key element in the cultural definition of (hetero)sexual offences, this was not the legal definition of most such offences. Until 1920, even rape law did not require "proof of emission of seed or total penetration to constitute the act of carnal knowledge."[45] Likewise, in theory, the statutes governing incest and carnal knowledge of a female under the age of 14 did not require corroboration that consent was lacking or obtained through threats, guile, and so on.

The overwhelming emphasis on evidence of consent and full penetration effectively marginalized or excluded all other forms of sexual touching that obviously affected case outcomes. The following testimony given by a doctor at the preliminary hearing in a 1931 carnal-knowledge case involving two accused and a 17-year-old complainant/victim, all of Russian origin, is typical:

> Pros.: Will you tell the court what you found?
> Dr.: I found the girl suffering from contusions and bruises and lacerations around the privates. The hymen and maidenhead was torn and lacerated in several places, and was still bleeding at that time. There was several scratches and bruises on the thighs....

Pros.: In your opinion as a medical doctor, what conclusion did you come to?

Dr.: I came to the conclusion that this girl, who was a virgin, had been forced to sexual intercourse with a good deal of violence....

Pros.: Why do you use the word, with a great deal of violence?

Dr.: There was a great deal of bruises, not only the parts, but around the pelvis and vagina.[46]

Moreover, notwithstanding the fact that medical examinations often took place long after the offence was said to have occurred, doctors did not necessarily qualify their conclusions when they gave evidence in court. At the preliminary hearing in a carnal-knowledge case in 1918, for instance, a doctor who had examined an eleven-year-old girl at the request of her father two weeks after the alleged sexual assault gave definitive testimony that she had not been raped:

I have to report that I could find no evidence of penetration. ... There was no evidence of bruising or discoloration of any kind. There was no abrasions or tearing which would indicate recent rupture of the Hymen. The Hymen was absent. I am of the opinion that this girl has never had sexual relation to the extent of penetration of the male penis.[47]

This is typical medical testimony, but the case outcome was quite atypical. Most often, especially when there was a large time gap between the alleged offence and the examination of the complainant/victim, such a definitive statement from a medical expert would have contributed to the non-prosecution or acquittal of the accused. However, the accused in this case was a male Chinese youth who was found guilty and sent to the Industrial School for two years. It is difficult to imagine that the inter-racial nature of the offence — a racialized boy accused of sexually assaulting a white girl — was not a factor in the outcome of this case.

ESTABLISHING THE CREDIBILITY OR NON-CREDIBILITY OF ACCUSED AND VICTIMS/COMPLAINANTS

The same medical evidence that reinforced legal and cultural definitions of sexual offences also established the credibility or non-credibility of victims/complainants. Were they morally fit or not? While the prosecution used doctors and other experts to try to construct the sexual victimization of young women and children, defence counsel were intent on discrediting medical testimony in order to portray the sexual promiscuity and moral delinquency of the victims/complainants in sexual-offence cases. Thus, the prosecution focused on evidence that attested to the sexual purity of complainants/victims at the time of the offence, their attempts to preserve virginity, and the physical and emotional trauma they experienced.[48]

Nowhere was this emphasis more evident than in cases involving an Aboriginal accused and a white complainant/victim. In a 1922 case on Vancouver Island, an "Indian" was charged with carnal knowledge of a 17-year-old young woman who was assaulted as she passed by reserve lands during her walk home after a music rehearsal. At the preliminary hearing, the prosecutor elicited the following medical testimony from the doctor who examined her after the assault:

> Dr.: [Miss B. was] in a condition of semi collapse and shock, and there were scratches and bruises on the front part and sides of her neck... I ordered her to bed, and transferred her after that to the hospital for the purpose of further examination, and owing to the fact that she was suffering so much from shock ... [At the hospital, I] found a bruising of the genitals and laceration...the pulse was fast. She was suffering from shock. ... In my opinion, penetration [by a man's penis] caused bruises on the hymen.[49]

The doctor went on to say that Miss B.'s bruises and scratches could have been caused by "attempts at choking" and that although she had "practically recovered" a week after being discharged from the hospital, "she is still nervous."[50] Arguably, this testimony contributed to the construction of the complainant/victim as purity defiled and, as indicated earlier, helped legitimate the sentence of 15 years in the B.C. Penitentiary meted out to the convicted man.[51]

In contrast to the prosecutorial strategy of introducing testimony about innocence spoiled or corrupted, the defence concentrated on the deconstruction of such testimony in an attempt to cast reasonable doubt on the veracity, and hence the purity, of the complainant/victim. The following exchange, taken from the preliminary hearing in a 1931 rape case involving a 22-year-old woman and in which both accused and complainant/victim were white, is typical of defence cross-examination strategies and tactics: Try to cast doubt on the expert witness himself and try to get the expert witness to admit that stains and physical marks on the complainant/victim and her clothing might not necessarily have been the result of a sexual assault.

DC: Have you given evidence in a rape case before?
Dr.: Yes.

DC: Have you examined the clothing of the girl?
Dr.: No.

DC: From a medical legal point of view, would the condition of the clothing have anything to do as to whether the girl had been raped?
Dr.: It might have.

DC: If the girl had been raped, would you expect to find torn clothes?
Dr.: It would be a natural thing.

DC: The marks on the girl could have been made by some other agency?
Dr.: Yes, that is very possible, a number of agencies could cause bruises.

DC: I suggest that an inflammation of the vagina, such as you say existed, could be from other causes than rape.
Dr.: There are a great many causes for it.[52]

While a doctor's testimony was never the sole determinant of a case outcome, his ability to withstand defence challenges was very important. In this case, for instance, the doctor's testimony was weakened through cross-examination. Arguably this was one of the factors that contributed to the conviction of the accused for the lesser offence of common assault with a strong recommendation for mercy. He received a suspended sentence; a conviction for rape would have meant time in prison.

Medical testimony about venereal disease in particular was important to determinations of sexual purity and impurity, since no other aspect of sexual-offence cases spoke so directly to the moral health or delinquency of the complainant/victim (and the accused). Doctors were routinely questioned about the presence or absence of disease and, in the vast majority of cases reviewed for this study, their medical examinations of complainants/victims revealed no evidence of VD. Not surprisingly, the ten cases in which VD was found evoked much jockeying between prosecution and defence, with the former trying to identify the accused and the latter attempting to depict the complainant/victim as the source of the disease.

The prosecution seems to have succeeded in targeting the accused when very young white children had contracted venereal disease. Two cases — one involving a ten-year-old girl and the other a six-year-old girl — resulted in conviction of the accused.[53] Defence counsel tried and failed to depict the ten-year-old as immoral and the six-year-old as an unreliable witness. At the preliminary hearing of the first case, for instance, the family doctor testified that he had treated not only the complainant/victim but also her brother and another young girl who lived in the same house (as did the accused) for gonorrhoea. However, the defence was unable to lead him to say that the girl could have been infected by her brother. Likewise, the police surgeon testified that, while he had found no evidence of active gonorrhoea in the accused, "there are some germs in there ... I should say it is an old attack." The defence was unsuccessful in getting him to state that the accused was probably not infectious when the children contracted VD.[54]

Defence counsel had an easier time constructing older complainants/victims as the source of disease, especially if they were not white. For instance, two intra-Aboriginal cases involving young women who were 12 and 19 years old resulted in outcomes of Not Guilty and No Bill respectively,[55] despite preliminary hearing testimony which revealed that both young women had contracted venereal disease after being sexually assaulted. In one case, a doctor had examined and found evidence of gonorrhoea in the accused as well as the complainant/victim."[56] Defence counsel were seemingly able to trade successfully on pervasive assumptions about the promiscuity of Aboriginal women, thereby transforming them into the carriers of disease.

What needs to be borne in mind, however, is that the prosecution and defence, as well as judges and non-legal experts, had a shared understanding of what differentiated founded from unfounded sexual-offence cases, of who was a "true" victim of such offences. They were in basic agreement that legitimate victims were women who were young and virginal; who were persuaded to consent to sex through false inducements or threats or, alternatively, were victimized in public spaces by predatory strangers; who strenuously resisted their attackers; and who could provide corroborating evidence of the offence. These ideological assumptions obviously influenced the way in which sexual-offence cases were processed in British Columbia (and elsewhere). Generally speaking, it is probably accurate to say that cases of incest, rape, carnal knowledge, indecent assault, and seduction which did not fit these ideological parameters could not be prosecuted successfully.

(Young) Women-in-Law

Clearly, then, the extent to which the testimony of a complainant/victim confirmed her status as a "legitimate" victim was key to the successful prosecution of sexual-offence cases as well. Regardless of medical and other testimony, her presentation of self could make or break a prosecutor's case. Although they frequently had class, "race," sexual orientation, and age in common, the (young) women who testified in sexual-offence cases did not (re)present themselves to the courts in uniform ways. By the time of the preliminary hearing, a complainant/victim usually had told her story a number of times — to parents or other caretakers, to the police, and perhaps to medical practitioners. Undoubtedly, the responses of these various adults to her account of events affected the way in which she presented her testimony at the preliminary hearing and, later, at the trial if the case went forward. Thus, some young women framed their experiences in terms of hegemonic, public, and professional discourses while others attempted to tell (or not tell) their stories in their own way.

figure 16.3

Miners' Union Dance, East Kootenay, 1 July 1903.

BC ARCHIVES C-00896. REPRODUCED BY PERMISSION.

In the British Columbia cases, complainants/victims' responses to questioning by prosecution and defence lawyers at preliminary hearings took three main forms. Some answered all questions directly and in "appropriate" language. Others answered all questions in their own way despite attempts to make them use "appropriate" language. Still others were reticent or totally unable to answer questions or to tell what happened to them. Their narratives of events (i.e., their testimony) demonstrate both accommodation to and non-compliance with the accounts constructed by medico-legal professionals.

FOLLOWING CONVENTIONAL SCRIPTS

In most of the cases examined, complainants/victims did respond to questioning in "appropriate" language. That is, they used the standard euphemisms for bodily parts and bodily functions that were part of public discourse and, sometimes, of medico-legal testimony as well: "in the family way," not pregnant; "sickness" or "my monthlies," not menstruation; "connection" or "interfering with me," not sexual intercourse, etc. Moreover, they seemingly did so without hesitation or pressure. The following excerpt from the testimony of an 11-year old girl in a 1918 carnal-knowledge case illustrates the language typically used by complainants/victims:

> [The accused] pulled up my clothes and pulled down my pants. ... He had his pants unbuttoned. I saw his *privates*. He tried to get his *privates* into me. It hurt a little bit. My *privates* have been feeling sore since.[57]

In a similar vein, the 15-year old complainant/victim in a 1911 carnal knowledge case described the actions of the accused as follows:

> He knocked me down on the couch, he lifted my clothes, he held me down, he had *connection* with me, he gave me money so as I would not tell my mother. ... The child was born on 15th August. The accused is [the] only man that ever *bothered with me.*[58]

Why did complainants/victims follow conventional scripts when they testified in court? One obvious explanation is that they were influenced, or even coached in advance, by the police, prosecution or other adults. Another compelling possibility is that complainants/victims themselves were imbued with dominant ideologies and discourses about sex/sexuality, gender relations, family, and so on. Therefore, the euphemistic language they often used to talk about bodily parts and functions was the public discourse employed by the majority of the (lay) population. In short, most complainants/victims in sexual-offence cases already were familiar with the scripts that they followed in presenting their testimony to the courts. Generally speaking, being white, as were the two complainants/victims quoted above, and adhering to a conventional script were necessary, albeit not always sufficient, conditions for achieving a successful case outcome.

FOLLOWING UNCONVENTIONAL SCRIPTS

While most complainants/victims in the British Columbia cases followed the norms of conventional discourses about sex and sexual offences in their court testimony, a few decidedly did not. Dispensing with euphemisms, they described their experiences in the explicit idiom of popular culture. As one young woman told the court in describing her experience of attempted rape by the accused: "He fucked me ... and left me lying there."[59] Her testimony, in conjunction with other testimony affirming her "moral delinquency," not surprisingly led to the acquittal of the accused. In a 1920 carnal-knowledge case, the 13-year-old complainant/victim used similarly graphic language about the accused. She explained to the court that he took down her pants and "started to f-u-c-k"; he hurt her with "his prick"; he put it "in my c-u-n-t."[60] Again, the girl's account reinforced other negative testimony about her that was presented at the preliminary hearing. As a result, a Grand Jury declared "No Bill" and this case did not even proceed to trial.

The complainants/victims in both of the above cases were white, although one was of Russian origin. But their "whiteness" could not compensate for their obvious familiarity with explicit sexual language and their knowledge of what sexual intercourse was about. "Pure" young women would not have such knowledge about sex and most certainly would never use anything but the acceptable euphemisms to speak about bodily parts and functions. Those who did clearly identified themselves as "moral delinquents" and non-credible witnesses whose testimony was suspect and ought not to be used to convict an accused.

FOLLOWING NO SCRIPTS

Relatively few young women used explicitly sexual language in the accounts of incest, carnal knowledge, rape, indecent assault, and seduction that they presented in court, however. A more frequent problem confronted by complainants/victims was extreme difficulty or even inability to testify at all. There were different reasons for this problem, but the age of a witness was among the more important factors. Among older witnesses, feelings of embarrassment and shame about their experiences were common, and speaking inaudibly in court was often the result. Fear and intimidation also made young women inarticulate or silent in court. Moreover, the legal authorities often lacked empathy for their situation, as the following excerpt from a 1925 incest case involving an 11-year-old girl attests:

> Court: Now there is no use in the girl whispering these things. If I
> can't hear the evidence I can't act on it, so that is all there is to that.
> Pros.: You will have to speak a little louder.
> Court: Speak up please. We can't wait all morning here. How long
> did your father sleep with you? Did he only sleep for one night
> with you?
> Witness: No.[61]

Another incest case was dismissed by the Court after the Crown's principal witness "failed in the box."[62]

A further problem arose when complainants/victims could not name or describe the bodily parts and actions involved in a sexual offence. Most often, this was an issue with very young female children whose descriptions of sexual assault incorporated the euphemistic "baby" language — referring to the "pee" of the accused, for instance — that they had learned from their parents or other adults. Being able to provide an accurate description of the sexual assault and to identify the body parts involved was required if the testimony of an unsworn child was to have any credence at all.

Sometimes she could deliver, as illustrated by the following excerpt from the preliminary hearing testimony of a six-year-old girl:

> [The accused] took down my pants and sucked me, then he hurt
> me. When I was alone in the room someone reached in the room
> and took a bottle or box out of the room. He undone his pants and
> laid his on top of me and hurt me. He told me to come back and
> asked me to kiss him and give me money to get ice cream [signed
> with an X].[63]

The child's account, in tandem with the medical evidence that she had contracted venereal disease after the date of the alleged offence, contributed to the conviction of the accused for indecent assault. More commonly, however, very young girls could not present such clear evidence in court. They made contradictory or inconsistent statements that ultimately were discounted; or they were not allowed to give evidence at all because they could not be sworn; or they could not give evidence because they were physically unable to appear in court.

An example of the latter situation occurred in a 1917 case in which the accused was charged with carnal knowledge of a four-year-old girl. At the preliminary hearing, the doctor testified that "there was so much injury that I sent her at once to the hospital" and that such injuries "would occur in an assault upon her with intention to rape I suppose." The little girl was still under treatment. A number of other witnesses saw the accused in and around the child's house on the night in question; at least two testified to the amount of blood "between her legs" the following morning, but no one was able to positively place him with the little girl. Although the case went forward to trial, the jury returned a Not Guilty verdict.[64] Obviously, whiteness and innocence were no guarantee that justice would be done.

Conclusion

In keeping with other research,[65] this analysis of sexual-offence cases suggests that it is important not to homogenize the experiences of jurisdictions that undergo similar, but not identical, historical change and development. Although the concerns of purity advocates and hygienists in British Columbia mirrored those of reformers elsewhere, they were expressed and acted upon in a unique historical context. In contrast to Ontario, for instance, reform campaigns and debates about citizenship issues in B.C. during the late nineteenth and early twentieth centuries occurred concomitantly with the transformation of the province: from a white settler colony in which the Anglo-Celtic population was a small minority, to a white settler society in which residents of British origin comprised the majority. Likewise, the scarcity of white women relative to men in British Columbia during the same period — 27 per cent of the non-Aboriginal adult population in 1870 and still only 46 per cent in 1941 — profoundly influenced the ways in which citizenship was conceptualized and regulated in the province.[66] Thus, the contribution of criminal law to the creation of a white settler society in the province was both similar to and different from the role played by law elsewhere.

Some might ask precisely how criminal law was implicated in the development of a white settler society in the province. After all, the British Columbia Supreme Court dealt with relatively few sexual-offence cases each year between 1885 and 1940. In B.C., as in other jurisdictions, "high justice" played a significant symbolic and ideological role.[67] The Criminal Assizes were one of the highlights of public life each spring and fall in Victoria, Vancouver, and all of the centres on the judicial circuit outside those cities. The judges and the cases being tried always received extensive coverage in local media and the trials were usually well attended. Arguably, then, the Supreme Court played an important educative role in disseminating and sustaining dominant conceptions of appropriate and inappropriate sexual and social relations.

My analysis of testimony by medico-legal professionals and "lay" complainants/victims in sexual-offence cases illustrates how criminal law worked symbolically and ideologically to reinforce and reproduce hierarchical social relations within the context of conceptions of purity and "fitness" that prevailed in the "West beyond the West." First, such testimony contributed to legal decisions that in effect distinguished between (racialized) "aliens" and "good" (white) citizens. Assumptions about the sexuality of Aboriginal, Chinese, and, to a lesser extent, eastern European populations in British Columbia disadvantaged both accused and complainants/victims in sexual-offence cases. As the literature documenting the way in which the sexuality of racialized men and women is equated with that of sub-humans reveals, racialized men are viewed as "natural" sexual predators and racialized women as innately wild and "promiscuous." With regard to the latter, various writers have pointed out that the "Madonna-whore" dichotomy applies only to white women; racialized women are either "prostitutes" or "beasts of burden."[68]

In the B.C. context, as discussed earlier, white men were rarely convicted of sexual offences against Aboriginal women; but Aboriginal and, most often, Chinese men accused of assaulting white women were convicted and punished. This conviction pattern, as well as the absence of medical testimony at preliminary hearings of many inter-racial cases, lends support to the argument that conceptions of sexuality are heavily racialized. Expert testimony was not crucial to the determination of moral health in such cases because the "purity" of white accused and the immorality of both racialized accused and complainants/victims were assumed *a priori*. What racialized people did among themselves and to each other was of little interest to white settler society since they posed no direct threat to the moral and social purity of the white population. What was of grave concern was the "pollution" of white women by racialized men and of white men by Aboriginal women. And the most threatening situations were those where Aboriginal peoples and Chinese men lived in close proximity or had daily contact with white settlement. Yet these situations were unavoidable because white settlements relied on the work performed and the goods and services provided by Chinese and Aboriginal peoples who therefore could not be confined to Chinatowns and reserves. Criminal law, and specifically Supreme Court judgments, reiterated and reaffirmed the boundaries between "alien" and "citizen" when breaches occurred.

Second, expert testimony as well as that of complainants/victims contributed to legal decisions that effectively distinguished between salvageable (white) women who, despite their defilement, could still be(come) "mothers of the race" and of future citizens, and those who were irredeemable. These distinctions were both class-based and gendered. Since most white accused and complainants/victims were from the working classes, court decisions in part were pronouncements on which of the parties could assume or resume a place in respectable working class society. Gendered assumptions about the innate sexuality of white women and men encapsulated in the sexual double standard more clearly disadvantaged complainants/victims than accused in court. As many writers have illustrated,[69] the ideas that men need sexual diversity and that women are instinctively maternal, even asexual, have exerted an enduring influence on legal decision-making. What law does is differentiate between the "Madonnas," who demonstrate their adherence to sexual norms, and the "whores," who do not.

Despite concerns about the lack of marriageable white women in British Columbia, a sizeable number of white complainants/victims in sexual-offence cases were found to be sexually "impure." Men were convicted in only a slight majority of the 455 cases that went to a Grand Jury and/or the Supreme Court between 1885 and 1940, most of which involved white accused and complainants. In the context of prevailing assumptions about Anglo-Celtic superiority, medical testimony became more and more important to the "scientific" determination of sexual (im)purity in intra-racial cases involving white women and men. Criminal law, including expert testimony, highlighted the gendered expectations of citizenship for white women and men and underlined the boundaries between the sexually "fit" and unfit." Whether they passed or failed the sexual fitness test, however, many white women undoubtedly left court and returned to the paternal authority of fathers and husbands or of the state.

Thus, the judgements of the British Columbia Supreme Court in sexual-offence cases helped to (re)produce and reinforce hierarchical relations of race, class, and gender as a white settler society and welfare state took shape in the province. It would be misleading, however, to leave the impression that legal decision-making was seamless and/or uncontested. For instance, the Supreme Court emphasis on the "rule of law" mitigated some of the more overt attempts to criminalize "aliens." Presumptions of "fairness" and "due process" seemed to work in favour of racial and ethnic minority accused in cases where charges seemed to be the direct result of racism and scapegoating on the part of white complainants/victims or, more commonly, their families. A number of cases involving Chinese or non-Anglo white men (e.g., Greeks or Italians) resulted in Not Guilty outcomes.[70]

Likewise, in keeping with research on sexual offences in other jurisdictions,[71] my data indicate that (young) women often proactively invoked law and that, when they testified about their experiences of incest, rape, and carnal knowledge, they were not merely passive objects who could be manipulated at will by medico-legal authorities. Nonetheless, the data on case out-comes also reveal that complainants/victims were fighting against the odds to achieve redress through law. Moreover, the best outcomes for com-plainants/victims in sexual-offence cases were achieved when they fitted into and accommodated themselves to the status quo: to the existing medico-legal framework, with its embedded assumptions about the normality of (het-ero)sexuality and hierarchical social relations, which was being continually (re)constructed by medico-legal experts. The irony is that, by doing so, they helped to entrench that framework. Ultimately, women's testimony in sex-ual-offence cases was more help than hindrance in the construction of a white settler society in British Columbia wherein their citizenship status was inextricably linked to their (re)productive "fitness."

Notes

1. An earlier version of this chapter was presented at the B.C. Studies conference, "Beyond Hope," in Kamloops, B.C., May 2001. Thanks to Robert A. Campbell for his constructive commentary, and to Robert Adamoski and Robert Menzies for additional comments, on that draft. I also am grateful to the Social Sciences and Humanities Research Council (SSHRC) for project funding that enabled me to complete the research on which this chapter is based. Tamara Vrooman and staff at the B.C. Archives provided invaluable assistance during the data-collection process.

2. British Columbia Archives (hereafter BCARS), Attorney General, Document Series 1857-1966, GR0419, v.244, #107, 1921. The quotation is excerpted from a handwritten draft of the Crown Attorney's address to the jury in a rape trial.

3. For a sampling of the vast literature on these movements, see Lucy Bland, *Banishing the Beast: English Feminism and Sexual Morality, 1885-1914* (London: Penguin Books, 1995); Michel Foucault, *The History of Sexuality*. vol.1 (New York: Vintage Books, 1980); David Garland, *Punishment and Welfare* (Brookfield, VT: Gower, 1985); Alan Hunt, *Governing Morals: A Social History of Moral Regulation* (Cambridge: Cambridge University Press, 1999); Angus McLaren, *Our Own Master Race: Eugenics in Canada, 1885-1945* (Toronto: McClelland and Stewart, 1990); Frank Mort, *Dangerous Sexualities: Medico-Moral Politics in England Since 1830* (London: Routledge & Kegan Paul, 1987); Nicole Rafter, *Creating Born Criminals* (Urbana: University of Illinois Press, 1997); Mariana Valverde, *The Age of Light, Soap, and Water* (Toronto: McClelland and Stewart, 1991); Judith Walkowitz, *Prostitution and Victorian Society: Women, Class and the State* (Cambridge: Cambridge University Press, 1980), *City of Dreadful Delight: Narratives of Sexual Danger in Late-Victorian London* (Chicago: University of Chicago Press, 1992).

4. In addition to the works listed in n.3 above, see also Kay Anderson, *Vancouver's Chinatown: Racial Discourse in Canada, 1875-1980* (Montreal: McGill-Queen's University Press, 1991); Constance Backhouse, *Colour Coded: A Legal History of Racism in Canada, 1900-1950* (Toronto: University of Toronto Press & The Osgoode Society, 1999); Clayton Mosher, *Discrimination and Denial: Systemic Racism in Ontario's Legal and Criminal Justice Systems, 1892-1961* (Toronto: University of Toronto Press, 1998).

5. Here I use quotation marks to indicate that race (and analagous terms such as white) is a socially constructed, historically and culturally specific concept. Hereafter, to avoid repeti-tion, I have not placed these terms in quotation marks.

6. See Mimi Ajzenstadt, "Cycles of Control: Alcohol Regulation and the Construction of Gender Role, British Columbia 1870-1925," *International Journal of Canadian Studies* 11 (1995): 101-20; Allan M. Brandt, *No Magic Bullet: A Social History of Venereal Disease in the United States Since 1880* (Oxford: Oxford University Press, 1985); Robert A. Campbell, *Sit Down and Drink Your Beer: Regulating Vancouver's Beer Parlours, 1925-1954* (Toronto: University of Toronto Press, 2001); Jay Cassel, *The Secret Plague: Venereal Disease in Canada 1838-1939* (Toronto: University of Toronto Press, 1987); John P.S. McLaren, "Chasing the 'Social Evil': Moral Fervour and the Evolution of Canada's Prostitution Laws, 1867-1917," *Canadian Journal of Law and Society* 1 (1986): 125-65; Robert Menzies, "Governing Mentalities: The Deportation of 'Insane' and 'Feebleminded' Immigrants Out of British Columbia From Confederation to World War II," *Canadian Journal of Law and Society* 12, 2 (Fall 1998): 135-73; Walkowitz, *Prostitution and Victorian Society*.
7. Although the first Canadian citizenship law was not implemented until 1947, the issue of who "qualified" or not for various forms of citizenship (e.g., civil, political, social) was a staple of public discourse and culture during the late nineteenth and early twentieth centuries in Canada. See, e.g., Anderson, *Vancouver's Chinatown*; Carol Lee Bacchi, *Liberation Deferred? The Ideas of the English-Canadian Suffragists, 1877-1918* (Toronto: University of Toronto Press, 1983); Catherine L. Cleverdon, *The Woman Suffrage Movement in Canada*, 2nd ed. (Toronto: University of Toronto Press, 1974); Renisa Mawani, "In Between and Out of Place: Racial Hybridity, Liquor and the Law in Late 19th and Early 20th Century British Columbia," *Canadian Journal of Law and Society* 15 (2000), 9-38; James W. St. G. Walker, *"Race," Rights, and the Law in the Supreme Court of Canada* (Toronto: The Osgoode Society for Legal History, 1997).
8. Carolyn Strange and Tina Loo, *Making Good: Law and Moral Regulation in Canada, 1867-1939* (Toronto: University of Toronto Press, 1997).
9. Katherine Arnup, *Education for Motherhood: Advice for Mothers in Twentieth-Century Canada* (Toronto: University of Toronto Press, 1994); Dorothy E. Chunn, "A Little Sex Can Be a Dangerous Thing: Regulating Sexuality, Venereal Disease and Reproduction in British Columbia, 1919-1945," in *Challenging the Public/Private Divide: Feminism, Law, and Public Policy*, ed. Susan B. Boyd (Toronto: University of Toronto Press, 1997); Renisa Mawani, "'Educational Prophylaxis': Venereal Disease Control and the Regulation of Sexuality in British Columbia and Canada, 1900-1930," (M.A. Thesis, Simon Fraser University, 1996).
10. Dorothy E. Chunn, *From Punishment To Doing Good: Family Courts and Socialized Justice in Ontario, 1880-1940* (Toronto: University of Toronto Press, 1992); Jacques Donzelot, *The Policing of Families* (New York: Pantheon Books, 1979); Garland, *Punishment and Welfare*; Linda Gordon, *Heroes of Their Own Lives: The Politics and History of Family Violence* (New York: Penguin, 1988); Mary Odem, *Delinquent Daughters: Protecting and Policing Adolescent Female Sexuality in the United States, 1885-1920* (Chapel Hill: University of North Carolina Press, 1995); Joan Sangster, *Regulating Girls and Women: Sexuality, Family, and the Law in Ontario, 1920-1960* (Toronto: Oxford University Press, 2001).
11. Although this chapter looks at sexual offences *per se*, reformers viewed criminal and non-criminal law as a vehicle for regulating all aspects of sex, sexuality, and reproduction, including abortion, birth control, sterilization, venereal diseases, prostitution, and related activities. See Cassel, *The Secret Plague*; Angus McLaren and Arlene McLaren, *The Bedroom and the State: The Changing Practices and Politics of Contraception and Abortion in Canada, 1880-1997*, 2nd. ed. (Toronto: Oxford University Press, 1997); McLaren, *Our Own Master Race*.
12. Lesbian relationships and marital rape were significant exceptions to this trend. New (hetero)sexual offences included indecent assault (female), carnal knowledge, bigamy; reform of old law included the criminalization of seduction. New (homo)sexual offences included indecent assault (male). In this paper, I focus on (hetero)sexual offences.
13. For discussions of this point in relation to British Columbia, see Karen Dubinsky and Adam Givertz, "'It was Only a Matter of Passion': Masculinity and Sexual Danger," in *Gendered Pasts: Historical Essays in Femininity and Masculinity in Canada*, ed. Kathryn McPherson, Cecilia Morgan, and Nancy M. Forestell (Toronto: Oxford University Press, 1999); Adele

Perry, *On the Edge of Empire: Gender, Race, and the Making of British Columbia, 1849-1871* (Toronto: University of Toronto Press, 2001).

14. Settler societies "[fall] along a continuum rather than within clear and fixed boundaries," but in general terms they are "societies in which Europeans have settled, where their descendants have remained politically dominant over indigenous peoples, and where a heterogeneous society has developed in class, ethnic and racial terms...." Daiva Stasiulis and Nira Yuval-Davis, "Introduction: Beyond Dichotomies – Gender, Race, Ethnicity and Class in Settler Societies," in *Unsettling Settler Societies: Articulations of Gender, Race, Ethnicity and Class*, ed. Stasiulis and Yuval-Davis (London: Sage, 1995), 3.

15. Here and throughout the chapter, I use the term "complainants/victims" to indicate that the (young) women involved in sexual-offence cases were active as well as reactive.

16. During this period, the Supreme Court of British Columbia operated as a circuit court. Twice a year, judges based in Victoria and the Lower Mainland travelled to smaller centres throughout the province (e.g., Kamloops, Prince Rupert, Nanaimo) to preside over trials. See David R. Verchere, *A Progression of Judges: A History of the Supreme Court of British Columbia* (Vancouver: UBC Press, 1988), 63-64.

17. The categorization of sexual offences in Canadian criminal law during this period is instructive of prevailing moral and social attitudes. Incest and seduction were classified as "offences against morality"; indecent assault (female), carnal knowledge, and rape as "offences against the person/reputation"; and abduction of a girl under the age of 16 as an "offence against parental rights." See *The Criminal Code*, 55-56 Vict., 1892, c.29.

18. I acknowledge the problems associated with reliance on case file data, but I concur with those who believe that, with judicious interpretation, such data can yield important historical insights. See Gordon, *Heroes of Their Own Lives*, 12-20, Appendix A; *On the Case: Explorations in Social History*, eds. Franca Iacovetta and Wendy Mitchinson (Toronto: University of Toronto Press, 1998).

19. For a study of (hetero)sexual offences in Ontario during this time period, see Karen Dubinsky, *Improper Advances: Rape and Heterosexual Conflict in Ontario, 1880-1929* (Chicago: The University of Chicago Press, 1993). See also Lynette Finch, *The Classing Gaze: Sexuality, Class and Surveillance* (Sydney: Allen and Unwin, 1993).

20. Perry, *On the Edge of Empire*, 3.

21. Jean Barman, *The West Beyond the West: A History of British Columbia*, 2nd ed. (Toronto: University of Toronto Press, 1996); Dara Culhane, *The Pleasure of the Crown: Anthropology, Law and First Nations* (Vancouver: Talonbooks, 1998).

22. John Porter, cited in Anderson, *Vancouver's Chinatown*, 47.

23. Perry, *On the Edge of Empire*, 13. See also Frances Abele and Daiva Stasiulis, "Canada as a 'White Settler Colony': What about Natives and Immigrants?" in *The New Canadian Political Economy*, ed. Wallace Clement and Glen Williams (Montreal: McGill-Queen's University Press, 1989), 240-77; Daiva Stasiulis and Radha Jhappan, "The Fractious Politics of a Settler Society: Canada," in *Unsettling Settler Societies*, ed. Stasiulis and Yuval-Davis, 95-131.

24. Barman, *The West Beyond the West*, 379.

25. Anderson, *Vancouver's Chinatown*, 47; see also Patricia Roy, *A White Man's Province: British Columbia Politicians and Chinese and Japanese Immigrants, 1858-1914* (Vancouver, UBC Press, 1989); Peter Ward, *White Canada Forever: Popular Attitudes and Public Policy Toward Orientals in British Columbia*, 2nd ed. (Montreal: McGill-Queen's University Press, 1990).

26. Barman, *The West Beyond the West*, 154; Culhane, *The Pleasure of the Crown*, 214.

27. See n. 25 above; see also Robert Menzies, "Race, Reason and Regulation: British Columbia's Mass Exile of Chinese 'Lunatics' Aboard the *Empress of Russia*, 9 February 1935," in *Regulating Lives: Historical Essays on the State, Society, the Individual and the Law*, ed. John McLaren, Robert Menzies, and Dorothy E. Chunn (Vancouver: UBC Press, forthcoming 2002).

28. Anderson, *Vancouver's Chinatown*, 92.

29. Jean Barman, "Taming Aboriginal Sexuality: Gender, Power and Race in British Columbia, 1850-1900," *BC Studies* 115-16 (1997-98), 237-66.

30. Barman, "Taming Aboriginal Sexuality"; see also Mawani, "In Between and Out of Place"; Perry, *On the Edge of Empire*, 48-78; Sylvia Van Kirk, *Many Tender Ties: Women in Fur-Trade Society, 1670-1870* (Winnipeg: Watson Dwyer, 1999 [1980]).

31. Barman, *The West Beyond the West*; Culhane, *The Pleasure of the Crown*.

32. Barman, *The West Beyond the West*, 379.

33. John McLaren, "Creating 'Slaves of Satan' or 'New Canadians'? The Law, Education, and the Socialization of Doukhobor Children, 1911-1935," in *Essays in the History of Canadian Law: British Columbia and the Yukon*, ed. Hamar Foster and John McLaren (Toronto: The Osgoode Society, 1995), 352-85.

34. McLaren, "Creating 'Slaves of Satan' or 'New Canadians'?"; see also Anderson, *Vancouver's Chinatown*; Culhane, *The Pleasure of the Crown*.

35. Barman, *The West Beyond the West*, 385.

36. Cleverdon, *The Woman Suffrage Movement in Canada*, 105-55.

37. Cleverdon, *The Woman Suffrage Movement in Canada*, 87.

38. Cleverdon, *The Woman Suffrage Movement in Canada*, 87-88.

39. Cleverdon, *The Woman Suffrage Movement in Canada*, 100-01. Full (white) male suffrage was introduced in 1876. Barman, *The West Beyond the West*, 101.

40. Elsie Gregory MacGill, *My Mother the Judge* (Toronto: PMA Books, 1981 [1955]), 118-19, 171.

41. Dorothy E. Chunn and Robert Menzies, "Out of Mind, Out of Law: The Regulation of 'Criminally Insane' Women Inside British Columbia's Public Mental Hospitals, 1888-1973," *Canadian Journal of Women and the Law* 10, 2 (1998): 306-37; Indiana Matters, "Sinners or Sinned Against? Historical Aspects of Female Juvenile Delinquency in British Columbia," in *Not Just Pin Money: Selected Essays on the History of Women's Work in British Columbia*, ed. Barbara Latham and Roberta Lazdro (Victoria: Camosun College, 1984); Robert Menzies and Dorothy E. Chunn, "The Gender Politics of Criminal Insanity: 'Order-in-Council' Women in British Columbia, 1888-1950," *Histoire sociale/Social History* 31, 62 (1999): 241-79.

42. Racial and ethnic identification of accused and complainants/victims was not clear in all cases, but approximately 80 per cent of the cases involved white women and men.

43. See BCARS, Attorney General, Document Series 1857-1966, GR0419, v.93, #63, 1902; v.116, #72, 1906; v.266, #32, 1923; v.271, #80, 1923. The respective sentences in these cases were 21 years (two convicted Aboriginal men); life imprisonment; 15 years; 15 years and 15 lashes. In contrast, if white men were convicted at all in cases involving Aboriginal women complainants/victims, overall they received less severe sentences, including prison terms. I am not suggesting that the Aboriginal accused were innocent and the white accused guilty, but only that the disparity in case outcomes is notable.

44. On "racialized" conceptions of sexuality, see Barman, "The Taming of Aboriginal Sexuality"; Patricia Collins, *Black Feminist Thought: Knowledge, Consciousness, and the Politics of Empowerment* (London: Harper-Collins, 1990); Perry, *On the Edge of Empire*.

45. Terry Chapman, "'Inquiring Minds Want To Know': The Handling of Children in Sex Assault Cases in the Canadian West, 1890-1920," in *Dimensions of Childhood: Essays on the History of Children and Youth in Canada*, ed. Russell Smandych, Gordon Dodds, and Alvin Esau (Winnipeg: Legal Research Institute of the University of Manitoba, 1991), 194-95.

46. BCARS, Attorney General, Document Series 1857-1966, GR0419, v.372, #36, 1931.

47. BCARS, v.214, #31, 1918.

48. See, e.g., BCARS, v.272, #36, 1931.

49. BCARS, v.266, #32, 1923.

50. BCARS, v.266, #32, 1923.

51. BCARS, v.266, #32, 1923. See n. 43.

52. BCARS, v.377, #49, 1931.

53. BCARS, v.167, #7, 1913; v.181, #231, 1913.

54. BCARS, v.167, #7, 1913.

55. BCARS, v.95, #11, 1903; v.176, #153, 1913.

56. BCARS, v.176, #153, 1913.

57. BCARS, v.214, #31, 1918, emphasis added.

58. BCARS, v.150, #64, 1911, emphasis added.

59. BCARS, v.177, #171, 1913.
60. BCARS, v.231, #11, 1920.
61. BCARS, v.297, #131, 1925.
62. *The Kamloops Telegram*, 2 June 1921, p.1.
63. BCARS, v.181, #231, 1913.
64. BCARS, v.210, #57, 1917.
65. See n. 13 above.
66. Barman, *The West Beyond the West*, 385.
67. Douglas Hay, "Time, Inequality and Law's Violence," in *Law's Violence*, ed. Austin Sarat and Thomas R. Kearns (Ann Arbor: University of Michigan Press, 1992).
68. See n. 44 above.
69. See, e.g., Dubinsky, *Improper Advances*; Finch, *The Classing Gaze*; Carol Smart, *Law, Crime and Sexuality: Essays in Feminism* (New York: Routledge, 1995).
70. For an analagous finding with respect to B.C. Supreme Court decisions, see John McLaren, "The Early British Columbia Supreme Court and the 'Chinese Question': Echoes of the Rule of Law," *Manitoba Law Journal* 20 (1990): 107-47.
71. See Chapman, "'Inquiring Minds Want to Know'"; Dubinsky, *Improper Advances*; Finch, *Classing the Gaze*; Gordon, *Heroes of Their Own Lives*; Sangster, *Regulating Girls and Women*.

chapter seventeen

"UNFIT" CITIZENS AND THE B.C. ROYAL COMMISSION ON MENTAL HYGIENE, 1925-28[1]

Robert Menzies

[T]his mental hygiene movement is a healthy, if precocious child. ...
Never has there been so bright a future; never has there been so
much encouragement; but never has there been so much need for
an intelligent understanding on the part of our average citizen. The
public must learn more and more that this is a national aim, and
just as the obliteration of tuberculosis, malaria and yellow fever was
achieved when they became national conceptions, so the same thing
is in the field of mental disorders. More experts are required in the
field, and the public must be taught to accept leadership as a duty to
society and the state. Mental hygiene must inevitably make its appeal
to you and to me, to everyone who enjoys the privilege of a home
and who appreciates the full significance of useful citizenship.[2]

A Commission is Launched

In Victoria on the afternoon of 18 November 1925, the Honourable William
Sloan, Provincial Secretary in Premier John Oliver's Liberal administration,
rose to address the B.C. Legislature on the vexing subject of mental hygiene.
Making the case for appointing a select committee to study "the whole question of the insane and feeble-minded" in British Columbia, the Minister
delivered an alarming exposé on the sinister tide of lunacy and deficiency
that was swamping the province. Sloan came armed with a battery of statistics and representations from a medley of concerned organizations and citizens. He solemnly reported that the province was at a critical crossroads in
its desperate war against a relentless onslaught of defect, disease, and disorder. According to hospital annual reports, the number of institutionalized

insane had mushroomed from 16 in 1872 to 1,884 in 1925. To date, these unsound humans had cost the B.C. taxpayers a stupefying $10,581,832 for their care and upkeep. Worse still, 70 per cent of psychiatric hospital inmates had been born outside the province. Compounding the crisis was the fact that some 1500 "subnormal and mentally defective"[3] children were alive in B.C. and, according to expert calculations, one out of every 285 residents of the province was mentally subnormal.

Rising to the occasion, Sloan stretched for allegories that would aptly capture this lurking calamity. "The farmer," he intoned, "is careful in selecting the seed whence his crop is to be sprung for he knows that as he sows so will he reap. But in the great field of humanity we are absolutely careless and indifferent and, accordingly, we are reaping as we have sown — a crop of human wastage and human misery." Who was to blame for this assault on the collective mentality of the province? According to Sloan, it was the "average person" who was accountable — the citizen who "gives little or no thought to the tremendous and vital issue," who expects the State to pay, seemingly oblivious to the fact that "you and I *are* the State."[4] By permitting the mentally unfit to immigrate, marry, and procreate, the people of British Columbia were committing "a sin of omission" that would condemn future generations to untold hardships and abet the propagation of "human derelicts" who were "a liability in peace and a menace in war." Such indifference to the evils inflicted on modern society by the scourges of insanity and feeble-mindedness was "unnatural, ... unChristian, ... immoral and unhuman." The only recourse was to reverse this national decline toward oblivion, by acknowledging "our duty to see that we build up a race true to the traditions and characteristics of the Anglo-Saxon." Luckily, all was not yet lost. "I am convinced," concluded the suitably exercised Provincial Secretary, "that there are in this House earnest, thoughtful and patriotic men and women who are ready, in the name of morality, to give their every effort and thought to a problem of such vital importance to the future of the race."[5]

The assembly greeted Sloan's oratory with a thunderous ovation. The Secretary's motion to strike a committee of investigation won a quick seconding and avowal of support from Liberal members and physicians E.J. Rothwell and H.C. Wrinch. Rothwell underscored the need to approach the matter of mental affliction through the cool and dispassionate lens of scientific inquiry. "Cut out sentimental wish-wash stuff," he advised. "It will not get you anywhere."[6] Sloan's resolution passed unanimously.

Within a month, as it became clear that the committee would have little opportunity to act before dissolution of the Legislature, Sloan moved to extend its mandate. Accordingly, on 30 December 1925, the provincial Cabinet through Order-in-Council[7] invoked the *Public Inquiries Act* to establish the B.C. Royal Commission on Mental Hygiene (BCRCMH). The Order empowered the Commission to investigate and make recommendations to the Legislature on five core issues:

1. The reasons for the increase in the number of patients maintained in the Provincial Mental Hospital and branches thereof;
2. The causes and prevention of lunacy in the Province generally;
3. The entry into the Province of insane, mentally deficient and subnormal persons;
4. The care and treatment of subnormal children;
5. All such other matters and things relating to the subject of insanity, especially as they affect the Province of British Columbia, as the said Commissioners may deem pertinent to their inquiry.[8]

Thus began British Columbia's grand inquiry, the most comprehensive in the province's history, into the mental makeup of its citizenry. During the two-year lifespan of the BCRCMH, the Commissioners probed and offered their prescriptions on a staggering range of political, medical, and legal problems that were obsessing the province around matters of the mind. Their investigations into mental illness and deficiency would have an enduring impact on state policies and practices. Perhaps even more important, during the mid- and late-1920s the BCRCMH became a lightning rod for official and community debate around myriad questions relating to matters of governance, citizenship, professional power, social justice, and public health.

In this chapter, drawing on the BCRCMH papers, the records and correspondence of government and private organizations, media clippings, scientific journals, popular publications, and secondary sources, I trace the activities of the BCRCMH through this tumultuous phase in mental hygiene history. Following the main themes of this book, I argue that ideas around citizenship figured prominently in health and welfare ideologies and practices that permeated British Columbia, and the country more generally, throughout the inter-war period. In chronicling the Commission's engagement with questions around immigration control, sterilization of the unfit, treatment of the insane, and segregation and training of the feeble-minded, I show how the BCRCMH both represented and fuelled the province's and nation's preoccupations with advancing modern civilization through the manufacture of good citizens and elimination of the unworthy.

Unsuited to Citizenship

As contemporary state officials, political theorists, and human rights advocates grapple with competing conceptions of "the new citizen" as this millennium unfurls,[9] it is illuminating to note that British Columbians, and Canadians more generally, were confronting similar debates around identity, entitlement, responsibility, and belonging nearly a century ago. For relatively young nation-states like Canada, the years 1900-1925 represented a critical era of transformation. In the midst of tidal transitions in the national and world order, long-held liberal models for managing the relations between government and populace, tradition and progress, private and public, entitlement and obligation were being held up to critical scrutiny. If nineteenth-century ideas about governance had rapidly devolved in the context of fin-de-siècle political culture, they imploded forever in the wake of World War I. As Dowbiggin observes, "once the Armistice was signed, much of the Canadian wartime unity began to unravel. ... Agrarian, labor, and sectional protests spread throughout the country, leading Canadians to long for a rebirth of citizenship and new leadership to help bring it about."[10]

In Canada, as elsewhere, it was the progressive movement that emerged to confront these manifold challenges to the *ancien régime*. A fresh generation of public servants, social engineers, planners, professionals and practitioners came to embrace a reconstructed vision of the body politic. No longer, according to the reformers for this new century, could a liberal state afford to dwell on the periphery of private life. The litany of social problems plaguing civilization — crime, disease, promiscuity, intemperance, disharmony, urban blight, worker unrest, political radicalism — demanded instead an interventionist and far-reaching program of scientific governance. Only by applying enlightened modern theories and methods could a truly moral, civil, patriotic, and industrious society issue forth. The great initiatives in public health, education, housing, labour relations, social welfare, recreation, and parenthood were all part of a wider impetus aimed at radically extending the ambit of state knowledge about, and regulation of, its citizenry. Individual Canadians came to be viewed increasingly as human embodiments of the public regime, as "not merely *constituents* of the state but constitutive *of* the state."[11] The manufacture of good Canadian citizens — virtuous, efficient, and adaptable contributors to public causes — was inseparable from the project of nation-(re)building itself.

But what of those who failed to measure up to the citizenship standards being brandished by the government officials, social reformers, and professional classes of a progressive post-WWI Canada? In particular, how could authorities contend with the masses of deficient, diseased, depraved, and degenerate beings who were not amenable to assimilation, education, treatment or training into conformity with the Canadian dream? Such unfit Canadians — and would-be Canadians — presented an enduring problem for those involved in the citizen-making business. Their very existence seemed to belie the belief that human beings were infinitely malleable and, therefore, ultimately perfectible.

In retrospect, it is scarcely surprising that early twentieth-century Canadian reformers gravitated so effortlessly toward the "science" of eugenics as a medium for articulating their anxieties.[12] Eugenics offered authorities a powerful set of discourses through which they could attribute the problem of flawed citizens, not to the deficits and prejudices of prevailing political ideas and social programs, but instead to the intrinsic genetic, biological, and cognitive inferiority of alien and subaltern groups who simply had no place in a modern Canada. The defective immigrant, the born criminal, the congenitally feeble-minded, and the hereditary insane became, figuratively and literally, enemies of the nation. Entire projects of identification, classification, exclusion, segregation, and even annihilation developed in science, law, and public policy, with the ambition of purging all traces of these aberrant beings, and the dysgenic germ plasm that they harboured, from the fragile tissue of Canadian society.

The twin perils of irrationality and subnormality were doubly menacing, as they threatened both to invade the nation from without and to subvert it from within. Beyond the national frontiers, as it appeared to many, swarmed untold multitudes of defective beings whose mass entry into Canada would toll a death-knell for the nation's health, welfare, and security. From the turn of the century through to the 1930s, immigration of the unfit remained a fixation among a succession of prominent Canadian medical authorities.[13] Prior to World War I, physicians were warning civilians that "[i]f in the years to come Canada is to hold its own among the nations ... none should be allowed to enter the Dominion save those who are physically fit to become good and useful citizens."[14] Helen Reid, head of the Immigration Division of the Canadian National Committee for Mental Hygiene (CNCMH), introduced W.G. Smith's well-publicized immigration study by asserting that "Canada cannot have a strong and healthy nation unless its people are mentally as well as physically sound. ... An immigrant with a lame or crippled mind is not a healthy immigrant, nor is he a whole man. Canada needs whole men."[15]

Domestically, the principal adversaries were congenitally feeble and deranged minds. A nineteenth-century invention[16] and artifact of the mental testing systems of modern mass education,[17] the feeble-minded subject was also, like the born criminal, a metaphor for wider trepidations about the instability of social order.[18] Likewise, the spectre of insanity seemed omnipresent as asylums swelled to overflowing and experts singled out heredity as the predominant cause. Insisting in 1921 that "[w]e must set as our objective an aristocracy of mind as the highest ideal of democracy," McGill University psychologist William D. Tait asked rhetorically, "Am I my brother's keeper?" The answer, he intimated, was "Yes, by preventing the necessity of calling him a brother, by keeping him in his place if he has arrived, by seeing to it that he does not beget his kind if he is one of the class that are of little use to humanity."[19] As F.C.S. Schiller added in the *Dalhousie Review*, the very future of the country was at stake:

> The license society allows at present to the criminal, the insane and the feebleminded to multiply at pleasure, and to have their worse than worthless offspring cared for at the public expense ... too much resembles the strange toleration shown by ant-bee-communities towards the moron parasites that infest their nests. ... If civilization is not to be submerged in a flood of congenital feeble-mindedness, there is no time to lose.[20]

Mental Hygiene in the West-Coast Province

Following World War I, the eugenics cause became inextricably interwoven with the rapidly ascending fortunes of the mental hygiene movement.[21] This cardinal engine of psychiatric ideology and practice from the 1920s through to the 1950s — this "offspring of a love for the human kind"[22] — was a formidable coalition of state authorities and private citizens, politicians and scientists, conservatives and progressives, academics and practitioners. It drew force from the sanguine idea, to quote Beers' canonical *A Mind That Found Itself*, that "[t]he greatest thing in the world is the human mind."[23] For professionals who had been confined to the inner wards of public asylums — bearing forlorn witness to the collapse of the great moral treatment campaigns of prior generations — mental hygiene offered an "escape route"[24] into a world that beckoned beyond the hospital gates. For psychiatry, long viewed as "the most backward of all branches of medicine,"[25] it constituted no less than a window into the twentieth century. Theorists and practitioners of mental hygiene envisioned a utopian future where, through the interventions of modern experts, in close alliance with the managerial state, the mentally deficient and diseased "would all be absorbed into the scientifically systematized social order, and be transformed into useful and contented members of society."[26] In Canada, this movement came of age in 1918 when the CNCMH formed under the leadership of C.K. Clarke and C.M. Hincks. Through to World War II and beyond, the CNCMH functioned as the nation's single most influential forum for mental hygiene research, government lobbying, policy promotion, and educational propaganda.[27]

What most distinguished the course of eugenics and mental hygiene during these years was the remarkable ability of these seemingly incommensurable worldviews to co-exist in the thoughts, words, and deeds of scientists, politicians, practitioners, and private citizens. In particular, experts of the mind proved themselves disarmingly adept at negotiating the spaces between destiny and agency, nature and nurture, despondency and hope, biology and mentality, eradication and prevention, expulsion and inclusion in their crusades to uplift the nation's mental health. Eugenicists and mental hygienists found common ground in their mutual allegiances to state and science as the twin instruments of social reform.[28] Moreover, exponents of both causes were seldom as philosophically committed as the public rhetoric might have often implied. Across the decades, authorities proved over and over that they felt little constrained by the dictates of ideological consistency.[29]

In British Columbia, the mental hygiene era had begun with the CNCMH provincial survey of 1919. Based on their searching investigations of psychiatric, correctional, social service, and educational facilities around the province, the CNCMH directors had concluded that "the most glaring need in British Columbia [is] the question of the treatment of acute cases [and] the rights of the insane to early scientific treatment."[30] Their report generated what would soon become the standard inventory of mental hygiene prescriptions for "heading off the stream at its source."[31] For the insane these included psychopathic wards[32] at the Vancouver General Hospital, an acute building at the Essondale institution in Coquitlam, more medical staff, a social service unit, a residential nurses' home at the Public Hospital for the Insane (PHI) in New Westminster,[33] voluntary admission provisions, occupational therapy, and a travelling psychiatric clinic attached to the PHI. The feeble-minded, for their part, were in "urgent" need of a training school, better diagnostic facilities, and more special classes[34] in the public schools.[35] Clarke and Hincks concluded by proposing that "there be appointed a Mental Hygiene Commission in British Columbia," the function of which "would consist in making a careful study of the problem of mental abnormality in the Province, and of developing a suitable plan for its solution."[36]

The years prior to and following the CNCMH report witnessed an avalanche of mental hygiene policy activity both in Canada and abroad.

Internationally, Britain produced the pioneering 1904-08 Royal Commission on the Care and Control of the Feeble-Minded (and the attendant 1913 *Mental Deficiency Act*).[37] Elsewhere in Canada, the Ontario Hodgins Commission of 1919[38] recommended, among other things, a provincial board of control and stringent segregation of the feeble-minded.[39] In Alberta, a citizens' committee, under the stewardship of Judge Emily Murphy, was conducting its own inquiries into the mental hospitals of that province.[40] Nova Scotia's Royal Commission Concerning Mentally Deficient Persons, chaired by W.L. Hall, would report to the government there in 1927.[41]

In British Columbia, the tempo also quickened. Declaring that "the feeble-minded and the progeny of the feeble-minded constitute one of the great social and economic burdens of our modern civilization,"[42] B.C. mental hospital superintendent C.E. Doherty (1905-20) and his successor H.C. Steeves (1920-26) pressed for state intervention. The Child Welfare Association of Vancouver publicly lobbied for marriage control and sterilization legislation, along with a custodial school for mentally defective children.[43] Women's organizations throughout the province, and especially the Local Councils of Women (LCWs), emulated their counterparts elsewhere in becoming key exponents of reform.[44]

In autumn 1925, Penticton MLA W.A. Mackenzie released his report chronicling the deplorable conditions of overcrowding inside the B.C. mental hospitals.[45] Mackenzie depicted the PHI as "a rambling structure, mostly of inflammable construction, ill suited and unfitted for the care of the large number of patients – mostly women – confined there." Feeble-minded children at Essondale, he continued, were "in constant danger of being roasted alive. ... These unfortunate sufferers," he admonished his colleagues, "are wards of the Government and the citizens of British Columbia and as such it is a public responsibility to see that they are properly housed."[46] Simultaneously, anti-immigration agitation also intensified. In November 1925 the Legislature resolved that "in the opinion of this House the strictest scrutiny of all immigrants coming into Canada as regards physical and mental condition be made by the Immigration Department."[47] A week later MLA Mary Ellen Smith followed suit, opining to her colleagues that, in the absence of immigration control, "we will have our jails, asylums and other institutions flooded with the flotsam and jetsam of humanity."[48]

The BCRCMH at Work

In a bipartisan gesture meant to reflect the gravity of these issues, Provincial Secretary Sloan appointed three Liberal and two Conservative members to sit on the BCRCMH. E.J. Rothwell, the elected chairman,[49] had won the New Westminster seat for the Liberals in Oliver's precariously slender election victory the previous June. Born in Ontario, Rothwell had graduated in medicine from the University of Toronto. After six years as a general physician in Trail, he relocated to the Royal City in 1902, where his practice brought him into contact with the nearby PHI.[50] Probably the most recognizable of Rothwell's co-Commissioners was the secretary, the redoubtable Vancouver Liberal member Brigadier-General V.W. Odlum. A fellow Ontarian by birth, Odlum was a long-time newspaperman who had served in both the Boer and First World Wars and was owner of the *Vancouver Star* between 1924 and 1932.[51] Their Liberal colleague was P.P. Harrison, a Cumberland lawyer who, following his short-lived political career, joined the judiciary and would eventually become a B.C. Supreme Court justice.[52] Reginald Hayward was a Conservative member from Victoria and former mayor of the capital city.[53] The remaining Commissioner, and second Conservative, was W.A. Mackenzie, who had written the report on overcrowding and would later become labour minister in Simon Fraser Tolmie's one-term Tory government.[54]

The first task of the newly-minted Commission was to inspect the mental hospitals at Essondale and New Westminster. The *Vancouver Province* conveyed a blow-by-blow rendition of their visit to the PHI on 11 January 1926. "Hour after hour," the reporter recounted, "the commissioners walked the long corridors leading from overcrowded dormitory to dormitory, where often the beds were separated by only a few inches, and from recreation room to recreation room where hundreds of human beings moved about in objectiveless purpose, or gazed in senseless wonder at the visitors." While the writer stressed that "every effort [was] being made to give comfort and care,"[55] it was apparent to all present that the resources and living space at both institutions had been stretched beyond toleration.

The members then met to parcel out their respective mandates. Mackenzie would address the matter of overcrowding, Harrison took on immigration, Hayward would delve into heredity, and Odlum would concern himself with "provincial repatriation of the insane." To Rothwell fell the issue of "psychopathic hospitalization with respect to its efficiency in preventing insanity in its incipient phases." Rothwell and Hayward would examine the California situation, and Mackenzie and Odlum would look into the operations in Ontario and Manitoba. Based on their inquiries and observations so far, the five MLAs developed a provisional list of proposals that included a new reception hospital and building for chronically afflicted women at Essondale, abandonment of the wood frame "feeble-minded building" at Essondale and removal of all deficients to New Westminster, appeal to the federal government for better mental screening of immigrants, an agreement for return of insane persons to their province of origin, legislation requiring mental certificates as prerequisites for marriage, sterilization, a psychopathic hospital in Vancouver, and "subnormal schools for those capable of receiving some useful instruction."[56]

figure 17.1

Rear of Admitting Building, Essondale, 1924.

BC ARCHIVES F-04732. REPRODUCED BY PERMISSION.

figure 17.2 • Provincial Mental Hospital, New Westminster, 1929.
BC ARCHIVES F-04737. REPRODUCED BY PERMISSION.

figure 17.3

Edwin James Rothwell, 1914.

REPRODUCED FROM *BRITISH COLUMBIA: PICTORIAL AND BIBLIOGRAPHICAL, VOL. 2* (S.J. CLARKE: WINNIPEG, 1914), PAGE 365.

Events unfolded apace through early 1926. The Commission opened its Vancouver offices and recruited J.A. Macdonald, an employee of Odlum at the *Vancouver Star*, as its assistant secretary.[57] Former publicity commissioner for Manitoba, Macdonald was an outspoken journalist who played a key role over the next two years in administering the inquiry, compiling a research library, and writing the official reports.[58] Immediately upon taking up the post, Macdonald launched into correspondence with an array of Canadian and international authorities. Meanwhile, the commissioners trained their sights on securing public support for their research and reform activities. Addressing the Victoria LCW in February 1926, Hayward transfixed his audience with accounts of the "idiot and low class imbecile type" children that he had observed in the hospitals, "a hopeless wreck of juvenile humanity, not one of them, who should ever have been born into this world ... some of whom are barely more than mere animals (their only resemblance of being human, is their shape)."[59]

The BCRCMH convened its Vancouver public hearings in the city's courthouse on 13-14 April 1926.[60] Vancouver mayor Louis D. Taylor gave the welcoming remarks. The internationally renowned Dr. C.B. Farrar, director of the Toronto Psychopathic Hospital and professor of psychiatry at the University of Toronto, was on hand as well. Over the two days of the proceedings, the elite of the Vancouver and Lower Mainland mental hygiene, public health, legal, and social welfare establishments[61] unleashed, one by one, their assorted tales of atrocity.

In the morning of the first day, H.C. Steeves echoed Mackenzie and Hayward before him in deploring the grave overcrowding that plagued his facilities. He pleaded with the government to fast-track plans for the Female Chronic Building and accommodations for the feeble-minded. Reporting that his physicians and staff were overwhelmed by the 135 mental cases arriving annually at their doors, Superintendent F.C. Bell of the Vancouver General Hospital added his voice to calls for a psychopathic hospital. P.D. Panton, Medical Officer of the Vancouver Police Department, offered a similar depiction of conditions at the city jail. Typifying the rabid eugenicist bent of many central Canadian psychiatrists, C.B. Farrar maintained that his colleagues were nearly united in considering that "any measure that could be taken to prevent reproduction of that kind of stock would be the finest thing that society could accomplish." Of particular concern to Farrar was the "intermediate group of higher grade defective." This type "is more prolific than any other group; they are the ones who fill our gaols and penitentiaries. They are in the poor quarters of the city and contribute to the thug and bandit class. ... That is the one group we should get hold of if we are to do anything toward preventing the accumulation of insanity, of poverty, of delinquents, and all the other tendencies which make for the social diseases."

When given his opportunity to speak, Vancouver psychiatrist J.G. McKay addressed the question of mental deficiency. According to this future member of the eugenics board, "[h]eredity is paramount. ... There is not a sane man associated with this work who won't agree with me." Reminding his audience that "it is an infringement of the law today to let inferior, unregistered stock run loose over the open prairie," McKay lamented that the regulation of low-quality humans could lag so far behind that of their bovine counterparts. For his part, J. Stuart Jamieson, police magistrate for Burnaby, stated that 40 per cent of juvenile offenders were of mentally defective stock. He offered up the case of an 18-year-old "girl" who had come before him accusing her male guardian of sexual assault. The charges were summarily dismissed, but Jamieson, to his chagrin, had no further power over her. "Now, that girl is a sexual pervert," he observed, "and she has cunning. ... In time, I feel sure, she will be on the street, and will probably have children. What will they be like? Her sister married a hunchback, and is raising a family who will be 100% feeble-minded and idiots. This type of person drifts into disease, and will likely add to the sum total of those suffering from syphilis." When queried about what should be done with this woman, Jamieson replied, "Segregation and sterilization. Sterilization would be perfectly safe, and she would be like a harmless child of 12. She could be put in an institution where she could learn something, some handicraft, and she could go out. She would be happier, and would be, more or less as a suitable citizen."

Against this general torrent of trepidation, however, flowed the testimony of other witnesses who contributed a rather more tempered account of B.C.'s mental problems. For Josephine Dauphinée, supervisor of Vancouver special classes for subnormal children, the image of mental defectives as dangerous untrainables was refuted by the experience, over the previous 15 years, of psychologists and educators. "[T]he majority of morons," asserted Dauphinée, were "not of that type. ... They can be trained so that they can live in the outside world. We teach them to be punctual, regular, cheerful and establish friendly relations with their fellow men, and good habits, good principles are necessarily associated with the business world."[62] Henry Shaw, Juvenile Court judge for Vancouver,[63] disputed the notion that most young offenders were biologically inferior: "These boys are for the most part absolutely normal, and their crimes are often deviltry and the result of high animal spirits." Only 15 per cent of the children appearing before his court could be considered in any way deficient. And even they were, for the most part, redeemable. "The public," continued Shaw, "should realise that the boys and girls of today are the men and women of tomorrow." For the fee-ble-minded child, "training will greatly strengthen his mentality and even render him, at all events, a useful citizen."[64]

Two days later the Commissioners reconvened in Victoria, where another retinue of professionals and social reformers awaited them. On behalf of the Victoria LCW and Social Service League, Emily May Schofield (wife of the capital city's Anglican bishop) recited the list of resolutions submitted by her organization, which included additional special classes for subnormal chil-dren, segregation of the feeble-minded and epileptic, relief of hospital over-crowding, and "stricter examination of all intending immigrants at the port of embarkation by doctors who have wide Canadian experience and under-stand the strain ... which newcomers to this country have to undergo." Her colleague on the LCW, Victoria physician Irene Bastow Hudson, declared herself an opponent of sterilization. When asked to elaborate, she obliged by stating that "allowing marriage after sterilization will create monsters of sex-perversion, and glorify sense gratification, making us and our future race ... lower than the mindless brute creation." As an alternative policy toward the subnormal, Hudson allowed that "[i]f they are a danger to society and liable to reproduce their kind without marriage; if they can't be trained, you must segregate them, and it is an economic impossibility to segregate them all. I think temporarily we might have to descend to the measure of castration."

But the main preoccupation of the Victoria hearings was plainly immigra-tion of the unfit. Dr. Arthur G. Price, the city's medical officer, protested that "Asiatics of low mentality are allowed to come into the Province, and many come from Europe who are undesirable from a mental standpoint." Speaking from his longstanding experience as provincial health officer and B.C. dele-gate to the Dominion Council of Health,[65] the imperious Henry Esson Young railed against the "promiscuous power" wielded by self-serving politicians to bypass sound scientific opinion and dilute the national stock through ill-advised admissions of defective aliens. According to Young, the federal gov-ernment's provisions for screening immigrants on corporal and mental com-petency had been grievously corrupted by ethnic influence-peddling. In particular, "the Jewish people there are very strong and very wealthy, and they are constantly besieging the Minister to get these people in."

As in Vancouver, despite the overall affinity of witnesses for eugenics-flavoured accounts of deficiency and disorder, the discourse was by no means univocal. On insanity, for instance, Arthur Price professed that "it is not heredity so much as we think." There were, he contended, innumerable sources for mental troubles, including "syphilis, toxin poisoning, injuries. ... poverty and poor living conditions; money losses; lack of work or ability to work; laxity in the family life, in the home; lack of control in the home and the uncontrolled desires of youth." For Victoria Medical Association representative E.M. Baillie, too, heredity was "allowed to play too great a part." On the subject of eugenic sterilization, even the otherwise zealous Young voiced his distaste except in the most "obvious" cases: "I don't believe in it ... In sterilisation you want to get rid of the recessive dormant seed; it would take eight thousand years to reduce it to 1%; at present it is 7%. There are cases that are not so obvious; where can you draw the line?"[66]

After the close of hearings, the Commissioners spent the remainder of 1926 undertaking their studies of selected mental hygiene issues,[67] communicating with consultants, and preparing their interim report to the Legislature. After relocating to Victoria in May, J.A. Macdonald commenced an ongoing correspondence with C.M. Hincks.[68] In July, the CNCMH medical director offered a typically loquacious letter that revealed some of the shifts in perspective taking place among the psychiatric elite during this pivotal period in mental hygiene history. Hincks was now persuaded that at most 50 per cent of mental deficiency cases were hereditary in origin — a quite spectacular revision downward from the 90-per-cent figure that was commonplace just a few years earlier. The emphasis in the field, according to Hincks, must now be on prevention. While he was careful to append "careful immigrant selection, and, perhaps, sterilization" to his list of prescriptions, Hincks was now accentuating wider programs of community interventions "by establishing Psychiatric or Habit clinics, by introducing mental hygiene into schools, by parent education [and] by incorporating mental hygiene in public health and social service endeavor."[69]

But not everyone had embraced such a balanced approach. Macdonald was also privy to the abundant outpourings of leading eugenicists across the United States (where 22 states had sterilization laws in place by the mid-1920s[70]). These included Paul Popenoe, E.S. Gosney, and E.O. Butler of California, where, from the codification of eugenics law in April 1909 through October 1925, 3,598 insane and 941 feebleminded inmates of state institutions had fallen under the sterilizer's scalpel.[71] The BCRCMH assistant secretary also absorbed a continuing barrage of pro-sterilization and anti-immigration rhetoric from provincial authorities such as McKay and Steeves. Meanwhile journalists persisted with their lobbying in the local media. In April, for example, the editorialists for the *Vancouver Sun* queried, "Is it not more humane and infinitely more reasonable to condemn the unborn unfit to non-existence than to permit them to be born and then condemn them to punishment and death? If civilization is to be protected from the rebellion and destructive tendencies of the underman, sterilization of those unable to bear the burden of civilization is essential."[72] Not to be outdone, their *Vancouver Province* counterparts chimed in: "we can not expect to build a successful and virile nation here if we allow the springs of our nationhood to be polluted by the mental defectives of other lands."[73]

Into this composite of divided opinion entered the report of psychologist Helen P. Davidson, Buckel Fellow in the Psychology Department at Stanford University, whom the BCRCMH engaged to document the genetic profiles of the province's insane inmates. A New Westminster native and former instructor in special classes for the feeble-minded,[74] Davidson reviewed the prevailing research and analyzed case files for the 3,883 persons admitted to the B.C. mental hospital system through the decade ending 30 June 1926.[75] Davidson proved to be a less than fervent proponent of the eugenic cant. "A cursory survey of the literature," she wrote, "shows remarkable disagreement among the authorities as to the amount of what is popularly termed insanity that is due to heredity."[76] Her study of the hospital records revealed that more than 70 per cent of B.C. insanity cases were traceable to factors other than heredity. Admittedly, Davidson did not dissociate herself entirely from hereditarian doctrine: her recommendations reprised the familiar clarion calls for immigration control, deportation, and sterilization.[77] But for the most part her recommendations concentrated on the imperatives of research, education, social service, prevention, treatment, and training.[78]

When it came to sterilization, the need for a circumspect approach was becoming increasingly apparent. While the hard line on immigration had garnered virtually no opposition,[79] eugenic surgery was a different matter altogether. There seemed to be too many potent counter-arguments around the impracticality of legislation, the questionable science of hereditarianism, and the implied threats to civil liberties.[80] Indeed, from the very beginning, the Commission had been inclined "to recommend, for a start, a mild permissive rather than compulsory law."[81] By November 1926, Macdonald confided that "I have begun to modify my own attitude" after finding "that apparently the majority of leading psychiatrists, if not exactly opposed [to sterilization], give it so inferior a place that they do not recommend its adoption in the face of the opposition it has already aroused." Despite these trepidations, Macdonald remained optimistic about the long-term prospects for eugenics legislation in B.C.: "If our Commission recommends a carefully modified law and it gets past the legislature, I do not anticipate much public opposition. Our people are like Cabell's[82] here — willing to try any drink once, which is the way of the west, in Canada as well as the U.S."[83]

Prescriptions for Reform

Into Macdonald's hands fell the task of synthesizing the vast array of facts and recommendations into the Commission's interim report.[84] After vetting the assistant secretary's draft, the Commissioners officially released the document on 4 March 1927. The report was a revealing study in compromise — a hybrid of populist and scientific, eugenic and mental hygiene reasoning. On the one hand, the BCRCMH wrote approvingly of the "revolution in methods of care and treatment" to which they had borne witness throughout their investigations to date, and of the "growth of public enlightenment on the subject in nearly all civilized communities" which "has forced radical changes in the attitude and sense of responsibility of society and the state towards the mentally afflicted."[85] Similarly, they argued that the quantitative growth of insanity in B.C. was not at all incommensurate with trends elsewhere, and that methods of treatment and care in the provincial hospitals "compare favourably with any on this continent."[86] On the other hand, the Commissioners warned that an acute overcrowding exigency, stemming in large part from the indiscriminate influx of foreign-born insane, was threatening to paralyze the province's asylum system.

The BCRCMH offered six main prescriptions for remedying this crisis: (1) a Provincial Board of Control to oversee the operations of B.C. mental hospitals, (2) a psychopathic hospital for Vancouver, (3) removal of mental deficients to suitable accommodation in a colony system or alternative care and housing, (4) voluntary sterilization of psychiatric inmates to eliminate "the danger of procreation with its attendant risk of multiplication of the evil by transmission of the disability to progeny,"[87] (5) consultation with other provinces around the payment of maintenance costs for inter-provincial migrant patients, and (6) representations to the Dominion government for better medical screening of unfit immigrants.

In the report's appendices, the Commissioners echoed Helen Davidson in equivocating on the heredity question. They referred to the "wide variance of opinion as to the proportion of insanity due, either partially or wholly, to this cause," and favourably quoted authorities such as Hincks, and A.T. Mathers of the Winnipeg Psychopathic Hospital, who attributed escalating mental inmate populations to improvements in institutional care, patient longevity, more liberal standards for admission, and "the increasing complexity of community life."[88] Moreover, their discussions around psychopathic hospitals and training of the feeble-minded were festooned with references to environmental influence and the need for social reform.

Yet on the vital topics of immigration and sterilization of the unfit, the BCRCMH members recited the customary eugenic liturgy. When it came to unfit foreigners, they predictably enjoined immigration authorities to enforce the existing prohibition of "idiots, imbeciles, feeble-minded persons, epileptics, insane persons, and persons that have been insane at any time previously."[89] The state, they declared, has a moral and legal obligation to debar those who would "add to the burden of the nation caused by mental abnormality."[90] Extolling the California program of reproduction control, the commissioners chose "to put greater reliance on the actual experience in that State than upon the theoretical objections of those who have not had the same opportunity of ascertaining by direct observation whether or not these objections are justified." They argued, too, that critics who cited civil liberties violations were simply missing the point. "Apart from any question," the BCRCMH claimed, "as to whether or not the rights of the individual may be held to be above the good of society at large, this argument has no application to the sterilization of a restricted class of the mentally abnormal..."[91] While the report arrived too late for legislative action in the current session, Rothwell was confident about the prospects for pushing it through "without serious contention" in January 1928.

In April, Macdonald distributed 1500 copies of the interim report throughout B.C., the rest of Canada, and the United States.[92] The document was generally well received. Clare Hincks, for one, proclaimed that "the Mental Hygiene Commission of British Columbia has performed a useful piece of work in studying mental hospital problems."[93] Media coverage was also approving. The *Vancouver Western Tribune* reserved special praise for the sterilization proposals.[94] The *Victoria Colonist* urged that "the Commission, whose report indicates that the problem has been given very careful study, should be allowed to continue its activities with the assistance of the best medical knowledge which is obtainable in the Province, and its main recommendations should be implemented without unnecessary loss of time."[95]

Throughout 1927, the BCRCMH mobilized in preparation for its final submission to the House. In March, Macdonald secured an appropriation to support his Commission work for a second year.[96] By summer, the Oliver government had approved a $2-million construction blueprint for the provincial hospitals, which included a 750-bed Women's Chronic Building and an additional wing for the Acute Building at Essondale, as well as a new apartment home for employees on the same grounds. But, to the Commissioners' chagrin, the long-awaited Vancouver psychopathic hospital, while obliquely mentioned, did not figure into the immediate plans.[97]

Then, in June, to the collective shock of his colleagues, E.J. Rothwell died of a stomach hemorrhage while vacationing in the interior B.C. town of Quesnel.[98] The death of their chairman — and the only medical professional on the Commission — prolonged the BCRCMH's work by several months. It would be September before they elected V.W. Odlum as Rothwell's replacement. Finally, several weeks after J.A. Macdonald moved back to Victoria in January 1928, the commissioners convened to authorize their final report.

On 9 March 1928, the four surviving BCRCMH members released that document to the provincial Legislature. For the most part the report recapitulated the proposals of its 1927 antecedent. When compared with the typically extremist rhetoric of American sources reprinted in its appendices,[99] the main body of the text seemed positively subdued. The Commissioners concentrated principally on the subject of mental deficiency. They declared that scientific inquiry had had the salutary effect of dampening the "alarmist attitude" toward subnormality that had dominated public attitudes earlier in the century. The BCRCMH by no means retreated from its eugenicist partialities around sterilization and immigration, but the Commissioners' main allegiance was now plainly to the environmentally-inclined mental hygienist agenda. They optimistically maintained that "[t]he key-note of a constructive programme for mental deficients is training, and nine-tenths of deficient children can be trained with greatest advantage in the public-school system. The problem, therefore, is educational rather than medical."[100]

Their drift away from the hard-line eugenicist agenda was also evident in the Commissioners' concluding recommendations. While they continued to advocate custodial confinement of "low-grade idiots and imbeciles" and public protection from the "dangerous anti-social" feeble-minded, now there was an accompanying emphasis on "vocational training of higher-grade mental deficients." Further, the BCRCMH endorsed special classes for subnormals in all B.C. population centres of 500 or more residents, provincial grants underwriting the vocational training of special class graduates, a provincial training school for deficients who were unsuited for special classes or lived in far-flung regions, public education regarding "the mentally handicapped," a separate *Mental Deficiency Act* along the lines of the 1913 English statute,[101] acceptance of the CNCMH's offer of matching funds for ongoing research, and the appointment of a provincial psychiatrist to counsel the government on mental hygiene matters. Even on the sterilization question their discourse was observed to thaw, as they advised "a carefully restricted and safeguarded measure of permissive sexual sterilization of certain suitable and definitely ascertained cases of mental abnormality ... with the object that such cases may be permitted safely to return to their normal place in the community."[102]

Aftermath

In tabling this final report, the BCRCMH ended its mandate. John MacLean, now premier, proclaimed that the document "will be of the utmost value in the consideration of the problem of insanity in this Province, and all of its recommendations will have the careful study of the Government."[103] But once again fate intervened. Before the Liberal government could act, the House dissolved and Tolmie's Conservatives swept to power in summer 1928. This changing of the B.C. political guard, along with the economic depression that descended in the following year, combined to retard implementation of the BCRCMH's mental hygiene agenda.

Indeed, the proposed psychopathic hospital for Vancouver never did materialize.[104] On other fronts, however, authorities slowly regrouped. Construction on the Female Chronic Building at Essondale carried forward, and the new facility opened in 1930. A year later the entire feeble-minded population relocated to the PHI (later renamed Woodlands School), under the superintendency of Louis Sauriol.[105] By autumn 1931, 23 special-class teachers for the subnormal were working in the Vancouver public school system.[106] Answering appeals dating back to the 1919 CNCMH survey, the government appointed A.L. Crease provincial psychiatrist in 1934.[107] By 1937, despite continuing economic stringency, the provincial mental hygiene operations expanded to encompass a Veterans' Building, a Home for the Aged, a Nurses' Home, and two re-modelled wards at the PHI. New services included a nurses' training school and post-graduate course,[108] an attendants' school, the hiring of three social workers,[109] and integration with provincial fieldwork services. The province also established a Child Guidance Clinic in Vancouver, and a travelling clinic for other areas, where "subnormal and feeble-minded children are dealt with, and parents and guardians receive advice."[110]

When it came to sterilization, the campaign continued as sexual surgery became increasingly identified with emerging eugenic ideas that attributed human problems "to poor parenting rather than to poor genes."[111] By the early 1930s it was incompetent mothers who became the main targets of sterilization crusaders.[112] As lobbyists intensified their efforts to suppress the reproductive functions of defective females, it became clear that this movement was primarily about controlling the sexuality of women and girls.[113] B.C. sterilization crusaders were all the more energized by the 1928 passage of eugenic legislation in Alberta,[114] by the avalanche of US statutes greeting the infamous 1927 Supreme Court judgment in Buck v. Bell,[115] and by the advocacy of sterilization by the 1930 Ontario Royal Commission on Public Welfare[116] and the Brock Committee in Britain four years thereafter.[117]

On 7 April 1933, the B.C. Legislature at long last enacted its own sterilization law,[118] in which it adopted the BCRCMH recommendation for voluntary provisions.[119] The legislation, a close replica of the Alberta code,[120] empowered a Eugenics Board to order the sexual sterilization of any mental hospital or industrial school inmate — on application of the institutional superintendent and consent of a marriage partner, parent, guardian or provincial secretary — who would otherwise be "likely to beget or bear children who by reason of inheritance would have a tendency to serious mental disease or mental deficiency."[121] The Board, comprising Justice H.B. Robertson, psychiatrist J.G. McKay, and Superintendent of Neglected Children Laura Holland, went into operation on 31 October 1933.[122] The government engaged Dr. W.S. Turnbull of the Vancouver General Hospital to perform the operations at $25 per patient.[123] However, British Columbia never embraced the legislation with the same ardency as did its Alberta and US neighbours. Between 1935 and 1945, 64 sterilizations of mental patients (of whom 57 were female) occurred,[124] and the Board attracted criticism for its generally phlegmatic performance.[125] Yet, while no more than 200-300 operations[126] ensued during the lifespan of the B.C. legislation — less than one-tenth of those occurring in Alberta — eugenic sterilization remained a potent weapon in the arsenal of provincial authorities until the law was finally rescinded in 1972.

In these ways, then, the inherent dualism of the mental hygiene movement — its mutually convergent yet ultimately irreconcilable allegiances to biology and social reform — continued to govern the course of psychiatric history in the province long after the BCRCMH submitted its final report to the Legislature. The medical establishment, and the various other helping and curing professions that emerged between the wars, never fully succeeded in resolving these contradictions or in forging a coherent program to enhance the mentality of the citizenry.

It is true that psychiatric and psychological practice was extending farther and farther out into the community, and that reformers like Hincks were increasingly insisting that "[i]t is a mistake to look upon the insane as essentially different from ourselves."[127] Yet by the early 1930s British Columbia's segregative mental institutions were also on the verge of an unprecedented surge of expansion that would not subside for more than two decades. Still further, a new era of somatic psychiatry was about to commence, as asylum keepers began to apply metrazol, insulin, mercury, electricity, and largactil to the bodies and brains of patients in their latest quest for a madness remedy.[128] As for the mentally deficient, after the "myth of the menace of the feeble-minded" began to evaporate during the 1930s, and once the cognitively disabled were forever separated from the insane and secreted away in "training schools," they "began to move from the centre of the political stage and lapse into obscurity."[129]

But ultimately the centre could not hold. Burdened with the legacy of their eugenicist past and unable to ignore the remorseless realities of mid-century institutional psychiatric practice, reformers elected *en masse* to abandon the mental hygiene concept altogether.[130] In 1950 even that national flagship of the movement, the CNCMH, reinvented itself as the Canadian Mental Health Association.[131]

In the end, the BCRCMH, and the interlocking reform enterprises that it both reflected and advanced, need to be appraised against the backdrop of these wider historical currents. Like most such ventures, the BCRCMH proved to be less an independent instrument of social change than a template on which the obsessions and forebodings, the preoccupations and longings of an entire generation were inscribed. In the mental hygiene movement, in British Columbia and beyond, legislators, professionals, and public all saw an uncommon opportunity to remake biology and history, and to fashion a political, scientific, and legal order that would accentuate human quality and realize the full potential of the citizenry. The enduring irony was that, in their crusades to transcend the nineteenth century, too often these citizen scientists and reformers succeeded only in reviving its most totalitarian tendencies. The tragedy was that the hygienists' route to utopia was impossibly congested with the countless thousands who, by virtue of their social status, bearing or mentality, failed to meet these capricious citizenship standards and were accordingly consigned to the nation's asylums, prisons, detention centres, training schools, and surgical slabs. In their grand experiment aimed at making ideal citizens, the mental hygienists showed just how fragile Canadian citizenship really was.

Notes

1. The research for this chapter benefitted enormously from a grant supplied by the Social Sciences and Humanities Research Council of Canada, in support of our collaborative project "Governing Bodies: Sexually Transmitted Diseases and the Politics of Citizenship in Canada, 1880-1945." My thanks go to Rob Adamoski, Dorothy Chunn, Joel Freedman and Jeffie Roberts; and to the professionals and staff of the BC Archives, National Archives of Canada, University of British Columbia Special Collections, University of Victoria Library, BC Legislative Library, Cumberland Museum (Lisa Baird and Barb Lemky), and Archives for the History of Canadian Psychiatry and Mental Health Services (John Court, Cynthia Cochrane, Cyril Greenland, and the late Jack Griffin).

2. "The Mental Hygiene Movement in Canada," *The Canadian Nurse* (1928): 59-62, 62. Although the editors fail to denote the author, it is almost certain that either C.M. Hincks or D.M. Le Bourdais of the Canadian National Committee for Mental Hygiene (CNCMH) contributed these words.

3. Throughout this chapter, in the interests of preserving the historical discourse, I use the popular and medical vernacular of the day ("feeble-minded," "defective," "subnormal," "lunatic," "insane") without qualification or commentary.

4. My emphasis.

5. "House Supports Drastic Measures Against Insanity," 25 Nov. 1925. This clipping, from which the above quotations are extracted, appears in the CMHA Scrapbook, Vol. 1, 1925-1930, Archives for the History of Canadian Psychiatry and Mental Health Services (hereinafter CMHA Scrapbook). It is likely derived from the *Vancouver Star*, which went out of print in 1933 and for which microfilm copies are unavailable. For other accounts of Sloan's speech, see "Steps Taken By Legislature to Guard Province," *Victoria Colonist*, 25 Nov. 1925; and "Sloan Says B.C. Gets Backwash," *Vancouver Daily Province*, 25 Nov. 1925, 16.

6. "Stern Measures, Including Sterilization of Lunatics, Proposed to Cure Insanity," *Victoria Times*, 19 Nov. 1925. CMHA Scrapbook.

7. Lieutenant-Governor Order-in-Council, *Public Inquiries Act*, 30 Dec. 1925. British Columbia Archives and Records Service (hereinafter BCARS), GR 865, box 1, file 4.

8. "Notice Under Public Inquiries Act," *Vancouver Star*, 7 April 1926. BCARS, GR 865, box 1, file 1.

9. See, for example, J.M. Barbelet, *Citizenship* (Minneapolis: University of Minnesota Press, 1988); "Symposium on Citizenship, Democracy, and Education," ed. Larry Becker and Will Kymlicka, *Ethics* 105 (April 1995): 465-579; T.M. Marshall and Tom Bottomore, *Citizenship and Social Class* (London: Pluto, 1992); Will Kymlicka and Wayne Norman, "Return of the Citizen: A Survey of Recent Work on Citizenship Theory," *Ethics* 104 (January 1994): 352-81; Ruth Lister, *Citizenship: Feminist Perspectives* (New York: NYU Press, 1997); Maurice Roche, *Rethinking Citizenship: Welfare, Ideology and Change in Modern Society* (Cambridge: Polity Press, 1992); *The Citizenship Debates: A Reader*, ed. Gershon Shafir (Minneapolis: University of Minnesota Press, 1998); Jeff Spinner, *The Boundaries of Citizenship: Race, Ethnicity, and Nationality in the Liberal State* (Baltimore: Johns Hopkins Press, 1994); Nancy Leys Stepan, "Race, Gender, Science and Citizenship," *Gender and History* 10, 1 (April, 1998): 26-52; Bryan Turner, "Outline of a Theory of Citizenship," *Sociology* 24, 2 (May, 1990): 189-217; Sylvia Walby, "Is Citizenship Gendered?" *Sociology* 28, 2 (May, 1994): 379-95.

10. Ian Dowbiggin, *Keeping America Sane: Psychiatry and Eugenics in the United States and Canada, 1880-1940* (Ithaca, NY: Cornell University Press, 1997), 174.

11. Matthew J. Lindsay, "Reproducing a Fit Citizenry: Dependency, Eugenics, and the Law of Marriage in the United States, 1860-1920," *Law and Social Inquiry* 23, 3 (Summer 1998): 541-85, 571.

12. Canadian writings on eugenics history include Terry L. Chapman, "Early Eugenics Movement in Western Canada," *Alberta History* 25, 4 (1977): 9-17; Ian Dowbiggin, "'Keeping This Young Country Sane': C.K. Clarke, Immigration Regulation, and Canadian Psychiatry, 1890-1925," *Canadian Historical Review* 76, 4 (December 1995): 598-627; Dowbiggin, *Keeping America Sane*; Ruth Marina McDonald, "A Policy of Privilege: The Alberta Sexual Sterilization Program 1928-1972" (MA Thesis, University of Victoria, 1996); Angus McLaren, "The Creation of a Haven for 'Human Thoroughbreds': The Sterilisation of the Feebleminded and the Mentally Ill in British Columbia," *Canadian Historical Review* 67 (June 1986): 127-50; Angus McLaren, *Our Own Master Race: The Eugenic Crusade in Canada* (Toronto: McClelland and Stewart, 1990); Monica Wosilius, "Eugenics, Insanity and Feeblemindedness: British Columbia's Sterilization Policy From 1933-43" (MA Thesis, University of Victoria, 1995). Some of the classic international works on eugenics are David Barker, "The Biology of Stupidity: Genetics, Eugenics and Mental Deficiency in the Inter-War Years," *British Journal for the History of Science* 22 (1989): 347-75; Mark H. Haller, *Eugenics: Hereditarian Attitudes in American Thought* (New Brunswick, NJ: Rutgers University Press, 1963); Marouf A. Hassian Jr., *The Rhetoric of Eugenics in Anglo-American Thought* (Athens: University of Georgia Press,

1996); Richard Hofstadter, *Social Darwinism in American Thought* (New York: George Braziller, 1969); Daniel J. Kevles, *In the Name of Eugenics: Genetics and the Uses of Human Heredity* (New York: Knopf, 1985); Kenneth M. Ludmerer, *Genetics and American Society: A Historical Appraisal* (Baltimore: Johns Hopkins University Press, 1972); Diane B. Paul, *Controlling Human Heredity* (Atlantic Highlands, NJ: Humanities Press, 1995); Steven Selden, *Inheriting Shame: The Story of Eugenics and Racism in America* (New York: Teachers College Press, 1999); Mathew Thomson, *The Problem of Mental Deficiency: Eugenics, Democracy, and Social Policy in Britain 1870-1959* (Oxford: Clarendon Press, 1998).

13. Peter H. Bruce, "Immigration in Relation to the Public Health," *Canadian Journal of Medicine and Surgery* 19, 4 (April, 1906): 203-10; C.K. Clarke, "The Defective and Insane Immigrant," *Bulletin of the Ontario Hospitals for the Insane* 2 (1908): 3-22; C.K. Clarke, "The Defective Immigrant," *Public Health Journal* 7 (1916): 462-65; C.K. Clarke, "Immigration," *Public Health Journal* 10 (1919): 441; A.H. Desloges, "Immigration and the Mentally Unfit," *Social Welfare* (1 March 1919): 138-39; J.D. Pagé, "Immigration and the Mentally Unfit," *Public Health Journal* 6 (1915): 554-58; J.D. Pagé. "Medical Aspects of Immigation," *The Canadian Nurse* 26, 8 (August, 1929): 395-9. Contemporary works on anti-immigration and the medical profession in Canada include Dowbiggin, "'Keeping This Young Country Sane'"; Zlata Godler, "Doctors and the New Immigrants," *Canadian Ethnic Studies* 9 (1977): 6-17; Robert Menzies, "Governing Mentalities: The Deportation of 'Insane' and 'Feebleminded' Immigrants Out of British Columbia From Confederation to World War II," *Canadian Journal of Law and Society* 13, 2 (Fall 1998): 135-73; Barbara Roberts, "Doctors and Deports: The Role of the Medical Profession in Canadian Deportation, 1900-20," *Canadian Ethnic Studies* 18, 3 (1987): 17-36. See generally Barbara Roberts, *Whence They Came: Deportation From Canada 1900-1935* (Ottawa: University of Toronto Press, 1988).

14. "Editorial," *Canadian Medical Association Journal* 2, 11 (November 1912): 1020-22.

15. Helen Reid, "Introduction," in W.G. Smith, *A Study in Canadian Immigration* (Toronto: Ryerson Press, 1920), cited in Kathleen J.A. McConnachie, "Science and Ideology: The Mental Hygiene and Eugenics Movements in the Inter-War Years, 1919-1939" (PhD Dissertation, University of Toronto, 1987), 85.

16. See J. David Smith, *Minds Made Feeble: The Myth and Legacy of the Kallikaks* (Rockville, MD: Aspen Systems Corporation, 1985); James W. Trent Jr., *Inventing the Feeble Mind: A History of Mental Retardation in the United States* (Berkeley: University of California Press, 1994).

17. McLaren, *Our Own Master Race*, 91.

18. Nicole Hahn Rafter, *Creating Born Criminals* (Urbana: University of Illinois Press, 1997), 238.

19. William D. Tait, "Democracy and Mental Hygiene," *Canadian Journal of Mental Hygiene* 3 (1921): 31-36, 33.

20. F.C.S. Schiller, "The Case For Eugenics," *Dalhousie Review* 4 (April 1924-January 1925): 405-10, 409, 410.

21. See Harley D. Davidson, "Scientific Parenthood: The Mental Hygiene Movement and the Reform of Canadian Families, 1925-1950," *Journal of Comparative Family Studies* 24, 3 (Autumn, 1993): 387-402; John D. Griffin, *In Search of Sanity: A Chronicle of the Canadian Mental Health Association, 1918-1988* (London, ON: Third Eye Books, 1989); McConnachie, "Science and Ideology"; David McLennan, "Beyond the Asylum: Professionalization and the Mental Hygiene Movement in Canada 1914-1928," *Canadian Bulletin of Medical History* 4 (1987): 7-23; Charles G. Roland, *Clarence Hincks: Mental Health Crusader* (Toronto: Hannah Institute and Dundurn Press, 1990); Harvey G. Simmons. *From Asylum to Welfare* (Downsview, ON: National Institute on Mental Retardation, 1982).

22. "The Mental Hygiene Movement in Canada," *The Canadian Nurse* (1928): 59-62, 59.

23. Clifford Beers, *A Mind That Found Itself* (New Haven, CT: Yale University Press, 1925). Beers is quoting from Professor William H. Burnham. BCARS, GR 865, box 1, file 9.

24. Dowbiggin, *Keeping America Sane*, 171.

25. C.M. Hincks, "Recent Progress of the Mental Hygiene Movement in Canada," *Canadian Medical Association Journal* 11 (1921): 823-25, 825.

26. "Reach Social Utopia Before the Year 2026," *Toronto Mail and Empire*, 20 May 1926. The quotation is extracted from an address in May 1926 by University of Toronto psychology professor W.E. Blatz to the Toronto Children's Aid Society. CMHA Scrapbook.

27. See note 20 above.

28. McConnachie, McLaren and Dowbiggin have all made this observation in, respectively, "Science and Ideology," *Our Own Master Race*, and *Keeping America Sane*.

29. Simmons, *From Asylum to Welfare*, 110-11.

30. "Mental Hygiene Survey Province of British Columbia," *Canadian Journal of Mental Hygiene* 2, 1 (1920): 3-59, 11.

31. "Mental Hygiene Survey Province of British Columbia," 51.

32. Psychopathic hospitals began to appear around North America during the second decade of the twentieth century, focussing on the short-term treatment of acute cases and on integration with university, community, and research services. Probably the most renowned was Boston Psychopathic, built in 1912, and operating in the mid-1920s with 110 beds under chief executive officer C.A. Bonner. Winnipeg Psychopathic, directed by Alvin T. Mathers, was the first such Canadian facility. In Toronto, a similar operation began on 30 November 1925 under C.B. Farrar. C.A. Bonner to J.A. Macdonald, 10 Sept. 1926. BCARS, GR 865, box 2, file 4; Editorial, "Manitoba's Progress in Mental Hygiene," *Canadian Journal of Mental Hygiene* 3 (1921): 280-84; C.B. Farrar, Transcript, "Public Hearings of the British Columbia Royal Commission on Mental Hygiene," 13, 14 April 1926, Vancouver Minister's Room, Court House, Vancouver. BCARS, GR 865, box 1, file 7.

33. The Public Hospital for the Insane (PHI) in New Westminster opened in 1878 as a replacement for the ramshackle Victoria Lunatic Asylum on Vancouver Island. The PHI was joined on 1 April 1913 by the Provincial Mental Home, Essondale, which occupied 1000 acres of land on a hillside in Coquitlam, just east of Vancouver.

34. The aims of special classes (which originated in Germany in 1863 and arrived in the United States in 1894, Toronto in 1910, and Vancouver a year later) "were to remove feeble-minded children from the regular school system where they were thought to constitute a disruptive influence on the regular pupils; to provide feeble-minded children with special education suitable to their needs and in particular one that would make them self-supporting; to protect them from harassment by children in regular classes; and to determine which among them was incapable of education and training and should be sent to custodial institutions." Simmons, *From Asylum to Welfare*, 90. Supervisor Josephine Dauphinée reported that, by 1926, there were 19 special classes operating in Vancouver (with 289 students), two in Victoria, and one in New Westminster. Transcript, "Public Hearings of the British Columbia Royal Commission on Mental Hygiene," 13, 14 April 1926. See also A. Josephine Dauphinée, "Vancouver's Sub-Normal Population," *Canadian Journal of Mental Hygiene* 3 (1921): 117-24; C.M. Hincks, "Recent Progress of the Mental Hygiene Movement in Canada," *Canadian Medical Association Journal* 11 (1921): 823-25.

35. "Mental Hygiene Survey Province of British Columbia," 51-55.

36. "Mental Hygiene Survey Province of British Columbia," 58.

37. *The Problem of the Feeble-Minded: An Abstract of the Report of the Royal Commission on the Care and Control of the Feeble-Minded* (London: P.S. King and Son, 1909). See Simmons, *From Asylum to Welfare*, 55-63.

38. "Investigation of Royal Commission Into the Existing Methods of Dealing With Mental Defectives in Ontario," *Canadian Journal of Mental Hygiene* 1 (1919-20): 88-92. See also McConnachie, "Science and Ideology," 59-62; Simmons, *From Asylum to Welfare*, 85-102.

39. Commission chair Justice Frank Egerton Hodgins took pains to quote the ubiquitous Walter E. Fernald, Superintendent of the Massachusetts School for the Feeble-Minded, to the effect that the feeble-minded constituted "a parasitic, predatory class, never capable of self-support or managing their own affairs." The women in particular were "almost invariably immoral, and, if at large, usually become carriers of venereal disease or give birth to children who are as defective as themselves." Simmons, *From Asylum to Welfare*, 93.

40. "Magistrate Murphy Reports on First Investigation of Asylums and Jails by Public Committee," *Medicine Hat News*, 28 May 1926. CMHA Scrapbook.

41. "Consults With Authorities on Mental Hygiene," *Halifax Herald*, 27 Jan. 1927; "Gives Lecture to Gyro Club," *Halifax Herald*, 26 May 1927; "Select N.S. Doctor for New Office," *Halifax Evening Mail*, 22 Sept. 1927. CMHA Scrapbook. See also Simmons, *From Asylum to Welfare*, 118.

42. C.E. Doherty, "The Care of the Mentally Disordered," unpublished paper. BCARS, GR 865, box 1, file 11.

43. "Discuss Problem of Mental Defectives," *Victoria Times*, 24 Nov. 1925. CMHA Scrapbook.

44. At the federal level, the National Council of Women (NCW) was the main clearinghouse for maternal feminist organizing. On feeble-mindedness and citizenship, for instance, the NCW convenor for mental hygiene, Dr. Elizabeth Smith Shortt, wrote in 1926 that "[t]he burden on the superior stock — the so-called normal — is tremendous ... segregation or operation or both, are means whereby we can save civilization." National Council of Women, *1926 Report*, 218. See generally Carol Bacchi, "Race Regeneration and Social Purity: A Study of the Social Attitudes of Canada's English-Speaking Suffragists," *Histoire sociale/Social History* 11 (1978): 260-74; Dowbiggin, *Keeping America Sane*; McLaren, *Our Own Master Race*; McConnachie, "Science and Ideology."

45. J.A. Macdonald to W.C. Laidlaw, Deputy Minister of Public Health, Alberta, 30 July 1926. BCARS, GR 865, box 1, file 2.

46. W.A. Mackenzie, "The Condition of Overcrowding in the Mental Hospitals of British Columbia," Report to the BCRCMH, nd, 1, 3, 4. BCARS, GR 865, box 2, file 10.

47. Members also resolved that the provinces should have the authority to re-examine all immigrants and, failing that, the Dominion should bear the expenses for any immigrant who becomes a public charge. Resolution of the B.C. Legislature, 25 Nov. 1925. BCARS, GR865, box 1, file 12.

48. "Sterilizing Defectives Urged as Aid to Nation." *Vancouver Star*, 2 Dec. 1925.

49. BCARS, GR 865, box 1, file 6.

50. "E.J. Rothwell, M.D., M.L.A," *Bulletin of the Canadian National Committee for Mental Hygiene* 2, 7 (July 1927): 2.

51. The Encyclopedia of British Columbia, ed. dir. Dan Francis (Madeira Park, BC: Harbour, 2000), 510; see also Scott Kerwin, "The Janet Smith Bill of 1924 and the Language of Race and Nation in British Columbia," *BC Studies* 121 (Spring, 1999): 83-114, 87-90.

52. Personal communication, Lisa Baird and Barb Lemky, Cumberland Museum. 5 July 2001.

53. William Sloan to H.C. Steeves, 13 Oct. 1925. BCARS, GR542, box 14, file 5.

54. Robin Fisher, *Duff Pattullo of British Columbia* (Toronto: University of Toronto Press, 1991), 218; Ian Donald Parker, "Simon Fraser Tolmie and the British Columbia Conservative Party 1916-1933" (MA Thesis, Simon Fraser University, 1970), 73.

55. "Mental Hospital has 700 in Rooms for 500," *Vancouver Province*, 11 Jan. 1926. CMHA Scrapbook.

56. Minutes, meeting of the BCRCMH, 13 Jan. 1926; V.W. Odlum to William Sloan, 13 Jan. 1926. BCARS, GR 865, box 1, file 6. See also "Lunacy Commission Outlines Programme," *Victoria Colonist*, 16 Jan. 1926; "Lunacy Inquiry Programme Made," *Victoria Times*, 15 Jan. 1926. CMHA Scrapbook.

57. Memorandum. "Expenses Re: Royal Commission." BCARS, GR 646, box 1.

58. J.A. Macdonald to C.M. Hincks, 2 May 1927. BCARS, GR 865, box 1, file 3; J.A. Macdonald to J.S. Woodsworth, 17 June 1926. BCARS, GR 865, box 1, file 2.

59. "Distressing Conditions Found by Commission in B.C.'s Asylums," *Victoria Daily Colonist*, 11 Feb. 1926, 3. Hayward discovered, to his pleasure, that the women "mostly seemed to agree on the matter of sterilization of mental defectives, and some said that stricter marriage laws should be enacted." Reginald Hayward to V.W. Odlum, 11 Feb. 1926. BCARS, GR 865, box 1, file 1. See also BCARS, GR 645, vol. 4.

60. J.A. Macdonald to V.W. Odlum, 4 May 1926. BCARS, GR 865, box 1, file 1.

61. From the outset it was apparent that the Commission's openness to full public debate was, to say the least, debatable. As Rothwell wrote in January of that year, "I don't think we are duty bound to hear every Tom, Dick & Harry." E.J. Rothwell to V.W. Odlum, 25 Jan. 1926. BCARS, GR 865, box 1, file 1.

62. Transcript, "Public Hearings of the British Columbia Royal Commission on Mental Hygiene," 13, 14 April 1926. See also "Low Mentality Great Cause of Delinquency," *Vancouver Sun*, 15 April 1926; "Mental Commission Adjourns Hearing," *Vancouver Province*, 14 April 1926; "Mental Commission to Sit Here Next," *Victoria Colonist*, 15 April 1926. CMHA Scrapbook. For a brief account of the hearings see also McLaren, *Our Own Master Race*, 96-97.

63. For more on Henry Shaw, see Alison J. Hatch and Curt T. Griffiths, "Child Saving Postponed: The Impact of the Juvenile Delinquents Act on the Processing of Young Offenders in Vancouver," in *Dimensions of Childhood: Essays on the History of Children and Youth in Canada*, ed. Russell Smandych, Gordon Dodds, and Alvin Esau (Winnipeg: Legal Research Institute, 1991), 233-66.

64. Transcript, "Public Hearings of the British Columbia Royal Commission on Mental Hygiene," 13, 14 April 1926.

65. The newly-established national Department of Health inaugurated the Dominion Council of Health in 1919 as a forum for provincial-federal consultation on health issues. J.J. Heagerty, "History and Activities of the National Health Division of the Department of Pensions and National Health," *Canadian Journal of Public Health* 26 (1935): 528-40, 540.

66. Transcript, "Public Hearings of the British Columbia Royal Commission on Mental Hygiene," 16 April 1926. Members' Room, Parliament Buildings, Victoria. BCARS, GR 865, box 1, file 7.

67. See P.P. Harrison. "Immigration and its Effects on the Increase of Insanity," Report to the BCRCMH, 8 Jan. 1927, 6, 7. BCARS, GR 865, box 1, file 12; Reginald Hayward, "Report on the 'Hereditary' Phase of the Cause of Insanity," Report to the BCRCMH, 15 April 1926. BCARS, GR 864, box 1, file 8.

68. From the outset, Hincks and the CNCMH had been highly interested observers of events unfolding on the west coast. See "Royal Commission on Mental Hygiene. British Columbia," *Bulletin of the Canadian National Committee for Mental Hygiene* 1, 7 (Dec., 1925): 3-4; "Mental Hygiene in British Columbia," *Bulletin of Canadian National Committee for Mental Hygiene* 2, 3 (April, 1926): 4-5; "Dr. Hincks Reports Optimistically on Mental Hygiene Progress in Four Western Provinces," *Bulletin of the Canadian National Committee for Mental Hygiene* 2, 7 (July, 1927): 1, 3.

69. C.M. Hincks to J.A. Macdonald, 16 July 1926. BCARS, GR 865, box 1, file 2.

70. See Harry Hamilton Laughlin, *Eugenical Sterilization in the United States* (Chicago: Psychopathic Laboratory of the Municipal Court of Chicago, 1922). Contemporary studies of sterilization history in the United States include Edward J. Larson, *Sex, Race, and Science: Eugenics in the Deep South* (Baltimore: Johns Hopkins University Press, 1995); Paul, *Controlling Human Heredity*; Philip R. Reilly, *The Surgical Solution: A History of Involuntary Sterilization in the United States* (Baltimore: Johns Hopkins University Press, 1991); *Sexual Sterilization*, ed. Jonas Robitscher (Springfield, IL: Charles C. Thomas, 1973).

71. See, for example, F.O. Butler, "Sterilization Procedure and its Success in California Institutions," State Department of Institutions, California, 12 Nov. 1925. In a typical passage from this report, Butler, Medical Superintendent of the Sonoma State Home for the Feeble-Minded, Eldridge, California, shares his views on the vital relationship between sterilization and the promotion of virile nationhood: "The very life of our Nation is its manhood and womanhood, and something must be done that we may beget none but sound offspring, and thus have a Nation physically and mentally strong." BCARS, GR 865, box 2, file 3, 9.

72. Editorial, "The Problem of the Unfit," *Vancouver Sun*, 16 April 1926. CMHA Scrapbook.

73. Editorial, "The Mentally Deficient," *Vancouver Province*, 2 Feb. 1927, 6.

74. "(Interim) Report of the Royal Commission on Mental Hygiene." BC Sessional Papers 1926-27, 3rd Session 16th Parliament, CC7.

75. V.W. Odlum to J.A. Macdonald, 16 Nov. 1926. BCARS, GR 865, box 1, file 2.

76. Helen P. Davidson, "A Report of the Heredity and Place of Origin of the Patients Admitted to the Provincial Mental Hospitals of British Columbia" (30 Nov. 1926), 4. The report is reproduced as Appendix G in the "(Interim) Report of the Royal Commission on Mental Hygiene," 33-54. A copy is also available in BCARS, GR 865, box 2, file 6.

77. Davidson, "A Report of the Heredity and Place of Origin," 49.
78. Specifically, Davidson recommended a "separate and appropriate institution for the care of the feeble-minded," special classes for the training of high grade morons (as she intimated, such special training would "enable the individual to be fitted into some small niche in the industrial world where he can be self-supporting and be a contented citizen. It is from such that the world obtains most of its 'hewers of wood and drawers of water'"); a psychopathic hospital; education of the public around insanity and mental deficiency; mental hygiene classes in the schools; social service workers for the mental hospitals; provincial research work on mental hygiene; and care of old folks suffering from senile dementia. Davidson, "A Report of the Heredity and Place of Origin," 49.
79. "Canada is now much more looked upon as the 'dumping ground' of Europeans whose people want to get rid of them. ... From everything I have been able to learn, you would be perfectly justified in reaching the conclusion that Canada has admitted an even greater proportion of unfit aliens than the U.S. and that the danger to be avoided in the immediate future is very great indeed." J.A. Macdonald to P.P. Harrison, 28 Sept. 1926. BCARS, GR865, box 1, file 2.
80. For a summary of the main arguments against sterilization, compiled by Macdonald as part of his research for the BCRCMH, see BCARS, GR 865, box 2, file 3.
81. J.A. Macdonald to C.M. Hincks, 28 June 1926. BCARS, GR 865, box 1, file 2.
82. This is a reference to characters in the novels of U.S. author James Branch Cabell, who garnered much controversy, not to mention accusations of obscenity, during the 1920s. See, in particular, Cabell's *Jurgen: A Comedy of Justice* (New York: R.M. McBride, 1919); *The High Place: A Comedy of Disenchantment* (London: John Lane, 1923); *The Silver Stallion: A Comedy of Redemption* (New York: R.M. McBride, 1926); and *Something About Eve: A Comedy of Fig-Leaves* (New York: R.M. McBride, 1927).
83. J.A. Macdonald to Paul Popenoe, 27 Nov. 1926. BCARS, GR 865, box 1, file 2.
84. J.A. Macdonald to V.W. Odlum, 22 Dec. 1926. BCARS, GR 865, box 1, file 2.
85. "(Interim) Report of the Royal Commission on Mental Hygiene," CC7.
86. "(Interim) Report of the Royal Commission on Mental Hygiene," CC6.
87. The members lifted these recommended criteria virtually unedited from the Alberta legislation. J.A. Macdonald to Malcolm R. Bow, Deputy Minister of Health, Alberta, 20 May 1927. BCARS, GR 865, box 1, file 3. Regarding the consent provision, as Rothwell advised Harry H. Laughlin of the Eugenics Record Office on Long Island, "[t]he Commission felt that it was best at this stage to recommend only a very restricted law, and that future action should be guided by actual results." They would obviously have preferred to go further. E.J. Rothwell to Harry H. Laughlin, 25 March 1927. BCARS, GR 865, box 1, file 3.
88. "(Interim) Report of the Royal Commission on Mental Hygiene," CC9-10.
89. *Immigration Act*, s 3(a).
90. "(Interim) Report of the Royal Commission on Mental Hygiene," CC30.
91. "(Interim) Report of the Royal Commission on Mental Hygiene," CC25-26.
92. BCRCMH Memorandum, 27 April 1927. BCARS, GR 865, box 2, file 10.
93. C.M. Hincks, "Dr. Hincks Reports Optimistically on Mental Hygiene Progress in Four Western Provinces," *Bulletin of the Canadian National Committee for Mental Hygiene* 2, 7 (July 1927): 1.
94. "Editorial," *Vancouver Western Tribune*, 19 March 1927. BCARS, GR 865, box 2, file 14.
95. "Commission on Insanity Urges Control Board," *Victoria Colonist*, 5 March 1927. CMHA Scrapbook.
96. J.A. Macdonald to J.L. White, Deputy Provincial Secretary, 8 April 1927. BCARS, GR 865, box 1, file 3.
97. "New Hospital For Essondale," *Vancouver Daily Province*, 28 July 1927, 3; "B.C. to Foot Big Bill For Insanity," *Victoria Daily Times*, 29 July 1927, 1.
98. J.A. Macdonald to C.M. Hincks, 30 June 1927. See also "Was a Noble Man, a Beloved Physician, and Worthy Citizen," *Bulletin of the Canadian National Committee for Mental Hygiene* 2, 7 (July 1927), 1.

99. For example, Appendix B comprised a report from the US National Committee for Mental Hygiene (NCMH), entitled "Mental Deficiency: A General Summary of the Problem," which claimed that "[f]eeble-minded persons are especially prolific and reproduce their kind with greater frequency than do normal persons, that through such reproduction provide an endless stream of defective progeny which are a serious drain on the resources of the nation." Alleging that "feeble-mindedness is one of the largest single factors in hereditary pauperism, juvenile vice and delinquency, adult crime and vagrancy, the spread of venereal disease, and the like," the NCMH deduced that "there is one sensible and really efficient measure that can be carried out, and that is to dam the stream near its source." "Final Report of the Royal Commission on Mental Hygiene," BC Sessional Papers, 1928, 4th Session, 16th Parliament, G10.
100. "Final Report of the Royal Commission on Mental Hygiene," BC Sessional Papers, 1928, 4th Session, 16th Parliament, G4.
101. For a review of the 1913 British legislation see, inter alia, Simmons, From Asylum to Welfare, 61-64.
102. "Final Report of the Royal Commission on Mental Hygiene," G5.
103. "Will Name Expert in Insanity," Victoria Times, 19 March 1928. BCARS, GR 865, box 2, file 14.
104. P.D. Walker. "Memo to Premier," 30 Aug. 1932. BCARS, GR 497, box 9, file 6. It was not until 16 November 1949 that the Crease Clinic of Psychological Medicine opened on the provincial mental hospital grounds at Essondale. A.L. Crease, "Director's Report," Mental Hospitals Report, 1949-50, BC Sessional Papers, 2nd Session, 22nd Parliament, 1950, V19.
105. See Val Adolph, In the Context of its Time: A History of Woodlands (Richmond: BC Ministry of Social Services, 1996).
106. A. Josephine Dauphinée to S.L. Howe, Provincial Secretary, 31 Oct. 1931. BCARS, GR 542, box 16, file 6.
107. In 1946 his title changed again, this time to Director of Mental Hygiene and Psychiatry. A.M. Gee, "Dr. Arthur L. Crease," Mental Hospitals Report, 1949-50, BC Sessional Papers, 2nd Session, 22nd Parliament, 1950, V13-4.
108. For a personal account of life at the Essondale nurses' school, see Agnes MacKinnon, I Carried a Key: Three Years in a Mental Hospital: A Nurse's Story (Vancouver: Hignell, 1996).
109. The head social worker, Josephine Kilburn, arrived in 1933, having been secured through the auspices of the CNCMH.
110. E.J. Ryan to C.M. Hincks, 27 Aug. 1937. BCARS, GR 542, box 22, file 5.
111. McLaren, Our Own Master Race, 111.
112. Allison C. Carey, "Gender and Compulsory Sterilization Programs in America: 1907-1950," Journal of Historical Sociology 11, 1 (March 1998): 74-105, 74; Molly Ladd-Taylor, "Saving Babies and Sterilizing Mothers: Eugenics and Welfare Politics in the Interwar United States," Social Politics (Spring 1997): 136-53; Deborah C. Park and John P. Radford, "From the Case Files: Reconstructing a History of Involuntary Sterilisation," Disability and Society 13, 3 (1998): 317-42; Jennifer K. Roberts, "'If Thine Eye Offend Thee, Pluck it Out': Sterilization and the Policing of Female Sexuality in Twentieth Century Western Canada" (MA Thesis, University of Victoria, 1999); Wosilius, "Eugenics, Insanity and Feeblemindedness."
113. As McConnachie observes, "The nativist fears that prompted the western provinces to initiate mental hygiene surveys in 1918 and 1919 also carried over into a pro-sterilization campaign. If immigration to Western Canada had slowed by the late 1920s fears about the 'foreigners in our midst' persisted. In the West, the strong support of women's organizations remained the bedrock of the pro-sterilization campaign." McConnachie, "Science and Ideology," 234. See Bacchi, "Race Regeneration and Social Purity"; Chapman, "Early Eugenics Movement in Western Canada"; Dowbiggin, Keeping America Sane, 178; McLaren, Our Own Master Race.
114. Timothy J. Christian, "The Mentally Ill and Human Rights in Alberta: A Study of the Alberta Sterilization Act," Unpublished paper, University of Alberta, nd; McDonald, "A Policy of Privilege"; Park and Radford, "From the Case Files"; Roberts, "'If Thine Eye Offend Thee, Pluck it Out.'"

115. In *Buck v. Bell*, 274 U.S. 200 (1927), the US Supreme Court under 86-year-old Justice Oliver Wendell Holmes upheld Virginia's compulsory sterilization legislation by an 8 to 1 margin, unleashing a new wave of legislation and surgery. See especially Reilly, *The Surgical Solution*, 67-68, 86-87. By the 1960s, US physicians had sexually sterilized 60,000 people in that country, two-thirds of whom were women. See Carey, "Gender and Compulsory Sterilization Programs in America," 74.

116. On F.P.D. Ross' Ontario Commission, see McLaren, *Our Own Master Race*, 112, 186; Simmons, *From Asylum to Welfare*, 113-19.

117. Desmond King, "Experts at Work: State Autonomy, Social Learning and Eugenic Sterilization in 1930s Britain," *British Journal of Political Science* 29 (1999): 77-107. In contrast to F.P.D. Ross in Ontario, Sir Lawrence Brock backed away from recommending compulsory sterilization law.

118. *An Act Respecting Sexual Sterilization*, 1933, c.59, 23 Geo. 5, 199-201. Assented to 7 April 1933.

119. In a letter distributed to several key exponents of stronger legislation, Deputy Provincial Secretary P.D. Walker disclosed that, while no one wanted a consent clause, "it was felt that the Act must be in a sense tentative, and that all we could expect was to establish the principle in some degree." P.D. Walker to C.M. Hincks, 10 April 1933. BCARS, GR 497, box 10, file 8.

120. P.D. Walker to A.L. Crease, 6 April 1933. BCARS, GR 542, box 17, file 1.

121. *An Act Respecting Sexual Sterilization*, s4.1.

122. P.D. Walker to A.L. Crease, 1 Nov. 1933. BCARS, GR 542, box 17, file 2. G.A. Minorgan, an Essondale physician, took over from McKay in April 1935, and Justice A.M. Manson replaced Robertson on 6 March 1936. A.L. Crease to P.D. Walker, 3 April 1935. BCARS, GR 542, box 17, file 5; Isobel Harvey to E.W. Griffith (Associate Deputy Provincial Secretary), 18 March 1944. BCARS, GR 542, box 11, file 4.

123. W.S. Turnbull to A.L. Crease, 7 Jan. 1935. BCARS, GR 542, box 11, file 4.

124. Margaret Stewart, "Some Aspects of Eugenical Sterilization in British Columbia with Special Reference to Patients Sterilized From Essondale Provincial Hospital Since 1935," 17 Aug. 1945. BCARS, GR 496, box 38, file 3.

125. Isobel Harvey to E.W. Griffith (Associate Deputy Provincial Secretary), 18 March 1944. BCARS, GR 542, box 11, file 4; see also J.D.M. Griffin, "Mental Hygiene in Canada," *Canadian Public Health Journal* 31, 4 (April 1940): 163-74, 170.

126. Since the Board of Eugenics records long ago disappeared, it is impossible to obtain a precise figure. This estimate is based on projections from the annual number of sterilizations occurring in the decade up to 1945, along with sporadic reports available in the BC Archives mental health services collections. BCARS, GR 133, box 6.

127. "Says Mental Ills Exact Heavy Toll," *Montreal Gazette*, 18 May 1928. CMHA Scrapbook.

128. Joel Braslow, *Mental Ills and Bodily Cures: Psychiatric Treatment in the First Half of the Twentieth Century* (Berkeley: University of California Press, 1997); Peter Schrag, *Mind Control* (New York: Pantheon, 1978); Elliot S. Valenstein, *Great and Desperate Cures: The Rise and Decline of Psychosurgery and Other Radical Treatments for Mental Illness* (New York: Basic, 1996).

129. Simmons, *From Asylum to Welfare*, 108.

130. As A.L. Crease confided to Deputy Provincial Secretary P.D. Walker on 30 Jan. 1939, "Mental Hygiene has been over-sold, and advertising only produces unfavourable comment and undue publicity and, in the end, does more harm to the cause than it does good. It starts correspondence by all the fanatics, bigots and paranoics." BCARS, GR 542, box 18, file 4.

131. Griffin, *In Search of Sanity*, 154-65.

CONTRIBUTORS

ROBERT ADAMOSKI chairs and teaches in the Criminology Department at Kwantlen University College. His research and publications have focused on the history and contemporary policies of child welfare agencies in British Columbia. Present interests include the contemporary restorative justice movement, and an historical study of boarding schools.

MARY LOUISE ADAMS teaches in the School of Physical and Health Education and in the Department of Sociology at Queen's University in Kingston. She is the author of *The Trouble With Normal: Postwar Youth and the Making of Heterosexuality*, published by the University of Toronto Press.

KATHERINE ARNUP is an historian who teaches in the School of Canadian Studies at Carleton University. She has written extensively on motherhood and child rearing, the history of the family, lesbian parenting, and feminist legal issues. She is the author of *Education for Motherhood: Advice for Mothers in Twentieth Century Canada* (University of Toronto Press) and the editor of *Lesbian Parenting: Living with Pride and Prejudice* (gynergy).

DENYSE BAILLARGEON is Associate Professor of History at the Université de Montréal. Her book *Ménagères au temps de la crise* (Remue-ménage, 1991 and 1993) has been translated under the title *Making Do: Women, Family and Home in Montreal during the Great Depression* (Wilfrid Laurier University Press, 1999). She is currently writing a new book on the medicalization of motherhood in Québec between 1910 and 1970.

JANINE BRODIE is the Chair of the Department of Political Science at the University of Alberta, a former Robarts Chair in Canadian Studies, and a past Director of the York Centre for Feminist Research. She is the author of several books and numerous articles on Canadian political economy, governance and gender and politics and is currently a co-investigator in a MCRI project on Neo-liberal Globalism.

DOROTHY E. CHUNN teaches in the School of Criminology and is co-director of the Feminist Institute for Studies on Law and Society at Simon Fraser University. Her current research projects focus on: the historical regulation of sex in the Canadian welfare state; feminism, law, and social change in Canada since the 1960s; and, poor women's experiences of health and housing.

CLAUDE DENIS is Associate Professor at the University of Alberta's Faculté Saint-Jean. He grew up in Montréal, and obtained his PhD in sociology from the University of Toronto. He is the author of *We Are Not You: First Nations and Canadian Modernity* (1997), and of articles on the practice and theory of "the state" in Canada, especially with regard to the conflict of nationalisms between anglophone Canada, Québec, and Indigenous peoples.

LORNA R. McLEAN is an Assistant Professor in the faculty of education at the University of Ottawa. Her research interests include gender, race, ethnicity, citizenship and education in early 20th century Canada. She recently co-edited the book *Framing Our Past: Canadian Women's History in the Twentieth Century*.

ROBERT MENZIES teaches criminology at Simon Fraser University. His current interests include psychiatric and public health history, medico-legal regulation of women and racialized peoples, and contemporary men's and fathers' rights movements. He is co-editor, with Susan C. Boyd and Dorothy E. Chunn, of *[Ab]Using Power: The Canadian Experience* (Fernwood, 2001); and, with John McLaren and Dorothy E. Chunn, of *Regulating Lives: Historical Essays on the State, Society, the Individual and the Law* (UBC Press, 2002).

BERNICE MOREAU is a faculty member in the School of Social Work at Carleton University. Her teaching and research interests include aging and social work from an international perspective, the political economy of the welfare state, the phenomenon of colour contusion, and the education of Black Nova Scotian women schooled in the early 1900s.

SEAN PURDY has an MA in History from Queen's University. He taught high school and Social Studies in Vancouver and currently teaches Language Arts and English as a Second Language in Sao Paulo, Brasil.

RONALD RUDIN is Professor and Chair of the history department at Concordia University. He has written a considerable number of articles and books on the economic, social and intellectual history of Quebec in the nineteenth and twentieth centuries. Most recently, he has published an examination of the historical profession in Québec: *Making History in Twentieth-Century Quebec*.

JOAN SANGSTER teaches History and is Director of the Frost Centre for Canadian Studies and Native Studies at Trent University, Peterborough. She has published articles and books on working-class and women's history, the most recent of which is *Regulating Girls and Women: Sexuality, Family and the Law, 1920-60* (Oxford University Press). *Girl Trouble!*, her forthcoming book on female juvenile delinquency, will be published by Between the Lines in 2002.

JENNIFER STEPHEN has published articles on historical constructions of citizenship, labour and welfare state policy formation. Her doctoral thesis at OISE/UT, "Deploying Discourses of Employability and Domesticity: Women's Training and Employment Policies and the Formation of the Canadian Welfare State, 1935-1947," was awarded the Canadian Policy Research Award Graduate Prize in 2000.

VERONICA STRONG-BOAG teaches in Women's Studies and Educational Studies at the University of British Columbia. A Fellow of the Royal Society of Canada and a former president of the Canadian Historical Association, she is the author or editor of numerous works including *Paddling Her Own Canoe: The Times and Texts of E. Pauline Johnson*, with Carole Gerson (2000), *Rethinking Canada: The Promise of Women's History*, 4th ed. with Mona Gleason and Adele Perry (2002), and *The New Day Recalled: The Lives of Girls and Women in English Canada, 1919-1939* (1988).

SHIRLEY TILLOTSON teaches Canadian History and Women's Studies at Dalhousie University. She is the author of *The Public at Play: Gender and the Politics of Recreation in Post-War Ontario*. Her scholarly interests in leisure and politics are being expressed at present in research on charitable fundraising as both a feature of associational life and a mechanism of state formation in twentieth century Canada.

INDEX

419